T0138946

Governing Health Systems

For Nations and Communities Around the World

Edited by
MICHAEL R. REICH
AND
KEIZO TAKEMI

Lamprey & Lee
an imprint of Bibliomotion, Inc.

First published in 2015 by Lamprey & Lee, an imprint of Bibliomotion, Inc
39 Harvard Street
Brookline, MA 02445
Tel: 617-934-2427
www.bibliomotion.com

Printed in the United States of America

Library of Congress Cataloging-in-Publication Data

Governing health systems (Reich)
    Governing health systems : for nations and communities around the world / edited by Michael R. Reich and Keizo Takemi.
        p. ; cm.
    Includes bibliographical references and index.
    ISBN 978-1-942108-00-9 (hardcover : alk. paper) — ISBN 978-1-942108-01-6 (ebook)
    I. Reich, Michael, 1950– , editor. II. Takemi, Keizo, editor. III. Title.
    [DNLM: 1. Health Services Administration. 2. Global Health. 3. Health Care Reform. 4. Organizational Case Studies. W 84.1]
    RA441
    362.1—dc23
                        2015000944

CONTENTS

Governing Local Health Systems

Governing National Health Systems

Contents   v

LIST OF TABLES

LIST OF FIGURES

AUTHORS' BIOGRAPHICAL INFORMATION

Uche Amazigo (Takemi Fellow, 1991–92) holds a PhD from Vienna University (Austria). Her work on onchocerciasis control fundamentally changed international perceptions of the disease and formed the scientific basis for the African Program for Onchocerciasis Control (WHO/APOC), launched in 1995. As APOC director from 2005–2011, she coordinated the control of river blindness in sub-Saharan Africa and worked to institutionalize the community-directed treatment (CDT) approach for drug delivery. In 2012, she received the Prince Mahidol Award in Public Health, to recognize her contributions to global health.

Lincoln Chen is president of the China Medical Board, and former Taro Takemi Professor of International Health at HSPH. He was the founding director of the Harvard Global Equity Initiative. Dr. Chen continues to serve on numerous boards, including the board of BRAC, the advisory committee to the FXB Center on Health and Human Rights at Harvard, the board of the Social Science Research Council, the Institute of Metrics and Evaluation (University of Washington), the Public Health Foundation of India, and the UN Fund for International Partnership (counterpart to UN Foundation).

Chunhuei Chi holds an ScD in health policy and management from the Harvard School of Public Health, and was a program associate of the Takemi Program as a doctoral student. He is an associate professor and coordinator of the International Health Program (IHP) at Oregon State University, where he established the master of public health in IHP in 1993. He developed a model IHP for the Japanese Ministry of Education at University of Tsukuba in 1999, assisted Taiwan in developing its first graduate IHP at National Yang-Ming University in 2002, and has mentored PhD students in IH research around the world. His expertise includes health systems finance, critical evaluation of IH programs, and health systems strengthening.

Nii Ayite Coleman (Takemi Fellow, 1996–97) is a public health physician, coordinator of the Health Policy and Leadership Program at the Ghana College of Physicians and Surgeons, and the focal person for National Health Insurance in Ghana's Ministry of Health.

T. R. Dilip is a demographer with a PhD from the International Institute for Population Sciences, India. He is based in Geneva as a consultant to the World Health Organization. He has prior experience in academia, the Ministry of Health and Family Welfare, New Delhi, and leading NGOs in India. His areas of interest include health and population data analytics, national health accounts, health system and policy analysis, social determinants of health, and maternal, newborn, and child health policies and programs.

Luiz Facchini (Takemi Fellow, 1996–97) is a Brazilian physician with a PhD in medical sciences and epidemiology. He is a member of the National Research Council of Brazil and was previously the president of the Brazilian Association of Collective Health. He currently coordinates the Primary Health Care Research Network in Rio de Janeiro, and is a titular member of the World Federation of Public Health Associations.

Anaclaudia Gastal Fassa (Takemi Fellow, 1998–99) has an MD and a PhD in epidemiology. She is an associate professor of the Department of Social Medicine at the Federal University of Pelotas, Brazil. She is the coordinator of the Specialization Course in Family Health through distance learning and professor of the postgraduate program in epidemiology. Her research interests include health services evaluation, primary health care evaluation, and occupational epidemiology.

Julio Frenk is dean of the faculty at the Harvard School of Public Health and Angelopoulos Professor of Public Health and International Development, a joint appointment with the Harvard Kennedy School of Government. Dr. Frenk served as the Minister of Health of Mexico from 2000–06, where he introduced a major health reform policy that is leading to universal health coverage. He was the founding director of the National Institute of Public Health of Mexico and has also held leadership positions at the Mexican Health Foundation, the World Health Organization, the Bill & Melinda Gates Foundation, and the Carso Health Institute.

Leila Posenato Garcia has a PhD in epidemiology and is currently a researcher at the Institute of Applied Economic Research, Brasilia, Brazil. She is also a professor in the postgraduate program in public health at the University of Brasilia, Brazil. She is editor-in-chief of *Epidemiology and Health Services*, a scientific journal of the Secretariat of Health Surveillance, Brazilian Ministry of Health.

Aya Goto (Takemi Fellow, 2012–13) is an associate professor of public health at Fukushima Medical University School of Medicine. Dr. Goto's main research areas are prevention of unintended pregnancy and parenting support. Her translational research in the past fifteen years has been conducted in close collaboration with local communities in Fukushima, Japan, and Ho Chi Minh City, Vietnam, and incorporates capacity building of local health care professionals in maternal and child health care as well as epidemiology.

Margaret Henning (Takemi Fellow, 2012–13) is an assistant professor in health science at Keene State College, in New Hampshire. Her work focuses on disparities, health education, community interventions, and maternal and infant health patterns from a cross-cultural perspective. Dr. Henning's work uses diverse yet complementary field techniques such as combining qualitative and quantitative methods in her research.

Richard Horton is editor-in-chief of the *Lancet*. He is an honorary professor at the London School of Hygiene and Tropical Medicine, University College London, and the University of Oslo. He writes regularly for the *New York Review of Books* and the *Times Literary Supplement*. Dr. Horton received the Edinburgh Medal in 2007 and the Dean's Medal from Johns Hopkins School of Public Health in 2009.

Masami Ishii became an executive board member of the Japan Medical Association in 2006, responsible mainly for international affairs and disaster and emergency medicine. He is also serving as vice-chair of council of the World Medical Association, and secretary general of the Confederation of Medical Associations in Asia and Oceania. After graduating from the Hirosaki Unversity School of Medicine in 1975 and its Graduate School of Medicine in 1979, Dr. Ishii opened the Ishii Hospital of Neurosurgery & Ophthalmology in 1985.

Young Ko is manager of the National Health Insurance Services (NHIS) in Korea. She graduated from Seoul National University in 1989, majoring in nursing. She earned her MPH from Seoul National University School of Public Health in 2004. She has been developing Korea's universal benefits coverage program since 2006 in NHIS.

Joseph Konde-Lule (Takemi Fellow, 1990–91) is a public health specialist and medical epidemiologist with more than thirty years of research and publications in various aspects of public health. Currently he is professor of epidemiology at the School of Public Health in the Makerere University College of Health Sciences in Uganda. His research focuses on infectious diseases and population surveys, and includes studies of HIV/AIDS, tuberculosis, trials for malaria treatment, health services management, and the role of private health practitioners in public health.

Hari Kusnanto (Takemi Fellow, 2001–02) is an Indonesian clinician and professor. After working with refugee populations on Gulang Island, he joined the School of Medicine at the Gadjah Mada University as a lecturer in epidemiology. His past research has looked at the effects of the Asian economic crisis on health, and he continues to work on the epidemiological basis of health policies and health system strengthening.

Soonman Kwon (Takemi Fellow, 2001–02) holds a PhD from the Wharton School of the University of Pennsylvania. He recently served as dean of the School of Public Health, Seoul National University, South Korea. He is also adjunct professor at the China Center for Health and Development, Peking University. He is on the editorial boards of *Social Science & Medicine, Health Economics Policy and Law, BMC Health Services Research*, and *Ageing Research Reviews*. Prof. Kwon is a member of the

Scientific and Technical Advisory Committee (STAC) of the (WHO) Alliance for Health Policy and Systems Research.

Udaya S. Mishra (Takemi Fellow, 2003–05) is a statistician and demographer at the Centre for Development Studies Trivandrum, Kerala, India. He is engaged in research and teaching on population and development issues and has published a number of articles both nationally and internationally. His research and teaching has concentrated on aging, health, nutrition, population policy, and program evaluation. Currently, he is researching measurement issues in health and equity in evaluation of outcomes.

A. Ngozi Njepuome is an international health consultant and technical adviser on neglected tropical diseases to WHO. She brings more than twenty years of experience in internal medicine and holds an MPH from the University of Manchester, UK. She is the past director of public health, Nigeria, a fellow of the National Post Graduate Medical College, and chairperson of Nigeria Community TB Committee.

Obioma Nwaorgu (Takemi Fellow, 1994–95) holds a doctorate in parasitology from the University of Cambridge, United Kingdom. She has worked actively internationally in public health parasitology and epidemiology. She is the president and founder of a nongovernmental organization, Global Health Awareness Research Foundation (GHARF). She pioneered two disease control programs in Enugu State, Nigeria (on Guinea worm and onchocerciasis) and was principal investigator in twelve TDR/WHO-supported research projects in the area of communicable disease prevention and control.

Bruno Pereira Nunes has an MSc in epidemiology and is completing his PhD at the Postgraduate Program in Epidemiology, Department of Social Medicine, Federal University of Pelotas, Brazil. His research focuses on health services assessment, primary health care evaluation, health inequalities, quality of care for chronic diseases, and co-morbidity.

Juhwan Oh (Takemi Fellow, 2008–10) is professor of International Health Policy and Management at Seoul National University College of

Medicine. He also serves as secretary of the JW Lee Center for Global Medicine at the same university. His work is centered on improving the health of underserved populations in resource-limited countries through Korea's Official Development Aid in Health and the JW Lee Center. His research addresses issues of national health insurance and maternal and child health.

Joseph Okeibunor (Takemi Fellow, 2010–11) is the regional adviser on social/anthropological aspects of immunization and vaccine development in the WHO Regional Office for Africa (WHO/AFRO). He has a doctorate in sociology/anthropology and is a professor in sociology in the Department of Sociology/Anthropology at the University of Nigeria, Nsukka. His research focuses on the social and behavioral aspects of health and health care in Africa, and he has published more than fifty scientific articles.

Friday Okonofua (Takemi Fellow, 1991–92) is a professor of obstetrics and gynecology at the University of Benin in Nigeria and fellow of the Nigerian Academy of Science. He has served as the executive director of the International Federation of Gynecology and Obstetrics (FIGO) and as honorary adviser on health to President Olusegun Obasanjo of Nigeria. Professor Okonofua is a global champion of women's health, and has published more than 240 journal articles. He currently serves as program officer at the Ford Foundation in Lagos.

Nkechi Onyeneho holds a PhD in medical sociology/anthropology from the University of Nigeria, Nsukka (UNN) and is a senior lecturer in the Department of Sociology/Anthropology, UNN. She is currently a visiting senior lecturer at the University of Malaya, Malaysia, and the UNN anchorperson in the AFRO-ASIAN Development University Network. She has participated in studies on health issues in Africa and published a number of scientific articles, including ones focused on the social and cultural aspects of disease control, health systems, and community participation strategies in health care and disease control.

Michael R. Reich is the Taro Takemi Professor of International Health Policy in the Department of Global Health and Population at HSPH, where he has been on the faculty since 1983. He received his PhD in political science from Yale University in 1981. Dr. Reich has written extensively about the political dimensions of public health policy, health reform, and pharmaceutical policy. He previously served as chair and acting chair of the Harvard School of Public Health's Department of Population and International Health (1997–2001) and as director of the Harvard Center for Population and Development Studies (2001–05), and continues as director of the Takemi Program in International Health.

Akihiro Seita (Takemi Fellow, 2003–04) is director of health programs at the United Nations Relief and Works Agency for Palestine (UNRWA). Prior to this appointment, he was coordinator for TB, AIDS, and Malaria for the Eastern Mediterranean Regional Office at the World Health Organization.

Suele Manjourany Silva has a PhD in epidemiology and is currently a professor for a specialization course in family health through distance learning at the Federal University of Pelotas, Brazil. Her research interests include health services evaluation, primary health care evaluation, and physical activity epidemiology.

Keizo Takemi (Takemi Fellow, 2007–09) is a member of the House of Councilors of Japan's National Diet and a senior fellow at the Japan Center for International Exchange (JCIE). He served as state secretary for foreign affairs of Japan in 1998–99 and senior vice-minister of Health, Labor, and Welfare of Japan in 2006–07. He is an internationally recognized advocate for global health and development, and played an important role in placing health at the center of the 2008 G8 summit in Japan.

Elaine Thumé (Takemi Fellow, 2008–09) has a PhD in epidemiology. She is an associate professor at Federal University of Pelotas, Brazil. Her research interests include health systems assessment, health inequalities, social networks and aging, and monitoring and evaluation of health programs. She is a researcher on collective health and a professor in the Postgraduate Nursing School at Federal University of Pelotas.

Elaine Tomasi has a PhD in epidemiology. She is an associate professor of the Department of Social Medicine and Postgraduate Program in Epidemiology at the Federal University of Pelotas, Brazil. Her research focuses on health service assessment, primary health care evaluation, health inequalities, and quality of care of maternal and child health.

Hacheong Yeon (Takemi Fellow, 1984–85) is a professor of comparative and welfare economics at KDI (Korea Development Institute) School of Public Policy and Management. Formerly, he was dean of the Graduate School and College of Social Science at Myongji University (1999–2010), president of the Korea Institute for Health and Social Affairs, director of the Center for North Korean Economic Studies, vice president of the Korea Development Institute, and a standing member of the Executive Committee of the Korean Economic Association.

Yoshitake Yokokura was elected as president of the Japan Medical Association in 2012 after serving as its vice president since 2010. He is now serving as council member of the World Medical Association, and councilor of the Confederation of Medical Associations in Asia and Oceania. He has also served as president of Yokokura Hospital since 1990. Dr. Yokokura graduated from Kurume University School of Medicine in 1969, worked for the surgery department of the university from 1969–1977, and for the surgery department of the Detmold Hospital in West Germany from 1977 to 1979.

CONGRATULATORY MESSAGE

Yoshitake Yokokura, President, Japan Medical Association

On behalf of the Japan Medical Association (JMA), I would like to deliver a message of congratulations on the thirtieth anniversary of the Takemi Program in International Health.

This international program is named after Dr. Taro Takemi, a distinguished physician-scientist and past president of the JMA, who served in that position for twenty-five years. Dr. Takemi's lifelong theme was "the development and allocation of medical care resources," and I believe that this theme continues to flow today at the core of the Takemi Program. This theme also became a high priority for the World Medical Association, as a broad-ranging fundamental issue that medical associations around the world continue to address today. "The development and allocation of medical care resources": these are important words that we as medical professionals must acknowledge once more today.

I would like to express my heartfelt respect and warmest congratulations to Dr. Julio Frenk, the dean of the Harvard School of Public Health, and to all the Harvard School of Public Health faculty who have sustained the Takemi Program for the past three decades, particularly Professor Michael Reich, who has overcome many difficulties and has played a central role in the program.

The JMA holds high expectations for the Takemi Program, which has the excellent achievement of producing a large number of Takemi Fellows—241 fellows from fifty-one countries around the world thus far—and has over many years endeavored to enhance and expand the program content. Recently the JMA established an internal committee on international health that is debating the issue of how the JMA should approach international health from various perspectives. The members of this committee include five former Japanese Takemi Fellows.

Japan is now facing the arrival of an aging society and the reality of a declining birthrate. In this situation, how to best protect the health of the general public under Japan's universal health insurance system is becoming an important and pressing issue. Such problems cannot be resolved from only a domestic viewpoint; they are problems that need to be tackled from a long-term perspective that incorporates dynamic international viewpoints.

While individual countries attempt to resolve domestic issues such as these, it is necessary that the world also seek solutions to medical issues—including both infectious diseases and natural disasters that have international consequences—from an international perspective that fosters the true cooperation of all countries.

It is my hope that the physicians and public health experts who are conducting their research in the Takemi Program continue to make great leaps forward in the future and continue to provide powerful research and policy insight on the key global health questions of our times. I am pleased to state that the JMA intends to proactively provide support for the Takemi Program's activities aimed at these objectives.

With the 30th Anniversary Symposium marking the close of one chapter and the beginning of another, I would like to conclude my congratulatory remarks by expressing my heartfelt hope that the Takemi Program will continue to greatly contribute to international health in the future.

Yoshitake Yokokura, MD
President, Japan Medical Association
August 2014

PREFACE

Julio Frenk

This book marks the thirtieth anniversary for the Takemi Program in International Health. This extraordinary program has been in existence since 1983, and it welcomed its thirtieth group of Takemi Fellows to Harvard in the fall of 2013. Over the past three decades, 241 people from fifty-one countries have participated in the Takemi Program. Beyond numbers, Takemi Fellows add immeasurably to the intellectual life at the Harvard School of Public Health (HSPH). We are pleased to celebrate some of the Takemi Program's achievements with this volume.

The Takemi Program's thirtieth anniversary coincided with the School of Public Health's centennial. In reflecting on the first century of our school, I think that historians will view the establishment of the Takemi Program as a key foundation block in the increasingly important role that HSPH has played in global health. It was a great pleasure, in October 2013, to welcome back to Harvard nearly eighty former Takemi Fellows, representing nearly every one of the program's thirty years. The Takemi Symposium and celebration marked an important event in the yearlong series of events recognizing the school's 100th anniversary.

The Takemi Symposium, on which this book is based, was a highly successful gathering, both substantively, in considering the issues of governing health systems, and socially, in marking a reunion of the network of Takemi Fellows. It was indeed an historic occasion—for the Takemi Program, for the school, for public health, and for Harvard.

The Takemi Program is known at HSPH and around Harvard University for its track record in attracting emerging leaders and for its contributions to global health. Those Takemi Fellows from the past are today's leaders in many countries around the world. Indeed, former Takemi Fellows are present at almost every global health meeting these days, engaging on topics from health financing reform to malaria control to innovative strategies for R&D and beyond.

Let me also offer some words of appreciation. For all of their efforts to support the Takemi Program, I would like to thank the program's key partner, the Japan Medical Association. I would also like to thank the core donors to the program, notably the Japanese Pharmaceutical Manufacturers Association, for their support over the years.

I would particularly like to thank Keizo Takemi for his dedication and commitment over three decades to supporting the program that is named after his father. And I must recognize the critical roles of the school's leaders, who had the foresight to establish and support this program at Harvard: Dean Howard Hiatt, a cofounder of the program; Dean Harvey Fineberg, who oversaw the first decade of the program and helped get it established in the school; and Dean Barry Bloom, who steadfastly supported the program. Professor Lincoln Chen, the first Taro Takemi Professor of International Health, gave foundational direction and support to the program. Finally, I also express our appreciation to the current Taro Takemi Professor of International Health Policy and the program's director, Michael R. Reich, who has been with the program since its inception.

The Takemi Program has played many special roles at the Harvard School of Public Health over the past thirty years. Takemi Fellows' presence in classes and discussions strengthen our intellectual life in global public health. Takemi Fellows' collaborations with our faculty and students have generated critical new areas of inquiry, and many Takemi Fellows continue to collaborate with Harvard researchers after they have left HSPH. The Takemi Program has been a key incubator for many other global health programs at Harvard. And the Takemi Program also enables the school to maintain a special relationship with Japan, as well as a network of people working in global health around the world.

The Takemi Program represents the longest continuing mid-career fellowship program in any field at the Harvard School of Public Health. I offer my congratulations to all for the legacy of the past thirty years, and I look forward to the next thirty years of continued innovation in global health leadership.

Julio Frenk, MD, MPH, PhD
Dean, Harvard School of Public Health
August 2014

CHAPTER I

Introduction and Overview for
Governing Health Systems

Michael R. Reich and Keizo Takemi

The way health systems are governed has gained increasing global attention in recent years. The global health community, after pursuing primary health care, followed by single-disease control strategies, health sector reform, and then health system strengthening, has now turned to governance questions in seeking to improve health. The crisis of pandemic Ebola in West Africa in 2014 has recently heightened global awareness about the critical importance of governing health systems and the tragic consequences of weak health systems. During this same time period, over the past thirty years the Takemi Program in International Health at Harvard School of Public Health has sought to cultivate cutting-edge researchers working on the allocation of limited resources for health. Governance of health systems has also become a prominent theme in the research of many Takemi Fellows.

The 30th Anniversary Takemi Symposium, held in October 2013 at Harvard University, focused on the challenges of governing health systems around the world. This book, based on the papers presented at the symposium, reports on the challenges facing local communities and entire nations as they develop and govern ever more complex health systems.

There are many different definitions of governance, and several chapters in this book offer perspectives on this question. For the purposes of this introduction and overview, we refer to one general definition provided by Dodgson and colleagues (2002, 6):

> [G]overnance can be defined as the actions and means adopted
> by a society to promote collective action and deliver collective
> solutions in pursuit of common goals. This is a broad term that
> is encompassing of the many ways in which human beings, as
> individuals and groups, organize themselves to achieve agreed
> goals. Such organization requires agreement on a range of mat-
> ters including membership within the co-operative relationship,
> obligations and responsibilities of members, the making of deci-
> sions, means of communication, resource mobilization and dis-
> tribution, dispute settlement, and formal or informal rules and
> procedures concerning all of these.

In considering questions of governance, we are increasingly aware
that it influences the performance of a health system but it is not clear
how governance affects performance or how improved governance can
produce better performance.

This book—using diverse perspectives and in different contexts, examining different institutional dimensions of governance—explores the
relationships between governance and performance in community and
national health systems. Each chapter provides an in-depth case study,
conducted with both qualitative and quantitative methods; they were prepared by former Takemi Fellows, now frontline health policy researchers in many countries, and their colleagues. This case study approach has
well-known methodological limitations, especially regarding whether the
findings can be generalized to other settings and countries. However, the
in-depth analysis of each case yields important findings, as well as contextual insights, which deserve serious consideration and may reflect more
general patterns related to governing health systems around the world.

The challenges inherent in governing health systems present core questions for global health policy makers today. These challenges will also continue to be important themes for the Takemi Program's research mission;
we have only begun to understand the questions, let alone the answers. We
hope that the studies presented in this book—deep examinations of illus-
trative examples—contribute to knowledge for global health researchers
and assist policy makers in dealing with the complex practical problems of
governing their own health systems. In short, this book addresses central
questions about governing health systems—and why governance matters.

GOVERNANCE AT THE COMMUNITY LEVEL

Questions about governing health systems often arise visibly at the local or community level. Public health has a long history of concern about community-level action—illustrated by the development of community-oriented primary care by Sidney Kark in South Africa in the 1950s (Tollman 1991) and by the global pursuit of primary health care policies in the 1970s. But this enthusiasm for community-oriented primary care has often confronted obstacles in implementation. One reason may be ambiguity in the way community-oriented primary care relates to the broader health system—in short, problems of institutions and governance.

The first half of this book explores five key themes of governing health systems at the community level. Although they are not the only issues related to community health systems that could be examined, they do represent core challenges for improving the delivery of health services in practice. The five case studies are: (1) the role of community participation in health management committees in Uganda; (2) the performance and management of district hospitals in Ghana; (3) the role of decentralized government in the state of Kerala in India; (4) community workers on the front lines of public health disasters in Japan and Zambia; and (5) the impact of community perceptions of health system performance in Nigeria. Here we briefly review the main questions and findings for each chapter in this section of the book, which explores governance in communities.

Community participation in health management committees: A key question in governing health systems at the community level is: How to cultivate meaningful community participation that helps improve the quality of care provided? There is a long-standing belief in public health that enhanced civil society participation will improve the quality of health service delivery in the community. How can this participation be promoted and institutionalized? In chapter 2, Joseph Konde-Lule examines community participation in the health sector in Uganda, focusing on the role of health unit management committees. He notes that health-sector governance includes three main sets of actors: *state actors*, such as policy makers and government technical officials; *health service providers* in public and private-sector health facilities;

and *beneficiaries*, including service users as well as the general public. The third group is usually considered to be "the community." Konde-Lule asks in his study how the beneficiaries of community health centers in Uganda participate in ensuring effective service delivery and accountability for resources, and in fulfilling government guidelines and regulations. In addition, he examines differences between public facilities and private facilities (with a focus on private nonprofit services from faith-based organizations).

A 2003 policy from the Ugandan Ministry of Health mandates that all health centers establish a health unit management committee. Konde-Lule's analysis explores the implementation of this government directive. The 2003 policy assigns many responsibilities and functions to the committees. Konde-Lule finds that management committees in the public sector face various challenges in their operations. They reportedly lack adequate funds; their existence is not well known in the community; and the committee members have limited managerial and technical experience.

By contrast, management committees in faith-based, mission-affiliated health centers were reportedly better organized. According to Konde-Lule's interviews, the members of these health unit management committees were selected from local church congregations, based on relevant qualifications. The committee members received training and support on committee responsibilities and complying with government guidelines. And the mission-affiliated committees had some actual managerial powers, including the power to hire and fire lower-level employees in the health centers.

Konde-Lule concludes that the two sectors show a striking difference in the implementation of community participation in health unit management committees, even though they are following the same guidelines and receive the same level of government financial support. Konde-Lule recommends that the public sector learn from the experiences of the faith-based private sector to make community participation in health unit management committees more effective. He offers a number of specific suggestions, based on the faith-based approaches, related to recruitment and training of committee members, monitoring of committee activities, and assurance that the committees comply with government rules. This chapter provides an insightful comparative analysis of how two different organizational environments, although operating in the same country and using the same governance structure, produce strikingly different performance results. The chapter also illustrates some specific challenges, found in many countries, to improving the performance of public-sector facilities and to creating meaningful mechanisms of community participation.

District hospitals and community governance: A related analysis, the assessment of institutional governance in district hospitals, is provided in chapter 3. How can a community provide effective representation and participation in the management of local hospitals? Does better community participation in governance lead to improved performance of local hospitals? These questions are especially important because of the pervasive problems of underperforming public hospitals in developing countries.

In chapter 3, Nii Ayite Coleman examines these questions in public district hospitals in the Eastern Region of Ghana. Coleman first places the district hospital within a broad review of the history of modern medicine in Ghana and the development of the nation's health system, beginning with the British colonial medical system. At the time of independence, in 1951, Ghana recognized the need to build a health system that met the needs of the population, with the capacity to deliver rural primary health care. The district hospital was considered the "apex" of the resulting district health system, and was assigned the roles of providing curative and preventive care, in addition to health-promotion activities. Despite these important roles for district hospitals and despite attention to them through various waves of health reform, they have remained "the weakest link in Ghana's health system," according to a recent assessment by Coleman. The reasons for their poor performance are attributed to serious problems in their organizational and managerial operations, including the lack of effective involvement of civil society.

Coleman presents his analysis of twelve (out of the fourteen) district hospitals in Ghana's Eastern Region (two hospitals did not respond to his requests for information). He distributed questionnaires to hospital staff to assess governance, asking about the existence of a hospital board, the duration of the board's existence, and its size, composition, leadership, and scheduled meetings. He found that only seven hospitals had a governing board, although they are required to establish one by Ghana's Hospital Strategy document. Further analysis of board practices found that all seven boards had mixed membership (from inside and outside the hospital) and leadership by non-health professionals, but none of them complied with the required quarterly meetings. In addition, Coleman created a proxy measure of hospital performance based on three-year trends in institutional mortality to categorize each facility as having high, medium, or low performance. This measure of performance showed no association with the existence or nonexistence of a governing board.

Based on this analysis, Coleman concludes, "[P]ublic district hospitals in Ghana consider governing boards to be optional," and even in hospitals with a governing board, the "accountability functions seem to have been lost." Coleman follows Ghana through "over half a century of successive health reforms," all of which failed to pay adequate attention to strengthening the governance, accountability, and performance of the district hospital. He hopes that this preliminary study will help put the district hospital on Ghana's health policy agenda. To that end, he recommends a number of concrete actions that could begin to address the weak link in the national health system.

Decentralized government and community health: A third major theme in governing health systems at the community level is how decentralized government structures contribute to better health and health systems. A recent study in England identified many governance issues that confront local health systems, including: coordination across government agencies, leadership tensions and ambiguity in accountability, challenges in effective management and performance monitoring, and the role of numerical health targets (Marks et al. 2010). Similar challenges occur in low- and middle-income countries for community health systems as well, especially given the trend toward decentralization in many nations. In chapter 4, Udaya S. Mishra and T.R. Dilip provide insight from India on these questions.

India has actively pursued a decentralization process through the formation of panchayati raj institutions, which were mandated in 1993 through two constitutional amendments. This process has included devolution of significant funds to the local self-government institutions so that they can plan and implement important community functions. Mishra and Dilip examine the roles of India's local self-government institutions in improving the community health system, by exploring the views of local stakeholders in one state.

The chapter looks in depth at the community health experiences of Kerala, which was the first Indian state to elect assemblies at the local level after the constitutional amendments. Mishra and Dilip's analysis is based on interviews with three key groups of stakeholders in the local health system: functionaries in local governments (193 people), health care providers (76 people), and community members (900 people). Through these interviews, the researchers identified strengths and weaknesses in the capacity of community institutions to manage the local health system.

Mishra and Dilip found growing acceptance of local government institutions in India, but also long-term challenges in institution building at the local level. Local government functionaries were aware of their responsibilities to create additional health infrastructure, improve community access to health services, and oversee both public and private health providers. However, the researchers also found reports of problems in the interviews: inadequate funding, lack of technical knowledge regarding public health, lack of community engagement, and lack of cooperation from health staff. Nearly all local health providers were aware of the health roles of local self-government, for example, in planning, financing, and monitoring community health programs. But Mishra and Dilip found strong resistance among local providers (60 percent of respondents) to the idea that they should be accountable to local self-government, because they considered the panchayats (the local assemblies) to be politically oriented, engaged in other priorities, lacking adequate administrative capacity, and lacking professional expertise in health.

Community members similarly showed a strong awareness of the local government's responsibilities to improve the community health system, including the delivery of preventive measures and curative services, and the identification of local health needs. But the researchers found that local residents continue to use private services instead of the public system because of a lack of physicians in public facilities and a sense that better treatment was provided at private hospitals, as well as "convenience, time saving, and immediate attention." These problems are typical not only of public-sector health services in India but in many other developing countries.

The chapter concludes with a discussion of significant challenges to improving the performance of Kerala's local self-government institutions in the health sector. Mishra and Dilip recommend strengthening the institutional capacity of local governments in public health, while recognizing major challenges in extending the authority of local government to cover the private sector and finding complementary roles for public and private health facilities. They also note the lack of community involvement and participation in the local health institutions. Resolving the conflicts between health providers and local government regarding their respective obligations and responsibilities, and building an environment of mutual trust remain two major obstacles to improving community health in Kerala.

Community workers and community health: A major question for governing health systems at the community level is: Who does the work of community health? Chapter 5, by Margaret Henning and colleagues, provides an innovative comparative study of this question. The authors explore the responses of public health nurses to the Fukushima nuclear disaster in Japan and the responses of public teachers to the AIDS disaster in Zambia. In both cases, women professionals (nurses and teachers) served as frontline community health workers in addressing major disasters that undermined public health and security.

While recognizing the vast differences between Japan and Zambia, as well as the different kinds of public health disasters involved in these cases, the authors uncovered common patterns and challenges for community workers in the face of a public health disaster. These relate directly to issues of governance: "One of the challenges in strengthening governance at the community level is identifying, giving voice to, and leveraging the key community players who can help transform the concept of health promotion into a community priority." From this perspective, nurses and teachers play critical roles in promoting both community health and community governance. The authors were particularly interested in strategies that could make these community workers more effective in their tasks. Henning et al. use Liberato's theory of building community capacity, which is based on an assessment of skills, resources, networking, leadership, and decision making, to examine and compare the roles of the nurses and teachers in the two cases (Liberato et al. 2011).

These two strikingly different cases showed some similarities: in both cases, frontline health workers (nurses and teachers) played a major role in bridging the gaps between science and society in communities during a public health disaster. The researchers found that nurses in Japan and teachers in Zambia both felt that they needed updated training (in the realm of skills), a shift in their tasks and responsibilities (related to resources), and enhanced coordination and information sharing (related to networking). Both kinds of community workers perceived the importance of *building trust* within the community as central to carrying out their task of helping local residents grapple with the personal and social dimensions of the disasters that are engulfing them. The nurses and teachers also felt they needed additional support to enhance their professional confidence as they confronted the complexities of the crises and sought to help their local communities heal and recover. The chapter concludes with four areas for action to strengthen community governance and community health "in ways that are strategic, sustainable, and cognizant of the importance of the historical role of community workers."

Community perceptions of the health system: A final theme related to governing health systems at the community level (which is suggested in the previous four cases) involves the perceptions of community members, especially regarding the way the public system delivers health care. These include perceptions of the health system, local government, and health providers. In chapter 6, Joseph Okeibunor and colleagues report on their analysis of community perceptions of health services in two states in southeastern Nigeria. They note, "The existing gap between objective measures to improve care delivery, in response to the Millennium Development Goal (MDG) targets on health, and current levels of service utilization as well as health indicators, calls for a critical examination of the perceptions of the health system among end users" because those perceptions may be contributing to the gaps in health system performance. They are particularly interested in "expressed satisfaction with the health service as well as the people's assessment of the attitude of the health staff." This chapter uses mixed methods (quantitative and qualitative) to explore people's perceptions in twenty-four communities. These include urban, peri-urban, and rural areas in Imo and Enugu states in southeastern Nigeria (one "strong-performing" state and one "weak-performing" state). The researchers used household questionnaires, in-depth interviews, and focus group discussions to explore and document perceptions.

Okeibunor and colleagues report that community members are "very much aware of the health facilities in their domain but utilization is low due to factors that relate to attitude of health workers, availability of equipment, and drugs." The study revealed that about half of the population uses health centers for care, around 40 percent use patent medicine vendors (private sector), and the remainder uses "other sources." Around 45 percent of respondents reported poor community involvement in the local health centers. And in nearly all cases, respondents said that they had to pay for medicines they received from public-sector health centers. The study found that local residents had a good understanding and high expectations of the government's obligations—to provide medicines, involve the community, provide personnel, construct hospitals, reduce family health care costs, and use local volunteers. But the study found a generally low opinion of the quality of health services delivered in the public sector. Around 50 percent of all respondents gave a "poor quality" rating, with little difference across sociodemographic groups. Community members reported they were willing to participate in the community health system, but they were disappointed when, for example, they helped to build a health center (as a form of participation), and the government did not then make it function properly.

Overall, the study found significantly higher ratings in the strong-performing state with regard to the way health care is delivered and the number of services actually delivered. But in both states, the study discovered a "generally low approval for the adequacy of government contributions." In short, people expect the government to do more and are highly dissatisfied with the current situation.

In the words of Okeibunor and colleagues, government efforts are considered "grossly inadequate and unsatisfactory," citing the lack of medicines in health centers and the poor attitudes of health workers toward clients. The authors conclude, "Health care seems only available depending on the financial capability of the clients, making access to essential health services unrealizable among the greater segment of the population." They note that these findings may not be generalizable to other parts of Nigeria, because of the great diversity of the country. In their conclusion, they urge both states and the federal government in Nigeria to analyze community perceptions of health services through-out the country, and to use those findings to improve the quality of the health care delivery in the public sector.

The challenges presented in these five case study chapters on community-level health system governance are familiar to people working in many countries, in both the developed and developing worlds. They reflect the real difficulties present when: creating effective mechanisms and institutions for meaningful community participation to improve quality of service delivery; building functional local government entities with public health expertise; supporting frontline community health workers (such as nurses and teachers); and, listening to the views of community members in ways that promote trusting and positive relationships with the health system.

In the next section of this chapter, we review the themes explored in the second set of case studies, which focus on governance at the *national* level.

GOVERNANCE AT THE NATIONAL LEVEL

Around the world many countries are enacting new policies designed to improve the performance of their national health systems. The issue of national health system performance has been a top item on the global health agenda since at least the early 2000s, as illustrated by the World Health Organization's *World Health Report 2000: Health Systems: Improving Performance*. In 2008, Japan promoted health system strengthening as an important issue for the G8 countries' action at the global summit held in Toyako (Reich et al. 2008). The World Bank similarly has addressed the topic through the Flagship Program on Health Sector Reform and Sustainable Financing, which by 2009 had trained nearly twenty thousand people around the world (Shaw and Samaha 2009), using a text that combines technical, ethical, and political analysis (Roberts et al. 2004).

Currently, the dominant global health policy theme related to national health systems is framed around the concept of universal health coverage. The World Health Organization (WHO) made "financing for universal health coverage" the theme of its *World Health Report 2010* (WHO 2010). The Rockefeller Foundation has developed an initiative on "transforming health systems," with universal health coverage as a major goal (Brearley and Marten 2013). And the Prince Mahidol Award Conference held in Bangkok, Thailand, in January 2012 was organized on the theme of moving toward universal health coverage. In these current debates about how to move countries toward universal health coverage, an underlying quandary is how to improve national health system governance at the same time.

The past decade has seen a huge expansion of interest not only in how national health systems work, but also in how their performance can be improved and measured. Various organizations have developed approaches for assessing and measuring "health governance" at a national level. WHO, for example, has proposed both rule/policy-based indicators and outcome-based indicators to monitor progress on health system governance (WHO 2008). The World Bank uses a *Country Policy and Institutional Assessment*, which provides a composite measure of governance across all sectors, with a subset for health and education policies (IEG 2009).

The second half of this book presents six chapters that examine different dimensions of governing health systems at the national level. These chapters analyze: (1) national policy reforms in Indonesia to move the country toward universal health coverage; (2) the family health strategy in Brazil and its implementation at the municipal level; (3) reforming Nigeria's national health system to reduce maternal mortality; (4) the process of reforming the United Nations health system for Palestinian refugees; (5) financial stability and accountability in the South Korean national health insurance system; and (6) the introduction of citizen participation in the decision-making process for the benefit package for national health insurance in South Korea. As with the chapters on community governance, these studies are in-depth single-nation case studies, with the inherent methodological strengths and limitations of this kind of research.

Governing toward universal health coverage: As noted above, many countries around the world have adopted the policy goal of "moving toward universal health coverage" for their national health system. Yet there are few analytical reports of how countries do this or of the obstacles and challenges in transforming a national health system. This kind of analysis should include an assessment of a reform's consequences, as well as probing the social-political dimensions of managing the reform process. What has worked well, and what has not worked so well? What roadblocks were encountered and how were they addressed? How did national governance change as the health system moved toward universal coverage? In chapter 7, Hari Kusnanto presents Indonesia's experiences in governing social health insurance as the country moves toward universal coverage. Indonesia is now in the midst of a major institutional reform. In the short time period of five years the country aims to create a national security system to cover the entire population.

Indonesia's first major effort to allocate significant national funds for social security emerged from the Asian economic crisis in 1997–98. Subsequently, in 2002 Indonesia amended its constitution to require a national security system; in 2004 the country passed a national law (the SJSN Law) to create this system, but without specifying the policy details. A second national law, the 2011 BPJS Law, created a single organizational unit and required the merger of existing social security plans. Indonesia is now implementing these laws in an effort to expand social health insurance coverage to the entire population. Kusnanto analyzes three governance issues related to the process of expansion and reorganization of existing systems in the health sector. These represent major institutional challenges that many countries confront in moving toward universal health coverage, especially if they are developing social health insurance organizations.

First, Kusnanto analyzes the *administration* of Indonesia's health insurance system. In moving toward universal health coverage, Indonesia has decided to create a single social security agency—combining existing social security organizations for civil servants, military personnel, and police officers, along with organizations for workers in the formal private sector and for poor families. One agency, for civil servants, is required to transform itself from a for-profit liability company into a nonprofit administrative entity, which is called BPJS Health. This entity is expected to increase its coverage from 17 million to 124 million in 2014, so that it will cover nearly half of the Indonesian population. Then by 2019 it should have increased to cover the full national population (of 258 million). Needless to say, this transformation involves multiple implementation challenges in organizational processes and capacity.

The second major governance challenge examined by Kusnanto is the *oversight* of national health insurance. The 2011 BPJS Law created a new supervisory body intended to advise on difficult decisions, such as the level of premium fees, the benefit package, and payment fees to health care providers—all highly contentious issues. But there are concerns that the new agency will lack the necessary technical expertise, and it has an ambiguous relationship to other government agencies. The third major area for governance issues in Indonesia's health system transformation is *quality assurance* in health services. Two key questions are: How do health professionals, such as the Indonesian Medical Association, participate in protecting quality of care? And, how are the views of beneficiaries used in assessing and improving quality of care? Ultimately, Kusnanto concludes that implementation of universal health coverage in Indonesia will take time (maybe more than the five years projected) and careful negotiation among the many groups involved.

National implementation in a decentralized system: Another major question in governing health systems is how national policies are implemented locally in a decentralized system. Further, how does that implementation affect the health system's performance? In large federal nations, the central government has limited legal responsibilities for implementation of health policy, which must be conducted by subnational government units (such as states or provinces). Examples of this include India, Nigeria, South Africa, and the United States. Brazil offers an important case study for examining decentralized implementation, due to its long history of a national health service (known as the Sistema Unificado de Salud [SUS], or the Unified Health System), which started in 1988 after democratization in Brazil. In 1994, Brazil introduced a new service, called the Family Health Strategy, which mandates multi-disciplinary teams of health professionals engaged in community outreach. This service is implemented at the municipal level, with key policy issues decided at the national level.

Chapter 8, by Luiz Facchini and colleagues, examines how municipalities have implemented the Family Health Strategy (as a proxy for governance) measured by forty-seven indicators of health system inputs, primary health care delivery, and health system performance. The researchers looked for trends in the outcome indicators across 5,565 municipalities in Brazil, according to the level of implementation of the Family Health Strategy. Facchini and colleagues report that the Family Health Strategy (FHS) has been implemented in 95 percent of Brazil's municipalities (5,309), reaching about 108 million people (or 56 percent of Brazil's total population). FHS covers a higher proportion of the population in smaller municipalities and in poorer areas of the country, especially in the Northeast region.

Their analysis shows a complex pattern of effects related to implementing the FHS. Overall, the results show that improvements in many indicators are associated with higher levels of FHS. Some indicators, however, declined as FHS coverage increased (perhaps due to poorer socioeconomic status of high FHS municipalities), and middle-sized municipalities also showed negative trends (compared to positive increasing trends in smaller and large municipalities). The researchers suggest that the problems of medium-sized municipalities deserve additional analysis by national policy makers. Other potential problem areas noted in the chapter include poor implementation of information (such as ombudsman telephone service and information to patients about services offered), and poor implementation of computer provision and access to the Internet (although larger municipalities tended to do better as FHS coverage increased). The analysis also found problems in the primary health care delivery system; these are illustrated by the general presence of a separate bathroom for employees (positive performance), but the general lack of a bathroom adapted for disabled persons (negative performance). Finally, on health system performance, the analysis found that 40 percent of mothers received no postpartum care, and this trend worsened as FHS coverage increased. Similarly about half of the municipalities did not have an acceptable infant mortality rate (below 15/1000 live births), and the trend worsened as FHS coverage increased (likely related to poorer socioeconomic status in those municipalities). The authors of chapter 8 call for an expansion of the Family Health Strategy in Brazil to additional municipalities and strengthening the FHS in municipalities where coverage is still low, while recognizing that additional efforts are also needed to address the implementation problems highlighted by their analysis.

National governance and maternal mortality: In recent decades, global attention has focused on the problem of high maternal mortality in certain regions and countries. Few researchers, however, have examined the role of national health system governance in contributing to high rates of maternal mortality or in helping to reduce maternal deaths in high-prevalence countries. In chapter 9, Friday Okonofua undertakes this analysis for Nigeria—which had one of the world's highest rates of maternal mortality in the 1980s. Okonofua posits that national governance exacerbated maternal mortality in Nigeria: under the military government, from 1985 to 1999, the lack of democratic governance "effectively ensured that none of the recommendations from the global conferences could be implemented in Nigeria." The return to democracy, in 1999, offered an opportunity for the Nigerian health sector to introduce mechanisms to reduce maternal deaths, but at the time the national health system suffered from multiple problems, and was ranked by the WHO as number 187 out of 191 countries in terms of overall performance (WHO 2000).

Okonofua shows that in recent decades Nigeria's democratic governments have given increasing political attention to strengthening health systems and reducing maternal mortality. He traces a series of health system reforms carried out between 1999 and 2007, and concludes they probably contributed to the reduction in maternal mortality that Nigeria recently achieved (dropping from 1,000 deaths per 100,000 live births in 2008 to 630 deaths per 100,000 live births in 2013). But the persistence of an extremely high rate of maternal mortality shows the limitations of these reforms. Okonofua writes that the policy changes demonstrated the political commitment of Nigeria's leadership, but "very few of these policies were actually implemented" and budgetary allocations for health did not result in significant spending to reduce maternal deaths.

Okonofua concludes his analysis by noting, "Political commitment alone is not sufficient." He offers several explanations for the disconnect between *the generation of political commitment* to improve maternal mortality in Nigeria (which occurred) and the *implementation of government policies* (which did not occur). He identifies three actions that could have been taken during this period. First, more advocacy could have been directed at the government technical bureaucracy, to push them to develop the same level of commitment as the political leadership. Second, the political leaders' commitment could have been integrated into broader political discourse and policy (for example, through national legislation on maternal mortality) so that successive national leaders would have had to show similar levels of commitment. Finally, stronger efforts could have been made to assure that Nigeria's economic growth contributed to improvements in the living conditions of the poor, thereby helping reduce maternal deaths. Okonofua concludes that much more can and should be done in strengthening the Nigerian health system in order to reduce the country's high maternal mortality.

Governing the health reform process: Most analyses of the way health reform happens agree that it is a complex and disorderly process, and therefore conclude that careful management is required to achieve positive results. In chapter 10, Akihiro Seita examines how the United Nations Health System for Palestine Refugees "moved mountains" in its health reform process. The UN Relief and Works Agency for Palestine Refugees (UNRWA) provides health services for around five million people in multiple countries, making it the largest health delivery system of all UN agencies. In 2006, UNRWA began to strengthen organizational development in all of its programs. Seita analyzes the process of reforming the UNRWA health system and presents lessons learned about governing the reform process. Through reform of its health activities, UNRWA sought to focus more on prevention and lifestyle changes that relate to noncommunicable diseases, to improve efficiency in order to reduce cost pressures on the health budget. The agency also sought

to give greater role to a "family doctor" model of primary care, in order
to improve the continuity of care for patients and thereby augment both
quality and efficiency.

UNRWA began the health reform process in January 2011. The
first step taken by the reform team was to conduct a political analysis
of stakeholders involved. They recognized that reform was "perceived
as reduction of services, and not improvement. In an effort to mitigate
this kind of thinking, we started stakeholder analysis and consultations
from the very beginning." They identified four key stakeholder groups:
Palestine refugees (the intended beneficiaries), UNRWA staff, host
governments, and donors—and analyzed their power, positions, and
perceptions of health reform prospects. Based on the political analysis,
the reform team decided on two key strategies for change: first, to put
the refugees at the center of the reform; and second, to identify strong
agents of change within UNRWA, the heads of the five field offices.
In chapter 10, Seita explains the compelling logic behind these two
strategic decisions, and then presents step by step what the UNRWA
health reform team did. He explains how they implemented the reform
plan for UNRWA, so that it would change practices in health centers
and change the experiences of patients and staff. He summarizes their
accomplishments succinctly:

> Over the course of two years, we were able to formulate the
> strategy for reform, acquire the buy-in of key stakeholders (six
> months), pilot the FHT [Family Health Team] in two sites (six
> months), and ultimately implement the FHT model in thirty-
> five health centers throughout UNRWA's service areas—
> excluding Syria (one year).... [J]oint assessments with partners
> and feedback from staff and clients confirmed that the desired
> results were achieved, and underlined the potential efficiency,
> effectiveness and sustainability of the reform.

Seita draws a number of lessons from the positive results of the
UNRWA health reform process. He notes: the importance of conducting an explicit political analysis of the environment and the players
involved; the benefits of moving quickly to try out the reform model in

pilot experiments; the positive role of a participatory approach to decisions about process, design, and implementation; and the advantages of building on the health system's existing strengths. Seita concludes by noting the significant challenges that UNRWA confronts in the region, due to the tense political and security environment, as well as budgetary constraints related to the global financial crisis. He writes, "UNRWA operates in one of the most politicized parts of the world, yet we have managed to deliver results by carefully creating an agenda that does not invite opposition and that is supported and promoted by key stakeholders and interested parties." It is indeed an impressive achievement.

National governance and financial accountability: One of the most recognized governance challenges for a national health system is finding adequate financial resources and managing those resources effectively so that services can be delivered in effective, efficient, and good-quality ways. The rapid development of Korea's national health insurance provides an instructive case study for analysis of financial issues. In chapter 11, Hacheon Yeon examines the historical expansion of Korea's health insurance system and the policy challenges it confronts today. Korea began compulsory national health insurance in 1977, starting with a scaled premium payment based on financial ability and the provision of uniform benefits, using a hybrid financial model that included some support from the government budget based on taxes (and covering about 8.8 percent of the total population). By 1989, Korea had achieved health insurance coverage for the entire population, by expanding coverage to self-employed people in rural areas, completing the process twenty-six years after the first Medical Insurance Act was adopted (in 1963). Then, in 2003, Korea carried out a second major institutional reform, merging the many insurance cooperatives into a single insurer. These policy reforms, over several decades, created a national health insurance system in Korea that is globally admired.

However, three long-term trends are now converging to create profound challenges for Korea: low fertility, an aging society with increasing life expectancy, and rising popular demand for more covered health services. Together, these three trends are creating a major challenge to the system's financial sustainability. As Yeon notes in his chapter, Korea is now confronting "a crocodile's mouth pattern" due to slower-rising national income (the lower jaw) and skyrocketing health care costs (the upper jaw). In short, revenues are not keeping up with expenditures. Korea's national system was initially based on low premiums, limited-benefit coverage, and low medical costs. But the package of health services covered by national health insurance has been gradually expanded, and costs have risen with an aging population. The financial imbalances have increased, "as the growing elderly population [and their growing health costs] must be supported by comparatively fewer members of the system and society." Yeon reports that according to one study the proportion of GDP spent on health could reach 13 percent in 2050—how will Korea pay for this?

Yeon recommends six policy shifts to address Korea's problems of financial sustainability: (1) improve efficiency of the health care delivery system; (2) expand resources available for national health insurance financing, especially for the elderly; (3) improve the premium-fee payment system, with attention to fairness of different levels; (4) change the system used for reimbursement of services, moving away from fee-for-service; (5) strengthen the delivery of primary care and promotion; and (6) rationalize the management of insured pharmaceutical costs. Yeon thus proposes another huge and complex reform agenda for Korea to address the converging long-term trends in demography and health insurance policy. Each of these six policies would change the political economy of Korea's national health insurance arena—as they redistribute resources among the various stakeholders. How Korea manages the conflicts inherent in this policy debate will be important to observe, as stakeholders struggle to reshape the financial sustainability of Korea's national health insurance system for the future.

Governing public participation in decisions: One critical area of national policy making for health involves decisions over which interventions and which conditions should be covered by public pooled funds. Who should make these decisions, and how? These decisions have obvious and critical implications for the financing of national health insurance and its budgetary implications, a major focus of the chapter by Yeon. In chapter 12, Juhwan Oh and colleagues report on an innovative experiment with deliberative democracy in health policy making in Korea. Recently, the Korean government has established a citizen's council to incorporate social value judgments in making decisions about benefits coverage for national health insurance. The fundamental ideas for this approach are derived from the "Accountability for Reasonableness" framework for priority setting (Daniels and Sabin 2008). Korea has explicitly used this framework and its four principles as a way to introduce deliberation and public participation into difficult policy decisions about which new benefits to include in health insurance coverage.

Oh and colleagues first conducted three pilot experiments (in 2008, 2010, and 2012). Each pilot had two phases: first, providing randomly selected citizens (from an applicant pool) with information about the decisions; and second, conducting a structured deliberation of the issues for a moderate amount of time. Each round involved questions about different ways that the government could expand insurance coverage to other types of services. The three experiments showed, according to Oh and colleagues, that participants were willing to increase their financial contribution to national health insurance to achieve better coverage, and were willing to reduce their support for expanding service coverage for some items, once information was provided and deliberation occurred. In short, the pilot rounds demonstrated that people could change their initial opinions about coverage expansion through educational and deliberative processes.

The next step was to include this approach in national policy making for actual coverage decisions. In September 2012, Korea's first Citizen Committee for Participation was held, with thirty people randomly selected out of a group of 2,650 applicants. The committee reviewed forty-five medical service items that were being considered for expansion by the Health Insurance Policy Committee (HIPC), the official decision-making body. The deliberations from the Citizen Committee were advisory; nevertheless, the HIPC ultimately accepted 69 percent of the Citizen Committee's recommendations. Oh and colleagues conclude, "Making decisions on benefits coverage is a key component of governing a health system, especially a national health insurance system. More than 1 trillion Korean won (equivalent to U.S. $1 billion) were allocated to cover the new items in the year 2013, with no political criticism or policy debate, partly because they were supported by the lay public participation body in the year 2012." The Citizen Committee for Participation thus worked effectively, according to the principles of Accountability for Reasonableness, using deliberative participatory processes to support decisions about benefits coverage for national health insurance.

Oh and colleagues conclude that the Korean experience of informed deliberation by the lay public is better than a formula-based decision process, such as the one used in the U.S. state of Oregon that "confronted obstacles from the public due to discrepancy between the lay public's value perceptions and the priority list generated mainly by cost effectiveness." They suggest that the Korean experience shows how a deliberative democratic decision-making process can lead to reasonable and accountable decisions under conditions of limited resources. They note: "The general public does not necessarily demand ever-increasing benefits, but can decide to keep benefits at a reasonable level once they understand the nature of public funding, financial sustainability, and cost effectiveness." The authors write that this process may help reduce "policy failure" in other contexts as well, if the results are due to common traits of human beings and do not depend on specific aspects of the Korean context. This experience in Korea, they believe, "deserves broad recognition around the world for its innovative approach to making difficult social decisions." This approach to using deliberative processes might also be able to address Korea's major challenge of financial sustainability (as described in chapter 10 by Yeon), which is looming on the horizon.

CONCLUDING REMARKS

The chapters in this book, summarized above, reflect the Takemi Program's efforts over the past thirty years to promote the development of leaders in health policy—Takemi Fellows. By participating in the Takemi Program at Harvard, these mid-career policy researchers and policy practitioners have developed an expertise in the design, analysis, and implementation of national health policies, using a multidisciplinary perspective. Many Takemi Fellows have assumed positions as policy practitioners in organizations around the world and have applied this perspective in creative ways to difficult health problems, thereby contributing to the solution of real-world health problems. The chapters in this book provide a vivid reflection of some of those experiences. The chapters also present some of the knowledge gained by Takemi Fellows in grappling with health policy challenges in their communities and their countries, and the implications for improving governance of health systems around the world. In this way the Takemi Program has played an important role in strengthening the capacity of problem solving in health at a global level.

Each chapter in this book illustrates efforts to solve real-world health problems at the community and national levels. And each chapter in the book analyzes how these problems are shaped by the quality of governance. The chapters show that in order to achieve common goals in the health sector, policy practitioners must seek ways to create both collective action and collective solutions, two of the fundamental challenges of governance. This process of creating shared value requires better practices in the community and in the nation—as illustrated by the chapters in this book.

It is now widely accepted that health problems represent a critical global challenge that goes beyond national boundaries. In short, health problems are among the most important global priorities for human civilization in the twenty-first century. Human society confronts many health issues that cannot be solved by the actions of individual nation-states. There is growing awareness among global policy makers about the complexity of today's problems in many spheres. The arena of global health is considered one field where the interests of individual nation-states are not as strong as other problems and where strengthening governance can have a significant policy impact in solving problems and improving human welfare. As a result, one of the critical goals for our generation is finding ways to strengthen governance mechanisms for health problems at the community, national, and global levels. We hope that the experiences presented in this book can help contribute to those efforts.

The Takemi Program's 30th Anniversary Symposium focused on governance at the community and national levels because in many ways human efforts at these levels are the most immediate; they make a difference in people's lives. Actions in the community and in the nation-state shape the policies that influence the living environment of communities and shape the actions of national and international organizations and the growing global networks of civil society organizations. We hope that the past thirty years of the Takemi Program have strengthened our understanding of governance in global health in ways that contribute to advancing public knowledge and promoting effective action. This book, we believe, provides examples and evidence of how research can make a difference in improving governance for health.

REFERENCES

Brearley, Lara, and Robert Marten. 2013. *Universal Health Coverage: A Commitment to Close the Gap.* London: Save the Children.

Daniels, N., and J. E. Sabin. 2008. *Setting Limits Fairly: Learning to Share Resources for Health,* 2nd ed. New York: Oxford University Press.

Dodgson, Richard, Kelley Lee, and Nick Drager. 2002. *Global Health Governance: A Conceptual Review.* Discussion Paper No. 1. Geneva: WHO Department of Health and Development.

Independent Evaluation Group. 2009. *The World Bank's Country Policy and Institutional Assessment: An Evaluation.* Washington, D.C.: World Bank, June 30.

Liberato, S. C., J. Brimblecombe, J. Ritchie, M. Ferguson, and J. Coveney. 2011. "Measuring Capacity Building in Communities: A Review of the Literature." *BMC Public Health* 11: 850.

Marks, L., S. Cave, and D. J. Hunter. 2010. "Public Health Governance: Views of Key Stakeholders." *Public Health* 124: 55–59.

Reich, Michael R., Keizo Takemi, Marc J. Roberts, and William C. Hsiao. 2008. "Global Action on Health Systems: A Proposal for the Toyako G8 Summit." *Lancet* 371: 865–69.

Roberts, M. J., William Hsiao, Peter Berman, and Michael R. Reich. 2004. *Getting Health Reform Right: A Guide to Improving Performance and Equity.* New York: Oxford University Press.

Shaw, R. Paul, and Hadia Samaha. 2009. *Building Capacity for Health System Strengthening: A Strategy That Works.* Washington, D.C.: World Bank Institute.

Tollman, Steven. 1991. "Community-Oriented Primary Care: Origins, Evolution, Applications." *Social Science & Medicine* 32: 633–42.

World Health Organization. 2000. *World Health Report 2000—Health Systems: Improving Performance.* Geneva: WHO.

World Health Organization. 2007. *Everybody's Business: Strengthening Health Systems to Improve Health Outcomes: WHO's Framework for Action.* Geneva: WHO.

World Health Organization. 2008. *Health Systems Governance: Toolkit on Monitoring Health Systems Strengthening.* Draft. Geneva: WHO, June.

World Health Organization. 2010. *World Health Report 2010: Financing for Universal Health Coverage.* Geneva: WHO.

PART I

Governing Local Health Systems

CHAPTER 2

Community Participation in Governance of the Health Care System: A Look at Health Unit Management Committees in Uganda

Joseph Konde-Lule

INTRODUCTION

Health System Governance

Governance has become increasingly recognized as of critical importance for the success of health programs, and it is also widely acknowledged that without due attention to governance, resources allocated to health may not achieve their intended results (WHO 2008). But what is governance? There have been many definitions and interpretations of governance. Some interpretations focus on technical government functions and how they are administered, but others are much broader. For example, according to the World Bank (2000, 9–11), governance is economic policy making and implementation, service delivery, plus the accountable use of public resources and of regulatory power. The "accountable use of public resources" is a complex issue, but it will be interpreted to mean the use of public resources according to the rules that regulate and are binding for all the concerned institutions and individuals. The rules enable society to hold the different actors responsible. These may include competitive elections, systems of judicial redress, transparency of information, advisory committees, and media access, among others.

Health governance has also been defined as "putting in place effective rules for policies, programs, and activities related to health-sector objectives" and how these are carried out at various institutional levels (Brinkerhoff and Bossert 2008, 3). The rules determine which institutional actors play what roles and their responsibilities. The same authors also state that "the popularity of governance as a conceptual and practical construct, however, has not led to clarity and agreement as to what it is or is not" (2008, 1). This, in my view, is not a weakness but rather a source of strength. It is a source of strength because it provides an opportunity for flexibility, enabling analysts to devise definitions that are most appropriate for different settings.

The WHO (2000) encouraged greater attention to health governance by introducing the concept of "stewardship," which constitutes six domains. These six are: generating intelligence (information and evidence); formulating strategic policy direction; ensuring tools for implementation through incentives and sanctions; building coalitions and partnerships; developing a fit between policy objectives and organizational structures and cultures; and ensuring accountability (Saltman and Ferrousier-Davis 2000; Travis et al. 2002). This concept of stewardship looks like a step-by-step way of guiding interested parties through some critical steps in the process of navigating the complex exercise of health system governance.

According to WHO (2008), there appears to be a general consensus that health systems should aim to attain three goals. These are:

1. Improvements in health status through more equitable access to quality health services and prevention and promotion programs
2. Patient and public satisfaction with health systems
3. Fair financing that protects against financial risks for those needing health care

These goals indicate that health systems should aim for equity and good governance as key components. Governments often see improvements in health as a public responsibility (World Bank 2004). The justification for this is based in the broader context of social justice as is outlined in the Universal Declaration of Human Rights (1948) and other international humanitarian conventions. The view is also apparently supported by the international endorsement of the UN Millennium Development Goals. Governments often demonstrate their responsibility by financing, providing, and regulating the services that contribute to health outcomes.

Uganda is counted among the poor countries in the world. According to the World Bank data, in 2011 Uganda had a GDP of $16.8 billion and a per capita GNP of $510. At the community level the frequency of poverty is quite high, and 24 percent of the population was reported to be below the poverty line (living on less than $1.25 a day). Providing services to the poor in any society is commonly associated with challenges, and some studies have indicated that the poor receive less than the average access to health care in their communities (Konde-Lule et al. 2010; Kiwanuka et al. 2008). In Uganda, as is the case in many societies around the world today, the services for the poor need to be protected by the authorities. In its 2004 World Development Report, the World Bank warned that broad improvements in human welfare would not occur unless the poor received wider access to affordable and improved services in "education, health, water, and sanitation and electricity" (2004, 1). The high level of poverty in Uganda makes these improvements a big challenge for the state.

In spite of a broad consensus on the importance of health governance as a catalyst for improving health outcomes, however, it is difficult to measure and it remains inadequately monitored and evaluated (WHO 2008). In health system governance many analysts have identified three sets of actors, and they are categorized as follows:

1. State actors, including policy makers and technical government officials
2. Health service providers, both public and private
3. Beneficiaries, including service users and the general public: this group constitutes (or represents) the community

These three pillars provide a framework for analyzing governance in the health sector (World Bank 2004; Brinkerhoff and Bossert 2008).

Health System Governance Analysis

The analysis of health system governance will be based on assessing how well each of the three sets of actors performs with regard to its designated roles. The yardstick should be the full list of activities that each set needs to perform. The WHO toolkit for monitoring health systems categorizes the indicators for measuring health systems governance into two groups. These are: (1) rules-based indicators, which assess the presence of appropriate laws, policies, strategies, and guidelines for governance; and (2) outcome-based indicators (WHO 2008). The outcome-based indicators measure whether rules and procedures are implemented effectively or enforced. While the three-pillars framework can be applied widely, it is clear that the rules and detailed roles may differ significantly between and within countries. There cannot be a single formula that fits all.

Community Participation in Health System Governance

The Declaration of Alma-Ata in 1978 during the International Conference on Primary Health Care identified community participation as one of the key requirements for achieving health care that is acceptable to the users (WHO 1978). From then onward, community participation became one of the cornerstones of primary health care, and it has been integrated in many national-level health policies and in disease control programs. It also became a standard item in the curricula of many public health training institutions. In Uganda, community participation policies are initiated at the national level, and is a process that embraces political leaders and Ministry of Health technocrats. The Alma-Ata Declaration, however, does not provide specific guidance on what kind of community participation is considered desirable. It is also silent on what effect the diversity between countries might have on the type of community participation that is required or on its measurement.

Working Definition

At health center level (representing the community-level health system) the indicators of good governance will be defined as "effective service delivery and adequate accountability for resources in accordance with relevant national and local government guidelines and regulations."

Research Questions

The research questions for this paper are:

1. How much do service users, beneficiaries, and members of the public get involved in ensuring effective service delivery and accountability for resources in the Ugandan community-level health centers?
2. How much do the general public, beneficiaries, and users of the Uganda health system participate in fulfilling government guidelines and regulations for the community-level health centers?

METHODS

This chapter is a literature review of both published and grey literature concerning health system governance, focusing on the community-level health system in Uganda. Searches were done over the Internet and also in the library at Makerere University School of Public Health and in the Ministry of Health library. The focus of the review is the district hospitals and lower-level health centers, which in effect represent the health system at community level. This chapter reviews the roles of different players in health system governance and analyzes the issues that promote or limit community participation in different settings. Following the finding of marked differences between the health unit management committees (HUMCs) in public health centers on the one hand and HUMCs in private health centers on the other, exploratory interviews were subsequently sought from the officers who supervise the HUMCs in the main faith-based organizations, to ask follow-up questions about these differences. This request was granted and responses were obtained from the Uganda Protestant Medical Bureau (UPMB) and from the Uganda Catholic Medical Bureau (UCMB).

At the community level in the Uganda health system, the three pillars of actors in health system governance can be clearly recognized in the following way:

1. **The state** provides the laws and regulations that define the roles of the different players. The main state actors are the Ministry of

Health and the district administrations. In Uganda several studies have found that there are many good laws and regulations for governing the health care system in the country, but the outstanding observation has been that these laws were in most instances not well enforced, and many practitioners broke or ignored them without facing any penalties (Kiwanuka et al. 2008; Konde-Lule et al. 1998; Okello et al. 1998).

2. **The health service providers** include a wide spectrum of providers, from public health centers to NGO health centers that are largely faith based to other private providers, mainly in private clinics, which are quite diverse. This chapter will focus on health centers, both public and private.

3. **Beneficiaries** include all service users, the general public, and any interest groups such as patient groups and the media. Some patient groups, including AIDS patients and cancer patients, have been very active advocates of change for various issues.

While the participation of the first two pillars in health system governance is the expected norm, the focus of this chapter is the degree of involvement of the third pillar, which includes service users, all beneficiaries, and the general public, in health system governance. Data from Uganda policy documents, together with data from national and international reports emanating from studies of health system governance in Uganda and elsewhere, which have been published in different forums, are the main sources of information for this review chapter. The focus of this chapter is the formal health facilities, including both public and private not-for-profit health centers. District hospitals are the referral level for these health centers and are therefore, strictly speaking, not community-level facilities, but they were used for comparison with health centers in some instances. The focus on health centers leaves out many community-level private health care providers in the Uganda health sector, both formal and informal. It also leaves out the community-based organizations (CBOs), which are private organizations that provide a wide range of preventive and promotive health services in the community. This focus is therefore a limitation, but it was necessitated by the desire to obtain a deeper analysis of governance and related issues in the community-level health facilities at health center category.

FINDINGS

The Uganda Model for Community Participation in Governance

The Uganda government has a policy that puts in place health unit management committees for health centers and hospital management boards for hospitals (Uganda MOH 2003). The HUMC policy was made in order to provide a standard guideline for the committees, which provide an entry point for the community to participate in governance of the health system at this level. It is a documented fact, however, that many health facilities, both public and private, had recruited management or advisory committees to support health unit managers on community-related issues many years before the policy was made. Such committees were very useful in matters requiring community mobilization, for example in relation to fund-raising for infrastructure development and other undertakings. They also played a key role in the management of user fees during the period when they were being levied in Uganda's public health facilities.

Historical Perspective on User Fees and Health Unit Management Committees

In Uganda, one of the issues that has greatly influenced community participation in health system governance at health center level is the management of user fees in public health units (Konde-Lule and Okello 1998). The concept of cost sharing through user fees in government health units was first floated during the late 1980s as a way of complementing health financing. It was resisted by many groups and was implemented for years without an official policy document to back it. Although the national parliament rejected the proposed policy in 1993, the scheme remained in place because it was very popular among health workers and it received support from the MOH technocrats. The decentralization policy that was introduced in the 1990s enabled many districts to enact bylaws that institutionalized user fees in their public facilities. Many studies, however, indicated that user fees were strongly resented by most health consumers in public facilities, and that they were described by many analysts as a barrier to access to health care, especially among the poor (Konde-Lule and Okello 1998; Asingwire 2000; Kipp et al. 2001; WHO 2000; Nabyonga-Orem et al. 2008).

During the period when user charges were being levied in Uganda's public health facilities, the HUMCs were the organs most directly concerned with managing the scheme. They fixed the appropriate fees for the unit, decided how fees were handled by staff, made waiver guidelines, determined what items the fees would be spent on, and provided overall oversight for the scheme. The MOH technocrats, together with some other agencies that were actively involved in matters related to health system governance at that time, were always available for consultation by the HUMCs, and they provided guidance and support. User charges commonly supported the purchase of supplies, staff welfare, and, in some instances, infrastructure development. The HUMCs had the power to modify this list according to the health unit priorities of the day.

User charges in public health units were suddenly abolished by the government in 2001, a decision that left HUMCs in these units practically redundant. There was no alternative activity requiring such heavy participation for the HUMCs to take on. The immediate consequence of this decision was that in 2001 the effective participation of HUMCs in public health system governance ended as abruptly as the user fees did. It suddenly looked like the HUMCs would disappear and be forgotten for good. In 2003, however, the quality assurance unit of the MOH drafted the HUMC policy, which clearly aimed to re-institutionalize community participation in the governance of health centers, which constitute the community-level health system. The policy outlines the roles of the HUMC with the aim of promoting quality of health care without reliance on user fees.

The HUMC Policy

According to the HUMC policy (2003), the main function of the management committee is "to monitor the general administration of the health unit within the policy and guidelines of the Ministry of Health." There is a provision in the policy to include ordinary members of the public in these organs. These committees play an oversight role and help to mitigate abuse of office and corruption. Because these committees are not full time and are required to meet only once every three months, there is a limit to what they can do, and many problems may pass unnoticed. Indeed, shortcomings have been identified in some studies.

One Uganda study found a lack of effective communication between the communities located near public health facilities and the management committees or boards (Rutebemberwa et al. 2009). The study found that committee members were not providing any feedback to the communities, nor were they receiving any input from the public. The reasons for this poor communication included the absence of an organized forum for such feedback and the widespread attitude among members of the public that health unit management committee members became part of the health provider system and always sided with the providers. The attitude that HUMC members suddenly change from being health consumers to being health care providers undermines the reasons for setting up the HUMC. If this attitude becomes very common in the community, it has the potential to so grossly undermine the HUMC that it has no value.

The organized or structured community participation in governance, as is envisioned for the health unit management committees, has limitations because of its narrow community catchment and participation. Many stakeholders feel that community participation needs to be opened up to a wide base of players. Singer (1995) defined community participation as "the sum total of actions taken by ordinary members of a political system in order to influence outcomes" (422). This type of opening up means that any suggestion or complaint from the public will, or should, constitute community participation in governance, especially if it comes to the attention of the relevant health care providers, managers, or policy makers. This means that attendance at political gatherings of any kind; stories in or comments to the media, including newspapers, and talk shows on radio or television; and statements from different levels of political leaders all constitute community participation in governance. The key variable for qualifying is any contribution to the betterment of the health care system. While such inputs are difficult to quantify, it is quite likely that in the Uganda setting, and probably in some other settings, they are more likely to produce policy or service delivery changes and improvements than the recognized or formal "structured" participation of the health unit management committees.

Challenges Facing Management Committees

The challenges that face the management committees include: a policy that demands a lot, or even too much, from the HUMC, shortage of funds, lack of publicity about the HUMCs, and shortage of managerial skills and technical knowledge among the HUMC members. These are outlined below.

A Policy That Demands a Lot from the HUMC

The government policy that outlines the responsibilities of the HUMCs provides a long list of what is expected of the HUMCs. The listed functions are quite numerous, and some of them require technical competence. There are four major categories of functions:

1. To monitor general administration of the health center on behalf of the local council and the Ministry of Local Government within the policy and guidelines of the Ministry of Health.
2. To manage funds from the district, specifically: supervise management of health center finances by ensuring that financial regulations and accountability instructions are observed; approve the annual budgets prepared by the health center management team; ensure that annual work plans are drawn up reflecting priority needs; monitor performance of approved budgets; ensure that funds released to the health center have been accounted for to the chief administrative officer through the health subdistrict; authorize the reallocation of funds within the health center budget lines if need arises and with approval of the health subdistrict; ensure that district funds are not diverted to other activities.
3. To advise upon, regulate, and monitor the collection, allocation, and use of finances from other sources.
4. To monitor the procurement, storage, and utilization of all health center goods and services in line with local government regulations. In particular, the HUMC should evaluate tenders and make subsequent recommendations to the district.

This is a long list of functions, and it is difficult to assess how well each HUMC fares with it. One common recommendation from various health system studies in Uganda has been "capacity strengthening" for HUMCs. If the limitations of the committees are put aside, and the listed functions of the HUMCs are assessed on the basis of their merits and potential contribution to effective community participation in governance, then this is without doubt a very good list of responsibilities. This list of responsibilities should certainly promote community participation in the governance of the health system at this level. The main concern is the lack of capacity for the HUMCs to fulfill these tasks, as the following challenges imply.

Shortage of Funds

The management committees are constituted by volunteers who get no regular pay and expect only a sitting allowance when they hold a meeting. At district hospital level this is not much of a problem because the boards' allowances are budgeted for in the hospital budgets. The hospital budget funds are released directly from the national Ministry of Finance. At health center level, however, the management committees are not so lucky, essentially because at district level the budgets are funded as part of "primary health care" costs and are quite small. The priorities for each health center, however, are commonly numerous, and any allowances must be modest in order to be approved by the district administration. Before user fees were abolished from public health facilities in 2001, they were a sure source of funding for health center–level health unit management committees' allowances. The shortage of funds is a problem because obtaining allowances depends on the goodwill of those in charge, which could in turn compromise the independence of the members.

Lack of Publicity

The health unit management committees have not been widely publicized as a channel through which the public could direct their views for improving health service delivery in their communities. Indeed, it has been found in a study done by Rutebemberwa et al. (2009) that most people in the community did not know about the existence of the committees. There is also inadequate or nonexistent publicity about the HUMC both inside and outside the health facilities. The public's ignorance of the HUMCs means that service users and the public cannot submit complaints or suggestions through this channel. This public ignorance about the HUMC is a big challenge, and one that almost renders the committees nonfunctional. Indeed, most people—including patients and many researchers—who make brief contact with health centers have been known to complete their requirements or tasks at health units without ever hearing about the HUMC. The typical finding is that there are no posters or any other form of advertisement for HUMCs.

Shortage of Managerial and Technical Experience

Although attempts are always made to nominate persons with an education and some managerial experience, like teachers and civil servants, some committees may be short of such members. If, in addition, there is no individual with any technical knowledge of the medical profession, then those with supervisory roles will face severe challenges. A dearth of knowledgeable and experienced committee members on a particular committee means that the health unit manager would be far more knowledgeable on all managerial and medical issues than anyone else on the committee, and he or she would therefore find it easy to dominate and control the committee. In such a situation the oversight role of the committee could easily be compromised. Although it has been argued from experience gained elsewhere that, given sufficient time, ordinary citizens can acquire the skills needed to participate in governance (Singer 1995), in the Uganda setting, with so many skills lacking, this could require a very long time.

HUMCs in Private Not-for-Profit (PNFP) Health Units

The HUMCs in PNFP units appear to be much better organized and more productive than their counterparts in public facilities. Because of this finding, the author chose to interview the national-level coordinators of HUMCs in the two largest PNFP organizations. Discussions were held with the Uganda Protestant Medical Bureau (D. Kiyimba, Institutional Capacity Building Program Officer, UPMB) and with the Uganda Catholic Medical Bureau (P. Asiimwe, Organizational Development Advisor, UCMB). The two officials were interviewed separately, but they provided information indicating that the two organizations have much in common. The similarities include having a designated unit within the organization that is concerned with the affairs of all affiliated HUMCs; a method of appointing HUMC members who have a high level of community participation; and a strong training and continuous support program for all affiliated management committees.

Appointment and Composition of HUMC Members

In both UPMB- and UCMB-affiliated health units, the process of selecting HUMC members starts in the local church congregation, where the best candidates are identified. The congregation is guided to identify people who are willing to offer voluntary service and who have a diversity of skills to offer for the good functioning of the committee. The parish council of the relevant faith nominates the best members, taking care of different interest groups and skills. The diocese vets the members and appoints the full committee for a three-year period. Every three years, the parish council elects a new committee and the parish priest becomes a member of the HUMC, representing the bishop.

Training and Support

In addition to an induction period that is provided to new committee members, all HUMC members get regular training for their roles at least once every year. During these regular training sessions, challenges to their roles and ways of solving those challenges are discussed with various experts. The training may be organized at either the diocesan or national level.

Roles of PNFP-Affiliated HUMCs

Both the UPMB and UCMB officials pointed out that their affiliated HUMCs actually follow the guidelines that are provided in the government policy for health unit management committees at health center level. The main difference is that the PNFP-affiliated committees receive regular training, advice, guidance, and encouragement to enable them to comply with the guidelines in the HUMC policy. Although the

PNFP-affiliated health centers belong to the dioceses, they are operationally quite autonomous. Each one generates its own budget, which is implemented quite strictly. The sources of funds include user charges and grants. The HUMCs are always encouraged to source for and to generate funds for their health units from a variety of sources.

Each UCMB-affiliated health unit also has a "charter" that guides it in the process of governance. The charter spells out the roles and responsibilities of each member of the staff and of the committee. The charter contains specific information that is unique for each health center, designed by the HUMC itself with the guidance and support of the national-level UCMB staff. It was made clear that the core content of the charter is extracted from the HUMC policy guideline of the Ministry of Health. The HUMC has the power to hire or dismiss the lower-level categories of the staff list. For the more senior professional staff, the HUMC may recommend disciplinary action to the diocese, where the final power is based. The HUMC members in PNFP health centers are also volunteers, and they receive sitting allowances that are in the same range as those for the committees in public health centers.

DISCUSSION

Differences Between Public and Private HUMCs

There is a big difference between the management committees in public health centers and those in private (PNFP) health centers. The committees in public health facilities provide the impression that participation in governance is a heavy burden because of the shortage of funds, low levels of publicity, lack of technical skills, and a policy guideline that demands too much from the committee. Conversely, the committees in PNFP-affiliated health centers appear to be performing the roles of participation in governance well, and they are not complaining about lack of publicity or skills. This is in spite of the two types of committees following the same policy guideline and receiving the same level of funding from the government's primary health care (PHC) funds. The key question is: What makes PNFP-affiliated HUMCs perform much better than those in public facilities? The outstanding differences between the two groups, which are likely to provide the explanation, are identifiable in the recruitment process, the types of individuals nominated for membership, regular training and guidance, and the pattern of monitoring and complying with all the rules and regulations in the policy guideline for HUMCs. A brief outline of these differences is presented in the following sections.

The Recruitment Process

In PNFP-affiliated committees, the recruitment process is heavily community based, beginning in the local church congregations. There, the most suitable candidates are nominated; this is unlike the process in the public facilities, where committee members are selected by politicians in the sub-county councils.

Types of Individuals Nominated for HUMC Membership

In PNFP-affiliated committees, the nominated members may be described as individuals who are ready and willing to perform voluntary service for the public good. Individuals with a diversity of skills are commonly targeted. Efforts are always made to appoint committees that include professionals in different disciplines and those with management experience, specifically targeting those who have retired from regular employment. In contrast, the HUMC members for public facilities are most commonly politicians from the local sub-county councils.

Regular Training

Participating in training is among the key requirements for all members of HUMCs in PNFP facilities. It is done as part of the induction for new committees and is performed regularly every year for all committees. The training is tailored to address challenges facing the committees. In public facilities there is no such training for the HUMCs.

Monitoring of HUMCs

The presence of a designated full-time office and personnel to monitor, plan for, and provide required assistance and advice to HUMCs is a significant difference between PNFP-affiliated HUMCs and those based in public health facilities. There is no such office for public facilities at either the district administration or in the Ministry of Health.

Complying with the Rules

In PNFP facilities, the practice of working according to the rules and following all guidelines in the government policy for HUMCs is one of the most important issues discussed, and the matter is given much attention during the training of HUMC members. It is emphasized during the monitoring process and in all the support visits to the health centers. There is apparently no such guidance for the HUMCs in public facilities.

How Can the HUMC Limitations in Public Facilities Be Addressed?

After comparing the operations of the HUMCs in public units with those in private health units, it is clear that the issue driving the challenges facing the HUMCs in public facilities is their failure to comply with the policy guidelines for HUMCs. In public facilities, all authority is vested in the hands of those in charge of the health unit. The role of the HUMC is apparently simply ignored. This problem is compounded by weak committees filled with members whose selection involves little or no community input and who are likely to be short on technical skills in key areas such as finance, management, and medical science. The failure of management committees in public facilities to exercise any authority over personnel or finances makes them redundant. These committees are viewed as practically nonfunctional, and their current role is advisory at best.

The HUMCs in public units therefore should learn a lesson or two from the committees in the PNFP health facilities, especially with regard to operating according to the rules laid out in the HUMC policy guidelines. This can happen only after these committees receive appropriate training and after arrangements have been made for ongoing support and advice with regard to exercising due authority over personnel and finances. Another practice that committees in public facilities could copy from those in PNFP facilities is representation from the umbrella organization. The parish priest performs this role in the committees that are based in PNFP-affiliated facilities. Such a member is best suited to providing advice and guidance during committee sessions. In the case of public facilities, this position would best be filled by a representative from the district administration.

Regular training and ongoing support by a designated unit are among the key attributes that have enabled HUMCs in PNFP facilities to fulfill the expectations set in the HUMC policy guidelines and to become effective and successful participants in governance. These two activities are therefore proposed as the main interventions to address the challenges of the committees in public health centers. The selection process for the committee members should also benefit from wider consultations with the public in order to identify individuals with a diversity of skills who are willing to become members. These changes are likely to enable the committees in public facilities to become more effective players in governance by exercising greater power over finances and personnel. These changes are necessary and need to be adopted, but as significant policy changes they would be most appropriately initiated by officials in the Ministry of Health. The potential benefits from the proposed changes justify the move. These changes have the potential to transform management committees in public health centers from dormant organs into effective organs of governance.

Publicity for HUMCs

The public's unfamiliarity with the HUMCs means that service users and the public cannot submit complaints or suggestions through this channel. It will be important to identify an effective method of publicizing the HUMCs. The communication trend in the country is rapidly shifting from verbal or print media to telecommunication via mobile telephones. These are getting more popular by the day, and many studies have indicated that most households own one or more of these phones. Adopting mobile phones to market the HUMCs and to solicit for comments using telephone messages could be an effective method of stimulating community participation in the governance of the community-level health system in the country. Mobile phone text messages have been found to be effective in various settings. For example, in

Kenya they were found to be effective in improving malaria treatment among health workers (Zurovac et al. 2011).

CONCLUSIONS AND RECOMMENDATIONS

Conclusions

Most health unit management committees in Uganda's public health centers are not performing the role of community participation in the governance of their health centers as effectively as they should. In contrast, the committees in the faith-based PNFP health centers are quite active, and they are performing the role of community participation in the governance of their health centers as outlined in the government policy guidelines for HUMCs at health center level. The reasons behind this difference include the handling of the recruitment process, which for PNFP units closely engages with the beneficiary communities; training for new HUMC members and regular refresher training for all HUMCs; close monitoring, guidance, and support of all affiliated HUMCs by the coordinating PNFP body; and the HUMCs closely following all regulations and guidelines during the process of conducting routine business. In public health centers there is currently minimal HUMC participation in governance. It appears that the main reason for this is the absence of training or any continuing guidance and support from either the district administrations or the Ministry of Health. There is no designated office tasked with monitoring, training, advising, and motivating HUMCs in public health centers. The current absence of effective community participation in the governance of public health centers has a negative effect on their performance and needs to be addressed.

Recommendations

On the basis of the findings in this report it is recommended that:

1. The leadership in both the Ministry of Health and at district level needs to work together to identify a coordinating office fully dedicated to HUMCs in public health facilities at district level. This office should take up the role of regularly training, monitoring, and advising public

facility–based HUMCs in the districts to enable them to conduct business according to the HUMC policy guidelines for effective participation in governance.

2. The selection process for the management committees should be modified to get a higher level of community involvement, and individuals with technical skills such as financial management should be targeted for membership if they are willing to offer voluntary service for the public good.

REFERENCES

Asiimwe, Peter. 2013. Personal communication regarding the role of the HUMCs in UCM-affiliated health centers, July.

Asingwire, Narathius. 2000. "The Impact of User Fees on Equity of Access to Health Services in AIDS-Affected Households in Rural Uganda: The Case of Tororo district." A research report for Makerere University SWSA Department, May.

Brinkerhoff, D. W., and T. J. Bossert. 2008. "Health Governance: Concepts Experience and Programming Options. A Brief Prepared for USAID for the Health Systems 20/20 Project." http://www.health systems2020.org/content/resource/detail/1914/.

Kipp, Walter, J. Kamugisha, P. Jacobs, G. Burnham, and T. Rubaale. 2001. "User Fees, Health Staff Incentives, and Service Utilization in Kabarole District, Uganda." *Bulletin of the World Health Organization* 79 (11): 1032–37.

Kiyimba David. 2013. Personal communication regarding the role of HUMCs in UPMB-affiliated health centers, July.

Kiwanuka S. N., E.K. Ekirapa, S. Peterson, O. Okui, M.H. Rahman, D. Peters, G. W. Pariyo. 2008. "Access to and Utilization of Health Services for the Poor in Uganda: a Systematic Review of Available Evidence." *Transactions of the Royal Society of Tropical Medicine and Hygiene* 102(11): 1067–74.

Konde-Lule, J. K., Sheba Gitta, Anne Lindfors, Sam Okuonzi, Virgil Onama, and Birger Forsberg. 2010. "Private and Public Health Care in Rural Areas of Uganda." *BMC International Health and Human Rights* 10 (1): 29.

Konde-Lule, J. K., and D. Okello. 1998. "User Fees in Government Health Units in Uganda: Implementation, Impact and Scope." Small applied research paper no. 2. Bethesda, MD: Partnerships for Health Reform Project, Abt Associates Inc., June.

Konde-Lule, J. K., D. O. Okello, R. N. Lubanga, and J. Arube-Wani. 1998. "Legislatory Framework for Private Medical Practice in Uganda." *East African Medical Journal* 75(9): 544–48.

Nabyonga-Orem, J., H. Karamagi, L. Atuyambe, F. Bagenda, S. Okuonzi, O. Walker. 2008. "Maintaining Quality of Health Services

After Abolition of User Fees: A Uganda Case Study." *BMC Health Services Research* 8: 102.

Okello, D. O., J. K. Konde-Lule, R. N. Lubanga, J. Arube-Wani, and J. Lwanga. 1998. "A Review of Regulatory Framework for the Emerging Private Health Sector in Uganda." *Journal of Clinical Epidemiology* 51 (suppl 1): S41.

Rutebemberwa, E., E. Ekirapa-Kiraso, and G. Pariyo. 2009. "Lack of Effective Communication Between Communities and Hospitals in Uganda: A Qualitative Exploration of Missing Links." *BMC Health Services Research* 9: 148.

Saltman, R. B., and O. Ferroussier. 2000. "The Concept of Stewardship in Health Policy." *Bulletin of the World Health Organization* 78: 6.

Singer, M.A. 1995. "Community Participation in Health Care Decision Making: Is It Feasible?" *Canadian Medical Association Journal* 153 (4): 421–24.

Travis P., D. Egger, P. Davies, and A. Mechbal. 2002. "Towards Better Stewardship: Concepts and Critical Issues." Geneva: World Health Organization.

Uganda Ministry of Health, Quality Assurance Unit. 2003. "Guidelines on Health Unit Management Committees for Health Centre III." Kampala, Uganda: Ministry of Health, Department of Health Assurance. http://www.health.go.ug/docs/Guidelines%20on%20Health%20Unit%20management%20committees%20for%20health%20Centre%20II%20(2003).pdf.

World Bank. 2004. *The World Development Report 2004: Making Services Work for Poor People*. Chapter 3. Washington, D.C.: World Bank.

World Bank. 2000. *Reforming Public Institutions and Strengthening Governance: A World Bank Strategy*. Washington, D.C.: World Bank, November. http://www1.worldbank.org/publicsector/Reforming.pdf.

World Health Organization. 1978. "Primary Health Care: Report of the Conference on Primary Health Care." Alma Ata, USSR, 6–12 September. Geneva: WHO.

World Health Organization. 2000. *World Health Report 2000: Health Systems: Improving Performance*. Geneva: WHO.

World Health Organization. 2008. "Health Systems Governance: Tool Kit on Monitoring Health Systems Strengthening." Geneva: WHO, June.

Zurovac, D., R. K. Sudoi, W. S. Akhwale, M. Ndiritu, D. H. Ham-
mer, A. K. Rowe, R. W. Snow. 2001. "The Effect of Mobile Phone
Text Message Reminders on Kenyan Health Workers' Adherence to
Malaria Treatment Guidelines: A Cluster Randomized Trial." *Lancet* 378 (9793): 795–803.

CHAPTER 3

Governance and Performance of Public District Hospitals in the Eastern Region of Ghana

Nii Ayite Coleman

According to many reports, Ghana's health system is underperforming. Although it performs reasonably well in comparison with other sub-Saharan African countries, when compared with other countries with similar incomes and health expenditures, such as Tunisia, Thailand, and the Kyrgyz Republic, its health outcomes for child and maternal mortality are worse (Saleh 2012).

Ghana's health system evolved from a colonial medical system that focused on promoting the well-being of European settlers. Prior to the arrival of Europeans in current-day Ghana in the late fifteenth century, the African population relied on health care services provided by traditional medicine practitioners. Western medicine was introduced to Africans during the slave trade in the sixteenth and seventeenth centuries by ships' surgeons on slave ships. It was extended to the indigenous populations by missionaries and the West African Army Medical Service, which later became the nucleus of colonial public health services. The colonial government's attempt in 1849 to use some of the poll tax revenue for health care delivery failed. Though unsuccessful, the 1849 attempt marked the first effort of the colonial government to formulate a health policy. From about 1890, an effective medical policy developed out of concern for the well-being of Europeans living in the country.

In *Evolution of Modern Medicine in Developing Countries: Ghana 1880–1960,*

Stephen Addae noted that the initial colonial medical policy had been directed primarily to safeguard the health of Europeans. Dispatches from the Colonial Office indicated that there was fear for European lives in any town that did not have a medical officer, and all efforts were made to provide medical help wherever the size of the European population merited it:

> The great concern for European well-being in the country evidently determined that all medical resources in the colony should be directed at securing the health of Europeans. A policy established in the early 1890s was to concentrate the affordable medical resources on the European populations and build hospitals in the big towns where there were large numbers of Europeans.
>
> Purely African townships had none [Europeans], with the inevitable consequences that hospitals and other health facilities were predominantly along the coast in particular and in the south of the country in general.... The medical facilities were primarily for use of European officials and non-officials, African government officials, troops, police, and the Hausa constabulary. (Addae 1996, 30)

The colonial medical system was based on a health policy that was Eurocentric, produced a health care system that was parochial, and made health care services inaccessible to the majority of indigenous Africans.

HEALTH SYSTEM REFORMS

Ghana's health system, like those of other African countries, has since independence, undergone cycles of reforms. In this section, we review four cycles: first, the independence health reforms of the 1950s and 1960s, to overturn the Eurocentric health policies of colonial government; then reforms under the banner of primary health care in the 1970s; next, the health sector reforms of the 1980s and 1990s under structural adjustment programs; and finally, the wave of reforms in the 1990s with the goal of universal health coverage.

Independence Health Reforms

The transition from the colonial medical system began after the colony adopted a new constitution in 1950. When the first African government of Kwame Nkrumah took power in 1951, it inherited a health system that had evolved over some seventy years and was predominantly curative, favored the south of the country, could handle about 20 percent of the population, had an organization that was outdated, and had grossly inadequate medical staff consisting mostly of European doctors and a small cadre of auxiliary medical staff. The new government started reforming the colonial medical system with the metamorphosis of the Medical Department to a Ministry of Health headed by an African, K. A. Gbedemah, with the administrative machinery also headed by an African, Dr. Eustace Akwei.

The independence health reform proceeded in two stages. The first phase was based on recommendations of the Maude Commission. After only a few months in office under the new constitution, the government appointed a committee headed by Sir John Maude. That committee was charged with holding a commission of enquiry into the health needs of the country, to enable it to formulate a policy on the development of health services in the country. The purpose of the commission was:

> ... [T]o review measures taken or projected in the Gold Coast either by government or private enterprise: for the development of preventive and social medicine, including health education; for the development of curative medicine, including the provision of hospitals, health centers and dressing stations, and the training of personnel; for medical research; to examine the adequacy of the administrative structure and organization of the Medical Department in relation to such development; and make recommendations. (Addae 1996, 84)

The Maude Commission recommended expanding the medical field units, improving hospital facilities, establishing health centers as nodal points in a network that embraced hospitals and dressing stations, increasing the number of dressing stations, and shifting emphasis from curative to preventive services. Addae illustrated the effect of the policy change:

> In 1951 there were three health centers in the country.... The African government implemented the Maude Commission recommendation of expansion of rural health centers with singular vigor. It was a more effective and rapid way of carrying health services to the people, the vast majority of who lived in the rural areas...By 1960, there were over 23 health centers in operation and 23 under construction. A Ministry of Health committee drew plans for 63 additional health centers spread over the entire country. (1996, 85–86)

The second phase of the expansion of the public health service was based on the proposals of Dr. David Brachott, who was part of an Israeli medical and technical assistance team to Ghana. The government hired him in 1962 to help reorganize the Ministry of Health and develop a ten-year medical plan for the country. The ten-year health service development program sought to deal with three major aspects of providing health care: a rural health service integrated into the system of hospitals, health centers, and other medical units; a countrywide hospital plan based on the health care needs of the population and on sound medical and economic consideration; and a training program for medical and paramedical personnel capable of achieving the ten-year health program goals.

Amenumey described the expansion of the health delivery system in reversal to the colonial policy for the development of health infrastructure:

> In the area of social services great progress was made. The government had planned to create a welfare state and raise the standards of living of the people. The government expanded health and social services. It built new hospitals, health centers, and clinics. It organized campaigns against diseases like small pox, yaws tuberculosis, and leprosy. By the end of 1960, it awarded scholarships to about 400 Ghanaians to study medicine abroad in order to increase the number of doctors in the country. (2008, 218–19)

During the 1950s, Ghana's economy grew rapidly. Between 1957 and 1960, gross domestic product (GDP) rose by 6 percent each year. The favorable economic conditions enabled Kwame Nkrumah's government to implement its socialist ideology. In May 1962 outpatient care became free for Ghanaian and non-Ghanaians at all government health care facilities (Arhinful 2003). In addition to the rapid expansion of the health care delivery system, the user fees policy, which had posed a formidable barrier to the utilization of health care services, was eliminated. The user fees policy, which was introduced by Governor Maxwell in 1894, gave way to a policy of financing health care by general tax revenue.

At the time of Ghana's independence struggle from British colonial rule in the 1940s and 1950s, the major health problem was lack of access by indigenous Africans, and the root cause was seen as colonialism coupled with its Eurocentric health-care policy. The solution comprised the elimination of colonialism through independence, reform of Eurocentric policy, and then extension of health care services to all citizens. The struggle for independence was about freedom, about social justice, and about equitable access to social services such as health and education. As a result, the independence health reform aspired to extend the health care system and services to all indigenous people (Coleman 2012).

Primary Health Care Reforms

During the 1960s, Ghanaian health planners saw the need to systematically improve methods of providing rural primary health care. Most doctors, nurses, midwives, and other health personnel were concentrated in large towns and cities. Local government health services were provided through rural health centers and health posts, but they were relatively few in number. To assist in initiating a rural family planning program, which would improve the health and welfare of the people, the Danfa Project began in 1966:

> The Danfa Comprehensive Rural Health and Family Planning Project is a service, research, and teaching project designed to help find solutions to health problems and to demonstrate feasible

methods of delivering effective health and family planning services in rural Ghana.

On health care delivery, the final report of the Danfa Project noted that:

> Because of economic difficulties over the past 15 years, it has become impossible to maintain existing health care facilities and programs at their former level of funding in constant dollars and it is difficult, therefore, to plan expansion of health care services.
>
> In considering the expansion of primary health care to rural areas such as the Danfa health district, it is important to be realistic and to consider only those service programs that can be implemented under existing national resources. The essential criteria for a feasible rural health care program for Ghana are: (1) it must deal with the major causes of morbidity and mortality to the extent feasible with existing technology; (2) it must be accessible to the entire population and result in high participation rates; (3) it must be feasible for implementation with existing resources; and (4) its most important objectives must be capable of being evaluated.
>
> It is likely that sufficient funds will not be available in Ghana in the next ten years to build, supply, and staff all the health centers and health posts that the Ministry of Health had previously planned. Even if they were to do so, the Danfa experience has shown that strictly health center–based care does not necessarily deal with the major causes of morbidity and mortality and that it is often not accessible or utilized by a large percent of the population who live more than three miles away. (University of Ghana Medical School 1979, CR1–CR2)

In fact, primarily for reasons of accessibility, the Danfa program evolved into a more village-based primary health care program. The report concluded that:

> The foremost needs in Ghana's health care system were: (a) the development of peripheral primary health care networks sensitive to the needs of various regions; (b) personnel to staff the

networks; (c) district-level supervisory staff; (d) a logistics system to coordinate supply distribution. (University of Ghana Medical School 1979, 1–6)

Various plans to strengthen health services in rural areas had been proposed, but acceptance and implementation were erratic. For that reason, the National Health Planning Unit was established by the Ministry of Health (MOH) in 1975. As stated in the *Primary Health Care Strategy for Ghana* (MOH 1978), the National Health Planning Unit demonstrated that "in spite of huge resources (both facilities and highly trained professionals) since 1960, there has been little improvement in the general health status of the nation in 15 years. In fact, certain communicable diseases have been increasing over the past 10 years" (MOH 1978, 3). The basic problem was that the health system, based on "passive service delivery (hospitals, health centers, and health posts)" (MOH 1978, 1), was ineffective because 70 percent of Ghanaians were unable to access services.

The planning unit used the findings of field projects at Danfa, Brong Ahafo, Bawku, and other areas to assist in the formulation of the Primary Health Care Strategy. This strategy was to be "an activating supplement to this system, particularly designed to reach the people of the rural areas and urban shanty towns" (MOH 1978, 1). The specific goal of the Primary Health Care System was:

> …to maximize the total healthy life of the Ghanaian people with the following targets achieved by 1990: (1) 80 percent coverage of the population by the introduction of the system to all villages with a population of 200 or more and (2) effective attack on the disease problems that account for 80 percent of the unnecessary deaths and disability afflicting Ghanaians. (MOH 1978, 9)

Implementation of the Primary Health Care Strategy began in 1978 with identification of five initial districts and District Medical Officers of Health. The Alma-Ata Declaration of 1978 on primary health care validated Ghana's Primary Health Care Strategy and provided impetus for its implementation.

In December 1981, the twenty-seven-month-old People's National Party government of Dr. Hilla Limann was overthrown and the government of the Provisional National Defence Council (PNDC) of Jerry Rawlings came to power. The Primary Health Care Strategy for Ghana was revised in 1982, and the revised policy expressed the unequivocal commitment of the PNDC government to primary health care, considering it a "revolutionary way of looking at the whole health system with a view to ensuring social justice to all citizens" (MOH 1982, 9). The revised policy emphasized the decentralization of health care services and the development of district health systems. The vision of the primary health care policy was captured in the words of the WHO:

> A district health system based on primary health care is a more or less self-contained segment of the national health system. It comprises first and foremost a well-defined population, living within a clearly delineated administrative and geographical area, whether urban or rural. It includes all institutions and individuals providing health care in the district, whether governmental, social security, non-governmental, private, or traditional. A district health system therefore consists of a large variety of interrelated elements that contribute to health in homes, schools, workplaces, and communities, through the health and other related sectors. It includes self-care and all health care workers and facilities, up to and including the hospital at the first referral level and the appropriate laboratory, other diagnostic, and logistic support services. Its component elements need to be well coordinated by an officer assigned to this function in order to draw together all these elements and institutions into a fully comprehensive range of promotive, preventive, curative, and rehabilitative health activities. (1988, 9)

The primary health care reform established a three-tier district health system: levels A, B, and C. At level A in the community, a village health worker treated minor ailments and a traditional birth attendant handled pregnancies and deliveries. Level B was the health center, where a medical assistant and a midwife operated. The district hospital was level C, the apex of the district health system.

Health Reforms Under the Structural Adjustment Program

The Ghanaian economy continued to deteriorate throughout the 1970s. The GDP annual growth rate declined to 0.4 percent by the end of the decade. Per capita income declined by 2.2 percent per annum in the 1970s. The World Bank summed up Ghana's economic situation in the early 1980s:

> Ghana's past economic policies were characterized by maintenance of overvalued exchange rates, declining real producer prices of export commodities, protection against imports that extended well beyond infant industry stage, a bias in favor of import substitution and against export promotion, wide variation in the degree of import protection across industries, low public utility prices which could cover only a fraction of utility costs, negative real interest rates, greater reliance on administered allocative mechanisms than on relative prices, overextension of the parastatal sector especially state monopolies and prevalence of sellers' markets that provided little inducement for productivity advances or for meeting users' needs. The situation was compounded by a succession of politically unstable governments who failed to take corrective action in time. The resulting drift and economic mismanagement culminated in severe distortion of the economy.... Ghana had made reasonable progress in providing health services but at present faces serious problems. (World Bank 1984, 2)

Total government expenditures, including spending on health, dropped precipitously. Ministry of Health expenditures in 1984 amounted to only 45.4 percent of what they had been in 1978 (Serageldin, Elmendorf, and Eltigani 1994).

In 1983, the government was forced by the dire economic circumstances to reopen serious discussions with the International Monetary Fund and the World Bank. In April 1983, in agreement with the International Monetary Fund and the World Bank to reverse the economic decline, the PNDC government embarked on an economic recovery program and adopted the International Monetary Fund's Structural Adjustment Program.

In response to the worsening economic conditions and reduced public finance for health services, Ghana had to reform various aspects of its health system. The approach to health care financing was identified as one of the fundamental causes of the problems in the health sector. According to the World Bank, efforts of government to provide free health care for everyone from general public revenues had resulted in chronic underfunding of recurrent expenditures, thus reducing the effectiveness of health staff and creating internal inefficiency of public programs (World Bank 1987). In its document entitled *The Agenda for Health Reform*, the World Bank provided four policy recommendations for adoption by developing countries undertaking the International Monetary Fund's Structural Adjustment Program. Two specific types of strategies were introduced by governments: reform of public-sector organization and procedures, and reform of financing strategies. The decentralization of health services and the charging of user fees for publicly provided health care were, probably, the most widely implemented reform strategies in Africa. The World Bank policy recommendation on decentralization gave impetus to the strengthening of district health systems.

Health-sector reforms under the Structural Adjustment Program reintroduced the user fees policy in 1983 through the repeal of LI 706 by Hospital Fees Regulation, 1983 (LI 1277). In 1985, the level of user fees rose significantly when LI 1277 was revoked by LI 1313.

When user fees were reintroduced in 1983, all fees collected by each health care facility were paid into a central account, and each facility was supplied with drugs and medical supplies from the central medical stores through the regional stores. Later health care facilities were permitted to retain 25 percent of the fees collected. By 1990, the percentage of fees retained rose to 100 percent, with health care facilities still obtaining drugs and medical supplies through the regional stores. The strategy enabled health care facilities to build seed capital to purchase drugs. In 1992, the seed capital was used to start revolving drug funds in all health care facilities. Health care facilities were no longer allowed to receive drugs from the medical stores free of charge; instead, they procured medicines on a cash-and-carry system. Health facility managers were forced to recover the full cost of drugs. Subsequently, cost recovery extended beyond drugs to cover medical supplies with total disregard for equity mechanisms and provisions in the legislation (Coleman 1997).

Once again, user fees became a formidable barrier to accessing health care services. Waddington and Enyimayew (1989) found that the increase in user fees in 1985 resulted in a significant reduction in the utilization of ambulatory care at district level. The reintroduction of user fee policy under the Structural Adjustment Program adversely affected the ambition to extend health care services to all.

Health Reforms Under the 1992 Constitution

Despite post-independence political instability and economic decline in the 1970s and 1980s, the independence aspiration of extending health care services to the entire Ghanaian population was never lost on government and health planners. The 1992 Constitution reaffirmed the independence aspiration to universal health coverage. Article 35, Clause 3, stipulates that "the State shall promote just and reasonable access by all citizens to public facilities and services in accordance with law." In response to the constitutional provision, the Fourth Republic legislature has enacted several laws reforming the organization and delivery of health care service, financing, and regulation. The Ghana Health Service and Teaching Hospitals Act of 1996 (Act 525) sought to increase access and improve quality of care. Section 3(1)(b) states that "The objects of the Service are (b) increase access to improved health services." Sections 3(2)(a), 3(2)(c), and 3(2)(d) endorse the primary health care and district health system strategy:

> For the purpose of achieving its objects, the Service shall perform the following functions—(a) ensure access to health services at the community, sub-district, district, and regional levels by providing health services or contracting out service provision to other recognized health care providers;... (c) plan, organize, and administer comprehensive health services with special emphasis on primary health care; (d) develop mechanisms for equitable distribution of health facilities in rural and urban districts.

Sections 25 and 26 provide for a District Director of Health Service:

> 25(1) There shall be appointed for each district a health professional to be known as the District Director of Health Service referred to in this Act as "District Director."
>
> 26(1) A District Director shall be responsible for the implementation of the policies and decisions of the Council in the district.

Section 23 provides the necessary flexibility to enable each district to make innovations in the development of its health system:

> For the purposes of effective health delivery, the Council may establish in each district such health areas as it considers necessary on advice of the Regional Director given after consultation with the District Director and the District Chief Executive concerned.

The Constitution of the Fourth Republic and legislation arising from it have incorporated elements of all postcolonial health reforms. The district health system has been endorsed as the basic unit of health care delivery. It has three levels of community health and planning services (CHPS) at the community level, a package of curative and preventive services at the sub-district level, and it is complemented by the district hospital. The district health system is therefore an integrated system of health centers supporting community health workers in CHPS zones and complemented by a district hospital.

The district hospital is designed to provide curative and preventive care as well as health promotion in the district. It offers clinical care by more skilled and competent staff than those of levels A and B. The clinical services include obstetrics and gynecology, child health, internal medicine, surgery including anesthesia, accident and emergency services, mental health, dental services, physiotherapy, and laboratory and imaging services. It is the first-referral hospital, provides training and technical supervision to lower levels, and forms an integral part of the district health system. It complements the services provided by lower-level health facilities and enables each district to provide access to comprehensive basic health services. The district hospital is a sine qua non of the district health system.

UNDERPERFORMING DISTRICT HOSPITALS

Ghana has made considerable progress in health systems reform. Health reforms since independence have focused predominantly on the organization and delivery of health services and the financing of health care (Coleman 2011). Until now, performance of the health system has been assessed by the number of hospitals and health care facilities built, as well as levels of service utilization. Omitted from the health agenda are measures of performance that reflect how well the health care delivery system is operating and whether services are being provided effectively and efficiently. At the current stage of its development, the government of Ghana could embark on additional optional reforms by building on its strengths while addressing its weaknesses in the areas of decentralization, governance, health service delivery, public health, and health financing (Saleh 2012).

Significant funds are being spent in Ghana's health sector, and there are concerns about spending effectiveness. Overall, hospitals are running more efficiently but improvements at lower levels could increase efficiency. Patients are bypassing clinics in favor of hospitals. More outpatient consultations are at hospitals than at clinics, a situation that is costly to the system. Patients are bypassing district hospitals in favor of regional hospitals for the same reason they prefer hospitals to clinics. A comprehensive assessment of Ghana's health system found that district hospitals receive a proportionately larger resource allocation relative to their production. Per capita spending at district hospitals is higher than at regional hospitals. They have substantially higher costs per bed or patient day. The assessment suggests that district hospitals form the weakest link in Ghana's health system.

Why are district hospitals so inefficient? According to the Hospital Strategy document prepared by the MOH and Ghana Health Service (2005), poorly developed management systems pose a major challenge to improving hospital performance. The document stated that the level of involvement of civil society in the management of hospitals is low and that there is a growing awareness that public-sector hospitals need to undergo organizational and managerial transformation. As the means to improve performance of hospitals the document proposed hospital autonomy with governing boards. Although many researchers and practitioners believe that good governance is positively associated with the performance of health care facilities, there is no empirical work in Ghana on this hypothesis.

This chapter examines a preliminary study of the governance and performance of public district hospitals in the Eastern Region of Ghana. The study sought to get an initial sense of the governance reality of public district hospitals in Ghana and to explore hypotheses about governance and performance of public hospitals. First, it argues that no major characteristic of hospitals is an independent driver of clinical performance or improvement and that all hospitals, regardless of type, could become high performers through effective clinical practice, sound management, and good governance. Second, it explores the relationship between governance and performance in health care systems, and concludes that existing studies do not provide clear answers about whether the corporate governance standards adopted positively or negatively affect the hospitals' performance. Next, it analyzes the hospital governance policy in Ghana and suggests that hospital governance policy in Ghana is ambiguous, obsolete, and requiring revision. Then, it presents the results of a study of governance and performance of twelve public district hospitals. Finally, it discusses some implications of the results; suggests short-term and long-term strategies for improving hospital governance in Ghana; and concurs with Frenk and Moon that governance challenges will continue to complicate the best efforts of nations to respond to urgent, complex, and serious global health problems.

Drivers of Hospital Performance

Are there specific institutional characteristics that lead to higher or lower clinical performance in some hospitals? According to the California Healthcare Foundation, "Few studies that previously examined this question had mixed, inconclusive results regarding a limited number of characteristics." In a study to "examine more comprehensively whether hospital characteristics were independently associated with hospital performance...No major category of hospital characteristics, including financial health, was determined to be an independent driver of clinical performance or improvement. The most striking finding was that a large majority of hospital characteristics never or rarely appeared in any way related to performance" (California Healthcare Foundation 2008, 1).

The Health Evidence Network at the WHO Regional Office in Europe acknowledges that "the principal methods of measuring hospital performance are regulatory inspection, public satisfaction surveys, third-party assessment, and statistical indicators, most of which have never been tested rigorously. Evidence of the relative effectiveness comes mostly from descriptive studies rather than from controlled trials. Statistical indicators can suggest issues for performance management, quality improvement, and further scrutiny; however, they need to be interpreted with caution. The effectiveness of measurement strategies depends on many variables including their purpose, the national culture, how they are applied, and how the results are used" (WHO 2003, 4–9).

In health, no single standard measure of effectiveness of care is universally acceptable but certain key elements are common to these measures. Govindaraj and Chawla (1996) used efficiency, quality of care, public accountability, equity, and resource mobilization as criteria for evaluating the performance of autonomous hospitals. The Institute of Medicine offers a framework in which a high-performing hospital should deliver effective health care in an economically efficient way (Institute of Medicine 2001). Using preference weightings, Kroch et al. (2007) combined three indicators (i.e., morbidity, complications, and mortality) into a single quality measure to provide a broad, robust performance indicator.

The report of the California Healthcare Foundation "suggests that researchers, policy makers, and others should discontinue the practice of separating hospitals by characteristics or type when attempting to assess performance or acting to improve it." They also "suggest that all hospitals, regardless of type, can become high performers by implementing effective practices" in clinical practice, management, and governance (California Healthcare Foundation 2008, 1).

Governance and Hospital Performance

Various studies have attempted to probe the relationship between corporate governance and a firm's performance. Unfortunately, most of the academic questions are yet to be answered satisfactorily. Questions examined include: Is one model (shareholder or stakeholder) of corporate governance better than the other? What are the benefits and costs associated with the different kinds of governance models in existence? The existing studies do not provide clear answers about whether the corporate governance standards adopted are positively or negatively affecting the firm's performance. Some of the studies indicate that poor governance accounts for much of the inefficiency in service provision in health care systems (Lewis and Petterson 2009).

Governance has multiple definitions and interpretations. In a review of fifty-three published governance studies Ruhanen et al. (2010) identified forty separate dimensions of governance, out of which the six most frequently included dimensions were: accountability, transparency, involvement, structure, effectiveness, and power. Cadbury noted, "Corporate governance is concerned with holding the balance between economic and social goals and between individual and communal goals...The aim is to align as nearly as possible the interests of individuals, corporations, and society" (Iskander and Chamlou 2000, vi). Operationally, governance is about the rules that distribute roles and responsibilities among societal actors and that shape the interactions among them.

Governance in health care systems is about developing and putting in place effective rules in defined institutional arenas for policies, programs, and activities related to fulfilling public health functions in order to achieve health-sector objectives (Bossert and Brinkerhoff 2008). There are three sets of actors involved in health care governance: (1) state actors, including politicians, policy makers, and other government officials; (2) health service providers, including public-, private-, and voluntary-sector providers; and (3) beneficiaries, service users, and the general public. Health care governance involves the rules that determine the roles and responsibilities of each of these categories of actors as well as the relationships and interactions among them.

D. W. Taylor (2000) proposed nine principles of good governance that could be applied to health care management. The first principle is about "knowing what governance is." The chief executive officer is responsible to the board for implementing its policies, plans, and strategic directions. The board is responsible for developing corporate policies and plans as well as monitoring and measuring organizational performance against those policies and plans. The board's governance responsibilities are to provide a linkage between the hospital and its moral ownership. Taylor's second principle is the "achievement of strategic ends." Hospital governance structure must be such that performance objectives can be measured and accomplished. The third principle is about the relationship between the board and the chief executive officer.

Principles four, five, and six are derived from classical management principles and concern the organization and mechanism for functioning of the board. Principle four is "unity of direction," five is "unity of command," and six is "unity of accountability and responsibility." Principle seven refers to "ownership needs" and points out that the board's ultimate accountability is to the organization's owners. The eighth principle covers the notion of "self improvement and quality management." It requires that continuous improvement be part of an organizational philosophy and permeate all hospital management and governance practice. Taylor's last principle, "understanding the cost of governance," addresses issues such as direct board meeting expenses, board members' personal opportunity costs, the costs associated with errors made by the board, and the costs of ineffectively structured governance-management-organization relationships. The governance process is therefore orchestrated by the board, which is charged with responsibility and accountability for the overall performance of an organization (Ditzel et al. 2006).

Bossert and Brinkerhoff (2008) identified four governance principles. First, governance rules should ensure some level of accountability of the key actors in the system to the beneficiaries and the broader public. Second, health governance involves a policy process that enables the interplay of the key competing interest groups to influence policy making on a level playing field. Third, health governance requires sufficient state capacity, power, and legitimacy to manage the policy-making process effectively. Finally, governance depends upon the engagement and efforts of non-state actors in the policy arena as well as in service delivery partnerships and in oversight and accountability.

"A weak system of accountability renders the task of public management difficult and the establishment of good governance unattainable" (Hugue 2011, 59). Good governance in health requires "the existence of standards, information on performance, incentives for good performance, and, arguably most importantly, accountability" (Lewis and Petterson 2009). Ackerman (2005, 6) described accountability as "a proactive process by which public officials inform about and justify their plans of action, their behavior and results, and are sanctioned accordingly." The existence of an effective board can enhance accountability. Al-Najjar (2012) analyzed the factors that affect board effectiveness and indicated that in the United Kingdom, board meetings, board composition, and board size are key indicators for good internal governance practices and, in turn, enhance board monitoring activities. He also found that board size and structure are positively related to the frequency of board meetings. And outside independent directors appear to strengthen corporate boards (Petra 2005). The governing board of a hospital thus provides the requisite mechanism by which health service providers and policy makers could "inform about and justify their plans, their behavior, and results" to beneficiaries, service users, and the general public.

Hospital Governance Policy in Ghana

The governance of public hospitals has received little attention in Ghana's health reform. The political system of Ghana, characterized by instability during the first four decades after independence in March 1957, has not fostered effective relationships and interactions among state actors and citizens. In a political system that until recently limited participation in decision making, it is no surprise that beneficiaries, service users, and the general public have limited relationships and interaction with both state actors and health service providers. Consequently, issues dealing with the relationship and interaction of these different sets of actors involved in health governance have remained obscure. The governance of health, like the governance of public-sector institutions, cannot be different from the governance of the entire state.

Ghana's public sector has the largest share of the market when it comes to health facilities, hospital beds, and health providers. The public sector has two organizational components: the Ghana Health Service focuses on service delivery, while the Ministry of Health is concerned with policy making for the entire health sector. The nonpublic sector includes the for-profit and the not-for-profit sectors. Of the 2,441 health facilities in the country, almost half belong to the nonpublic sector, and at least 34 percent of hospital beds belong to the nonpublic sector. Public hospitals include teaching, regional, district, and specialist hospitals, and are owned by government and managed by the Ghana Health Service as a public-service provider.

Data from 2009 indicate that Ghana has 153 district hospitals; 62 percent of them were under the Ghana Health Service and the rest were owned by the Christian Health Association of Ghana (CHAG). Overall, 42 percent of districts had at least one hospital, 11 percent had more than one, and 42 percent had none. The number of beds in district hospitals range from eighty to 180. District hospitals are managed by a team of three comprising the physician in charge, a medical administrator, and the nursing officer in charge.

The community participation paradigm of primary health care in the late 1970s put governance on Ghana's health agenda. When hospitals were authorized to spend fees collected as part of the user fee policy of the late 1980s, the Hospital Administration Act of 1988 (PNDCL 209) established management committees to govern all public hospitals. The management committees of public district hospitals were drawn from the local community and the hospital, and were designed to enhance the relationship and interaction among service providers and users. For example, between 1988 and 1990 Worawora Hospital's management committee was chaired by Mr. Dabo, a former district commissioner in the immediate post-independence era, and had representation from the community including a chief and a local pastor. The management committees were in essence boards that offered some accountability for public hospitals.

Unlike the Hospital Administration Act of 1988, the Ghana Health Service and Teaching Hospitals Act of 1995 (Act 525) made provision for governance of teaching and regional hospitals. Under Act 525, teaching hospitals were granted autonomy and governing boards were appointed. Govindaraj and Chawla (1996, 59) concluded that "the experiment to give autonomy to teaching hospitals in Ghana has not yielded many of the hoped for benefits in terms of efficiency, quality of care, and public accountability."

Act 525 stipulates the appointment of regional and district health committees, and is silent on the governance of regional and district hospitals (Coleman 2009). Health reforms since the reintroduction of democratic rule in 1992 have failed to pursue a district hospital governance agenda.

The change in health care financing policy in Ghana from predominantly general tax revenues first to user fees and then to health insurance has exposed weaknesses in the management and governance of public hospitals. Sakyi et al. (2012) observed that the National Health Insurance Scheme has brought many organizational and service management challenges to hospitals. The identified problems confronting hospital management include cash flow delays from the health insurance authority; lack of capacity to procure essential drug and nondrug consumables; and an inability to take initiative and carry on effective administrative work. In a performance audit report on the generation and management of internally generated funds in public hospitals presented to the speaker of parliament dated January 30, 2011, the auditor-general highlighted improper record keeping, inadequate and poor maintenance of infrastructure, and insufficient maintenance of equipment and machinery leading to frequent breakdowns as key management challenges facing public hospitals. User fees and health insurance have thus exacerbated the constraints on the institutional capacity of hospitals (Gilson and Mills 1995).

The weak institutional capacity of hospitals also reflects a dysfunctional oversight system lacking accountability. Ghana's reform efforts have failed to introduce clear lines of accountability both downward to communities and upward to higher management levels through hospital boards. Cassels (1993) proposed three characteristics without which reforms are unlikely to succeed; among them is accountability of managerial decisions. A study by Abor et al. (2008) revealed numerous differences in the governance structures in private and public hospitals in Ghana. It concluded that some of Taylor's principles of good governance were not observed in current hospital governance systems.

Study Methods and Limitations

This is a preliminary study of public district hospitals in the Eastern Region of Ghana. The study seeks to get an initial sense of the governance reality of public district hospitals in Ghana and explore hypotheses about governance and performance.

The study analyzed data from twelve out of fourteen public district hospitals in the Eastern Region of Ghana. Two hospitals did not respond to a questionnaire sent and could not be reached by telephone for interview.

The study assumes that the governance entails institutionalized accountability, a process orchestrated by the governing board of an organization. The assessment of governance therefore focuses on the functioning of the hospital board. In this study, governance practice is assessed in terms of the existence of a governing board, board size and composition, board leadership, and board meetings.

Hospital performance is measured by trends in hospital mortality rates. Hospitals with mortality rates of less than 2 percent over the period of study are classified as high performing, those with mortality rates between 2 and 4 percent as medium, and those with mortality above 4 percent as low performing. Routine institutional data is used in this analysis. The measurement excludes the efficiency dimension of performance.

This study is limited to a small sample of public district hospitals in the Eastern Region of Ghana. The selection of hospitals from a single region is meant to eliminate variations that could be explained by supervisory styles of different regional directors of health services. The findings do not apply to other district hospitals owned by the nonpublic sector because they are guided by different management and governance regulations.

KEY FINDINGS

The public district hospitals examined in this study vary in size, with a range of sixty to 170 beds. Table 3.1 shows the governance practices of the hospitals. Institutionalized accountability defined by a governing board with statutory functions varies across this sample of twelve public district hospitals in Ghana.

TABLE 3.1 Governance Practices of Public District Hospitals

Hospital	Beds	Board existence	Size	Composition	Leadership	Meetings
Atibie	169	Less than 1 year	15	Mixed	External	Quarterly
Kibi	104	No board				
Kade	61	No board				
Oda	170	8 years	11	Mixed	External	Quarterly
Atua	122	4 years	16	Mixed	External	Quarterly
Asamankese	66	No board				
Akuse	60	7 years	13	Mixed	External	Quarterly
Asesewa	61	7 years	12	Mixed	External	Quarterly
Enyiresi	70	3 years	14	Mixed	External	Quarterly
Nsawam	135	No board				
Suhum	124	3 years	15	Mixed	External	Quarterly
T. Quarshie	129	No board				

Five out of the twelve hospitals (42 percent) have no governing boards. In Kibi the board had not been "reactivated" when it became nonfunctional as a result of attrition. In Nsawam the board was dissolved because of the "personalities...they were confusing the day to day activities" of the hospital. In Tetteh Quarshie it was "dissolved" because "Act 525 does not provide for boards of district hospitals."

Seven hospitals—58 percent of the sample—had governing boards with varying sizes and composition. Board size ranged from eleven to sixteen members. The boards of all seven hospitals had mixed composition of external and internal members. The composition of the boards was not uniform in terms of internal and external representation, interest group, or field of expertise. The boards of all seven hospitals were led by external members with varied professional backgrounds.

Board meetings in all seven hospitals were irregular. All the boards were scheduled to meet quarterly. None of the hospitals, however, reported that the boards met regularly as scheduled.

Trends in Mortality

The mortality trends in these twelve hospitals are shown in Figure 3.1 and Table 3.2. Four (33.3 percent) of the hospitals (Asesewa, Enyiresi,

Kade, and Suhum hospitals) were high performing. Four others (33.3 percent) (Akuse, Asamankese, Kibi, and Nsawam hospitals) were medium performers. The other four (33.3 percent) (Atibie, Atua, Oda, and Tetteh Quarshie hospitals) were low performers.

TABLE 3.2 Performance of Hospitals

PERFORMANCE	HOSPITAL	TREND
High (< 2%)	Asesewa	Unstable
	Enyiresi	Worsening
	Kade	
	Suhum	Worsening
Medium (2-4%)	Akuse	
	Asamankese	
	Kibi	
	Nsawam	
Low (> 4%)	Atibie	Improving
	Atua	Improving
	Oda	
	Tetteh Quarshie	Worsening

FIGURE 3.1 Trends in Hospital Mortality Rates

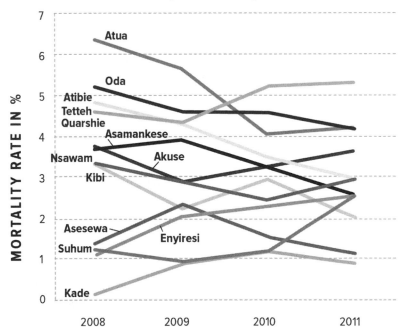

Performance and Governance

As Table 3.3 indicates, this study is inconclusive about the relationship between governance and performance of public district hospitals.

TABLE 3.3 Summary of Governance Practices

Performance	With board	Without board	Total
High	3	1	4
Medium	1	3	4
Low	3	1	4
Total	7	5	12

DISCUSSION AND CONCLUSIONS

This study, though preliminary and inconclusive, corroborates the view that accountability is rare in most public health systems worldwide (Lewis and Petterson 2009). The findings suggest that public district hospitals in Ghana consider governing boards to be optional. Differences in the Ghana Health Service and Teaching Hospitals Act of 1996, which is silent on governance of district hospitals, and the Hospital Administration Act of 1988, which establishes management committees to govern public district hospitals, could explain the observed variation in governance practices. The ambiguous situation created leaves public district hospitals without effective governing boards and with gaps in accountability systems.

Even in hospitals with governing boards, the accountability functions seem to have been lost. Managers of hospitals judge the performance of boards by their ability to bring in additional resources. The management of Atua hospital, which is a low-performing hospital, believes that the board contributes to the performance of the hospital because "it helps in seeking and lobbying for financial and material support for the hospital." This is contrary to Taylor's first principle of good governance: knowing what governance is.

Ghana's drive to achieve the Millennium Development Goals and its own form of universal health coverage has focused predominantly on access to health care and utilization of services. Further gains in health outcomes will only result from attention to quality, costs, and accountability. This study suggests that the rules determining the roles and responsibilities of each category of actors in health, and the relationships and interactions among them, are not working effectively. It will be a difficult challenge to continue improving overall health outcomes in Ghana unless health systems challenges such as accountability and governance are addressed with effective measures (Saleh 2012).

In general, the key to improving spending effectiveness is accountability. Yet, in Ghana accountability systems are weak, reporting and assessment of expenditures are limited, and reporting of health service indicators is incomplete. Civil society has little information about public-sector activities, and the level of its involvement in the management of hospitals is low. Mechanisms to improve accountability must reform and strengthen the governance of public hospitals and improve the performance of public hospitals. The governing board of a hospital is an essential instrument of accountability. It provides, as Ackerman (2005, 6) noted, the "proactive process by which public officials inform about and justify their plans of action, their behavior and results, and are sanctioned accordingly." The hospital board is the only structured mechanism that could involve beneficiaries, service users, and the general public and give them power to transparently assess the effectiveness of hospitals. Promoting good governance of district hospitals could encourage the efficient use of resources through accountability for the stewardship of those resources.

IMPROVING GOVERNANCE OF HOSPITALS

What could be done to improve the governance of public district hospitals? Improving governance of public district hospitals would require research, short-term action by the Ghana Health Service, and long-term action involving legislative reform.

Frenk and Moon (2013, 941) have indicated that "Rigorous research and analysis of the achievements and shortfall of past experiences in governance arrangements are needed and merit attention from the academic community." This study is helping to put governance of public district hospitals on Ghana's policy agenda but is not adequate to offer the level of understanding and evidence to support effective intervention. The director general of the Ghana Health Service has expressed interest in the study and has proposed a larger study to better understand the relationship between governance and performance for public district hospitals. The regional director of Health Services for the Eastern Region intends to work with the Health Policy and Leadership Program of the Ghana College of Physicians and Surgeons to address the challenges of hospital governance in the region. This study, together with a subsequent larger study, will contribute to efforts to improve both the governance of district hospitals and performance of the health system. Both short- and long-term actions by Ghana's parliament and the director general of the Ghana Health Service will require a better understanding of how governance influences hospital performance.

In the short term and at the agency level of the Ghana Health Service, intervention is possible without changes to legislation. This is possible because the Ghana Health Service and Teaching Hospitals Act does not specifically forbid the existence of governing boards for district hospitals. The Hospital Strategy has recommended "limited autonomy for district hospitals" through the appointment of boards. That recommendation provides the mechanism for action by the director general of the Ghana Health Service.

In the long term, changes in legislation are required in order to reconcile the provisions for hospital governance between the Ghana Health Service and Teaching Hospitals Act of 1996 and the Hospital Administration Act of 1988. Ongoing decentralization reforms have made amendment of the Ghana Health Service and Teaching Hospital Act of 1996 imminent, so there is an opportunity to revise the provisions for governing public district hospitals. Amending legislation, however, requires action by the Parliament of Ghana and is a long and complicated process.

NATIONAL CHALLENGES OF GOVERNING HEALTH IN AFRICA

Ghana's narrative is not unique. Many nations in Africa have, since independence, undertaken a series of health reforms similar to those undertaken in Ghana. To reverse Eurocentric health care policy under colonialism, most African countries at independence initiated health reforms. And a significant number of nations went the way of Ghana.

Killick (2010, 1) noted that "most African leaders shared many of [Nkrumah's] views and what was done in Ghana was repeated in other African states as they won their independence." Similarly, the primary health care reforms were undertaken across many counties in Africa. At its thirteenth session in September 1980, the Regional Committee of the WHO Regional Office for Africa invited member states to reorient their health systems to give support to primary health care (WHO AFRO 1980). By July 21, 1981, thirty-five member states out of forty-four had signed the Charter for Health Development of the Africa Region. The charter was a tool for reorientation of existing medical services and integration of new institutions into real national health systems (WHO Technical Paper No. 20).

In response to worsening economic conditions, many African countries adopted the World Bank's Agenda for Health Reform under the Structural Adjustment Program. District-based health care was therefore practiced widely in countries such as Tanzania, Botswana, and Zimbabwe, partially in Benin, Guinea, Mali, and Nigeria, and on an experimental basis in Burundi and Senegal (World Bank 1994). As a result, the "preferred management level is usually the district, where the management of primary and secondary level services can be integrated and planned for a defined population" (Gilson and Mills 1995, 292). A survey of thirty-seven sub-Saharan African countries showed that thirty-three had cost-recovery programs or planned to introduce one (Nolan and Turbat 1993). The importance of user charges to health care financing policies at the time was endorsed in Windhoek, Namibia, in 1993 by participants at a meeting of senior health officials from twelve African countries (WHO 1994).

In recent times, there is a new wave of health reforms in many African countries, including Ghana, that seek to establish social health insurance plans. Countries such as Rwanda, Mali, Kenya, and Nigeria have introduced national health insurance reforms aimed at providing financial protection against the cost of basic health care services. These social health insurance reforms are indications that many African countries still hold onto the independence aspiration of universal health coverage.

And many African countries have enshrined this aspiration to universal health coverage in their respective national constitutions. The principles of state policy in the constitutions of nations such as Nigeria, Sierra

Leone, and Gambia all oblige the state to progressively extend health care service to their entire populations. Articles 13, 14, 17 (3) c and d of Nigeria's 1999 Constitution; Articles 211 and 216 (4) and (7) of the 1997 Constitution of Gambia; and Articles 4, 5, 8 (3) c and d, 12 a of the 1991 Constitution of Sierra Leone in varying forms articulate respective national aspirations to universal health coverage. The 2010 Kenyan Constitution stipulates in Article 6 (3) that "A national State organ shall ensure reasonable access to its services in all parts of the Republic, in so far as it is appropriate to do so having regard to the nature of the service." The 1995 Ugandan Constitution states in Article XIV that as one of the general social and economic objectives, "The State shall endeavor to fulfill the fundamental rights of all Ugandans to social justice and economic development and shall, in particular, ensure that (ii) all Ugandans enjoy rights and opportunities and access to education, health services, clean and safe water ..." Article XX on medical services is more specific: "The State shall take all practical measures to ensure the provision of basic medical services to the population."

Evidently, Ghana's health system, and that of many other African nations, has since independence been orienting itself toward progressive realization of universal health coverage through half a century of successive health reforms: independence health reform, primary health care reform, health-sector reform under Structural Adjustment Program, and, more recently, national health insurance reforms. Progress toward universal health coverage has been impeded by population growth, challenged by medical and technological advancement, and disrupted by political instability and economic decline in the last quarter of the twentieth century.

Today, several national health systems in Africa have in place strategies, policies, and programs for the World Health Organization's (WHO) three conceptual dimensions of universal health coverage (UHC): population, benefit package, and financial protection. But it is not enough to have good strategies, policies, and programs for all three conceptual dimensions of UHC. UHC strategies, policies, and programs must be complemented by efforts that seek to institutionalize performance measurement and accountability in the health care system. The measurement of performance, coupled with institutionalized accountability, constitutes the structural elements, the essence, of good governance.

The next and logical stage of health reform across Africa must focus on governance and accountability, if childhood and maternal mortality goals of the Millennium Development Goals are to be achieved.

In their article on "Governance Challenges in Global Health," Frenk and Moon (2013) indicated that good governance for health should exhibit effectiveness, equity, and efficiency in achieving outcomes. In Ghana, and apparently across Africa, achievement of these goals is hampered by entrenched governance challenges that are embedded in the structure of national systems. National health systems are confronted with complex challenges that demand engagement outside the traditional health sector. Frenk and Moon (2013, 941) noted that "governance challenges will continue to complicate our best efforts to respond to urgent, complex, and serious global health problems." And a robust response to the complex situation requires improved governance of health systems with credible and legitimate decision-making processes. Efforts to strengthen national and global health systems should focus on identifying new governance arrangements that are more effective, equitable, and accountable, and that can be fully implemented at the district level in the governance of hospitals, as analyzed in this chapter.

REFERENCES

Abor, Patience A., Gordon Abekah-Nkrumah, and Joshua Abor. 2008. "An Examination of Hospital Governance in Ghana." *Leadership in Health Services* 21 (1): 47–60.

Ackerman, J. M. 2005. *Social Accountability in Public Sector: A Conceptual Discussion.* Washington, D.C.: World Bank.

Addae, S. 1996. *Evolution of Modern Medicine in a Developing Country: Ghana 1880–1960.* Bishop Auckland: Durham Academic Press.

Al-Najjar, Basil. 2012. "The Determinants of Board Meetings: Evidence from Categorical Analysis." *Journal of Applied Accounting Research* 13 (2).

Amenumey, D. E. K. 2008. *Ghana: A Concise History from Pre-Colonial Times to the 20ᵗʰ Century.* Accra: Woeli Publishing Services.

Arhinful, D. K. 2003. *The Solidarity of Self-Interest: Social and Cultural Feasibility of Rural Health Insurance in Ghana.* Leiden, The Netherlands: African Studies Center.

Brinkerhoff, D., and T. Bossert. 2008. *Health Governance: Concepts, Experience, and Programming Options.* Health Systems 20/20. Washington, D.C.: U.S. Agency for International Development, February. www.healthsystems2020.org.

California Healthcare Foundation. 2008. *Measure for Measure: Analyzing California Hospital Characteristics and Performance.* Issue brief. December.

Cassels, A. 1993. *Perspectives on Health Sector Reform in Health Sector Reform, Report on Consultation.* Geneva: World Health Organization, December 9–10.

Coleman, N. A. 1997. *The Uneven Implementation of User Fee Policy in Ghana.* Boston, MA: Takemi Program in International Health, Harvard School of Public Health. Unpublished.

Coleman, N. A. 2009. *Concept Note on Strengthening Regional and District Hospital Boards.* Accra: Coleman & Partners.

Coleman, N. A. 2011. *A Journey to Universal Health Coverage: Ghana's Transition to National Health Insurance.* Seattle, WA: PATH.

Ditzel, Elizabeth, P. Strach, and P. Pirozek. 2006. "An Inquiry into Good Hospital Governance: A New Zealand-Czech Comparison." *Health Research Policy and Systems* 4: 2.

Frenk, J., and S. Moon. 2013. "Governance Challenges in Global Health." *New England Journal of Medicine* 368: 936–42.

Gilson, L., and A. Mills. 1995. "Health Sector Reforms in Sub-Saharan Africa: Lessons of the Last 10 Years," in *Health Sector Reforms in Developing Countries*. Edited by Peter Berman, Harvard University Press.

Government of Gambia. 1997. Constitution of Gambia.

Government of Ghana. 1996. Ghana Health Service and Teaching Hospitals Act (Act 525).

Government of Ghana. 1992. Republican Constitution of Ghana.

Government of Ghana. 1988. Hospital Administration Act of 1988 (PNDCL 209).

Government of Ghana. 1971. Legislative Instrument 706.

Government of Ghana. 1983. Legislative Instrument 1277.

Government of Ghana. 1985. Legislative Instrument 1313.

Government of Kenya. 2010. Constitution of Kenya.

Government of Nigeria. 1999. Constitution of the Federal Republic of Nigeria.

Government of Sierra Leone. 1991. Constitution of Sierra Leone.

Government of Uganda. 1995. Constitution of Uganda.

Govindaraj, R., and M. Chawla. 1996. *Recent Experiences with Hospital Autonomy in Developing Countries—What Can We Learn?* Boston: Data for Decision-Making Project, Harvard School of Public Health.

Hugue, Shafiqul. 2011. "Accountability and Governance: Strengthening Extra Bureaucratic Mechanisms in Bangladesh." *International Journal of Productivity and Performance Management* 6 (1).

Institute of Medicine. 2001. *Crossing the Quality Chasm: A New Health System for the 21st Century*. Washington, D.C.: Institute of Medicine.

Iskander, M. R., and N. Chamlou. 2000. *Corporate Governance: A Framework for Implementation*. Washington, D.C.: World Bank.

Killick, T. 2010. *Development Economics in Action: A Study of Economic Policies in Ghana*. New York: Routledge.

Lewis, M., and G. Petterson. 2009. *Governance in Health Care Delivery: Raising Performance*. Policy Working Paper 5074. Washington, D.C.: World Bank.

Ministry of Health/Ghana Health Service. 2005. Hospital Strategy.

Ministry of Health. 1978. *A Primary Health Care Strategy for Ghana*. Accra: National Health Planning Unit, Ministry of Health.

Ministry of Health. 1982. *Health Policy of Ghana*. Accra: Ministry of Health.

Nolan, B., and V. Turbat. 1993. *Cost Recovery in Public Health Services in Sub-Saharan Africa.* Washington, D.C.: World Bank (draft paper).

Petra, Steven T. 2005. "Do Outside Independent Directors Strengthen Corporate Boards?" *Corporate Governance* 5 (1).

Ruhanen, L., Noel Scott, Brent Ritchie, and Aaron Tkaczynski. 2010. "Governance: A Review and Synthesis of the Literature." *Tourism Review* 65 (4).

Sakyi, Emmanuel K., Roger A. Atinga, and Francis A. Adzei. 2012. "Managerial Problems of Hospitals Under Ghana's National Health Insurance." *Clinical Governance: An International Journal* 17 (3).

Saleh, Karima. 2012. *The Health Sector in Ghana: A Comprehensive Assessment.* Washington, D.C.: World Bank.

Serageldin, I., A. E. Elmendorf, and E. E. Eltigani. 1994. "Structural Adjustment and Health in Africa in the 1980s." In *Research in Human Capital and Development.* Greenwich, CT: JAI Press Inc.

Taylor, D. W. 2000. "Facts, Myths and Monsters: Understanding the Principles of Good Governance." *The International Journal of Public Sector Management* 13.

University of Ghana Medical School and University of California Los Angeles. *Danfa Project Final Report, Ghana.* 1979. Accra: University of Ghana; Los Angeles: UCLA.

Waddington, C. J., and K. A. Enyimayew. 1989. "A Price to Pay: The Impact of User Charges in Ashanti-Akim District Ghana." *International Journal of Health Planning & Management* 4 (1): 17–47.

Waddington, C., and K. A. Enyimayew. 1989. "A Price to Pay: The Impact of User Charges in the Volta Region of Ghana." *International Journal of Health Planning & Management* 5: 287–312.

World Bank. 1984. *Ghana: Policies and Program for Adjustment.* Washington, D.C.: World Bank.

World Bank. 1987. *Financing Health Services in Developing Countries: An Agenda for Reform.* Washington, D.C.: World Bank.

World Bank. 1994. *Better Health for Africa: Experiences and Lessons Learned.* Washington, D.C.: World Bank.

WHO Regional Office for Africa. 1980. Resolution AFR/RC.30/R9 (1980).

WHO Regional Office for Africa. 1985. *Twenty Years of Political Struggle for Health.* AFRP Technical Papers No. 20. Brazzaville, Republic

of the Congo: WHO Regional Office for Africa. WHO/SHS/
DHS/87.13 WHO/SHS/DHS/88.1/Rev.1.

World Health Organization. 2003. *How Can Hospital Performance Be Measured and Monitored?* WHO Regional Office for Europe's Health Evidence Network (HEN). World Health Organization/SHS/ DHS/88.1/Rev. 1.

CHAPTER 4

Managing Grassroots Health Systems in Kerala: The Roles and Capacities of Local Self-Government Institutions

Udaya S. Mishra and T. R. Dilip

INTRODUCTION

After independence of India from colonial rule in 1947, the Constitution advocated for a centralized federal parliamentary system; the *panchayat* system, an alternative form of political and economic organization, was encouraged within these limits. However, the centralizing policy framework faced challenges, beginning with the introduction of the Community Development Program (CDP) in 1952. After a series of policy framework reviews, the government of India introduced the Seventy-Third and Seventy-Fourth Amendments to the Constitution and enacted them in 1993. The passage of these amendments marked a new era in the federal democratic structure of the country and provided constitutional status to the *panchayati raj* institutions (PRIs). Today, decentralization is recognized as a key element in contemporary development discourse around the world. Almost all countries, both developing and developed, have adopted decentralization and strengthening local governments in their development policy agenda for improving governance.

Decentralization is often viewed as a prerequisite for the reduction of poverty and the empowerment of poor and politically marginalized groups in India (Drèze and Sen 1996). In India, the idea of decentralization is not new, but it gained momentum through the exhortations of Mahatma Gandhi. In Gandhi's vision, an independent India was a highly decentralized polity, with its villages having extensive political and economic autonomy; this is the concept of *gram swaraj* (village self-rule). However, the capacity of existing PRIs to implement development projects is suspect on account of various factors, including the shortage of local-level technical expertise for planning and an inability to exercise the power accorded them by the Constitutional Amendments. Allocation of funds within a panchayat is often linked to electoral politics rather than to real demand for investment.

Clearly, an effective process of decentralized planning requires an efficient *gram panchayat* (governing structure made up of elected representatives) and a vigilant *grama sabha* (the represented community). However, a major constraint in decentralized planning is the limited expenditure discretion that has been given to local governments (World Bank 2004). Though local governments are empowered to generate revenue, it is rarely done, due to weak administration and unwillingness to enforce the tax laws, among other reasons. The paucity of funds has reduced the panchayats to mere agents to implement state- and centrally sponsored schemes.

Kerala state has more than a decade of experience with decentralized planning; it enjoys the distinction of being the first Indian state to have elected panchayats after the Seventy-Third and Seventy-Fourth Amendments. Kerala's model of democratic decentralization with a special focus on people's participation is frequently acknowledged in debates on decentralized governance in India and beyond. Implementation of the decentralization process in Kerala started with a "people's campaign on decentralized planning," conceived and orchestrated by the Planning Board, a relatively autonomous state agency, with the political support of the Communist Party of India (Marxist) (CPM). This effort is seen as the most ambitious and concerted state-led effort to build local participatory democratic governance institutions ever undertaken in the subcontinent (Heller, Harilal, and Chaudhuri 2007).

The campaign resulted in the creation of local self-governments with new resources and authority. The public response to decentralization is evident: about 10 percent of the electoral population in the state, 1.8 million people, attended the planning grama sabhas in the first two years (Chaudhuri and Heller 2003). Importantly, women account for

40 percent of participants, and participation among the scheduled caste/scheduled tribe (SC/ST) population is well above their share in the total population. Overall, 35 percent to 40 percent of the state's budget outlay for projects and programs drawn up and implemented by local bodies is utilized through this people's planning campaign. Since the 1990s, each successive state government has played a key role in continued promotion of decentralized planning in Kerala.

With the transition in governance mechanisms giving a greater emphasis to decentralization, PRIs have an enhanced role in promoting human development in Kerala, including efficient and equitable delivery of health care and health services. However, there are a number of lacunae in the public health system of India, including poor coverage of health facilities, shortage of human resources, inadequate supply of drugs, and limited financial resources. Therefore, the current challenge before the PRIs is correcting existing inequalities in health care services and transforming them into an efficient system through community participation.

The existing literature offers mixed evidence regarding the success of PRIs in improving local health systems. For instance, a few studies noted that the quality of health care services, as well as outreach to vulnerable sections of society, has not improved significantly over time (Vijayanand 2001; Eapen and Thomas 2005). On the other hand, others have observed an overall improvement in delivery of health care services (Narayana and Kurup 2000; Chaudhuri et al. 2004). Ramankutty (2002) highlights some positive effects of decentralized planning on local governments and communities, including increased space and more choice in overall planning for health. But there is also contrasting evidence indicating that the panchayats allocate a lower proportion of resources for health care than was allocated before decentralization by the state government (Varatharajan 2004). Likewise, Ramanathan et al. (2005) acknowledge that women's participation in democratic political participation has increased substantially, but conventional gender norms continue to govern conservative approaches to reproductive health issues. The studies also report friction between the PRIs and higher-level functionaries in the health system. Assessing the evidence can be difficult, as some of the studies suffer from significant biases (see Heller et al. 2007).

This chapter undertakes a comprehensive review of major concerns raised by the growing relevance of decentralized planning in health and health care delivery. The views of key stakeholders in the local health system are analyzed, including elected representatives of PRIs, health care providers, community members, and state-level functionaries. In particular, the chapter assesses the capacity of the PRIs to oversee and guide the local health system, and examines the views of two key stakeholder groups—health care providers and community members—on the role of PRIs in health system management. With this backdrop, the remaining part of the chapter is organized as follows: the next section provides information regarding data and methods. Following that, the third section presents the results and description. This section is divided into four subsections, and these describe the opinions of grassroots health system functionaries, roles and capacities of PRIs, providers' perspectives on PRIs, and community perspectives on PRIs, respectively. Finally, the chapter concludes with a brief discussion of the results and policy implications.

DATA AND METHODOLOGY

A multicentric study was carried out across five states in India in 2007–08; one of the states included was Kerala, the front runner in India in adopting decentralized governance. The three-tier system of rural local bodies in Kerala is comprised of 991 *grama panchayats*, 152 block *panchayats*, and 14 *zilla panchayats*. Grama panchayats in Kerala have larger catchment areas and populations than they do in other states in India. Three major groups of stakeholders were identified when evaluating the roles and capacities of PRIs in delivering health services at the grassroots level, namely health providers, PRI members, and beneficiaries (community members). This study includes respondents from all three groups of stakeholders, who were guided through a structured questionnaire. In addition, state-levels officials were interviewed on issues relating to transfer of power owing to decentralization in the health sector, using a structured questionnaire.

As per the study protocol, three districts were selected in each state; within each district, the zilla panchayat, two block panchayats, and six grama panchayats (three from each of the two block panchayats) were included. Thus, the total sample for Kerala state comprises three districts, six blocks (two from each district), and eighteen village panchayats (three from each block). Between eight to ten members of each PRI were interviewed; a total of 193 PRI members were interviewed in this study. The sample requirements for health care providers in each state were: eighteen male health workers, eighteen female health workers, ten female health supervisors, ten Behavioral Health Educators/Inspectors, ten medical officers in primary health centers (PHC), and ten senior medical officers (chief medical officer, district medical officer, or deputy chief medical officer). Overall, information was collected from seventy-six providers. For respondents representing beneficiaries and community members, twenty-five males and twenty-five females between eighteen and fifty years of age were randomly selected from each grama panchayat in the study. In total, nine hundred persons were interviewed from the eighteen grama panchayats selected for the study. In addition, in-depth interviews were conducted with ten state-level officials.

The three districts were selected, based on the district-wise human development index reported in the Kerala human development report, to represent low, middle, and high levels of human development across the state. According to the 2005 human development report of Kerala, Ernakulam ranked first, Kollam ranked sixth, and Waynad ranked thirteenth, so these districts were selected to represent the disparate levels of development across districts of the state. To select blocks within the districts, three indicators were considered: literacy rate, percentage of male main workers as cultivators, and population sex ratio. Among these indicators, greater variation was noticed regarding the percentage of male main workers as cultivators; the selection of two blocks each was made based on this indicator from each of the selected districts. The selected blocks represented two extremes in terms of this particular indicator within the districts. Thus, the Aluva and Muvattupuzha blocks were selected in Ernalulam district; Kottarakara and Krunagapally blocks in Kollam district, and Vythiri and Mananthavadi blocks in Wayand district. Following the block selection, three village panchayats were selected at random from a list of village panchayats.

Data were collected by conducting interviews using structured questionnaires for the three groups of stakeholders. Three different questionnaires were used to obtain information from stakeholders on the actions and perceptions of the functioning of the grassroots health system. The questionnaire for the PRI members emphasized their knowledge and awareness regarding the powers and functions of the panchayat in governance and intervention in the health system at the grassroots level. In addition, information was collected regarding their involvement and participation in providing health care in the community. Similarly, the questionnaire for health providers aimed at understanding their specific roles and functions in health care delivery, as well as documenting initiatives taken by them to improve health care provision.

Further, they were probed regarding the involvement of PRI functionaries in designing, planning, and implementing specific plans for better health care provision according to the needs of the community. These grassroots-level health providers were also asked about their level of satisfaction with the interventions of PRI functionaries in day-to-day running of the sub-center/PHC/CHC. Finally, the questionnaire for the community asked the perceptions of potential health system users/beneficiaries regarding the functioning of the grassroots health system, particularly related to any changes in conditions following decentralization and devolution of powers to local institutions.

RESULTS

PRIs and Grassroots Health System

Nearly half of the 193 PRI members interviewed represented grama panchayats, and the remaining respondents represented block and district panchayats. Of these, 152 respondents were elected members; twenty-six and fifteen of them were head and vice-head of their institutions, respectively. The sex of the respondents reflected the prevailing proportions of men and women in the panchayati raj institutions. The surveyed members adequately represented different religious and caste groups (detailed demographic statistics are available from the authors). The educational profile, when disaggregated by sex, showed that female PRIs were mostly qualified above secondary level, while male PRIs were more likely to have stopped at primary education. Nearly one third of the respondents worked in the service sector and another third worked in agriculture and business. The sample of PRIs included house-wives and unemployed people at one extreme and professionals on the other. This occupational variety suggests that the PRIs in Kerala come from a wide range of occupational backgrounds and are not necessarily dominated by a single category of individuals.

The study sought to understand the perceptions of PRI members regarding the defined roles and functions of the PRI, as well as the limits of the jurisdiction. While almost all respondents stated that their primary function is to solve the problems of the people, there were divergent opinions on specific functions that they need to perform. The second important function, implementing development programs, was stated by nearly one third of them. Other functions that were mentioned included attending or arranging meetings to facilitate the functioning and activi-ties of the panchayat. When asked directly about holding meetings, a substantial proportion of them answered in the affirmative; 73 percent of the PRIs stated that meetings take place monthly, with a few others reporting that meetings are less frequent. Apart from questions about members' understanding of their perceived functions as well as partici-pation/conduct of meetings, specific enquiry was made as to their power relating to health programs and their execution. Most (98 percent) PRI members believe that they have the power to intervene in relation to planning and execution of health programs. A set of specific functions was mentioned by the interviewers to determine individual PRI mem-bers' opinions about these functions. While almost all of them identified their primary function to be solving the problems of the people, fol-lowed by implementation of developmental programs, they were almost equally divided over other functions.

When it comes to the PRI's role in addressing health concerns of the population in its jurisdiction, it depends largely on its power and func-tions to intervene in the local-level health system. Such an intervention may not only be in a regulatory role but also in its proactive role in addressing emerging health issues. This requires fund allocation, priori-tization of issues, and so on. On this count, an assessment of PRIs' dif-ferent budgetary allocations was made to assess prioritization in health care. This budget is spent on a variety of activities, which primarily involve disease prevention and health promotion activities. Apart from this, there is allocation toward water and sanitation, social security, and welfare of the underprivileged. The share and magnitude of the PRIs' allocations to health were collected to determine its priority level.

As part of the panchayat's involvement with the health system, 81 percent of the PRIs felt that the panchayat could always ensure regular supply of medicine in the public health facility primarily through monitoring and supervision. Some of the PRIs added that regular supply of medicine and equipment could also be achieved through proper coordination between the panchayat and the health facility, as well as consideration of public demand. The most common health problems cited by the PRIs are waterborne diseases, communicable diseases, and chronic diseases. However, other water/sanitation–related and nutrition-related ailments were also mentioned by a few of the PRIs. With regard to the role of the panchayat in ensuring universal immunization of children, the PRIs consider immunization the role of the auxiliary nurse midwife (ANM), health workers at the sub-center level, or the primary health care/community health centers (PHC/CHC).

The above findings indicate a significant engagement of PRIs with the grassroots-level health system to facilitate their effective functioning. In fact, their involvement sounds positive in terms of making the health system cater to local needs. On this count, more than half of the respondents report that their respective panchayat has a specific health program of its own. These programs include preventive, promotive, and social security–related programs. The PRIs seem to be aware of the state of functioning of the health facility in the panchayat as well as any deficiencies. There is an equal share of sampled PRIs agreeing on adequate manpower and infrastructure in their respective health facility. In the case of inadequacies, more than 90 percent of PRIs reported they have acted upon it. There are various ways of addressing such inadequacies, including informing the government and approaching the zila parishad. Some of the respondents raised the issue with the district medical authorities as well. However, cases that were not acted upon were justified with the understanding that the PRIs had no jurisdiction over the health system or the absence of adequate funds. According to the surveyed PRIs, they often provide guidance and advice on ways to improve functioning of the health system. Such guidance involves evaluation and monitoring as well as promoting preventive measures to control the spread of diseases.

Roles and Capacities of PRIs

The roles and capacities of PRIs are vital to the kind of contribution they can make toward improving the grassroots health system. Such roles and capacities involve the PRI's awareness of its mandate and operational jurisdiction related to intervening in the health system as well as ensuring better health for people. In either case, PRIs need to have an environment that enables them to serve the cause of improved and efficient health care provision. As part of this enabling condition, many panchayats have formed health committees that seek to recognize the health needs of the people and oversee the functioning of the health system to serve people better. About three-fourths of the PRIs reported having a health committee constituted in their respective panchayat. This formation of health committees was by government order in 36 percent of the instances, whereas in 38 percent of instances committees were formed through the self-initiative of the panchayat. Apart from these two types of cases, thirty-six PRI members attributed the formation of the committee to statutory requirement while two other PRIs related it to a department initiative. On the whole, the formation of a health committee in the panchayat has been largely by way of the panchayat's initiative or government order.

With regard to the responsibilities and activities of the committees, about 52 percent of the PRI members identified the committee's role in terms of disease prevention; this is followed by other roles such as setting up health awareness programs and administration and management, as well as meeting and discussion to make decisions about interventions. When asked about the functioning of the health committee by the PRIs, it was observed that PRI members were unaware of the jurisdiction of these committees in regard to intervention in the health sector. Therefore these committees are unlikely to offer effective means of bringing changes if needed to improve health care services among the people.

Among the one-fourth of PRI members who denied having any health committees in their respective panchayats, the prevailing opinion was that this type of committee lacked relevance; others expressed simple ignorance about the committees. More than one-half of them also referred to welfare committees taking care of health-related issues. The panchayat's role in terms of health programs, as stated by these PRI members, was confined to disease prevention and health promotion followed by administration and monitoring.

Whenever any specific issue concerning health is notified to the panchayat authorities, either by the community or the health functionaries, the panchayat ought to take some remedial action. In either situation, panchayat authorities have a systemic role for intervening in the matter. However, such interventions depend on their powers and functions. With regard to the efforts made by the panchayat toward resolving problems, about 46 percent of the PRIs respond in terms of reporting to the higher level of administration. Alternative recourses as reported by the PRIs include resolving through coordination, bringing the problem to the notice of the government, and trying to create infrastructure. The fact that reporting to a higher level of administration was the most frequently reported solution indicates the PRIs' lack of inherent capacity in resolving problems at hand.

The views of the PRIs regarding the location of the PHC/CHC from an accessibility perspective indicate that in most (82 percent) of the cases accessibility is not an issue. The kind of prevention and promotion activities that the panchayat engages in was probed to gauge the extent and pattern of their involvement. In the context of family welfare programs, one-third of the PRI members reported panchayats conducting awareness classes; another third reported no activity by the panchayat. Similarly, in relation to health education programs, more than 81 percent of the PRI members reported on a panchayat conducting health education programs. Such health education programs are mostly carried out in the form of awareness/cultural programs as well as camp/seminars and classes.

A significant proportion of PRI members (about 76 percent) believe that people receive appropriate treatment from the public health facility, apart from prevention and promotion activities carried out by the panchayat. However, the 20 percent who find the public health facility inadequate in terms of treating patients attributed this to the absence of efficient medical officers as well as the lack of medicines. PRI members reported that the panchayat can take steps toward resolving this situation, including reports to higher authorities as well as better administering and monitoring of the system. In any case, the panchayats' role seems limited in resolving problems by itself, as it prefers to draw the attention of higher authorities. Despite this, it is interesting to observe the role of panchayats in terms of obtaining health services for the poor. About 62 percent of PRI members report that their panchayat facilitates health care for the poor or provides financial assistance for obtaining health care. This is perhaps indicative of the social security initiatives of the panchayat with regard to provision of basic needs.

Nevertheless, with all positive intentions, panchayats are often unable to effectively implement their plans of action. When asked about the kind of problems faced by the panchayat in carrying out its responsibilities, the PRIs cited a host of reasons. The most prominent reason, lack of funds, was expressed by 96 percent of the PRIs. The next frequently mentioned reason is lack of technical know-how, which calls for capacity building among the PRIs to bolster expertise in various fields of activities. Along with these reasons, lack of community participation (50 percent) and lack of cooperation of health staff were cited as reasons that panchayats are unable to carry out their responsibilities. Given the stated constraints of panchayats' functioning, there were also suggestions made regarding measures to alleviate such constraints. A large proportion of PRIs have reported the need for increased infrastructure and manpower as well as more funds for health programs.

Providers' Perspectives on PRIs and Health

Health providers are key stakeholders in this evaluation, as they are the instruments of change in terms of health system functioning. While the hierarchical infrastructure of health institutions remains the same, decentralization in the health sector changes the powers, functioning, and management of these institutions. In the process, the providers at the grassroots level are exposed to new forms of governance within which they need to deliver. Under such circumstances, the providers' perceptions and opinions regarding the changed conditions, their roles, and their levels of involvement might provide valuable clues regarding the outcome of health-sector decentralization. This exercise therefore included a structured questionnaire among health providers at different levels to explore their views and perceptions regarding the intervention. The total number of health providers interviewed for the study was seventy-six and comprised four categories: village-level health workers, health supervisors, health inspectors, and medical officers. Eighteen interviewees were village-level workers known as junior public health nurses (JPHNs). Twenty-eight were health inspectors, twenty were doctors, and ten were health supervisors. More than half of our sample work at PHCs and less than a quarter are from sub-centers. This distribution is primarily in keeping with the availability of providers at these levels. Sex composition of the health providers was forty-five women and thirty-one men.

To bring about a change in the grassroots health system, the health providers must be responsive to the local needs in terms of designing specific programs. In this regard, the primary requisite is their awareness regarding the jurisdiction of the local government to implement needed interventions and programs. This awareness is more or less universal among health functionaries at varied levels of the hierarchy, with a minor exception: a few health providers working at the sub-center level were unaware. When asked about the power of the panchayat with regard to the implementation of health care programs, seventy-five out of seventy-six providers interviewed answered in the affirmative. This awareness was universal among providers at the PHC and CHC level. Such awareness varied not only between providers at different levels but also according to the provider's place in the hierarchy. This hierarchy includes JPHN at the bottom and medical officers at the top. Awareness was universal among male providers but not among female providers.

Given that there is more or less universal agreement among health providers on the jurisdiction of the panchayat to implement health care programs, it is appropriate to ask about the kind of programs that the panchayat should engage in. Lists of possible health programs were mentioned by the providers, of which the most common were maternity care, water, and sanitation. The other programs mentioned were: control of TB, leprosy, blindness, and malaria. Providers were also asked about the main functions of the panchayat with regard to health system functioning. Nearly 90 percent of the providers consider the panchayat's functions ideally to be planning, financing of health care, and performance monitoring of the health programs.

A majority of health providers agreed on a common set of functions that include financing, planning, and generating health awareness, as well as sharing health information among PRI members. Among the respondents, 99 percent and 96 percent, respectively, said that the main functions of the panchayat are registering births and deaths and sharing health-related concerns with the PRI members. More than 90 percent also held the view that the main functions of the panchayat are to provide financial help for health care programs, plan health care programs, and create awareness about primary health care activities.

When asked about the status of record maintenance of health activities by the health providers, 92 percent of respondents answered in the affirmative, that providers do maintain records; six out of seventy-six providers seem to not be maintaining any health records. Three-quarters of the health providers agreed that records were being utilized by the panchayat officials for planning. Health providers report on the measures being taken by the panchayat to improve health services, which are primarily intended to improve basic infrastructure facilities for health; other measures included spreading awareness regarding health, sanitation, and health education and allocating resources to the health sector. Apart from these, few of the providers reported any measures adopted by the panchayat toward improving nutrition or the health care of women and children.

According to the sample of health providers, the major health-related problems in their respective areas were infectious diseases and environment-related problems. The other less prominent health problems reported include malnutrition and water-borne diseases. Eighty-eight percent of the health providers believe that PRIs can help to improve the public health system. The means of such improvement include allocating adequate funds and proper utilization of funds, as well as regular communication with higher authorities. Nine out of seventy-six providers who disagreed with the possibility of PRIs being instrumental in improving the efficiency of the public health system based their opinions on the lack of financial allocation as well as lack of interest among the PRIs. In the case of providers, sixty-three out of seventy-six have benefited from the financial support of the panchayat for health activities.

As mentioned above, seventy-four out of seventy-six providers reported that their respective panchayats have a health committee. The specific activities of these committees are to plan preventive activities and find solutions for emerging health issues, along with planning and execution of health programs. With regard to the frequency of meetings of these committees, only 37 percent of the providers reported that they meet as and when necessary; otherwise, the reported frequency is largely monthly or quarterly. These committees are said to be making useful contributions to improving health by three-fourths of the providers. Health providers' participation in these committee meetings indicate that around 62 percent of them attended such meetings regularly, while others attended sometimes or occasionally.

The health providers' level of interaction with panchayat officials was probed in terms of its frequency. Frequency of these interactions varied according to the level of the panchayat official. Two-thirds of the providers reported one or two interactions with the head of the panchayat in the previous month. Such interactions, when assessed over a one-month period and a three-month period, do not show much of a change, indicating that there is a moderate level of interaction between health providers at the grassroots level and the panchayat functionaries in Kerala.

Only 38 percent of the providers assert that panchayats have initiated some health program on their own. Such health programs include housing and safe drinking water as well as organization of health medical camps. In relation to the sanctioning of adequate manpower and infrastructure in the health facility, only about 60 percent of the providers find it satisfactory. There is dissatisfaction among health providers with regard to furniture, medical equipment, and medical supplies. Despite this inadequacy in manpower and infrastructure, 88 percent of the providers trust that PRIs can strengthen the system and 84 percent of them acknowledge that panchayats have made efforts in this direction.

Two-thirds of the interviewed providers have had specific issues or problems brought to their notice by the PRIs. These problems were addressed through either intervention or advice. Given that the health providers' responses were positive about the PRIs' cooperation with regard to addressing the health issues, their opinion was sought as to whether there was any improvement in the health facility following the transfer of power to local governments. About 60 percent of the providers answered this query in the affirmative. Providers were also asked about changes regarding availability of drugs and supplies, as well as overall functioning of the health system, and their responses about improvements on these two areas (drugs and supplies, and overall functioning) were not very different. Despite this mixed response to the changes in health provisioning, the providers' opinion of the transfer of power to local government was positive among two-third of respondents and negative or uncertain for the rest of them. The nature of the existing relationship between the health providers and the local governance was in tune with the providers' approval of the transfer of power to local bodies.

There was greater opposition, however, regarding the accountability of health staff to the local bodies. About 60 percent of the providers did not agree that they were accountable to local bodies (24 percent agreed that they were accountable to local bodies and 19 percent had no opinion on this issue). Those who agreed to be accountable to the local bodies reasoned that panchayats are the local authority and recognized its role in provisioning of health. Those who disagreed that they were accountable to the local bodies reasoned that panchayats are political bodies and do not possess any professional expertise in the health arena. Following this diverse opinion on health providers' accountability, providers were asked whether they believed that the panchayat authorities had the expertise necessary to manage the local health system, and 52 percent answered in the negative while one-third answered in the affirmative. Of those who questioned whether the panchayat had the expertise to manage the health system, 47 percent agreed that it would be possible to make the panchayat competent in this regard. The means of making the panchayat competent included providing training and making the members more aware of health issues.

The negative opinion of the providers regarding the competence of the panchayat relates to the lack of interest in health compared with other items on the panchayat's agenda. The opinions of the providers about improving the functioning of the local health system hints at improving health infrastructure as well as making the PRI members more sensitive to the health needs of the population. Capacity building is one of the best means toward making the panchayat competent to manage the local health system, as stated by the health providers. The other means cited include additional funds and additional staff to be provided to the panchayats.

The providers who considered panchayats to be incompetent in managing the local health system have their own reasons for saying so. The prime reason is that panchayats have no funds or proper administrative system to address health system–related issues. Also, panchayats are felt by providers to be overloaded with administrative work of a varied nature and therefore PRI members cannot be the direct contacts for health workers. Clearly, to bring about a change at the grassroots level of the health system, the health providers need to be responsive to local needs and design specific programs that cater to them. In this regard, the primary requisite is awareness that the PRIs have the jurisdictional authority to implement the needed interventions and programs. This awareness is more or less universal among health functionaries.

Community Perspectives

To understand the performance of the grassroots health system in the context of PRIs, it is important to examine the perspectives of those who would benefit from any changes in the mode of governance. For this purpose, twenty-five men and twenty-five women each from the eighteen grama panchayats were selected for the study, resulting in a total of about nine hundred respondents, with three hundred from each district. The inquiry among the beneficiaries largely covered their awareness and perceptions regarding the functioning of the panchayat institutions, as well as their corresponding role in serving local health needs. This inquiry allows comparisons with the opinions of the PRI functionaries and health providers regarding their activities. People's perceptions were also solicited regarding the reality of this arrangement and its efficiency in delivering better health care.

The sample respondents were aged between eighteen and fifty years; 44 percent were above the age of forty years. The sample included

20 percent younger respondents (below the age of thirty years) and the rest were between thirty and forty years of age. The sex composition of the sample was balanced, with half men and half women. The educational composition of the respondents presents a more or less normal distribution, with less educated and highly educated respondents representing smaller numbers, compared with those in the middle spectrum. While 4 percent of the respondents reported themselves illiterate, 2 percent stated that they had a postgraduate or professional degree. A large share of respondents (46 percent) had a secondary or high school level of education, and the remaining portion had a primary school education. The occupational profile of the sample respondents comprised a wide range, including manual workers, professional and businesspersons, and housewives (these three groups represented two-thirds of the sample). This mix of educational and occupational composition of respondents provides a strong basis for interpreting the range of opinions and perceptions found in the study.

While gauging the perception regarding the improvement in provision of health care in the locality, the study found that 47 percent of the respondents felt that there had been improvement in health care; 34 percent disagreed and the rest were indifferent. This perception, evaluated against other parameters, reveals a pattern of consistency as well as other factors shaping this perception. These factors include the constitution of a health committee, the stated role of the panchayat in addressing health problems, and the control of health providers by the panchayat. With regard to the constitution of health committees, about 25 percent of the respondents reported the existence of a health committee in their panchayat and the rest either denied having a panchayat health committee or were unaware of any such committee being in place. When this information was compared with the perception of improvement in health, it was observed that those who said "yes" to having a health committee also perceived an improvement in health, to a large extent. Those who were either unaware of a panchayat health committee or stated that such a committee was entirely absent largely disagreed that there had been improvements in health.

Respondents were asked for their opinions on the role of panchayats in resolving health problems in the community. It was observed that about two-thirds of the respondents answered in the affirmative and the rest were either unsure or negative. These answers are quite consistent in relative terms; among those who consider panchayats to have a significant role in solving health problems in the locality, the perception regarding the felt improvement in health was also positive. Similarly, among those who deny the panchayat's role in resolving health problems, the perception regarding improvement in health was also weak. Ultimately, the conviction regarding the role of the panchayat in health provision governs the perception regarding the felt improvement in health.

In addition to the panchayat's role in resolving health problems, further inquiry was made with regard to the conditions of health providers under the jurisdiction of the panchayat. Here, people's perception on improvement in health was contrasted with their awareness that the health providers were under the control of the panchayat. About 88 percent of the respondents said that the health provider is under the control of the panchayat—this perception went along with the perception of felt improvement in health only 50 percent of the time. The perception of health improvement was lower among those who were either unaware or unsure whether the health providers were under the control of the panchayat.

While 78 percent of the respondents reported believing that the panchayat is competent to manage the local health system, 88 percent were aware that the health providers are under the control of the panchayat. Next, it was examined whether comments on the panchayat's ability to manage the local health system depend on views on health providers being under its jurisdiction. In fact, there is a strong association, although respondents unsure of the panchayat's control over the health providers also spoke in favor of the panchayat's capacity to manage the health system. This reflects the prevailing positive perception of decentralized governance in the region, which could also be viewed as a strong expectation for the panchayat among the population.

The study also probed areas in which the intervention of the panchayat resulted in improvement in health status. This inquiry was made with an open-ended query, and responses were put into three broad categories: adopting preventive measures, improving health care provision, and recognizing local needs/opportunities. A majority of respondents

(64 percent) felt that progress in health status resulted from the panchayat's involvement in improving health care provision; this was followed by "adopting preventive measures." A very small percentage of respondents (6 percent) stated "recognition of local needs" to be a successful strategy adopted by the panchayat in its effort at improving the health system.

People's perception of the strategies adopted by panchayats reveals lacunae in health care provision and the roles that panchayats can take to improve the situation. Finally, beneficiaries' views on the role of health workers were collected to explore the prominent services that the local health providers offer to the people. From a list of activities that was provided, one-third of the respondents listed provision of prenatal care, as well as inquiring about diseases and patient health, as the primary activity of the health worker. The analysis shows the opinion of beneficiaries about the improvements in different fields of health through the intervention of the panchayat. Such opinion includes the panchayat's engagement in prevention and awareness as well as sanitation activities.

DISCUSSION AND CONCLUSIONS

This assessment of decentralized governance in improving grassroots health systems in Kerala was based on the opinions and perceptions of three key groups: panchayat functionaries, local-level health providers, and the system's beneficiaries. While there are varying views on the central issue of the impact of decentralized governance, there is definite recognition of change by all three groups of stakeholders. This analysis presents findings from the three different stakeholder groups. There are contrasts and contradictions in the views expressed by the three groups on the issues, along with certain patterns related to the attributes and behaviors of the three groups.

An analysis of information obtained from respondents reveals that people's perceptions regarding the panchayat's role in bettering health care provision are reasonably positive, and there is an awareness regarding the changes that have taken place in decentralized governance in relation to control and jurisdiction of health providers at the local level. There seems to be a greater degree of knowledge regarding the limits of the panchayat and its roles and responsibilities, as well as optimism about its role in delivery of services. Respondents in general believed there is a systematic role for the panchayat in improving the provision of health care. However, the respondents' convictions regarding the role of the panchayat in health provision shape their perceptions regarding the felt improvement in health.

Given a mixed pattern of utilization of health care facilities in both private and public sectors reported by the respondents, beneficiaries were asked about the reasons for using private facilities. These reasons also serve as a clue to understanding problems in the performance of public facilities. The prominent reasons cited were unavailability of doctors in public facilities, as well as better treatment and cooperation from private hospitals. Apart from these prominent reasons, other reasons stated by respondents include convenience, time saving, and immediate attention. This response reflects the limitations of public facilities and may suggest why people's perceptions are positive in terms of the panchayat's role in addressing such limitations.

To bring about a change in the grassroots health system, health providers need to be responsive to local needs and design specific programs that cater to them. In this regard, the primary requirement is their awareness regarding the jurisdiction of the local government to implement the needed interventions and programs. This awareness is more or less universal among health functionaries at all levels of the hierarchy, except for the sub-center level, which is unaware of it. Further, health providers' opinions about the benefits of decentralization to the health service delivery is based on their individual perceptions about decentralized governance as well as their relationship with the PRI members. Among providers who were positive about the decentralized form of governance, a majority had a sound relationship with the panchayat members. And this perception of the providers may depend primarily on the kind of relationship they have with the PRI members.

Capacity building is one of the best means of improving the competence of the panchayat to manage the local health system, according to health providers. The other means cited by some providers was additional funds and staff for panchayats. The providers who considered the panchayats unable to manage the local health system have their own reasons for saying so. The prime reason was that the panchayats have no funds or proper administrative system to address health system–related issues. Also, panchayats were felt to be overloaded with administrative work of a varied nature that made PRI members less engaged with health-related activities.

In a positive environment of decentralized governance, as exists in Kerala state, strengthening the grassroots-level health system lies squarely on the shoulders of the panchayat. However, a number of issues need attention in the state of Kerala. There is conflict between health providers and local governments with regard to their obligations and responsibilities. These involve whether local government should be a regulator or an administrator of grassroots-level health functionaries, as well as whether health functionaries should act on the suggestion or instruction of panchayat-level officials. Moreover, there is a question of whether health providers' assertions regarding the deficiency and lacunae in the health system should be routed through the panchayat for rectification. If the answer is yes, what is the extent to which the panchayat could provide remedies? Also, it is critical to know that mechanisms are in place before working further to build a healthy and constructive interaction between panchayat officials and health functionaries.

If changes in governance and accountability structures are made, the impacts can also depend on other existing operational structures, especially service provision. The altered structure of governance and transfer of power to local bodies will influence health and education differently. Unlike the educational infrastructure in the state, which had a structure of community involvement and participation, the health infrastructure was more centralized, dictated by district and state authorities. To obtain positive results for this alternative governance structure, there needs to be space made for similar community involvement and participation in evolving health institutions at the local level. The institutional structure of health provision could perhaps be revolutionized, with more of a regulatory role for the government. In addition, public-private partnerships could be encouraged, to ease public financing limitations and increase accountability.

Given the mix of public and private health care facilities in Kerala, the expectation of public provision will always fall short of the ideal. Hence, there should be complementarities in health care provision between the public and the private facilities (or the so-called private sources need to be made part of health care provision under the local bodies). Private facilities should fall under the jurisdiction of local bodies as well.

If priority setting in health care provision is to be included on the agenda of local panchayat bodies, then the local bodies need to possess the organizational capacity required for recognizing and planning health needs. However, negotiating those local health needs with the health functionaries may be effective, if health functionaries are instructed to follow the agenda set by the local authorities and if mechanisms exist to hold the functionaries accountable for implementation. Lastly, judicious allocation and prioritization of public health needs by the local panchayat bodies will depend on the values and actions of the panchayat members and also on the people's participation and involvement to assure that the panchayat members reflect the local community.

Acknowledgment: The paper on which this chapter is based was derived from a larger study on "Roles and Capacities of Panchayati Raj Institutions in Managing the Health System," funded by the Indian Council of Medical Research, New Delhi.

REFERENCES

Bardhan, P. 1996. "Decentralised Development." *Indian Economic Review* 31 (2): 139–56.

Chaudhuri, S., K. N. Harilal, and P. Heller. 2004. "Does Decentralisation Make a Difference? A Study of the People's Campaign for Decentralised Planning in the Indian State of Kerala." Unpublished. Thiruvanathapuram: Centre for Development Studies.

De Souza, P. R. 2003. "The Struggle of Local Government: Indian Democracy's New Phase." *The Journal of Federalism* 33 (4): 77–89.

Eapen, M., and S. Thomas, 2004. Gender Analysis of Selected Grama Panchayats Plan Budgets in Trivandrum District. Discussion paper no. 11. New Delhi: Human Development Resource Centre, UNDP.

Ghatak, M., and M. Ghatak. 2002. "Recent Reforms in the *Panchayat* System in West Bengal: Towards Greater Participatory Governance?" *Economic and Political Weekly* 5 (January): 45–58.

Government of Kerala. 2006. *Kerala Human Development Report 2005.* Thiruvananthapuram: State Planning Board Government of Kerala.

Government of Kerala. 2008. *Economic Review 2007.* Thiruvanathapuram: State Planning Board, Government of Kerala.

Heller, P, K. N. Harilal, and S. Chaudhuri. 2007. "Building Local Democracy: Evaluating the Impact of Decentralisation in Kerala." *World Development* 35 (4): 626–48.

Isaac, T., and R. W. Franke. 2000. *Local Democracy and Development— People's Campaign for Decentralized Planning in Kerala.* New Delhi: Left World.

Johnson, C. 2003. *Decentralisation in India: Poverty Politics and Panchayati Raj.* Working paper 199. London: Overseas Development Institute.

Narayana, D., and K. K. H. Kurup. 2000. *Decentralisation of Health Sector in Kerala: Some Issues.* Centre for Development Studies Working Paper No 298. Thiruvanathapuram: CDS.

National Institute of Rural Development. 2007. *Rural Development Statistics 2005–2006.* Hyderabad: National Institute of Rural Development.

Ramanathan, M., D. Varatharajan, A. Vijayan, Sukanya, and P. Nanda. 2005. *Political Decentralisation and Primary Health Care System: Examining the Potential for Improving Women's Reproductive Health Care in*

Kerala. CHANGE working paper. USA: Center for Health and Gender Equity.

Ramankutty, V. 2000. "Health Planning and Decentralisation: The Kerala Experience." Unpublished document. Thiruvanathapuram: Health Action People.

Varadarajan, D., R. Thankappan, and S. Jayabalan. 2004. "Assessing the Performance of Primary Health Centres Under Decentralised Government in Kerala, India." *Health Policy and Planning* 19 (1): 41–51.

Vijayanand, S. M. 2001. "Poverty Reduction Through Decentralisation: Lessons from Experience of Kerala State in India." Paper presented in the Asia and Pacific Forum on Poverty: Reforming Policies and Institutions for Poverty Reduction, held at The Asian Development Bank, Manila.

World Bank. 2000. *Overview of Rural Decentralization in India, Volume I.* Unpublished report. Washington, D.C.: World Bank.

World Bank. 2004. *India Fiscal Decentralization to Rural Government, Report No 26654-IN.* Washington, D.C.: World Bank, Rural Development Unit, South Asia Region.

CHAPTER 5

Leveraging the Voice of Community Workers in Health Governance: A Two-Case Study from Zambia and Japan

Margaret Henning, Aya Goto, Chunhuei Chi, and Michael R. Reich

INTRODUCTION

We present two cases of major public health challenges: HIV/AIDS in Zambia and a nuclear power plant accident in Japan. Our focus is on the roles of frontline community workers: teachers in Zambia and public health nurses in Japan. While we recognize the striking differences between these two cases—the obvious differences in job functions as well as the economic, social, and geographic differences between the two countries—we are also drawn to uncovering similar patterns and challenges for community workers. Both teachers and public health nurses are often members of the community to which they are delivering services. In these two cases, both faced unplanned events and challenges that were not part of their formal training or regular functions.

The existing literature provides support for the effectiveness and critical role of community health workers, but there are still insufficient policy and practice recommendations (Avey and Fernandez 2012). First, we must understand the health governance architecture that provides a structural overview for the many ways in which people organize themselves to achieve common goals. This usually includes agreed-upon rules and institutions that collectively promote and protect health (Dodgson et al. 2003). One of the challenges in strengthening governance at the community level is identifying, giving voice to, and leveraging the key community players (Dodgson et al. 2003) who can help transform the concept of health promotion into a community priority. Further, such priority should be the community's decision rather than externally imposed.

One essential part of community governance is community participation in making decisions (Heritage and Dooris 2009). The importance of community participation in promoting good health was clearly recognized in the Alma-Ata Declaration in 1978, as the key to the attainment of "health for all," and based on the ethical principle of self-determination. More than a decade later, practical strategies for health promotion were discussed in the Healthy Cities and Communities Initiatives (Liberato et al. 2011). Central to the initiatives is the emphasis on the role of local government, strengthening community capacity, and the process of taking action (Hancock 1993). In the World Health Organization's (WHO) guidelines (WHO Regional Office for the Western Pacific 2000), the first step for developing a healthy cities project is the coordination of key players, including policy makers, service providers, and community members.

Our aim in this study was to analyze and discuss the roles of teachers and nurses in promoting community health and community governance, and how they are strategically positioned, standing between the modernity of science and the traditionalism of community (Inkeles and Smith 1999). In our exploration of these two kinds of community workers, we (1) address their participation as a means of leverage for community governance; (2) examine the circumstances under which teachers and nurses work; and (3) identify conditions that support their expanded responsibility in community governance. Through this comparative study we identify shared strategies to promote the roles of community workers in these two countries, rather than highlighting the constraints that are specific to each country because of differing social, economic, and political environments. In sum, by examining two strikingly different cases located in two very different countries, we seek common themes and common challenges in understanding how community workers can be more effective in promoting community health and community governance.

COMMUNITY PARTICIPATION

One of the reports from the WHO's Healthy Cities Initiative acknowledges diversity in the way community participation is defined and, further, how this can cause difficulties at the operational level. The working definition that the report developed, thus, was "a process by which people are enabled to become actively and genuinely involved in defining the issues of concern to them, in making decisions about factors that affect their lives, in formulating and implementing policies, in planning, developing, and delivering services, and in taking action to achieve change" (WHO Regional Office for Europe 2002, 10). Although this definition is a concise normative description of community participation, it leaves the definition of "participation" vague and does not address the problem of how to apply the concept at the community level. As is, the definition does not describe what exactly is meant by "active" and "genuine" involvement of people in defining issues and decision making, and yet it goes beyond superficial involvement to specify "taking action." Community participation based on the concept of self-determination of community is not merely the community's physical participation, but involves working with an understanding that the community should be at the center of deciding what forms of participation members of the community prefer, and what system of community governance they desire (Deci and Ryan 2000). Contextualization, rather than generalization, therefore, is also an important principle in community participation.

In another study, the researchers Heritage and Dooris used Davidson's (2009) wheel of participation, which consisted of different levels of information, consultation, participation, and empowerment, to describe various types of community participation in different political, social, economic, and organizational contexts. Their work recognizes various types of actions aimed at increasing community participation, but still fails to answer the fundamental questions of who might best implement the processes and how they should be implemented. When community participation is maximized in the Davidson's wheel model, it should be by the community people themselves. They do not, however, work alone, and internal and external resource mobilization is needed to leverage community (Maclellan-Wright et al. 2007). As mentioned above, the Healthy Cities project calls for a local government as the central governing agency coordinating other key players (WHO Regional Office for the Western Pacific 2000). In Canada, the emerging model is one in which regional health authorities are assisted by a staff of health professionals (Frankish et al. 2002).

Of the key players listed in the WHO Healthy Cities project guideline (WHO Regional Office for the Western Pacific 2000), we explore the capacity building of community workers (service providers) as facilitators of community participation. This work compares different types of community workers in different countries, in an effort to explore and provide consideration for approaches to sustainable solutions that are purported to be feasible, culturally appropriate, community centered, and in turn can promote a community's self-determination capacity.

COMMUNITY WORKERS

Community educators and healers have existed worldwide for centuries (Arvey and Fernandez 2012). Rosenthal (1998) identified the community health worker's role as cultural mediation, informal counseling and social support, providing culturally appropriate health education, advocating for individual and community needs, assuring that people get the services they need, building individual and community capacity, and providing direct services. The roles of nurses and teachers in this work are positioned under the umbrella of community health worker, with consideration given to the psychocultural factors influencing modernization as an important factor in the process of development (Inkeles and Smith 1999). Nurses interact and may share views with traditional community residents, among whom will be some, but not all, who may distrust the new and undervalue any actions that are perceived as not directly related to their own daily living.

More recently, the community health workforce has been termed "frontline health workers," often being the first point of connection for those in need of health care. For nurses this is a clear connection, but for teachers, although providing care is a reality, it is often not identified as such in the job description. Both types of worker serve either directly or indirectly a component of the public primary health care system, which ideally should be integrated into the broader health system; teachers and nurses act as a pivot point between the community and the health system. The profile of the employee is that she or he has local roots, has an understanding of the specific society and culture, holds a degree of training, and is often selected by merit at a low cost with a high level of effectiveness (Avey and Fernandez 2012). In the cases that we have identified, nurses are likely to be women, and community health workers have historically been women. Our work examines merging the traditional community worker with the need to develop or mobilize community resources, and we propose an expanded strategy that would allow nurses and teachers to be more effective as community-based professionals, thus serving as a bridge for development between science and society.

STUDY METHOD: A CROSS-NATIONAL CASE STUDY

The two cases from Lusaka, Zambia, and Fukushima, Japan, illustrate ways to leverage key community workers; Tables 5.1 and 5.2 give an overview. A cross-national comparison is challenging given differences in historical, cultural, economic, and political contexts, but it facilitates the construction of generalizable claims (Gómez 2011). A case study methodology does not statistically test a hypothesis, but it has an advantage in that it identifies a new variable or hypothesis, and facilitates a better understanding of a complex structural relationship within a specific context (George and Bennett 2005). Applying case studies to cross-national comparison, therefore, focuses more on examining the underlying contextual structure and processes, while also identifying shared principles that may be common across nations.

TABLE 5.1 Country Profiles: Zambia and Japan

Data in 2011[a]	Zambia	Japan
Total population (thousands)	13,475	126,536
Gross national income (PPP[b] international $)	1,490	35,330
Life expectancy at birth (both sexes, years)	55	83
Under-5-years-old mortality rate (per 1,000 live births)	83	3
Maternal mortality ratio[c] (per 100,000 live births)	440	5
Prevalence of HIV (per 100,000 population)	7204	6

[a] Data are extracted from World Health Organization's country health profiles (2013).
[b] Purchasing power parity.
[c] Data in 2010.

TABLE 5.2 Health Events of the Two Cases: Zambia and Japan

	HIV/AIDS Epidemic in Zambia	Radiation Contamination in Japan
Biological	HIV is found in the blood, semen, or vaginal fluid of someone who is infected with the virus. Retroviruses have a long latent time period between initial infection and the beginning of serious symptoms. Co-occurring health issues increase risk.	1. An increase in cancer risks has been reported for radiation exposure of 100mSv. The exposure level in the acute phase for most of the residents in Fukushima is below 2mSv. 2. There is no dose-response relationship between the radiation exposure and mental health risks.
Status	Chronic issue	Recently occurring chronic issue
Health Impacts	High impact on mortality	Little impact on immediate mortality. Long-term impact on mental health.
Economic	1. Disproportionately affects most productive age groups 2. Limited resource allocation in the education sector	1. Unemployment among evacuees 2. Decline in local products marketing 3. Shortage of Health Care Workers
Sociocultural	Stigma toward people living with HIV/AIDS	Stigma toward local people living in contaminated areas
Relational	Family and community separation	Family and community separation
Legal	Free primary education policy	The Act on Special Measures for Fukushima Reconstruction and Revitalization
Political	1. Concern that resources will be taken from other health priorities 2. Logistic and economic barriers to care and support	1. Perceived slow cleanup and other response activities 2. Distrust toward government 3. Accountability issue
Psychological	Expected long-term negative consequences on mental health	Expected long-term negative consequences on mental health

Public health practitioners often evaluate community projects by quantifying outputs and outcomes. An equally important but more difficult task, which we attempt to do here, is to assess the nature of health governance at the community level (Smith et al. 2006). In analyzing each case, we will follow the five major components of building community capacity as framed by Liberato and colleagues (2011). First, "skills" refers to identification of knowledge gaps and provision of training opportunities. Second, "resources" includes funds, people, facilities, and time. Third, "networking" within and across communities refers to the potential to develop programmatic capacity that is culturally competent, encourages realistic goals, and is driven by community needs. Fourth, "leadership" motivates community to participate in reaching the goal; key aspects include understanding the "big picture," with the ability to cultivate community input, action, and trust. Fifth, "decision making" is defined as being actively involved in identifying community root concerns and in problem solving. In this framework of analysis, we are examining the process of governance rather than output or outcome.

We'd like to point out that in applying this theory, the "community (players)" we have focused on is the group of workers who are facilitators of community participation, but not the community laypeople with whom they work. For this case study, nurses are directly related to the health system, whereas teachers are not formally a part of a health system, but they often address health concerns. However, both often take on the role of health advocate and can be effective because they share the culture of the population they serve (Rhodes et al. 2007). This type of structured comparison, however, is often difficult to carry out in collaborative research when a different scholar undertakes each case study (George and Bennett 2005). In order to overcome the potential methodological shortcoming, we asked an outside researcher to monitor each case in order to assure that each case included a sufficient description of the five components. The two cases were compared and combined to draw common conditions for community governance.

CASE IN ZAMBIA

The first case examines the role of teachers as HIV-prevention educators, with attention given to their emphasis on the principle of self-determination. An estimated 30 million people are living with HIV worldwide; 22.5 million live in sub-Saharan Africa (Claeyé and Jackson 2011). The effect of the disease extends well beyond the families, community, and nation by hindering economic growth, challenging the provision of social services, and further exacerbating poverty and stress in an already vulnerable population. In Zambia, it is critical to understanding the systemic views among a given population in order to accurately explore the influence of individual and contextual variables that affect and/or relate to cultural influence on HIV/AIDS education.

This case shows that teachers are well positioned to be HIV-prevention educators. School-based HIV-prevention programming, starting as early as primary school, is supported in the literature as a necessary step to protect the general population from further infection (Barnett et al. 1995; Finger et al. 2002; Kaaya et al. 2002). Schools are an ideal environment for an extensive and systematic response to the HIV epidemic with prevention education (Mathews et al. 2006; Tijuana et al. 2004). The educational sector is already established as a framework in the community to reach children and young people, and as such can be leveraged as a preventive measure against HIV infection. Zambia's draft HIV/AIDS strategic plan for education provides a concrete example of an approach for community participation in addressing HIV/AIDS— specifically calling for all schools and colleges to participate in responding to the AIDS-related needs of their communities (Katjavivi and Otaala 2004).

Zambia's national education program consists of primary school (grades one through nine), secondary school (grades ten through twelve), and tertiary education (university or college). The Ministry of Education (MoE) guides the delivery of education components, ensuring that educational activities meet requirements for advancement.

Schools in Zambia are divided into three main types: community, private, and government. All school types are divided into primary, secondary, junior secondary, and upper secondary. Primary grade levels consist of years one to seven. Primary schooling is followed by five years of secondary education, with an entrance age of fourteen. Currently, the Zambian government is placing emphasis on ensuring the provision of primary education. In 2005, Zambia had 6,962 basic schools with 2.8 million learners and 463 high schools with more than 136,000 learners (Zambian Ministry of Education 2006).

In sub-Saharan Africa, many young people leave the system before completing secondary school (Chondoka 2006). Despite the introduction of free basic education in 2002, many girls and other vulnerable groups drop out of school before they complete primary school largely because of poverty and the impact of HIV/AIDS on families. Less than 20 percent of the children are age appropriate for secondary school level (fourteen), with older children and younger children sharing mixed classroom settings.

Currently, a shortage of health workers is an obstacle in the effort to scale up HIV services and education. Adopting a task-shifting approach represents one strategy for rapid expansion of the health workforce (Fulton et al. 2011). Central to this discourse is a shift in thinking, which endeavors to: "emphasize the capacity of people to be creative reflexive human beings, that is, to be active agents in shaping their lives" and their communities (Williams et al. 1999, 2).

Skills

Under the MoE, there are fourteen teacher colleges responsible for the training of educators in Zambia. Typically, teachers either obtain certification through an institution that provides a recognized certificate-teaching program—the Examinations Council of Zambia certifies these programs—or they enroll in a diploma program, certified by the University of Zambia.

Zambia, like many countries, struggles with an increasing burden of disease and a complex and fragmented health system. The health system, including health education, has major limitations in both material and human resources. There is a significant gap between the skills of those providing health care interventions and the needs of the community. "A comprehensive health systems framework considers the connection between education and health systems" (Frenk et al. 2010, 5). A systems approach is necessary to leverage the role educators have within the community, including delineating the link between health workers and teachers. These health professionals ultimately provide care and health information to the population.

In Zambia, teachers might be the only source of professional health information, including mental, physical, and/or social support in most communities for children. However, teacher training in health is narrow and limited. The current system offers courses of study that fall under the umbrella of "study areas." These study areas include groupings of topics, such as HIV and AIDS education, drug abuse, and environmental education. The grouping of topics, however, makes it difficult to identify whether a specific subject is taught and the extent of its overview. The MoE recognizes that quality education requires the availability and use of textbooks and other educational materials, that these may be limited, and that teachers lack training and resources (Ministry of Education in Zambia 1996).

There is an opportunity to bring attention to the broader contextual environment where health care and education take place. In addition, there is a critical need to match health priorities and training with a broader contextual understanding. Further, Zambian society will need to establish a system that allows the community to voice its preference in coordinating and prioritizing the role of teachers versus community health workers in providing essential education. This will have a profound impact on the way Zambia trains and prepares its teachers.

Resources

Once a middle-income country, Zambia began an economic decline in the 1970s when copper prices fell on world markets. Slow progress in diversifying the economy and high levels of borrowing and debt services are contributing factors to the country's economic struggle (Bureau of African Affairs 2007). The ensuing impact on the educational system has been devastating, causing a decline in revenue to help support educational initiatives over the past several decades. Despite these setbacks, Zambia remains committed to recovering and reforming its educational efforts by reaffirming its commitment to the Millennium Development Goals (MDGs) and Education for All. The MDGs for Zambia have focused efforts on the enrollment of children in primary education and on increased construction of schools, and the country was able to remove school fees in 2002 and adopt free basic education and reentry policies. However, the economic situation and cultural factors, combined with gender inequality, create a hospitable environment for the spread of HIV infections. The HIV/AIDS pandemic remains one of the most formidable challenges within the education sector. The combination of a strained economy and a high HIV-transmission rate has strapped the country.

In 2002, as part of Zambia's efforts to address poverty reduction and education for all, the MoE outlined in its strategic plan the introduction of a free primary education policy. The adoption and implementation of this policy has increased accessibility of schooling for all students, resulting in a massive increase in student enrollment (Ministry of Education 2003). Educators now have more opportunities to engage students and families. These increased points of contact have the potential to transform models of health-education delivery.

Networking

The complexity of HIV-education programs range in type but may include lectures, role playing, group exercises, audiovisual materials, essay writing, debates, and development of artistic activities such as poems, songs, plays, games, and posters, as well as co- or extracurricular activities. There is also variation in session length and frequency of HIV-prevention education programs (Gallant and Maticka-Tyndale 2004). Most interventions are supported and headed by nongovernmental organizations (NGOs). NGOs, both domestic and international, are the networks that support teachers' HIV-prevention efforts in the school systems.

Leadership

There are opportunities to strengthen HIV education in the school but the focus has been on legislation in education; an outdated act of parliament has guided the sector since 1966. There have been many developments and policy pronouncements by the Zambian government. However, the NGO sector has taken the strongest initiative and stepped forward in leading development campaigns. Examples of successful interventions include: Education Quality Improvement

Program (EQUIP2); Quality Education Services Through Technology (QUESTT); Community Health and Nutrition, Gender and Education support (CHANGES2), and the Textbook and Learning Materials Project (TLMP).

In the late 1980s, Zambia became perhaps the first country in the world to set up an anti-AIDS club, and by 1992 there were 1,150 registered clubs, primarily based out of schools (Baker 1993). The goal of the clubs was to share messages about safer behavior and compassion for those living with HIV/AIDS. Television, radio, and the press have also proved to be influential in raising awareness and decreasing stigma, even though not all people have direct access to them. Some 71 percent of urban and 36 percent of rural youth saw the Helping Each other Act Responsibly Together (HEART) campaign, a media campaign to convey information to young people ages thirteen to nineteen years about sexually transmitted infections, HIV, and acquired immune deficiency syndrome transmission and prevention (Underwood et al. 2006). Oftentimes, programs attempt to do too much with too few resources and thus are spread thin (Bryant et al. 2012). Although there are successful examples of education as a point of intervention, there are limited formal opportunities for teachers to voice or take leadership roles in directing the community needs.

Decision Making

Green (1986) has long contended that community involvement, including decision making, is a core element of health promotion. Putting health workers at the center of the system is essential because the system works through these professionals. The MoE has primary responsibility for and decision-making power over teachers, starting with where they are trained to where they are posted at the completion of their training. Postings are often restricted by funding and by the preference of the teachers; most request urban areas rather than rural ones. Lack of housing is a major obstacle to teacher recruitment and retention in rural areas (World Bank 2006).

As was the case in other studies (Pattman and Chege 2003), this study found that many teachers know how to prevent HIV but are not sure what to teach or how to teach the material. In the researcher interactions, some teachers indicated that talking about HIV and AIDS challenges ideas of childhood innocence and could possibly "encourage" sexual promiscuity. Teachers commonly expressed the need for community acceptance of their role as HIV educators. As a government school teacher said, "We need the community to see this as important and support this information. I am not going to teach and lose my job." Again, we see the importance of considering the cultural and social contexts specific to this phenomenon. Another government schoolteacher said, "I have been trained in HIV and prevention, but it is hard to talk about. Some parents may be mad and what language do I use? We need to support these children beyond school—it needs to be mixed with the community as their lives are here, but also at home." The voices of teachers suggest that they do feel responsible for general education and HIV-prevention education, but have concern for the community's reaction and level of support (Henning et al. 2011). Reports of a disconnect between teachers and the community might be because of a lack of clarity about the teacher's role in health education and the community's perceptions of the role of the teacher.

Summary of Zambia Case

Teachers in Zambia are well positioned to provide support for children affected with HIV. However, appropriate "resources" must be allocated to address challenges in the form of training, and a formalized structure is required to deliver prevention and intervention efforts. While Zambia's education sector, along with supporting NGOs, has taken initiative in the development of programs such as anti–AIDS clubs in schools, there is room to further explore the structure and relationship between NGOs and teachers. This work suggests strengthening the link between teachers, NGOs, and the community, to ensure teachers are fully supported in prevention efforts. To support teachers in their role as HIV educators, the MoE will need to be involved throughout the process to formalize the teacher's role, while ensuring "leadership" for HIV education is cognizant of governance from a horizontal and vertical angle.

CASE IN JAPAN

The second case explores the empowerment of public health nurses in the restoration processes of the nuclear power plant accident in Fukushima Prefecture in 2011, which created, among other widespread problems, a worrisome gap between science and community. Although the cancer risk of low-dose exposure far below 100mSv is at a level any epidemiological investigation may fail to detect (Boice 2012), many families have evacuated. Within a year after the disaster, there was a nearly 10 percent decline in the population of children under five years of age in Fukushima City, located seventy kilometers from the plant. In an environment of uncertainty caused by an unexpected crisis, people have difficulty processing information and their risk perception is not always congruent with the actual risk level (Rudd et al. 2003).

It is likely that the issues of care, compensation, and cleanup related to radiation contamination will persist (Reich 2011), as will adverse mental health consequences—particularly among mothers (Bromet 2012). In the Japanese health system, public health nurses are the key providers of community health services. They are national-board-certified public health professionals with a nursing license, many of whom work at prefectural and municipal level health centers in the public sector. Historically, they have played a major role in national health promotion activities (Marui 1991) not only by providing a wide range of health care for children, adults, and elders, but also by carrying out community assessments through interactions with local residents and formulating plans to solve identified problems (Murashima et al. 1999). In Fukushima City, public health nurses are expected to act as frontline service providers to understand and respond to local mothers' concerns about radiation exposure, which is expected to be long lasting.

The deliberative processes of promoting public participation and discussion in a community have a long history of application in environmental health issues, but at the same time, there is concern that these discussions are more difficult to execute in a crisis situation that requires making hard decisions (Abelson et al. 2003). The nuclear power plant accident has become such a case, and thus, the role of public health nurses to bridge local government and community residents becomes all the more important.

Skills

Under the Act on Public Health Nurses, Midwives, and Nurses established in 1948, a public health nurse was defined as a person who engages in health guidance using the title of public health nurse under the license of the Minister of Health, Labor, and Welfare (Japanese Nursing Association 2011). To become a public health nurse, three years of basic nursing education and one or more years of specialized education in public health at the college level are required. The existing training provided, however, may not be sufficient preparation for a nuclear accident setting. In a survey among public health nurses who were in charge of health crisis management and were working in a prefecture with a nuclear power plant and in two adjacent prefectures, most who were interviewed said that they had anxiety with regard to undertaking required tasks in the event of disaster (Kitamiya 2011). A lack of knowledge and concerns over their own safety were the major factors contributing to their anxiety.

Resources

Public health nurses in Japan work in a vertical local government health system. There are public health nurses working at the prefectural and municipal-level health centers. The Community Health Act in 1994 assigned the prefectural health centers to provide specialized services (e.g., home visits for low-birth-weight infants) and to supervise municipal health centers that provide more common services (e.g., child health checkups) (Hirano et al. 2011). Since the autonomy of cities has been strengthened after the Omnibus Decentralization Act in 2000, even the home visit program for low-birth-weight infants was transferred to the municipal level in 2012.

Financial and human resource allocations in general are provided for the smooth operation of assigned services. However, disaster restoration activities are causing excessive workloads among public health nurses in Fukushima City; one of these activities was provision of radiation dosimeters and turning over the results to residents. The new transfer of a specialized home visitation program may create further burdens among public health nurses. Currently, Fukushima City faces a shortage of public health nurses, which in turn leads to a shortage of time for the nurses to acquire new knowledge and skills. This may cause a lack of motivation and opportunity for them to implement any new health promotion activities that parents could benefit from in the post-disaster environment. Even in the normal setting in the pre-disaster period, the vertical local government system made it difficult for nurses to implement any new activity that was not included in the tasks specified by the upper governments (Japanese Nursing Association 2012) and was not included at the time when the annual activity and budget plan was formulated in the previous year.

Networking

The public health nurses in Japan consider networking to be one of the important tasks inherent in their goal of health promotion in the community. In the Hirano and colleagues (2011) survey among 834 public health nurses, 84 percent answered that they perceived coordinating an organization as their most important task; this was the highest priority among the six tasks that were asked about. The "coordination" in their report was explained as linking health, medical, and welfare services, which requires lateral networking of staff working in different sectors in a local government office.

The Japanese Nursing Association, which manages the continuous nursing education, has recently launched a capacity-building project for public health nurses at the municipal level to improve their skills in identifying community problems, planning activities, and evaluating their effects through networking within their organization (Japanese Nursing Association 2012). After the nuclear disaster, city public health nurses needed information sharing among their peers in the city and other municipalities, with other city personnel working in different sectors, and with local academic institutes in order to respond to a new environmental issue that affected many aspects of residents' lives. In the post-disaster period, training workshops were organized in collaboration with the local university, in order to provide city public health nurses an opportunity to learn new knowledge and share opinions among themselves.

Leadership

Japanese public health nurses are involved in the networking of residents' groups and organizations such as child-care circles, which is supported by local government funding. Through such activities, public health nurses' leadership competence is established and recognized in local communities (Hirano et al. 2011). Especially in rural areas, a qualitative study reported that building trust with the community is central in the work of public health nurses (Yamashita et al. 2005). Another case study explained how a public health nurse visited households in her village, held community meetings, and tried to understand the underlying meaning of residents' words, through which she earned community trust (Hatashita and Anderson 2004). This theory is also applicable in urban areas. A large-scale mixed-method study (Negishi et al. 2010), targeting more than seven hundred public health nurses in the central part of Japan, identified connectedness to community as a specific factor determining their professional identity.

The most difficult challenge, however, in the post-disaster phase in Fukushima City is the building of a trust relationship between communities and organizations. Fukushima regional culture has now given rise to some groups of residents who are deeply skeptical about any government or government-involved activities and information, and this skepticism is preventing public health nurses from taking a leadership role (Goto et al. 2014). The national Fukushima Nuclear Accident Independent Investigation Commission reported that the central government was not only slow in informing local governments and residents about the occurrence and severity of the nuclear power plant accident, but also failed to provide timely information about a safer evacuation route (The National Diet of Japan 2012).

Decision Making

This study also found that in addition to the activity of trust building of public health nurses is another major important construct: identifying and responding promptly to community needs (Yamashita et al. 2005). Another similar study described and identified three major components that influenced public health nurses' confidence in their work:

these components are managerial skills, health counseling abilities, and scientific evidence-based evaluation capabilities (Ogawa and Nakatani 2012). The second component of health counseling included familiarity and communication with the community, reflecting the importance of qualitative approaches. It is noteworthy that the third component addressed more quantitative skills in relating to the community, as an independent dimension in this analysis. The nuclear disaster brought in a new factor negatively affecting parenting, so public health nurses had to conduct needs assessments to plan and provide adequate parenting supports.

SUMMARY OF JAPAN CASE

Public health nurses in Japan were trained in a well-defined national training system, which did not, however, prepare them to respond to nuclear disaster issues. They work in a government system, which allocates resources for routine work but not for extra tasks in a disaster setting. The work ethics of these nurses include networking and building trust with the community, missions that were challenged after the disaster. Unexpected disaster tasks required more information sharing among their peers, and the community's distrust of government agencies demanded reassessment of people's needs and involved regaining their trust.

In the National Mental Health Center's recent efforts to revise disaster mental health guidelines, they could not reach agreement on defining the roles of public health nurses in a disaster setting despite their recognition of nurses as major community health service providers (Suzuki et al. 2012). Reasons cited were nurses' different levels of skills and experiences working during disasters and their unpredictable availability in emergencies. This example emphasizes that public health nurses need adequate training, resources, and better integration into the health system in order to enhance their roles in disaster responses.

CONDITIONS FOR COMMUNITY GOVERNANCE

Using the five-components analysis in this study, we found commonalities between our cases in Lusaka and Fukushima (Table 5.3).

TABLE 5.3 Commonalities of the Two Cases in Zambia and Japan

Five components:	Teachers in Zambia and public health nurses in Japan:
Skills	1. Have formal education 2 Provide health information to community at the front line 3. Need updated training of specific topics
Resources	1. Function in the government system 2. Experience excessive workloads that may restrain their willingness to address emerging community needs
Networking	1. Need coordination and information sharing among themselves and with other groups
Leadership	1. Are financially supported by the local government 2. Perceive building trust with the community as central to their work
Decision Making	1. Perceive confidence in their work as important 2. Need managerial, material, and technical supports for their capacity, autonomy, and legitimacy in representing community voices

On the basis of these commonalities, we propose a framework (Figure 5.1) that can help leverage community workers to strengthen community governance. Good governance is both a means of achieving development and a development objective in itself. The World Bank has defined good governance as "epitomized by predictable, open, and enlightened policy making; a bureaucracy imbued with a professional ethos; an executive arm of government accountable for its actions; and a strong civil society participating in public affairs; and all behaving under the rule of law" (World Bank 1994, vii).

However, this definition, as well as the previously mentioned WHO definition of community participation, does not identify the critical issue of who makes decisions. It only includes a weak form of community participation, failing to emphasize community ownership of decision making. Our framework (Figure 5.1) puts more emphasis on the ultimate goals of community workers to reach good governance, which are to earn community trust (outcomes) and to achieve community well-being (outcomes). These ultimate goals are achieved by strengthening the workers' leadership capacity built on their professional confidence (outputs). For the community workers to fulfill their responsibilities, they first need training and networking to improve their knowledge and skills (inputs). Second, they need their work to be authorized and

FIGURE 5.1 Framework for Community Health Workers

FRAMEWORK FOR COMMUNITY HEALTH WORKERS

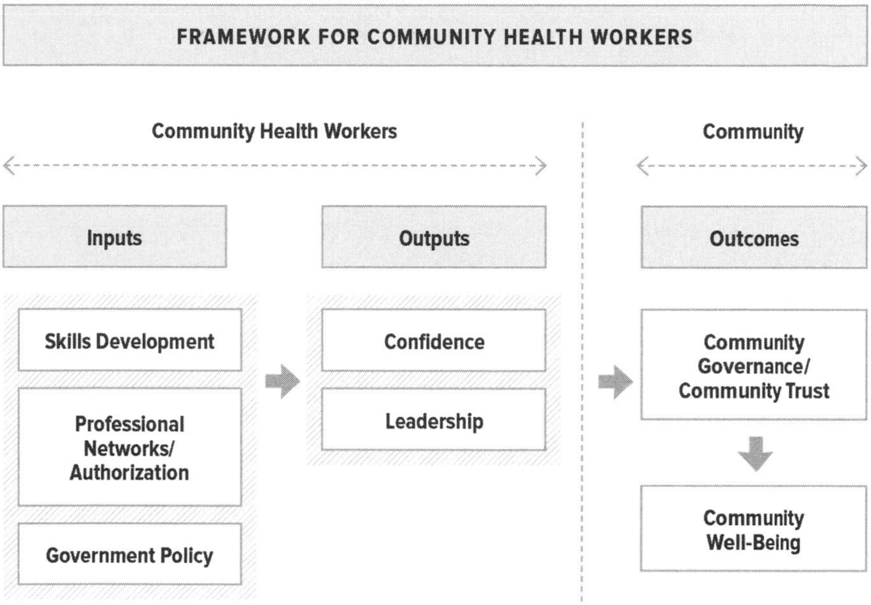

framed within government policy, so their autonomy to plan and implement community activities will be protected and enhanced. We explain each item included in inputs, outputs, and outcomes.

At the input level, this study identified four important indicators: skills development, professional network building, authorization, and government policy support.

1. **Skills development:** Teachers in Zambia and public health nurses in Japan are community residents' entry point to scientific evidence. Teachers needed skills in health education, nurses needed skills in nuclear disaster management, and both needed training in communication skills. A competency-based approach, adapted to local conditions to address both present and emerging factors (such as the case of Fukushima), is needed (Lehmann and Sanders 2007). Teachers in Zambia are already perceived by their communities as an HIV-education resource, however, this effort involves task shifting, defined as delegating tasks to existing or new cadres with less training (Fulton 2011), leading to suitability and sustainability (Fellin 2001). In the case of nurses in Fukushima, the need for task shifting was unexpected—responding to a

nuclear accident. At the same time, there is similarity with teachers in Zambia, in that institutional capacity and governance are required to make this emergency transition of preparing nurses to shift tasks in a timely and competent manner.

2. **Professional network building:** The community workers in both countries needed opportunities to share information among themselves and with other professional groups. Teachers in Zambia needed a formalized link connecting the teachers, MoE, and clinically skilled workers and health facility–based services. Public health nurses needed continuous support from a local university. In both countries, it made sense to promote transprofessional education, with an emphasis on professional networks. Both key players have a role in the health system, which, if better integrated and supported, can facilitate referrals and counter-referrals from teachers to health services and vice versa. Linkage points allow opportunities for increased supply chain, services, and data collection (The Earth Institute 2013).

3. **Authorization:** Teachers in Zambia are already perceived by their community as an HIV-education resource, but need supportive task shifting to be integrated into a health system to take part in HIV/AIDS education. Public health nurses in Japan are already playing a central role in community health activities, but need more flexibility in their work to plan actions to respond to residents' emerging needs after the disaster. Community workers need certification or authorization, which follows appropriate training mentioned above and ensures their professional autonomy to organize themselves and community activities. This requires legitimacy and backup support in order for the workers to fully integrate into a health system where their voices are represented and they are positioned to make decisions for the larger communities they serve (Kane et al. 2010; Anand and Bärnighausen 2012). We should, however, consider an argument that when professional activities are managed for efficiency, this priority may suppress socially intimate and responsive activities (Gilbert 2005). Community workers need authorization that supports their autonomous activities but does not distort their close relationship with community.

4. **Government policy support:** Teacher involvement in the health sector in Zambia needs to be legitimized. The successful integration of teachers into HIV response can expand teachers' roles as change agents for future health challenges other than HIV/AIDS. Public health nurses in Japan, on the other hand, were well incorporated into the health system but needed better work-management strategies to secure an adequate number of staff and more time to comply with the increasing number of tasks after the disaster. Collaborative dialogue in policy making brings together interdependent stakeholders, who together can generate policy solutions to problems (Innes and Booher 2003). In both cases, the implementation of policy should consider contextual determinants.

At the output level, the study emphasized the importance of confidence in and leadership of community workers, so that they can effectively contribute to delivering services to community residents engaged in the improvement of their own health. According to Ruiz and colleagues (2012), core competency-based training can successfully affect community health workers' perceived confidence. Teachers and nurses need to be supported in ways that build their confidence and leadership to support translational change in a community.

At the outcome level, the study highlighted how community workers perceive community trust as critical in providing services aimed at improving community well-being. Trust is a complex construct, the specific elements of which vary between settings and relationships (Gilson et al. 2005). Both the HIV crisis in Zambia and the nuclear disaster in Japan have medical and social dimensions, and teachers and nurses could be positioned to bridge the gaps between science and society. When they improve their skills and are leveraged to communicate with local residents, community workers can fulfill their leadership role and augment community trust. This enhanced sense of trust about given services in a community can lead to heightened life satisfaction among local residents (Tang 2013). We use the term "well-being" as a subjective measurement that reflects a community's physical, mental, and socioeconomic dimensions, and which has gained increasing attention as a component in making economic and political decisions (Diener

2008). Our work suggests that supporting teachers and nurses is likely to result in a positive shift in a community's overall sense of well-being.

CONCLUSIONS

These two cases of community workers are different in many ways, each grounded in local economic, cultural, political, and environmental contexts; yet, strikingly, both cases aim to find a common ground in the governance of health crises. Both teachers in Lusaka and public health nurses in Fukushima work in the community and perceive community acceptance and trust as important for them to fulfill their roles, which were challenged by the HIV/AIDS epidemic and the nuclear disaster. Both cases, one in a high-income and one in a low-income country, are faced with chronic health issues that influence capacity building, information sharing, and the ability to provide systemic support of a voice for those on the front lines of health and disease prevention. This study provides suggestions for strategies that can help scale up efforts to strengthen community governance and community health in ways that are strategic, sustainable, and cognizant of the importance of the historical role of frontline community workers—and, as such, provide a critical pathway forward in meeting future health challenges.

Acknowledgment: The authors wish to acknowledge Luzma Gonzalez PhD, MHA, Associate Professor, Autonomous University of the State of Morelos, Mexico, for her support in the case analysis of this work.

REFERENCES

Abelson, J., P. G. Forest, J. Eyles, P. Smith, E. Martin, and F. P. Gauvin. 2003. "Deliberations About Deliberative Methods: Issues in the Design and Evaluation of Public Participation Processes." *Social Science & Medicine* 57: 239–51.

Anand, S., and T. Bärnighausen. 2012. "Health Workers at the Core of the Health System: Framework and Research Issues." *Health Policy* 105: 185–91.

Avey, S. R., and M. F. Fernandez. 2012. "Identifying the Core Elements of Effective Community Health Worker Programs: A Research Agenda." *American Journal of Public Health* 102: 1633–37.

Baker, K. 1993. "Zambia: Anti-AIDS Clubs." *Children Worldwide* 20: 60–63.

Barnett, E., K. de Koning, and B. Francis. 1995. *Health and HIV/AIDS Education in Primary and Secondary Schools in Africa and Asia.* Overseas Development Administration, Education Resource Group, Serial No. 14.

Boice, J.D. 2012. "Radiation Epidemiology: A Perspective on Fukushima." *Journal of Radiological Protection* 32: N33–40.

Bromet, E. J. 2012. "Mental Health Consequences of the Chernobyl Disaster." *Journal of Radiological Protection* 32: N71–N75.

Bryant, M., J. Beard, L. Sabin, M. I. Brooks, N. Scott, B. A. Larson, G. Biemba, C. Miller, and J. Simon. 2012. "PEPFAR's Support for Orphans and Vulnerable Children: Some Beneficial Effects, but too Little Data, and Programs Spread Thin." *Health Affairs* 31: 1508–1518.

Bureau of African Affairs. 2007. Third Annual Report to Congress on PEPFAR. http://www.pepfar.gov/press/c21604.htm.

Chondoka, Y. A. 2006. *Situation Analysis of Community Schools in Central Province of Zambia.* Lusaka, Zambia: University of Zambia.

Claeyé, F., and T. Jackson. 2011. "Project Delivery in HIV/AIDS and TB in Southern Africa: The Cross-Cultural Management Imperative." *Journal of Health Organization and Management* 25: 469–86.

Deci, E. L., and R. M. Ryan. 2000. "The 'What' and 'Why' of Goal Pursuits: Human Needs and the Self-Determination of Behavior." *Inquiry Psychological* 11: 227–68.

Diener, E., P. Kesebir, and R. Lucas. 2008. "Benefits of Accounts of Well-Being—For Societies and for Psychological Science." *Applied Psychology* 57, Supplement s1: 37–53.

Dodgson, R., L. Kelley, and D. Nick. 2002. *Global Health Governance: A Conceptual Review.* Discussion paper no. 1. Geneva: WHO Department of Health and Development.

Fulton, B. D., R. M. Scheffler, S. P. Sparkes, E. Y. Auh, M. Vujicic, and A. Soucat. 2011. "Health Workforce Skill Mix and Task Shifting in Low Income Countries: A Review of Recent evidence." *Human Resources for Health* 9 (1): 1.

Finger, B., M. Lapetina, and M. Pribila. 2002. *Intervention Strategies That Work for Youth: Summary of the FOCUS on Young Adults End of Program Report.* Virginia: Family Health International.

Frankish, C. J., B. Kwan, P. A. Ratner, J. W. Higgins, and C. Larsen. 2002. "Challenges of Citizen Participation in Regional Health Authorities." *Social Science & Medicine* 54: 1471–80.

Frenk, J., L. Chen, Z. A. Bhutta, J. Cohen, N. Crisp, T. Evans, H. Fineberg, P. Garcia, Y. Ke, P. Kelley, B. Kistnasamy, A. Meleis, D. Naylor, A. Pablos-Mendez, S. Reddy, S. Scrimshaw, J. Sepulveda, D. Serwadda, and H. Zurayk. 2010. "Health Professionals for a New Century: Transforming Education to Strengthen Health Systems in an Interdependent World." *Lancet* 376: 1923–58.

Fulton, B.D., R. M. Scheffler, S. P. Sparkes, E. Y. Auh, M. Vujicic, and A. Soucat. 2011. "Health Workforce Skill Mix and Task Shifting in Low Income Countries: A Review of Recent Evidence." *Human Resources for Health* 9: 1.

Gallant, M., and E. Maticka-Tyndale. 2004. School-Based HIV Prevention Programmes for African Youth. *Social Science & Medicine* 58: 1337–51.

George, A. L., and A. Bennett. 2005. *Case Studies and Theory Development in the Social Sciences.* Cambridge, MA: MIT Press.

Gilbert, T. P. 2005. "Trust and Managerialism: Exploring Discourses of Care." *Journal of Advanced Nursing* 52: 454–63.

Gilson, L., N. Palmer, and H. Schneider. 2005. "Trust and Health Worker Performance: Exploring a Conceptual Framework Using South African Evidence." *Social Science & Medicine* 61: 1418–29.

Gómez, E. J. 2011. "An Alternative Approach to Evaluating, Measuring, and Comparing Domestic and International Health Institutions: Insights from Social Science Theories." *Health Policy* 101: 209–19.

Goto, A., M. R. Reich, Y. Suzuki, H. Tsutomi, E. Watanabe, and S. Yasumura. 2014. "Parenting in Fukushima City in the Post-Disaster Period: Short-Term Strategies and Long-Term Perspectives." *Disasters* 38, Suppl. 2: S179–89.

Green, L. 1986. "The Theory of Participation: A Qualitative Analysis of Its Expression in National and International Health Policies." *Advances in Health Education and Promotion* 1: 211–36.

Hancock, T. 1993. "The Evolution, Impact and Significance of the Healthy Cities/Healthy Communities Movement." *Journal of Public Health Policy* 14: 5–18.

Hatashita, H., and E. T. Anderson. 2004. "Public Health Nurses Make a Difference: A Japanese Rural Village Benefits." *Journal of Community Health Nursing* 21: 101–10.

Henning, M., C. Chi, and S. K. Khanna. 2011. "Factors Associated with School Teachers' Perceived Needs and Level of Adoption of HIV Prevention Education in Lusaka, Zambia." *International Electronic Journal of Health Education* 14: 1–15.

Heritage, Z., and M. Dooris. 2009. "Community Participation and Empowerment in Healthy Cities." *Health Promotion International* 24: 45–55.

Hirano, M., K. Saeki, M. Kawaharada, and I. Ueda. 2011. "Awareness of the Importance of Public Health Nursing Activities in Japan." *Journal of Community Health* 36: 765–771.

Inkeles, A., and D. H. Smith. 1999. *Becoming Modern: Individual Change in Six Developing Countries.* Cambridge, MA: Harvard University Press.

Innes, J. E., and D. E. Booher. 2003. "Collaborative Policy Making: Governance Through Dialogue." In *Deliberative Policy Analysis: Understanding Governance in the Network Society,* edited by M. A. Hager and H. Wagenaar. Cambridge, U.K.: Cambridge University Press.

Japanese Nursing Association. 2011. *Nursing in Japan.* http://www.nurse.or.jp/jna/english/pdf/nursing-in-japan2011.pdf. [In Japanese]

Japanese Nursing Association. 2012. *Review of Health Activities in Municipalities.* http://www.nurse.or.jp/home/publication/pdf/senkuteki/23-houkoku-shichoson.pdf [In Japanese].

Kaaya, S. G., W. Mukoma, A. J. Flisher, and K. I. Klepp. 2002. "School-Based Sexual Health Initiatives in Sub-Saharan Africa: A Review." *Social Dynamics* 28: 64–88.

Kane, S. S., B. Gerretsen, R. Scherpbier, M. Dal Poz, and M. Dieleman. 2010. "A Realist Synthesis of Randomised Control Trials Involving Use of Community Health Workers for Delivering Child Health Interventions in Low and Middle Income Countries." BMC *Health Services Research* 10: 286.

Katjavivi, P. H., and B. Otaala. 2004. "African Higher Education Institutions Responding to the HIV/AIDS Pandemic." *African Universities in the Twenty-First Century: Knowledge and Society* 2.

Kitamiya, C. 2011. "Activities and Awareness of Public Health Nurses Working at Local Government Facilities and Health Centers Regarding Potential Nuclear Accidents. *Nihon Koshu Eisei Zasshi*" 58: 372–81. [In Japanese.]

Lehmann, U., and D. Sanders. 2007. *Community Health Workers: What Do We Know About Them?* Geneva: World Health Organization.

Liberato, S. C., J. Brimblecombe, J. Ritchie, M. Ferguson, and J. Coveney. 2011. "Measuring Capacity Building in Communities: A Review of the Literature." *BMC Public Health* 11: 850.

Maclellan-Wright, M. F., D. Anderson, S. Barber, N. Smith, B. Cantin, R. Felix, and K. Raine. 2007. "The Development of Measures of Community Capacity for Community-Based Funding Programs in Canada." *Health Promotion International* 22: 299–306.

Marui, E. 1991. "Public Health Nurses, Midwives, Nurses and Public Health." *Hoken No Kagaku* 33: 419–21. [In Japanese.]

Mathews, C., A. Boon, J. Flisher, and H.P. Schaalma. 2006. "Factors Associated with Teachers' Implementation of HIV/AIDS Education in Secondary Schools in Cape Town, South Africa." *AIDS Care* 18: 388–97.

Ministry of Education. 1996. *Educating Our Future.* Lusaka, Zambia: Ministry of Education.

Ministry of Education, Zambia. 2003. *HIV/AIDS Guidelines for Educators.* Lusaka, Zambia: Teacher Education Department. Ministry of Education, Zambia. 2006.National ICT Policy., Lusaka, Zambia: Ministry of Education.

Murashima, S., Y. Hatono, N. Whyte, and K. Asahara. 1999. "Public Health Nursing in Japan: New Opportunities for Health Promotion." *Public Health Nursing* 16: 133–39.

Negishi, K., K. Asahara, and H. Yanai. 2010. Developing a Professional Identity Scale: Identifying Factors Related to Professional Identity of Government-Employed Public Health Nurses. *Nihon Koshu Eisei Zasshi* 57: 27–38. [In Japanese.]

Ogawa, T., and H. Nakatani. 2012. "Professional Confidence of Public Health Nurses and Related Factors." *Nihon Koshu Eisei Zasshi* 59: 457–65. [In Japanese.]

Patman, R., and F. Chege. 2003. *Finding Our Voices: Gendered & Sexual Identities and HIV/AIDS in Education.* UNICEF, Eastern and Southern Africa.

Reich, M. R. 2011. "A Public Health Perspective on Reconstructing Post-Disaster Japan." *Nihon Ishikai Zasshi* 140: 1480–85. [In Japanese.]

Ravensbergen, F., and M. VanderPlaat. 2010. "Barriers to Citizen Participation: The Missing Voices of People Living with Low Income." *Community Development Journal* 45: 389–403.

Rhodes, S. D., K. L. Foley, C. S. Zometa, and F. R. Bloom. 2007. "Lay Health Advisor Interventions Among Hispanics/Latinos: A Qualitative Systematic Review." *American Journal of Preventive Medicine* 33: 418–27.

Rosenthal, E. L. 1998. *A Summary of the National Community Health Advisor Study.* Baltimore, MD: Annie E. Casey Foundation.

Rudd, R. E., Comings, J. P., and J. Hyde. 2003. "Leave No One Behind: Improving Health and Risk Communication Through Attention to Literacy." *Journal of Health Communication* 8, Suppl 1: 104-15.

Ruiz, Y., S. Matos, S. Kapadia, N. Islam, A. Cusack, S. Kwong, and C. Trinh-Shevrin. 2012. "Lessons Learned from a Community–Academic Initiative: The Development of a Core Competency–Based Training for Community–Academic Initiative Community Health Workers." *American Journal of Public Health* 102: 2372–79.

Smith, L. T., D. B. Johnson, E. Lamson, and M. Sitaker. 2006. "A Framework for Developing Evaluation Tools Used in Washington State's Healthy Communities Projects." *Preventing Chronic Disease* 3: A64.

Suzuki, Y., M. Fukasawa, S. Nakajima, T. Narisawa, and Y. Kim. 2012. "Development of Disaster Mental Health Guidelines Through the Delphi Process in Japan." *International Journal of Mental Health Systems* 6: 7.

Tang, L. 2013. "The Chinese Community Patient's Life Satisfaction, Assessment of Community Medical Service, and Trust in Community Health Delivery System." *Health and Quality of Life Outcomes* 11: 18.

The Earth Institute, Columbia University. 2013. *One Million Community Health Workers*. Technical taskforce report. http://1million healthworkers.org/files/2013/01/1mCHW_TechnicalTaskForce Report.pdf.

The National Diet of Japan. 2012. The Official Report of the Fukushima Nuclear Accident Independent Investigation Commission. Executive summary. http://www.nirs.org/fukushima/naiic_report .pdf.

Tijuana, J. T. A., W. Finger, R. C. Daileader, and S. Savariaud. 2004. *Teacher Training: Essential for School-Based Reproductive Health and HIV/AIDS Education—Focus on Sub-Saharan Africa*. Arlington, VA: Family Health International, YouthNet Program.

Underwood, C., H. Hachonda, E. Serlemitsos, and U. Bharath-Kumar. 2006. "Reducing the Risk of HIV Transmission Among Adolescents in Zambia: Psychosocial and Behavioral Correlates of Viewing a Risk-Reduction Media Campaign." *Journal of Adolescent Health* 38 (1): 55–e1.

Williams, F., J. Popay, and A. Oakley. 1999. *Welfare Research: A Critical Review*. London: UCL Press.

World Bank. 1994. *Governance: The World Bank's Experience*. A World Bank Publication Development in Practice Energy Series.

World Bank. 2006. *Zambia Education Sector Public Expenditure Review*. Washington, D.C.: World Bank.

World Health Organization. 2013. *Countries*. http://www.who.int/ countries/en/.

World Health Organization Regional Office for Europe. 2002. Community Participation in Local Health and Sustainable Development: Approaches and Techniques. http://www.euro.who.int/__data/ assets/pdf_file/0013/101065/E78652.pdf.

World Health Organization Regional Office for the Western Pacific. 2000. Regional Guidelines for Developing a Healthy Cities Project. http://whqlibdoc.who.int/wpro/2000/a78396.pdf.

Yamashita, M., F. Miyaji, and R. Akimoto. 2005. "The Public Health Nursing Role in Rural Japan." *Public Health Nursing* 22: 156–65.

CHAPTER 6

Community Perception of Health Services in South East Nigeria: A Reflection of Health System Governance in Nigeria

Joseph Okeibunor, A. Ngozi Njepuome, Obioma C. Nwaorgu, Nkechi G. Onyeneho, and Uche V. Amazigo

INTRODUCTION

Despite huge global investments in strengthening health systems, there are yawning gaps between health service provisioning and the health needs of the people, especially those in resource-poor environments. The uptake of health interventions is generally low due largely to a disconnect between the health systems and the end users. The quest for a health system that responds to the health needs of the populations served was the major motive behind many declarations in the health sector. Beyond this, however, Roberts et al. (2004, 90) proposed a set of performance goals for the health system that could contribute to the evaluation of the health service and ipso facto the uptake of health services by the people. These include "(1) health status of the population, (2) the satisfaction citizens derive from the system, and (3) the degree to which citizens are protected from financial risks of ill health."

The existing gap between objective measures to improve care delivery, in response to the Millennium Development Goal (MDG) targets on health, and current levels of service utilization, as well as health indicators, calls for a critical examination of the perceptions of the health system among end users. Individuals' subjective perception of health service and inadequate health workforce may contribute to the apparent gap (Roberts et al. 2004; Forchuk et al. 2008; Gregor et al. 2005; Nyamathi et al. 2004).

In Nigeria, as in many developing countries, health services financed by the state have mostly the poor, elderly, uneducated, and unemployed as their clientele. It is often practically impossible for these people to evaluate what is provided because, in many cases, they lack a basis for comparison, having experienced only what they receive. Thus, perceptions and judgment about what they get are determined by assessing factors their traditions and culture consider important; they can assess and judge factors such as courtesy, responsiveness, attentiveness, and perceived competence of the health staff (Singh et al. 1999). Perceptions, here, are seen in the context of the expressed satisfaction with the health service as well as the people's assessment of the attitude of the health staff.

For instance, guided by the Alma-Ata Declaration of 1978, the World Health Organization (WHO) launched the primary health care (PHC) approach, with intent to focus health services on shared key commitments and community participation in health service provisioning (WHO and UNICEF 1978; Lawn et al. 2008; WHO/AFRO 2012). The recognition of the potential contributions of the people to governing health systems and ensuring effectiveness also provided justification for the Addis Ababa Declaration (WHO 2006; WHO 2008a) and the Ouagadougou Declaration (WHO 2008b). These declarations stressed people-centered principles as the drivers for universal health coverage.

A people-centered health service promotes community participation, which is largely influenced by the people's perceptions of the current health service. It has been widely acknowledged that feedback from the people is vital if a health system's deficiencies are to be identified and improvements achieved (Singh et al. 1999). Here, community participation in health care delivery is the process by which people are enabled to become actively and genuinely involved in defining the issues of concern to them, in making decisions about factors that affect their lives, in formulating and implementing polices, in developing and delivering services, and in taking action to achieve change. This is largely influenced by the community perception, which is seen here as the views individuals and communities have about health services. It can be influenced by outcomes of previous health care experiences and patient satisfaction

(Roberts et al. 2004). Experiences in the development of community participation (Muller 1979; Atkinson et al. 2000; Atkinson et al. 2005) and community health financing strategies have shown the importance of community context (Criel 2004).

The health system in Africa has continued to exhibit symptoms of weakness and inefficiency, as attested to by the delay in realizing the health-related MDGs 4, 5, and 6. Consequently, there has been renewed focus on strengthening the health systems (G8 Health Experts Group 2008; Reich et al. 2008). However, efforts to strengthen the health systems have focused disproportionately on improving the workforce, increasing funding, and expanding the knowledge base about how to make the health systems work better (WHO, 2008c), to the disregard of health governance issues and the views of the people on what makes a good health system.

Many approaches to health systems have focused on increasing inputs without adequate attention to how these inputs are used, leading to inefficiency in these systems. It takes more than increased finances, expanded inputs in health service delivery, a surge in human resource capacity, and enhanced availability of health technology or commodities to produce improved health outcomes (WHO/AFRO 2012; Travis et al. 2004; WHO 2000). To achieve the desired performance goals, there is an urgent need to understand the people's perception of the health delivery services. This forms the focus of this chapter.

The utter disregard of the people could be attributed to the mutual avoidance between the health policy makers and the end users. The structural participation of the people in governing health systems is germane to improving the performance and efficiency of the health systems and universal health coverage (WHO 2010). It is important to note here that there are six key elements of health systems, namely, service delivery; health workforce; information; medical products, vaccines and technologies; financing; and leadership and governance (WHO 2007; WHO 2006; Sambo and Kiriga 2011). These make up the WHO building blocks approach, which mainly uses inputs and does not provide a good analysis or role for popular perceptions. On the contrary, however, citizen perceptions that derive largely from satisfaction with previous experiences go a long way in determining their evaluation of the system and, of course, their willingness to use the system in the future.

It follows, therefore, that a major barrier to realizing the health MDGs has been the neglect of the issues of leadership and governance, which include the involvement of the people in decision making or accommodation of the people's perceptions of health service. Involving people with diverse perspectives in the development of the health system could serve to promote acceptance and support. According to Roberts et al. (2004, 32), "Giving potential supporters a role in the design process can help transform them into actual supporters." Several tested health system–strengthening mechanisms have demonstrated that health interventions can be effectively implemented when government and communities take responsibility for the health service (Amazigo et al. 2007; Amazigo et al. 2012; Okeibunor et al. 2011). Experiences from some community-driven health interventions have shown high performance where the perceptions of local communities have been given a central role. A typical example is the African Program for Onchocerciasis Control (APOC) strategy for control, where communities play the central role and make major decisions on the implementation of health interventions (Amazigo et al. 2007).

Based on empirical data, APOC has promoted a community-directed strategy of community involvement as the main delivery mechanism for ivermectin, providing more than 140,000 villages with consistently adequate coverage for nearly seventeen years. This approach has been employed in a number of other disease-control interventions in the African region and can be used for other health services with greater efficiency (Katabarwa et al. 2010; Njepuome et al. 2009; Blackburn 2006).

Ironically, health decision makers have anchored their decisions on the views of health providers with little or no concern shown for the views of end users, despite the recognition of the roles of communities in stimulating demand and in actual delivery of health care (WHO/AFRO 2012). This chapter documents the perceptions of communities in southeastern Nigeria as a reflection of health system governance in Nigeria and provides evidence on the weaknesses of health services delivery, which needs to be addressed to optimize the components of leadership and governance. The study used mixed methods (quantitative and qualitative) in order to better capture an understanding of users' perceptions of the health system and covered urban, peri-urban, and rural communities alike.

MATERIALS AND METHODS

Study Design

This study was designed to allow a description and analysis of community perceptions and expectations of health and health care in the context of district-based health systems in the South East geopolitical zone of Nigeria. Community perception of health and health care is viewed from the perspective of a model that recognizes an interaction among a number of variables (WHO/AFRO 2012). These include the environmental and sociodemographic realities of the people as well as their past experiences with the health system. The various sociodemographic and environmental realities of the people constitute the independent variables. On the other hand, the model accounts for past experiences with PHC in explaining the intermediate factors that influence perceptions and expectations of the PHC system. See Figure 6.1 for details. The design ensured the determination of key factors for community engagement and empowerment in the governance and management of local health systems.

This multidisciplinary study combined two analytical designs, namely, cross-sectional survey and qualitative inquiry. The survey research was based on an interviewer-administered household survey instrument. The qualitative inquiry was based on in-depth interview and focus-group discussion methods. These two designs contributed to an in-depth, triangulated understanding of community perceptions and perspectives of health systems in South East Nigeria.

Nigerian political structure comprises thirty-six states and the federal capital territory (FCT) distributed into six geopolitical zones (GPZs). These GPZs are made up of states with semiautonomous health systems that independently develop strategies for attaining health targets in line with the national health policy. The GPZs represent broad clusters of political, cultural, and linguistic realities in Nigeria. They are the fundamental context for understanding Nigeria's ethnic diversity. The realities represented by this spread go a long way to influence the health services and health behavior of the people. The South East GPZ is predominantly Igbo, one of the three largest ethnic-sociocultural groups in Nigeria. Five states comprise this GPZ. Beyond being culturally

FIGURE 6.1 Analytical Framework for Community Perception of Health and Health Care

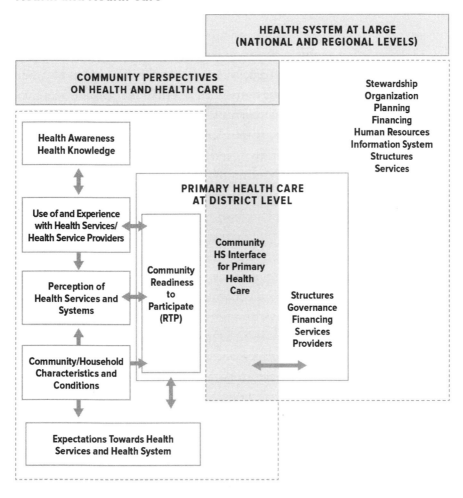

"Communities":
(Key) individuals
Households
Specific groups
Source: WHO/AFRO, 2012

homogenous, the zone had the highest average zonal immunization coverage, 66.9 percent, albeit below the desired 80 percent expected at local government area (LGA) levels. The other zones—South West, South South, North Central, North East and North West—had average zonal coverage of 66.5 percent, 54.2 percent, 43.4 percent, 12.4 percent, and 9.11 percent, respectively.

Given the variability of the PHC development at state and LGA lev-els, two states were randomly selected in two stages. States in the South East GPZ were grouped into two categories of "strong" (well perform-ing) versus "weak" (less well performing) based on DPT3 coverage in the 2008 Nigeria Demographic and Health Survey (NPC & ICF Macro 2009). The zonal average DPT3 coverage for the South East was 66.9 per-cent. Thus, any state within the zone with less than the zonal average was classified as weak. Imo and Anambra states, with 77.0 percent and 76.3 percent coverage respectively, were classified as "strong," while Ebonyi (60.1 percent), Abia (58.8 percent), and Enugu (50.0 percent) were clas-sified as "weak." Imo and Enugu states were randomly selected from the clusters of strong and weak performing states, respectively.

Population and Sampling

The LGA in each of the two selected states were classified and grouped into three clusters of urban, peri-urban, and rural. Three LGAs, one each from urban, peri-urban, and rural segments of each sampled state, were randomly selected, for a total of six LGAs. From the list of the commu-nities in each sampled LGA, four communities were randomly selected. These formed the sampling clusters from which eligible respondents were drawn. Again, this followed a two-stage sampling. The communi-ties were grouped into two clusters of far (>5km) and near (<5km) to the LGA PHC center. Two communities were randomly selected from each cluster. This gave a total of twenty-four communities.

Using a 50 percent assumed rate of awareness of health services in the communities, and a confidence interval of 95 percent with an estimated 3.5 percent error margin, a sample size of 770 ± 27 was computed. The sample size was, however, rounded up to 840 households, taking into account a 5 percent contingency rate. Approximately thirty-five house-hold heads were interviewed in each of the twenty-four communities.

To select the households, a central location in each of the randomly selected communities was identified, and this served as the starting point for data collection in the selected community. Two data collec-tors were assigned to cover each community cluster. The interviewers moved in opposite directions from the identified starting point in each community. Interviewers continued to turn right at any junction until the desired number of respondents was attained. On occasions where the number required in any community was not reached, interviewers moved into an adjacent community to complete the number.

Research Instruments

Five different research instruments were employed in the study, each targeting different sources of information for investigating the research questions. Each method has implications for different aspects of the study unit of analysis and the specific information needs of the research questions. These instruments include:

- *Household survey instrument:* Administered to the thirty-five heads of household in each of the study communities

- *Guides for in-depth interviews:*
  - In-depth interview (IDI) guides to interview community leaders and representatives of community-based organizations (CBOs)
  - In-depth interview (IDI) guides to interview community health volunteers
  - In-depth interview (IDI) guides to interview health workers at national, state, and LGA levels

- *Focus group discussion (FGD) guide for group interviews with community groups:* Twelve FGDs (three adult females and three adult males; three adolescent females and three adolescent males) with between eight and ten persons in each session were held in each health region

Data Analysis

All quantitative data were computer processed with EPI Info version 6 and analyzed with SPSS version 19. Simple descriptive statistics were employed in characterizing the respondents. However, multivariate analyses were also conducted to detect the predictive powers of certain demographic characteristics of the respondents on their perceptions of health systems in South East Nigeria.

Qualitative data consisted of textual data, mainly transcripts from interviews and discussion data. All qualitative data were analyzed using Atlas.Ti. All interviews were tape-recorded and detailed notes taken simultaneously, including verbal citations. Tape-recorded interviews were transcribed according to standard rules and translated into English. All textual data were entered into Atlas.Ti software, coded according to an established code list. Citations, by code and memos, were analyzed according to emerging themes using the network visualization abilities of the Atlas.Ti software for qualitative analysis.

Ethical Approval

Ethical approval was obtained through the University of Nigeria Teaching Hospital Ethical Review Board.

RESULTS

Sociodemographic Characteristics of Survey Respondents

Key sociodemographic characteristics of the sample population are summarized in Table 6.1. The sex distribution of the respondents follows the trend in most African countries, where there are more male household heads in the population. Most of the people interviewed were engaged in income-generating activities (86.8 percent), mainly in the form of artisanship (22.9 percent) or farming (20.6 percent), followed by business (19.1 percent), small-scale trading (18.5 percent), and paid employment (16.0 percent). The sample comprised equal numbers of respondents from urban (280), peri-urban (280), and rural communities (280). More than two-thirds of the respondents were married (73.2 percent), with a slightly higher proportion of the respondents in the rural communities (27.1 percent) reporting widowhood. This could be due to the fact that the rural sample had a relatively higher proportion of older persons (46.8 percent aged fifty-five or older, n=280) compared with the urban and peri-urban sites. The mean age of the respondents in the entire

TABLE 6.1 Sociodemographic Characteristics of Respondents, by Locality

SOCIODEMOGRAPHIC CHARACTERISTICS		LOCALITY (% IN PARENTHESES)			TOTAL (%)
		Urban	Peri-Urban	Rural	
Sex	Male	202 (72.1)	226 (80.7)	195 (69.6)	623 (74.2)
	Female	78 (27.9)	54 (19.3)	85 (30.4)	217 (25.8)
Age	25-34	29 (10.4)	14 (5.0)	10 (3.6)	53 (6.3)
	35-44	78 (27.9)	59 (21.1)	57 (20.4)	194 (23.1)
	45-54	87 (31.1)	77 (27.5)	82 (29.3)	246 (29.3)
	55-64	46 (16.4)	69 (24.6)	64 (22.9)	179 (21.3)
	65+	40 (14.3)	61 (21.8)	67 (23.9)	168 (20.0)
	Mean	*49.16*	*53.25*	*54.02*	*52.15*
	STD	*12.03*	*12.16*	*12.44*	*12.38*
	Median	*48.00*	*53.00*	*52.00*	*50.00*
	Minimum	*26.00*	*30.00*	*30.00*	*26*
	Maximum	*85.00*	*90.00*	*92.00*	*92*
Level of Education Attained	None	44 (15.7)	36 (12.9)	75 (26.8)	155 (18.5)
	Primary	81 (34.3)	121 (49.6)	110 (53.7)	312 (45.5)
	Secondary	98 (41.5)	90 (36.9)	69 (33.7)	257 (37.5)
	Post-secondary	41 (17.4)	31 (12.7)	19 (9.3)	91 (13.3)
	Vocational	15 (6.4)	2 (0.8)	7 (3.4)	24 (3.5)
	Nonformal/Arabic	1 (0.4)	0 (0.0)	0 (0.0)	1 (0.1)
Income-Generating Activities	None	41 (14.6)	38 (13.6)	32 (11.4)	111 (13.2)
	Farming/fishing/livestock	32 (13.4)	47 (19.4)	71 (28.6)	150 (20.6)
	Small-scale trading	54 (22.6)	34 (14.0)	47 (19.0)	135 (18.5)
	Paid employment	37 (15.5)	46 (19.0)	34 (13.7)	117 (16.0)
	Artisanship	56 (23.4)	63 (26.0)	48 (19.4)	167 (22.9)
	Business	56 (23.4)	41 (16.9)	42 (16.9)	139 (19.1)
	Other	4 (1.7)	11 (4.5)	6 (2.4)	21 (2.9)
Marital Status	Single	5 (1.8)	7 (2.5)	3 (1.1)	15 (1.8)
	Married	215 (76.8)	212 (75.7)	188 (67.1)	615 (73.2)
	Widowed	51 (18.2)	49 (17.5)	76 (27.1)	176 (21.0)
	Divorced	6 (2.1)	10 (3.6)	8 (2.9)	24 (2.9)
	Separated	3 (1.1)	2 (0.7)	5 (1.8)	10 (1.2)
Religious Affiliation	Christian	56 (23.4)	41 (16.9)	42 (16.9)	139 (19.1)
	Muslim	4 (1.7)	11 (4.5)	6 (2.4)	21 (2.9)
	African traditional	5 (1.8)	2 (0.7)	12 (4.3)	19 (2.3)
	No religion	1 (0.4)	0 (0.0)	0 (0.0)	1 (0.1)

SOCIODEMOGRAPHIC CHARACTERISTICS		LOCALITY (% IN PARENTHESES)			TOTAL (%)
		Urban	Peri-Urban	Rural	
Length of Stay	< 1 year	3 (1.1)	2 (0.7)	1 (0.4)	6 (0.7)
	1-4 years	23 (8.2)	13 (4.6)	7 (2.5)	43 (5.1)
	5-10 years	62 (22.1)	27 (9.6)	29 (10.4)	118 (14.0)
	11-20 years	60 (21.4)	56 (20.0)	54 (19.3)	170 (20.2)
	>20 years	132 (47.1)	182 (65.0)	189 (67.5)	503 (59.9)
	Mean	*25.9*	*32.2*	*34.5*	*30.9*
	STD	*20.2*	*19.5*	*20.4*	*20.3*
	Median	*20.0*	*30.0*	*31.5*	*30.0*
	Minimum	*1*	*1*	*1*	*1*
	Maximum	*75*	*85*	*92*	*92*
Source of Health Information	Radio	142 (50.7)	151 (53.9)	113 (40.4)	406 (48.3)
	Television	12 (4.3)	4 (1.4)	6 (2.1)	22 (2.6)
	Pamphlets	1 (0.4)	0 (0.0)	1 (0.4)	2 (0.2)
	Billboard	1 (0.4)	2 (0.7)	0 (0.0)	3 (0.4)
	Community/ town crier	39 (13.9)	63 (22.5)	90 (32.1)	192 (22.9)
	Friends & relatives	33 (11.8)	26 (9.3)	15 (5.4)	74 (8.8)
	Churches & health centers	44 (15.7)	32 (11.4)	54 (19.3)	130 (15.5)
	Don't know	8 (2.9)	2 (0.7)	1 (0.4)	11 (1.3)

sample was 52.15 years with a median of 50.00 years (52.15±12.38SD). More than two-thirds (80.1 percent) of the respondents had lived in the specific sites for eleven years or more, and thus were able to relate to community events and activities around the health service with confidence. The respondents were predominantly Christians (96.7 percent) and had a formal education (81.4 percent). Radio was the commonest source of information (48.3 percent), irrespective of the locality.

Perception of Services Rendered and Utilized in Health Facility

Treatment of ailments was the commonest service offered in the health centers nearest to the respondents, with 73.2 percent mentions. This is commonest in the urban communities, with 81.1 percent, and least in the rural communities, with 68.7 percent mentions. Other services include prescription for treatment (32.2 percent) and dispensing of drugs (30.4 percent). The peri-urban and rural communities mentioned child delivery care, with 52.5 percent and 43.9 percent, respectively. Similarly, more of the peri-urban respondents (57.0 percent) and rural respondents (51.1 percent) than the urban respondents (42.5 percent) mentioned immunization. Table 6.2 also shows services by state performance category.

The qualitative data revealed that people in the community are very much aware of the health facilities in their domain but utilization is low due to factors that relate to the attitude of health workers, and availability of equipment and drugs. According to a community leader of a rural community in the strong-performing state:

> We encourage our people to avail themselves of these opportunities. But like I said, most of the time, it ends up being talk shows. We have not been feeling direct impact of some of these opportunities you talk to us about. I hope by this visit I think we would rather move from talking to practical.

In the weak-performing state, the picture is the same. A health worker who was recently transferred to the rural area observed:

> The health facility is not functioning well.... The women and the children are not much after this health center. They prefer private hospitals instead of coming here. They are not patronizing the health center. Though there are many problems that make them not to come to the health centers ....

A community health worker in the weak-performing state summarized the situation and called for action in these words:

> Some communities don't even have roads to reach health center. Even when we have health centers, the communities do not utilize them. Some pregnant women prefer to go to a traditional birth attendant because they say that it is cheap and close

TABLE 6.2: Perceived Services Provided in Health Facilities, by State Category

Health Service Provided	STATE PERFORMANCE CATEGORY (% IN PARENTHESES)		
	Strong (n=420)	Weak (n=420)	Total (N=840)
Treat ailments	323 (76.9)	275 (69.4)	598 (73.3)
Counsel patients	81 (19.3)	75 (18.9)	156 (19.1)
Prescribe treatment	126 (30.0)	137 (34.6)	263 (32.2)
Dispense drugs	135 (32.1)	113 (28.5)	248 (30.4)
Referral	22 (5.2)	38 (9.6)	60 (7.4)
Diagnosis	69 (16.4)	45 (11.4)	114 (14.0)
Prenatal care	166 (39.5)	104 (26.3)	270 (33.1)
Delivery care	231 (55.0)	109 (27.5)	340 (41.7)
Postnatal care	145 (34.5)	67 (16.9)	212 (26.0)
Infant & child care	132 (31.4)	65 (16.4)	197 (24.1)
Immunization	264 (62.9)	145 (36.6)	409 (50.1)
Nutritional care	12 (2.9)	13 (3.3)	25 (3.1)
Malaria treatment	74 (17.6)	53 (13.4)	127 (15.6)
TB diagnosis	8 (1.9)	6 (1.5)	14 (1.7)
HIV screening	19 (4.5)	11 (2.8)	30 (3.7)
Health education	32 (7.6)	19 (4.8)	51 (6.3)

to them. They should use health centers so that our workers can be encouraged. Government should go to these communities, and educate their leaders, and tell them the importance of using health centers.

Figure 6.2 shows some differences in the services offered in the health facilities located in the strong-performing and the weak-performing states. For instance, while the strong-performing state offered up to ten services, the low-performing state offered only eight services, with median scores of 4 and 3 respectively. Table 6.2 revealed that maternal and child health services were poorly represented among the service provided in both the strong- and weak-performing states.

Another variable of interest used is their perception of the number of services delivered in the health facilities. This was categorized into "high" and "low" using a cutoff point of four services; approximately

FIGURE 6.2 Perceived Number of Services Offered in Health Facilities, by State Performance Category

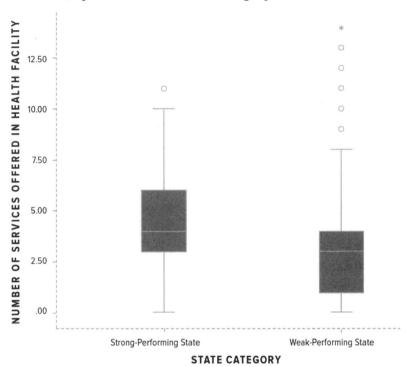

half (52.2 percent) of the respondents mention between four and eleven services. Where the number of services ranged from zero to three services, the health facilities were grouped under "low" in service delivery in the area of operation. On the other hand, where the number of services ranged from four to fourteen, the facilities were categorized as "high" in service delivery. This is later employed, along with other background characteristics of respondents, in a multivariate correlation model to evaluate factors that influence their perceptions of services of the health facility in the community, community involvement in health service provision, and feelings about the way health care is provided.

Health-Seeking Behavior of Respondents

With respect to the type of location at which they seek health services, about half (50.2 percent) of the respondents cited a health center and

40.4 percent mentioned a patent medicine vendor. The highest mention here came from the peri-urban area, while the lowest came from the urban area, with 50.0 percent and 26.4 percent, respectively. Patent medicines are drugs that are allowed to be sold over the counter (OTC) and that Nigerian regulatory authorities, such as Pharmaceutical Council of Nigeria (PCN), judge safe for unsupervised public use, as long as they are sold in their original manufacturer packages (Okonkwo and Okonkwo 2010; Onyeneho and Chukwu 2010; Brieger et al. 2005; Ross-Degnan et al. 1996; Egboh 1984, 9–11). OTC drugs include common drugs like pain-relieving tablets, antimalarials, cough syrups, and so forth (Okonkwo et al. 2010).

Health centers and patent medicine vendors were very popular for management of different health problems, irrespective of location. For instance, 57.1 percent of the 840 respondents cited patent medicine vendors for the management of aches and pains, while 40.1 percent cited health centers. Health centers were also popular for health problems like difficulty moving around, difficulty engaging in vigorous activities, difficulty caring for oneself, and difficulty recognizing people. Health centers were less popular in the rural areas than in the urban or peri-urban areas.

Participants in the qualitative inquiry blamed lack of responsive services in the government health centers for their preference for the patent medicine stores. Respondents in the qualitative study also complained of lack of drugs and attitude of health workers in the health center:

> It is heart breaking that when a sick person gets to the health center, he or she will not get the drugs needed. [Participant: FGD, Adult Male in Imo, Peri-urban]
>
> The attitude of the health workers does not help matters. They treat us with no respect. In many cases they respond to you based on their estimation of your social standing or wealth. The poor are ignored for the rich and even where they attend to you, they are very rude. [Participant: FGD, Adult Female in Enugu, Rural]

Experience with Health Care Services

About a third (39.6 percent) of the respondents had just one health facility to visit for health care. More of the urban respondents sought health care in private for-profit hospitals/clinics.

> When they are really sick, they look out for hospitals with qualified medical doctors…and other specialist medical personnel, whom they will not find at the primary health centers. [Respondent: IDI; Health Worker in Owerri, Imo State]

In the weak-performing state, however, a community leader in Ezeagu said,

> Because we don't have a good hospital here, when people are sick they go to the bush and start looking for leaves and roots to boil and drink or they will go to the chemist to buy drugs that may be fake or just pray for the sickness to go away in God's time.

In about two-thirds (64 percent) of the cases in which respondents sought health care within thirty days before the survey, the drugs they needed were not available. The implication is that the patients had to buy the prescribed drugs from medicine vendors at prices with profit markups. In 7.3 percent of the cases, none of the prescribed drugs were available in the health facilities, with the rural communities being worse hit. About two-thirds (70.2 percent) of the respondents got the drugs from medicine shops.

Health Financing/Insurance Plan

In virtually all cases, the patients paid for drugs they got from the health facilities, irrespective of locality. There is no system of reimbursement for the drugs the people collected and paid for in the health facilities. There is also no health insurance plan in the twenty-four communities covered in the study. According to a community member in the low-performing state:

> We don't have any health financing here. The only thing we
> have here is those free drugs like Mectizan® that are given to us
> to share to the people, otherwise you are on your own.

Respondents in the urban communities have no way of recovering the
cost of treatment in the health facilities. Twenty-five percent of the rural
respondents indicated that support for health costs comes from community efforts. Government free health programs also provide health support
for the peri-urban (75 percent) and rural (75 percent) respondents.

Perception of Health Care Service/System

Respondents were asked to rate the services provided in the health facilities. About half (50.4 percent) of the respondents rated their health care
services as bad, with the highest negative rating by the rural dwellers
(55.4 percent) and equal negative ratings of 47.9 percent each from the
peri-urban and urban respondents.

More than half (58.6 percent) of the urban respondents rated community involvement in health care delivery as bad. According to a health
officer in the weak-performing state, "we give opportunity, but they
are not participating." In the urban area of the strong-performing state,
involvement in health care delivery appears to be high because, according to the head of the Health Department, "they are organized in different committees, like the health facility development committee, where
they carry out monthly meetings; the chairman of this committee must
be an indigene." A majority of the respondents demanded that drugs be
provided in the health facilities (74.9 percent). The highest proportion
of respondents demanding that drugs be put in the health facilities come
from the rural communities (80.0 percent). Figure 6.3 also revealed that
very high proportions of the respondents were dissatisfied with the provision of health care, irrespective of locality.

There was a general low rating (≤50 percent in many cases) for the
way health service is delivered in the community. Furthermore, this low
rating cuts across the different sociodemographic backgrounds of the
respondents. As shown in Table 6.3, a significantly higher proportion
of the respondents from the strong-performing state gave a high rating to the way health care is delivered in their community ($p < 0.001$).

FIGURE 6.3 Perception of Health Service/System, by Locality Type

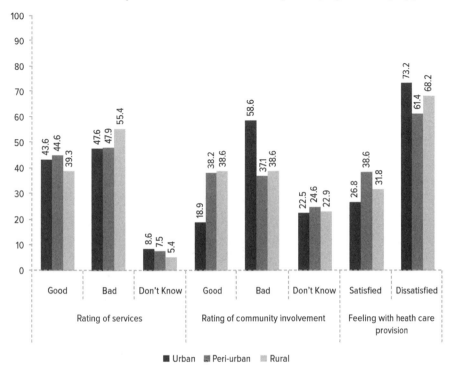

The results also revealed that a significantly higher proportion of those from areas where the health facilities are perceived to give more services assigned higher ratings to health care in their community than their counterparts in areas where services are reported to be low (p<0.001).

A patient summarized her frustration with poor services, remarking that:

> If I had gone to a private hospital, I would have paid more money, but would have saved my time. I would be paid attention because the workers know that I'm bringing in money. They would be here on time to do their jobs but here, it is not like that. It is only poverty that will bring me here again.

Significantly more (43.3 percent; p<0.001) of the respondents from the strong-performing health state than their counterparts in the weak-performing state gave high ratings for the level of involvement of the communities in decision making with regard to the delivery of health care. A higher proportion of peri-urban (38.2 percent) and rural (38.6) than urban (18.9 percent) respondents approved of the level of involvement of the communities in health care delivery. The finding is supported by qualitative data. According to the community leader:

> When the health center at Afuigiri was almost a no-go area, people like us, from our little resource, gave out money to repair some of the wards and the leaking roofs and we made the place a little bit habitable. With all the medical teams that are sent to work in our health center in most cases, the village women would buy beans and rice, plantain, oranges and give to them. We try to make them feel comfortable in delivering their services and I think so far it has been a very cordial relationship.

Further, a health worker reported that the community members participate in safeguarding the health equipment and commodities. This shows that community members are willing to get involved in the process of health care delivery when they are invited to play a role.

> They do, when they are given opportunities, and they do participate and support health activities to the extent they can. Some of them assist us in providing cold-chain logistics using their domestic freezers to produce ice. They also donate generators when we need to keep some drugs cold. Some (traditional rulers) donated their town halls as a makeshift health center. In some communities, they *built* the structures themselves and asked government to equip it. [Respondent: IDI; Rural; Female; Health officer, Imo State]

However, in the urban area the highest form of involvement is for the women to bring their children for immunization. The respondents also differed by their perception of the number of services provided in the health centers. For instance, more (41.0 percent) of the respondents from areas where the health centers are perceived to deliver more services approved of the level of involvement of their communities in the delivery of health services (p<0.001).

Despite variations by locality, the results show that more (49.0 percent) of the respondents from the strong-performing state were satisfied with the way health care is delivered. More of the respondents in peri-urban

TABLE 6.3 Demographic Factors and Ratings of Services in Health Facility; Community Involvement in Health Service Provision; and Feelings About Ways Health Care Is Provided

DEMOGRAPHIC FACTORS			RATINGS				Feelings About the Way Health Care Is Provided	
			Services of Health Facility in Community		Community Involvement in Health-Service Provision			
Factors	Category	Number	% Good Rating	x^2 Statistic; p value	% Good Rating	x^2 Statistic; p value	% Good Rating	x^2 Statistic; p value
State	Strong	420	63.1	$x^2=145.84$; P< 0.001	43.3	$x^2=51.11$; P< 0.001	49.0	$x^2=106.57$; P< 0.001
	Weak	420	21.9		20.5		15.7	
Proximity	Near	420	44.8	$x^2=2.01$; P= 0.366	34.5	$x^2=5.62$; P= 0.060	35.0	$x^2=2.632$; P= 0.061
	Far	420	40.2		29.3		29.8	
Locality	Urban	280	43.6	$x^2=5.24$; P=0.263	18.9	$x^2=41.42$; P<0.001	26.8	$x^2=8.95$; P=0.011
	Peri-Urban	280	44.6		38.2		38.6	
	Rural	280	39.3		38.6		31.8	
Sex	Male	623	41.3	$x^2=5.69$; P=0.058	31.9	$x^2=1.60$; P=0.449	31.3	$x^2=1.29$; P=0.147
	Female	217	46.1		31.8		35.5	
Education	Formal	685	43.4	$x^2=1.53$; P=0.466	32.6	$x^2=1.00$; P=0.608	32.8	$x^2=0.368$; P=0.306
	Non Formal	155	38.7		29.0		30.3	
Engage in Income Activity	Yes	729	41.4	$x^2=3.29$; P=0.193	33.1	$x^2=3.48$; P=0.175	32.0	$x^2=0.44$; P=0.287
	No	111	49.5		24.3		35.1	
Length of Stay in the Area (in years)	<1	6	50.0		33.3		16.7	
	1-4	43	51.2	$x^2=6.24$; P=0.621	30.2	$x^2=21.09$; P=0.007	30.2	$x^2=3.41$; P=0.491
	5-10	118	45.8		23.7		30.5	
	11-20	170	36.5		21.8		28.2	
	>20	503	42.9		37.4		34.6	
Age (in years)	Young (<50)	368	43.2	$x^2=0.22$; P=0.897	32.1	$x^2=0.23$; P=0.891	33.2	$x^2=0.18$; P=0.364
	Old (50+)	472	41.9		31.8		31.9	
Source of Health Information	Radio	406	45.4		28.8		34.8	
	Television	22	54.5		36.4		40.9	
	Pamphlet	2	50.0		50.0		50.0	
	Billboard	3	0.0	$x^2=6.24$; P=0.621	66.7	$x^2=21.09$; P=0.007	33.3	$x^2=11.75$; P=0.109
	Town Crier	192	43.2		42.2		35.9	
	Friend/ Relatives	74	35.1		23.0		28.4	
	Church/HF	130	34.6		31.5		21.5	
	Don't know	11	54.5		9.1		18.2	
Number of Services in Health Center	Low (0-3)	426	34.0	$x^2=6.24$; P=0.621	25.4	$x^2=21.09$; P=0.007	26.1	$x^2=21.24$; P<0.001
	High (4-14)	390	54.1		41.0		41.4	

(38.6 percent) and rural (32.6 percent) LGAs, compared with their urban counterparts, were satisfied with the way health care is delivered in their communities. One of the patients interviewed during the exit interview had this to say: "An injection that I should have taken at 6:00 a.m. is given to me at 11:45 a.m. because of their lateness; that is what I mean."

Perception of Government and Community Contributions

The main contribution of government to delivery of health care in the communities is the provision of under-five immunization, which was mentioned by 55.4 percent of the respondents. The highest mention in this regard came from the peri-urban communities, with 61.1 percent mentions, and the lowest was from the urban communities, with 47.1 percent mentions; more than half (57.9 percent) of the rural respondents also believed that government contribution to the health of the communities is in the area of immunization for under-five-year-old children. Another large segment (44.6 percent) believed government makes contributions toward the provision of health facilities. This belief is popular among the rural respondents, where more than half (53.2 percent) mentioned this. Less than half of the urban respondents and just a third of the peri-urban respondents considered government contribution in this regard as satisfactory. However, more than two-thirds (72.3 percent) of the respondents considered the contributions of government to the health of the people as inadequate. According to a community member:

> Recently, the local government dug a bore hole at the health center, but it is not functioning yet. We need a plant as a substitute to NEPA electricity; when there is no light the plant can be used, this is very important...to make the health center up to the required standard. [Participant: FGD; Peri-urban; community member]

In terms of the contribution of the communities, the respondents were also of the view that the communities were not doing enough, though they were not as critical as they were of government contributions. Slightly more than half (50.1 percent) of the respondents perceived their contributions as inadequate, with the highest critics coming from the rural communities, with 53.6 percent mentions. Smaller proportions of the peri-urban and urban respondents were dissatisfied with the contributions of the communities, with 49.6 percent and 47.1 percent respectively.

A comparative analysis of the peoples' perception of the contributions of government and community to health care shows that comparatively more respondents were dissatisfied with the contributions of government when compared with the contributions of the communities (Figure 6.4). Respondents' judgments of the adequacy of government and community contributions to health service provision in the communities were further examined against the background characteristics of the respondents.

Generally, the respondents perceive as inadequate the contributions of government to the provision of health care in the communities (Table 6.4). The highest score, from respondents in the strong-performing state, was <40 percent. This is a demonstration of low acceptance of government

FIGURE 6.4 Perceived Adequacy of Government and Community Contributions to Health Care

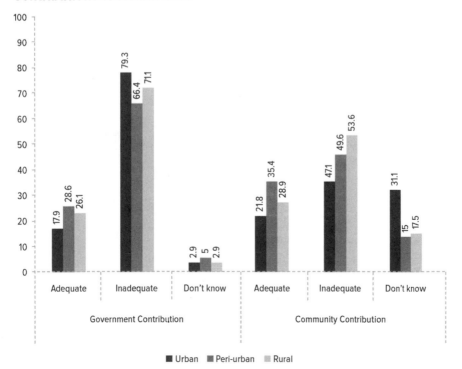

contribution by respondents. This cuts across the different backgrounds of the respondents as well as categories within the different backgrounds.

Statistically significant differences were only noticed between the low- and high-performing states. Here, the data showed that respondents in the high-performing state were significantly more likely to view government contributions as adequate compared to respondents in the low-performing state ($p<0.001$). Similar differences were noted among the different localities, but the differences were not statistically significant. More of the urban residents disapproved of the level of government contribution ($p=0.012$). More of the males than the females disapproved of government contributions ($p=0.025$). The data also revealed that the higher the number of services delivered in the health centers, the more the approval rating of government contribution to the delivery of health care in the communities.

All the same, there is generally low approval for the adequacy of government contributions to the health service. This position is also supported by the qualitative data. A good number of the people engaged in the qualitative segment of the study demonstrated their disapproval of the level of government contribution to the health of the people. For most of them, government stops at providing the health facilities, and in some cases when the communities construct the facility, government fails to provide the medical personnel and other equipment and health commodities needed in the facilities. Several statements from the qualitative data support the quantitative data that the contributions of government toward health care delivery are grossly inadequate:

> We have been writing, all these things are very important. [The government] should give us qualified nurses and midwives, they should equip the center, not when we finish building a health center, they will leave it for the community to suffer, then they start going from one place or another looking for quack nurses and doctors, [the government] are helping to kill the people. They should equip the centers with medicine and manpower. [Participant: FGD; Peri-urban; Community member, Imo State]
>
> Are we not part of Nigeria? They should give us doctor, they should give us drugs; not tomorrow again they will send some other people to come and ask us our needs and interview us. We have managed to build this health center. The government, we are

TABLE 6.4 Demographic Factors and Perceived Adequacy of Government Contribution to Health of Community

Factors	Category	Number	GOVERNMENT % Adequate	GOVERNMENT x^2 Statistic; p value	COMMUNITY % Adequate	COMMUNITY x^2 Statistic; p value
State	Strong	420	35.7	x^2=64.232; P<0.001	38.8	x^2=42.462; P<0.001
	Weak	420	12.6		18.6	
Proximity	Near	420	26.0	x^2=1.841; P=0.398	27.9	x^2=0.581; P=0.748
	Far	420	22.4		29.5	
Locality	Urban	280	17.9	x^2=12.948; P=0.012	21.4	x^2=30.214; P<0.001
	Peri-Urban	280	28.6		35.4	
	Rural	280	26.1		29.3	
Sex	Male	623	21.8	x^2=7.346; P=0.025	29.5	x^2=2.578; P=0.276
	Female	217	30.9		26.3	
Education	Formal	685	23.6	x^2=0.977; P=0.614	29.3	x^2=1.308; P=0.520
	Non Formal	155	26.5		25.8	
Engage in Income Activity	Yes	729	24.8	x^2=1.528; P=0.468	29.6	x^2=2.392; P=0.302
	No	111	19.8		22.5	
Length of Stay in the Area (in years)	< 1	6	33.3	x^2=8.053; P=0.428	16.7	x^2=32.663; P<0.001
	1-4	43	27.9		39.5	
	5-10	118	21.2		21.2	
	11-20	170	18.8		22.4	
		503	26.2		31.8	
Age (in years)	Young (<50)	368	26.4	x^2=2.802; P=0.246	26.1	x^2=7.804; P=0.020
	Old (50+)	472	22.5		30.7	
Source of Health Information	Radio	406	26.4	x^2=11.636; P=0.636	29.3	x^2=39.936; P<0.001
	Television	22	18.2		9.1	
	Pamphlet	2	50.0		0.0	
	Billboard	3	0.0		33.3	
	Town Crier	192	24.5		35.4	
	Friend/ Relatives	74	23.0		21.6	
	Church/HF	130	20.8		26.9	
	Don't know	11	0.0		0.0	
Number of Services in Health Center	Low (0-3)	426	20.2	x^2=10.637; P=0.005	22.5	x^2=19.636; P<0.001
	High (4-14)	390	30.0		36.7	

not sure whether they are still functioning, tomorrow they will come and ask for our votes. [IDI: Rural; Community leader, Imo]

Respondents also strongly decried the shortage of essential drugs in government health facilities:

It is not good: now that we have a health center, we still keep searching for a place to get treatment and cure, as was asked earlier about people seeking alternative treatment. The reason is that when we go to the health center, we do not get the necessary drugs to cure our illness, so we look for cure elsewhere. At most, what they have at the health center are some drugs for children, what about the adults? Any sickness that affects the head of the house is the most dangerous, so they should be considered too, their health should be taken care of so that they can care for their families. Drugs should also be supplied for adults. [IDI: Rural; Adult male; Community leader, Imo State]

What is important in our health center is that whenever you go there, the workers are there. But they do not have most of the drugs, especially drugs for children, they have difficulties with this. Sometimes, they will promise that it will come, a promise which fails most of the time. This is not the fault of the workers, it is the fault of the government. The government should supply us with drugs, good and effective drugs for children and adult, please help us we do not have any other facility but the health center, it is the nearest to us, please help us. [Participant: FGD; Peri-urban; Community member, Enugu State]

Approval rating for the level of community contributions against the demographic backgrounds of the respondents was examined. The results, as revealed in Table 6.4, show a slightly higher approval rating for the adequacy of community contributions than the government contributions to health care delivery in the communities. All the same, the ratings were generally low (<40 percent). Another major difference between the ratings for government contributions and those for the communities is in the fact that there were more variations between and among the categories of the different background characteristics of the respondents. For instance, one observes that in addition to the statistically significant difference between the strong- and weak-performing states ($p<0.001$), significant differences exist among the different localities. The urban residents disapproved more of the contribution of the communities ($p<0.001$). Also, significant differences exist among the respondents in terms of the length of time they have spent in the communities, their ages, and the number of services rendered in the community health facilities.

More than two-thirds (69.0 percent) of the respondents were willing to contribute to health care delivery in the future, with the highest coming from those in the rural area (69.3 percent); equal proportions of the peri-urban and urban respondents indicated their willingness to contribute in the future in assisting in caring for patients (39.7 percent) and maintenance of health facilities (32.9 percent).

The main reason that some of the respondents do not want to make any contributions in the future is poverty. More than half (52.9 percent) of those who indicated that they will not make any contribution in the future blamed it on the fact that they have no money. This is particularly true of the peri-urban and rural respondents (55.8 percent and 54.7 percent, respectively). Another major reason is that the people believe it is the responsibility of government to provide health care for the people.

DISCUSSION

The health system in the South East GPZ, at the LGA levels, are reputed mainly for the treatment of ailments, prescription and dispensing of drugs, prenatal care, immunization services, childbirth delivery, counseling patients, and malaria treatment and prevention in line with the PHC system, which expects the first course of care to take place at the health district and community levels. Secondary and tertiary care are obtainable at the state and national levels.

The PHC system in Nigeria, as elsewhere in Africa, was based on community participation in health care delivery, following the Alma-Ata Declaration in 1978, which recognized the role of communities in health care delivery. After the Alm-Ata Declaration came other local efforts to domesticate the declaration in Africa and even Nigeria in the 1980s. Thus, the institution of PHC got seriously underway in Africa in the mid-1980s, with the decision of African health ministers at a meeting in Lusaka, Zambia in 1985 to strengthen their national health systems using the PHC approach. The guiding principles were community participation and empowerment for sustainable health programs as well as collaboration between the community and the usual health services, leading to strengthening of the national health system, which thus becomes community-appropriate. These ideals were vigorously pursued under the tenure of Olikoye Ransome Kuti, who, as Minister for Health (1985–1993), provided a foothold for the institutionalization of PHC in Nigeria. With the help of partners, the health sector was revamped and restructured to make the health district and community the cornerstone of the implementation of PHC, in which community health and related activities would support community economic and social development.

However, with the weakening of other institutions in Nigeria, following incessant change in government and governance ideologies, came very tenuous commitment to health care in the country generally, and indeed to PHC and health care in the communities. It is not surprising, therefore, that in this study the people rated government contributions to health service in the communities, as well as community participation, as inadequate. Consequently, the people relied on patent medicine vendors and private for-profit health facilities. This is due to the poor infrastructure, out-of-stock syndrome, and poor personnel in these facilities. In some cases, the people constructed health facilities with their own resources and expected the government to stock them with health commodities and personnel, but this remains a mirage. Government is often unable to maintain the health facilities. The result was the poor rating of the health systems and government contributions by respondents, irrespective of state and locality.

Respondents complained that the health care delivery falls short of their expectations vis-à-vis the PHC minimum health package. The urban residents were more critical about the contribution of government to the health of the people. This may be attributed to the fact that most of the urban dwellers provide for their health needs by patronizing private for-profit health outfits in the urban areas, hence the suggestion that there are other services the government ought to provide for the good health of the people.

Universal coverage designed for improved equity in service delivery, people-centered health systems, public policy to promote and protect the health of communities, and leadership to expand stakeholder base and hold leaders accountable are yet to be fully felt. There is no universal coverage, as health is for the highest bidder. Health care seems available depending on the financial capability of the clients, making access to essential health services unrealizable among the greater segment of the population. Access, here, is defined not just as availability of health services but also proper utilization (Frost and Reich 2008). According to Roberts et al. (2004, 114), "...utilization is only partially a reflection of effective availability, as patients may choose not to use services, even if they are available." In other words, low use of the health services is a reflection of patient choice, which is often influenced by their perception of the services. The urban dwellers are more likely to be able to afford the cost of services in these profit-oriented facilities than the rural poor.

The general perception of health and health service was poor across all the study areas (urban, peri-urban, and rural). There was a general dissatisfaction with the provision of health care based on the cost of services, which were considered high in the rural and urban areas, while the peri-urban area reported satisfaction with the provision of services. Common health problems in all the study districts were malaria and fever. The signs of good health were based on physical activities such as the ability to work and move around. This poor understanding of the definition of health, which includes social and mental fitness, could be attributed to the respondents' level of education and exposure. The respondents viewed staying healthy as arising from healthy eating, followed by hygiene, sanitation, and regular checkups, and these are in line with standards of best health practices.

Solutions to health problems were sought mainly from government and private hospitals mostly outside the study districts. There were, however, people with ailments such as mental illness and convulsions who were not taken to the hospitals. These people were mostly taken to traditional healers and spiritual healers, based on cultural beliefs of the respondents. The household heads were mainly responsible for ensuring good health in the community, irrespective of classification of districts. This is not unusual in the African setting, where men play significant roles in decision making.

Experiences of community engagement with the health system were facilitated by the avenues through which information reached people. The major source of information was the radio (48.3 percent) followed by community announcement (22.9 percent). There was no barrier to information on health and health service delivery, suggesting good awareness on health issues. This was also confirmed by community involvement and participation in health issues irrespective of the districts.

A comparative analysis of how the sources of information influenced perceptions revealed no difference with respect to perceptions on services of health facilities in the communities, community involvement, and satisfaction with the way health care is provided in the communities. Similarly, the source of health information did not influence perception of the adequacy of government contributions to the health of the community. All of these point to a general low perception of the performance of the health system and government in terms of health care delivery in the communities. However, with respect to the contributions of the communities, the source of health information affected perceptions significantly. Significantly more (35.4 percent) of the 192 respondents who got their health information from community announcers (town criers) rated community contributions as adequate.

The community members were able to express their opinions freely on health issues through their community leaders; community leaders serve as the major channel of communication between the community and the government, which government recognizes and responds to. For example, governments have put in place a drug-revolving plan in response to community needs. There are other initiatives as found in the study (such as free maternal and child care). This is particularly true of Enugu State, the low-performing health state. To address the problem of poor maternal and child health, the government instituted the free maternal and child health (FMCH) program. Under this program, the government provided free prenatal and postnatal care for mothers and their children. Unfortunately, however, this has generated other concerns, as the men complained that they are not cared for. Worse still, the program seemed to function only in the urban and, to a limited extent, the peri-urban area, while rural communities know very little about the program, having only heard about it over the radio.

In many cases, community members who received care and got prescriptions sourced drugs from medicine stores. Nishtar (2007) documented a similar scenario in her appraisal of health care delivery in African countries. She reported that in developing and underserved areas, a mixed health system is the norm, in which out-of-pocket payments and market provision of privately delivered services co-exist along with publicly financed government health delivery.

Respondents in the quantitative and qualitative studies indicated readiness (willingness and capability) to participate in health service delivery. They cited cases of past contributions to health care delivery such as construction of health centers, school buildings, and market stalls, among other projects. They also mentioned cases where they helped with the distribution of health commodities when asked to do so. On the participation of communities in the organization of rural health services, Taylor (2004) noted that based on their contributions in areas such as maintenance of the health facility, assisting in caring for patients, sanitation, management of the health facility, and in some cases selection of volunteers and provision of health commodities, communities have helped in the provision of health care.

In the two study states, Imo and Enugu, community volunteerism has been entrenched in health care delivery. The APOC community-directed treatment with ivermectin (CDTI) program provided the vehicle for community involvement in health care, as it did in other African countries where the CDTI approach is the major strategy for the treatment of communities in which onchocerciasis is endemic (Okeibunor et al. 2004). In Imo State, for instance, volunteers commonly referred to as community-directed distributors (CDDs) gave and regarded their free services as their corporal work of mercy and service to their communities. In addition, community members perceived their roles as that of providing support to government initiatives through awareness creation and ensuring compliance to treatments. Effectiveness in playing these roles was enhanced by health promotion on the benefit of the interventions (Okeibunor et al. 2011). Identified impediments to effective participation in health care activities were attributed to shortage of commodities, poor access to the health facilities, affordability, and lack of basic amenities. This was also noted in the report on community-directed interventions in major health problems in Africa (WHO 2008).

In conclusion, the findings of the study revealed poor community perception of health service. The respondents in the study gave poor ratings to the health systems. Government contributions to health care delivery were rated grossly inadequate and unsatisfactory.

Community expectations and responsiveness on health service delivery were not met. The lack of health facilities in some communities, shortage of commodities, inaccessibility especially during the rainy season, and lack of basic amenities in the community such as potable water were identified as impediments to peoples' participation in delivering health. Communities (urban, peri-urban, and rural) expressed disappointment for the grossly inadequate health care services available to them, which are characterized by the acute shortage of drugs in health facilities, poor attitude of health workers, and lack of health insurance.

Communities were willing and making contributions to health service delivery by assisting in caring for patients. Other forms, such as sanitation and maintenance of health facilities, were rated inadequate. The self-help spirit is high in these communities and the people have a history of constructing health facilities and supporting the delivery of health care.

This study about people's perception of health services by governments in South East Nigeria is the first attempt made to listen, document, and analyze the views/perceptions of end users of health services. However, given the ethnic diversity in Nigeria, the findings in this study (of one region) may not be generalizable to other regions of Nigeria. Given this limitation, the states and federal governments are encouraged to conduct more in-depth multidisciplinary studies to gain an understanding of the characteristics of a good health system based on the perspectives of users and ways of improving government facilities using already existing channels. Such studies should also explore ways to improve attitudes of health personnel by considering modification of the curriculum and training module for faculties of medical and health sciences programs, making the programs more people-centered. The studies should also determine ways that communities and end users of health services can be sensitized and motivated to patronize health facilities.

Acknowledgments and Funding: *The chapter is based on a study that was implemented with funding from the World Health Organization African Program for Onchocerciasis (WHO/APOC) and the World Health Organization Regional Office for Africa (WHO/AFRO), Brazzaville.*

REFERENCES

Amazigo, U., J. Okeibunor, V. Matovu, H. Zoure, J. Bump, and A. Seketeli. 2007. "Performance of Predictors: Evaluating Sustainability in Community-Directed Treatment Projects of the African Program for Onchocerciasis Control." *Social Science & Medicine* 64: 2070–82.

Amazigo, U. V., S. G. A Leak, H. G. M. Zoure, N. Njepuome, and P. S. Lusamba-Dikassa. 2012 "Community-Driven Interventions Can Revolutionize Control of Neglected Tropical Diseases." *Trends in Parasitology* 28 (6): 231–38.

Atkinson, S., R. L. R. Medeiros, P. H. Oliveira, and R. D. de Almeida. 2000. "Going Down to the Local: Incorporating Social Organisation and Political Culture into Assessments of Decentralised Health Care." *Social Science & Medicine* 51 (4): 619–36.

Atkinson, S., L. Fernandez, A. Caprara, and J. Gideon. 2005. "Prevention and Promotion in Decentralised Rural Health Systems: A Comparative Study from North-East Brazil." *Health Policy and Planning* 20 (2): 69–79.

Blackburn, B. G., A. Eigege, H. Gotau, G. Gerlong, E. Miri, W.A. Hawley, E. Mathieu, and F. Richards. 2006. "Successful Integration of Insecticide-Treated Bed Net Distribution with Mass Drug Administration in Central Nigeria." *American Journal of Tropical Medicine and Hygiene* 75 (4): 650–55.

Brieger, W., A. Unwin, G. Greer, and S. Meek. 2005. *Interventions to Improve the Role of Medicine Sellers in Malaria Case Management for Children in Africa.* London, U.K., and Arlington, VA, U.S.: The Malaria Consortium and BASICS for the United States Agency for International Development; prepared for Roll Back Malaria's Sub-Group for Communication and Training and Malaria Case Management Working Group.

Criel, B., C. Atim, R. Basaza. P. Blaise, and M. P. Waelkens. 2004. "Community Health Insurance (CHI) in Sub-Saharan Africa: Researching the Context." *Tropical Medicine and International Health* 9 (10): 1041–43.

Egboh, A. 1984. *Pharmacy Laws and Practice in Nigeria.* Ikeja, Nigeria: Literamed Publications.

Forchuk, C., S. A. Brown, R. Schofield, and E. Jensen. 2008. "Perceptions of Health and Health Service Utilization Among Homeless and Housed Psychiatric Consumer/Survivors." *Journal of Psychiatric and Mental Health Nursing* 15: 399–407.

Frost, L. J., and M. R. Reich. 2008. *Access: How Do Good Health Technologies Get to Poor People in Poor Countries.* Cambridge, MA: Harvard Center for Population and Development Studies.

G8 Health Experts Group. 2008. Toyako Framework for Action on Global Health: Report of the G8 Health Experts Group. http://www.mofa.go.jp/policy/economy/summit/2008/doc/pdf/0708_09_en.pdf, accessed January 28, 2013.

Gregor, K. L., M. J. Zvolensky, and A. R. Yartz. 2005. "Perceived Health Among Individuals with Panic Disorder: Associations with Affective Vulnerability and Psychiatric Disability." *Journal of Nervous and Mental Disease* 193: 697–99.

Katabarwa, M., P. Habomugisha, S. Agunyo, A. McKelvey, N. Ogweng, S. Kwebiihae, F. Byenume, B. Male, and D. McFarland. 2010. "Traditional Kinship System Enhanced Classic Community-Directed Treatment with Ivermectin (CDTI) for Onchocerciasis Control in Uganda." *Transactions of the Royal Society of Tropical Medicine and Hygiene* 104 (4): 265–72.

Lawn, J. E., J. Rohde, S. Rifkin, M. Were, V. K. Paul, and M. Chopra. 2008. "Alma-Ata: Rebirth and Revision 1. Alma-Ata 30 Years On: Revolutionary, Relevant, and Time to Revitalise." *Lancet* 13 372 (9642): 917–27.

MacLean, L. M., M. Meyer, and A. Estable. 2004. "Improving Accuracy of Transcripts in Qualitative Research." *Qualitative Health Research* 14 (1): 113–23.

Monekosso, G. L. 1989. *Accelerating the Achievement of Health for All African: The Three-Phase Health Development Scenario.* Brazzaville, Republic of the Congo: WHO Regional Office for Africa.

Muller, F. 1979. *Participación Popular en Programas de Atención Sanitaria Primaria en America Latina.* Colombia: Universidad de Antioquia.

National Population Commission (NPC) [Nigeria] and ICF Macro. 2009. *Nigeria Demographic and Health Survey 2008.* Abuja, Nigeria: National Population Commission and ICF Macro.

Nishtar, S. 2007. "Politics of Health Systems: WHO's New Frontier."
    Lancet 370: 935–36.

Njepuome, N. A., D. R. Hopkins, F. O. Richards, Jr., I. N. Anagbogu,
    P. O. Pearce, M. M. Jibril, et al. 2009. "Nigeria's War on Terror:
    Fighting Dracunculiasis, Onchocerciasis, Lymphatic Filariasis, and
    Schistosomiasis at the Grassroots." *American Journal of Tropical Medi-
    cine and Hygiene* 80 (5): 691–98.

Nyamathi, A., H. Sands, A. Pattatucci-Aragón, J. Berge, B. Leake, J.
    E. Hahn, and D. Morisky. 2004. "Perception of Health Status by
    Homeless US Veterans." *Family and Community Health* 27: 65–74.

Okeibunor, J. C., M. K. Ogungbemi, M. Sama, S. C. Gbeleou, U.
    Onyene, and J. H. F. Remme 2004. "Additional Health and Devel-
    opment Activities for Community-Directed Distributors of Iver-
    mectin: Threat or Opportunity for Onchocerciasis Control?"
    Tropical Medicine and International Health 9 (8): 887–96.

Okeibunor, J. C., M. Amuyunzu-Nyamongo, N. G. Onyeneho, Y. F. L.
    Tchounkeu, C. Manianga, A. T. Kabali, and S. Leak. 2011. "Where
    Would I Be without Ivermectin? Capturing the Benefits of Com-
    munity-Directed Treatment with Ivermectin in Africa." *Tropical
    Medicine and International Health* 16 (5): 608–21.

Okeibunor, J. C., B. C. Orji, W. Brieger, G. Ishola, E. O. Otolorin, B. Raw-
    lins, E. U. Ndekhedehe, N. Onyeneho, and G. Fink. 2011. "Preventing
    Malaria in Pregnancy Through Community-Directed Interventions:
    Evidence from Akwa Ibom State, Nigeria." *Malaria Journal* 10: 227.

Okonkwo, A. D., and U.P. Okonkwo. 2010. Patent Medicine Vendors,
    Community Pharmacists and STI Management in Abuja, Nigeria.
    African Health Sciences 10(3): 253–65.

Onyeneho, N. G., and J. N. Chukwu. 2010. "Is There a Role for Patent
    Medicine Vendors in Tuberculosis Control in Southern Nigeria?"
    Journal of Health Population and Nutrition 28 (6): 567–77.

Reich, M. R., K. Takemi, M. J. Roberts, and W. C. Hsiao. 2008.
    "Global Action on Health Systems: A Proposal for the Toyako G8
    Summit." *Lancet* 371: 865–69.

Roberts, M. J., W. Hsiao, P. Berman, and M. R. Reich. 2004.
    *Getting Health Reform Right: A Guide to Improving Performance and
    Equity.* New York: Oxford University Press.

Ross-Degnan, D., P. Goel, P. Berman, and S. Soumeari. 1996. "Retail Pharmacies in Developing Countries: A Behaviour and Intervention Framework." *Social Science & Medicine* 42 (8): 1155–61.

Sambo, L. G., and J. M. Kirigia. 2011. "Africa's Health: Could the Private Sector Accelerate the Progress Towards the MDGs?" *International Archives of Medicine* 4: 39.

Singh, H., E. D. Haqq, N. Mustapha. 1999. "Patients' Perception and Satisfaction with Health Care Professionals at Primary Care Facilities in Trinidad and Tobago." *Bulletin of the World Health Organization* 77 (4).

Taylor, J. 2004. *Community Participation in the Organization of Rural General Medical Practice: Three Case Studies in South Australia,* PhD thesis, Department of Health Sciences, University of SA, Adelaide.

Travis, P., S. Bennett, A. Haines, T. Pang, A. Bhutta, A. A. Hyder, N. R. Pielemeier, A. Mills, and T. Evans. 2004. "Overcoming Health-Systems Constraints to Achieve the Millennium Development Goals." *Lancet* 364 (9437): 900–06.

UNDP/World Bank/WHO Special Program for Research and Training in Tropical Diseases (TDR). Community-Directed Treatment of Lymphatic Filariasis in Africa. 2000. *Report of a Multi-Center Study in Ghana and Kenya.* 2000, TDR/IDE/RP/CDTI/00.2.

WHO. 2000. *The World Health Report: Health Systems. Improving Performance.* Geneva: World Health Organization.

WHO. 2006. *The Addis Ababa Declaration on Community Health in the African Region.* Joint UNAIDS, UNICEF, World Bank and WHO International Conference on Community Health in the African Region to Ensure Universal Access to Quality Health Care and a Healthier Future for the African People. Addis Ababa: November 20–26, 2006. Brazzaville, Republic of the Congo: World Health Organization Regional Office for Africa.

WHO. 2007. *Everybody's Business: Strengthening Health Systems to Improve Health Outcomes. WHO Framework for Action.* Geneva: World Health Organization.

WHO. 2008. *Community-Directed Interventions for Major Health Problems in Africa: A Multi-Country Study: Final Report.* http://apps.who.int/tdr/svc/publications/tdr-research-publications/community-directed-interventions-health-problems.

WHO. 2008a. *The World Health Report: Primary Health Care (Now More Than Ever)*. Geneva: World Health Organization.

WHO. 2008b. *The Ouagadougou Declaration on Primary Health Care and Health Systems in Africa: Achieving Better Health for Africa in the New Millennium*. Brazzaville, Republic of the Congo: World Health Organization Regional Office for Africa.

WHO. 2008c. *Closing the Gap in Health Equity Through Action on the Social Determinants of Health*. Geneva: World Health Organization Commission on Social Determinants on Health. http://www.who .int/social_determinants/thecommission/finalreport/en/index .html, accessed January 29, 2013.

WHO/AFRO. 2012. *Health Systems in Africa: Community Perceptions and Perspectives*. Brazzaville, Republic of the Congo: WHO/AFRO.

WHO/UNICEF. 1978. *Primary Health Care: Report of the International Conference on Primary Health Care, Alma-Ata*, USSR. Geneva: World Health Organization.

PART II

Governing National Health Systems

CHAPTER 7

Governing Social Health Insurance Systems for Universal Coverage: The Case of Indonesia

Hari Kusnanto

INTRODUCTION

Social protection and community welfare are mandated by the Indonesian Constitution as the responsibilities of the government. Article 25H, Clause 3, of the Constitution says that social security is the right of each individual Indonesian citizen. However, not until the Asian economic crisis in 1997–1998 did the government allocate significant resources for social protection in the forms of free health care, cash transfer, food for work, and other social insurance and social assistance measures (Ananta 2012, 179). Then, in 2002, Article 34 clause 2 of the Constitution was amended to require the government to develop a national security system, covering the whole Indonesian population, and empower the poor according to human dignity principles.

Law No. 40 of 2004, commonly known as the SJSN Law, has provided a framework for how the social security system should be designed. The law is an important milestone in the history of social protection in Indonesia. For the first time the Indonesian government mandated a social security program that would cover all Indonesian citizens, including formal sector and informal sector workers, the unemployed, and the poor. However, the law does not specify the health insurance benefits, contribution rates, collection and investment of funds, or sanctions if the funds are misappropriated; it left these issues to the respective ministers,

such as ministers of finance, health, home affairs, and manpower (Arifianto 2006, 62).

The SJSN programs include health insurance, a benefit pension system
paying monthly annuities, a lump-sum benefit at retirement, and worker
accident insurance and death benefits for survivors of deceased beneficiaries. The SJSN Law stipulates the establishment of a National Social
Security Council (referred to as DJSN), composed of fifteen members
representing the government, experts, and organizations of employers
as well as workers. The main functions of DJSN are to formulate policies and evaluate the implementation of the National Social Security
System (SJSN). Presidential Regulation No. 44 of 2008 specifies the
role of DJSN as helping the president in "formulating general policies
and synchronizing the implementation of SJSN programs" (Article 1,
Clause 1). The DJSN members are appointed by and responsible directly
to the president.

As a priority in SJSN programs, social health insurance is to be implemented beginning in 2014, while the SJSN law anticipates that universal coverage should be achieved in a phased manner. Currently, only
the social health insurance program is approaching the one originally
intended by the SJSN Law (Widjaja 2012, 188). According to Presidential Regulation No. 12 of 2013, the coverage of the social health insurance in the first phase (beginning January 1, 2014) includes members of
ASKES (state-owned limited liability health insurance company) and
JAMSOSTEK (state-owned social security system for the labor force
other than government employees), and recipients of a contribution subsidy, known as PBI (for whom the government pays premium fees). In
the second phase, coverage would be expanded to the rest of the population, so that universal coverage would be accomplished by January 1,
2019.

Law No. 24 of 2011, also known as the BPJS (Social Security Administration Agency) Law, specifies two organizing bodies: one organizes
the social health insurance programs and the other is responsible for programs related to the welfare of workers, comprising pensions, old-age
benefits (lump sum funds at retirement), employment injury insurance,
and death benefits for the heirs of deceased persons. The law requires a
merger of government-owned limited liability companies to create one
universal program under two organizing bodies (BPJS Health and BPJS

Employment), to promote cross-subsidization, decrease administrative costs, and enhance equality in benefits (Lagomarsino et al. 2012, 937).

There are at least three major governance issues related to the social health insurance mandated by the SJSN law: (1) the administrative capacity of the overall health insurance system; (2) the structure of oversight by DJSN and supervisory bodies, supported by consistent regulation and transparency of information; and (3) the health care quality system, in which professional associations and beneficiaries are involved. This chapter focuses on the governance issues of social health insurance leading to universal coverage for the Indonesian people. The chapter is structured into four sections: first, an assessment of the general capacity for social health insurance system administration; second, a description of the structure and functions of social health insurance governance; third, a look at the quality assurance of health care provided to the beneficiaries, involving health care professional associations and the recipients of health care services; and fourth, discussion and conclusions.

CAPACITY FOR SOCIAL HEALTH INSURANCE SYSTEM ADMINISTRATION

History of the Social Health Insurance System in Indonesia

The current social security system reform taking place in Indonesia does not begin in a vacuum. During the colonial period of the East Indies (now Indonesia), the Dutch established a compulsory health-financing plan for civil servants and delivered comprehensive benefits through government facilities. Elements of social security among government employees have been in place for almost fifty years. ASKES, TASPEN, and ASABRI have been running the social security system for civil servants, military personnel, and police officers. These agencies are state-owned enterprises, required to make a profit, pay dividends to the government, and pay corporate income tax. JAMSOSTEK is also a state-owned enterprise serving the formal labor force, other than civil servants and the military or police officers, with four programs: (1) health care benefits, (2) employment injury benefits, (3) old-age benefits, and (4) death benefits (Table 7.1).

TABLE 7.1 Social Security Providers Covering Certain Employees in Indonesia

NAME OF PROVIDERS	YEAR ESTABLISHED	BENEFICIARIES (NUMBER)	BENEFIT
ASKES	1968	Civil servants (14.7 million), retired military police officers, veterans and patriots (1.7 million), state officials (46.5 thousand) and their dependents	Health care and maternity care (primary, secondary and tertiary medical care)
TASPEN	1969	Pensioners (2.3 million) and active civil servants making contributions (4.6 million)	Monthly pension and lump sum old-age savings benefit
ASABRI	1968	Military and police personnel and civil servants working in the Department of Defense (1.2 million)	Pension and retirement benefit, disability benefit, funeral compensation, cash benefit for those who resign or are dismissed, survivors' benefit for death before retirement or in line of duty, health care through clinics and hospitals and owned by military and police institutions for active personnel
JAMSOSTEK	1977	Workers in formal, private sectors (9.3 million)	Employment injury insurance, life insurance, old age savings, and health insurance (the first three programs are mandatory)

In recent years ASKES developed commercial health insurance, an expansion of its services, to cover private companies and individuals. In 2005, ASKES became the administrator of ASKESKIN (health insurance for poor families) funded by the government from general income tax. Using panel data for 8,582 households observed in 2005 and subsequently in 2006, it was found that ASKESKIN indeed targeted poor families and those at the highest risk for catastrophic out-of-pocket health payments. Utilization of outpatient services increased, and out-of-pocket spending among the insured urban poor also increased, likely due to only partial coverage of inpatient care (Sparrow et al. 2013, 271).

At the same time that ASKESKIN was implemented, several local governments also provided free health care to poor people, often as part of a political campaign. In 2005, representatives of East Java parliaments and administrators of provincial health insurance for poor people in East

Java Province filed a judicial review to the Constitutional Court. They argued that Article 5, Clauses 2, 3, and 4 of SJSN Law undermined their constitutional right and responsibilities to provide health insurance benefits to the people in their province. The court ruled that Article 5, Clauses 2, 3, and 4 of SJSN Law is a statement to convert ASKES, TASPEN, ASABRI, and JAMSOSTEK into a single social security administering agency. Hence, local governments are allowed to provide social security benefits to the local population.

The goal of universal health coverage, to ensure that all people obtain affordable health care, is inspired by the notion of health as human right, mandated by the Constitution (Article 28H) and Health Act of 2009 (Article 4). SJSN Law specifies social health insurance as a way to achieve universal coverage and the integration of social insurance companies into a trust fund as single payer. The existing social security providers initially resisted being merged into the trust fund, until the parliament enacted Law Number 24 (BPJS Law) of 2011, which stipulates that ASKES will become the sole administrator of the social health insurance system nationwide (social security provider for health insurance or BPJS Health) after integrating the health insurance division of JAMSOSTEK into its own organization. According to the BPJS Law, ASKES is required to change itself, without liquidation, from a for-profit liability company to a not-for-profit administrative entity, which will be called BPJS Health. Government regulations will provide technical guidance on how ASKES and JAMSOSTEK will be merged, while leaving alone military and police institutions, which are used to managing their own hospitals and providing health care insurance for active military and police personnel.

Health Insurance for the Poor

ASKESKIN, health insurance for poor families, was introduced in 2004 and implemented in the second half of 2005 as the first phase of the plan to achieve universal health coverage in Indonesia. The main objective of ASKESKIN was to remove financial barriers against health care for poor households unprotected by any health insurance. It initially targeted the poorest forty million people.

Poor people eligible for ASKESKIN benefits were entitled to free medical services from primary to tertiary health care. ASKES paid claims for services rendered by health care providers every three months. The Ministry of Health allocated money to ASKES on a yearly basis.

At the end of 2006 ASKES had to pay 248 billion rupiah (U.S. $27.5 million) to health care providers, about half of the total claims of 545 billion rupiah (U.S. $60.5 million), while no more funds allocated for beneficiaries of ASKESKIN were available to the insurance company. The verification processes conducted by teams employed by ASKES failed to contain spending by health care providers. The shortage of funds for covering beneficiaries of ASKESKIN was often attributed to the low tax-based "premium," which was only 6,000 rupiah (U.S. $0.52) per capita per month, while high expenditures for the treatment of cardiovascular diseases, strokes, chronic renal diseases, and cancers were fully covered.

National and Local Health Insurance Plan for the Poor

In 2008 ASKESKIN evolved into JAMKESMAS (community health insurance); the Ministry of Health took over from ASKES most administrative functions, including payment to health care providers, and created a more comprehensive benefit package. The providers were public and private health care clinics or hospitals. The beneficiaries of JAMKESMAS were increased from 40 to 76.4 million households. Outpatient care could only be obtained from public community health care clinics or hospitals. Beneficiaries of JAMKESMAS were allowed to utilize emergency care (direct visit) and inpatient care (upon referral from primary outpatient care only) at 926 hospitals, including 220 private hospitals for certain procedures.

JAMKESMAS is funded through general tax revenue, administered by the Ministry of Health, and supported by ASKES for the verification of payment to health care providers. Expenditure for JAMKESMAS in 2010 amounted to 5.1 trillion rupiah (U.S. $443.5 million), roughly equivalent to 0.07 percent of GDP; this increased to 7.3 trillion rupiah (U.S. $634.8 million), nearly equivalent to 0.09 percent of GDP, in 2012.

In 2005 BPS (National Statistics Agency) carried out a National Poverty Census Survey using a proxy means test with fourteen asset indicators to identify poor households based on estimated consumption level. BPS produced a list of quotas for eligible households to be members of JAMKESMAS in each district. The staff of the health offices in the districts validated and verified data from BPS and enrolled poor households in JAMKESMAS; those household members then received JAMKESMAS cards. Members of JAMKESMAS cannot directly access hospital outpatient or inpatient care, except for emergency medical care. They have to be referred to secondary care facilities by primary health care clinics, and verified by ASKES, which is responsible for maintaining JAMKESMAS membership database. The Government Regulation Number 12 of 2013 required BPJS to administer financial compensation if health care facilities are not available.

According to the National Socioeconomic Survey in 2010, the beneficiaries of JAMKESMAS included 20 percent of the population in the top three deciles, 32.4 percent of those in the middle four deciles, and 47.6 percent of those in the lowest three deciles, indicating a substantial proportion (52.4 percent) of poor households targeted that did not join the plan. Mistargeting of poor households to become members of JAMKESMAS could be due to differences in the criteria used for proxy-means testing; there were also a few reports accusing fraud and political clientelism (Harimurti et al. 2013, 13).

JAMKESDA is a social health insurance system implemented by districts or provinces to fill the gaps in health care coverage for the local community not enrolled in JAMKESMAS (the actual number of poor people in the districts might outnumber quotas allocated based on the list produced by BPS). In addition to the 76.4 million people covered by JAMKESMAS (funded by central government), 31.6 million people not covered by JAMKESMAS are insured through JAMKESDA (funded by local governments).

One example of a local health insurance plan leading to universal coverage is KJS (Jakarta Health Card), which was launched by the governor of Jakarta (capital of Indonesia) in November 2012. Under the initial phase of the program, 4.7 million people were eligible for primary care clinics and hospital services, including inpatient care in the third-class wards (the cheapest hospital room, each of which may be occupied by more than two patients). By 2014, all residents of Jakarta should be covered by the health insurance plan.

The Jakarta Health Card Program is considered a good policy on the demand side, as the program encourages poor people to seek health care from health centers and hospitals. However, the supply side of health care provision is complex, requiring an adequate number of trained doctors and paramedical personnel, pharmaceuticals, medical equipment, hospital beds and basic amenities, a safe disposal system for wastes, and medical record and information technology, among other necessities. A good referral system is also an essential element of cost-effective health care delivery. The Jakarta Health Card Program has caused a surge in the number of patients visiting hospitals, but these institutions are unprepared to deal with the excessive workload, and are paid through a case-based reimbursement system.

Two private hospitals (Thamrin and Admira hospitals) withdrew their participation in the program due to their reluctance to bear the substantial losses incurred from providing services to patients covered by the Jakarta Health Card Program. ASKES has been appointed to manage the funds that finance the Jakarta Health Card Program, for which the Jakarta administration has earmarked 1.2 trillion rupiah (U.S. $104.35 million) to cover the program in 2013. Salaries of personnel and other infrastructure of public hospitals are supported by the government through national and local budgets. This is not the case with private hospitals, which have to bear the brunt of the surge in the cost of providing health care to poor patients while receiving lower revenue. The immediate effects of universal health coverage associated with the Jakarta Health Card Program were similar to the impact of the massive expansion of health insurance in Japan on the substantial increase in the utilization of health care (Kondo and Shigeoka 2013, 16).

BPJS Leading to Universal Coverage

As mandated by the BPJS Law (Law Number 24 of 2011), ASKES will be transformed into BPJS Health. There are several competitive advantages of making ASKES the trust fund as the single payer for the social health insurance system, such as: (1) its more than forty years of experience serving government employees and, more recently, poor people; (2) its existing networks with primary health care clinics, hospitals, local governments, pharmacies, and laboratories; (3) its experience dealing with structured health care (gatekeeper and referral system), selected drug lists, utilization review, capitation, and case-based reimbursement; (4) it is in good standing financially with a satisfactory track record; and (5) it has an interconnected management information system with a membership database, payment to providers, and a verification system.

It is expected that at the beginning of social health insurance implementation in 2014, BPJS Health will cover 124,338,408 people. The government will fully subsidize a total of 98.9 million of the poor and indigent. Government Regulation Number 101 of 2012 set criteria for who is eligible to receive the government subsidy for premium payment. By January 1, 2014, BPJS Health will cover 49 percent of the Indonesian population (Figure 7.1).

Expansion and integration of membership will be accomplished in five years, so that by 2019 the whole population (estimated to be 257.5 million) will be served by BPJS as a single payer. Presidential Regulation

FIGURE 7.1 Estimated Coverage of Social Health Insurance in Indonesia at the Beginning of 2014

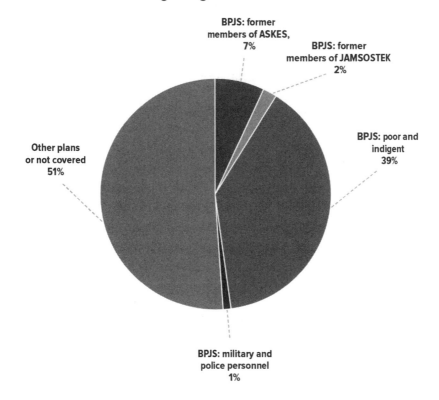

Number 12 of 2013 addresses social health insurance membership, premium payment, benefits package, referral system, and methods of payment to providers.

The capacity for social health insurance system administration is evaluated based on key performance indicators, including membership management, fund management (collection of contribution payment, insurance administration fund, and reserves), and payment to health care providers. The Ministry of Health has organized a BPJS task force to develop an information system and technology action plan, including the use of National Identification Numbers, improvement of district and provincial health office information systems, integration of hospital information systems with the case-mix billing system, and strengthening of e-health leadership and coordination. ASKES has also improved the information system platform to integrate a membership database that includes members of JAMKESMAS and JAMSOSTEK as well as active military and police personnel, and which links to the National Identification Number. BPJS trials have been conducted in three provinces (Aceh, West Java, and Jakarta). Preliminary results of the BPJS trial in Jakarta suggested that the third-class wards of hospitals were increasingly overcrowded by patients (40 percent with mild illnesses), while visits to community health centers were relatively unchanged (Dewi 2013). Referral system or "gatekeepers" did not function as intended by the program.

Law 24 of 2011 specified the role of BPJS to collect revenue, make financial investments, develop and terminate contracts with health care providers, negotiate the level of payment to providers based on case-mix principles, monitor the compliance of providers and beneficiaries, and produce reports. According to the principles of prudence, accountability, and transparency, BPJS is responsible for producing accountability reports, including: (1) program accountability reports, covering program performance, investment performance, liquidity and solvability of the program, and financial position and (2) financial accounting reports, according to generally accepted accounting principles as a nonprofit entity (including financial statements, comprehensive income, changes in equity, cash flows, net revenue, and expenses of trust funds), statutory accounting practices, and management accounting reports. These reports should be made accessible to the public, as stipulated by Law No. 14 of 2008 on public information disclosure.

Health promotion, especially through regulation, advocacy, and social policy, is financed from general tax revenue. BPJS is mainly responsible for providing promotive, preventive, curative, and rehabilitative care to individual beneficiaries. There are two types of provider payment by BPJS: (1) capitation fees paid to primary health care providers, comprising community health centers, family doctors, and dentists, and (2) case-based payment for secondary and tertiary care of outpatients and inpatients. Previous experiences with case-based payment for patients covered by JAMKESMAS suggest that on average hospital expenditures for surgical cases, cancer patients undergoing chemotherapy, and patients with certain procedures were higher than the amounts paid through the diagnosis-related-group payment system. Incomplete recording of diagnoses and comorbidities/complications became one of the reasons for underpayment to health care providers (Indriani 2013, unpublished dissertation).

OVERSIGHT OF THE SOCIAL HEALTH INSURANCE SYSTEM

The National Social Security Council (DJSN) is an oversight body representing stakeholders and experts. As a political entity, DJSN is responsible for helping the president in protecting the interests of health insurance members, and at the same time assuring efficient and fiscally sustainable operations of the social health insurance system. The technical operations of BPJS should be closely monitored without being heavily influenced by political interests. It has been argued that DJSN might not have the technical expertise or legal support necessary for supervisory functions. According to the SJSN Law (2004) and the BPJS Law (2011), the role of DJSN is to make assessment, provide advice and consultancies, and prepare reports concerning the performance of SJSN every six months (Table 7.2).

The SJSN Law also stipulates that DJSN is composed of fifteen members, who are appointed by the president. As a matter of fact, DJSN has been in operation since 2009 with the primary role of recommending investment policy and proposing the government's budget for subsidies for the poor. The BPJS Law emphasized the marginal role of the DJSN as an advisory body to the president, reporting on the implementation of SJSN and as an "external" supervisory body serving as a consultant to the BPJS.

TABLE 7.2 Mandates of DJSN According to SJSN Law (2004) and BPJS Law (2011)

THE LEGAL MANDATES OF DJSN	
SJSN Law (2004)	BPJS Law (2011)
DJSN is responsible to and appointed by the president	DJSN submits SJSN monitoring and evaluation report every 6 months
DJSN formulates general policies and helps the president to synchronize the administration of SJSN	DJSN proposes directors and supervisors for SJSN administration
	DJSN receives copies of BPJS programs and financial reports
DJSN carries out evaluation and research, proposes investment policies, and proposes budget for subsidized premiums for the poor	DJSN provides consultations to BPJS regarding the format and content of reports
	DJSN is an external supervisory body to BPJS

DJSN proposed the targeting of potential beneficiaries in the private, informal, and self-employed sectors, those who live in remote areas, and populations already provided social health insurance by provincial or district government, and suggested ways to integrate health insurance plans already implemented by many institutions. Stages of developing a full-fledged social health insurance system leading to universal coverage in 2019 were designed by DJSN as a "road map" (Table 7.3).

TABLE 7.3 Stages of Social Health Insurance Under BPJS Leading to Universal Health Care Coverage

YEAR	2014	2015	2016	2017	2018	2019
Members of BPJS	121.6 million	Integration of district and provincial health insurance into BPJS				257.5 million (total population)
Coverage According to Employment Size	20% large 20% medium 10% small 10% micro	50% large 50% medium 30% small 25% micro	75% large 75% medium 50% small 40% micro	100% large 100% medium 70% small 60% micro	100% small 80% micro	100% micro
Measuring Satisfaction of Services	Surveys will be conducted every 6 months, with the expectation that 85% of beneficiaries are satisfied with the services of BPJS by 2019					
Evaluation	Benefits and services will be evaluated annually					

Sustainability of the social health insurance program can be achieved if the program is acceptable to stakeholders (especially health insurance beneficiaries and health care providers) and offers an effective and satisfactory benefit package, efficient provider payment, and low administrative cost (no more than 10 percent of operational cost); it must also be able to prevent moral hazard through utilization review, medical audit, and other quality assurance measures. Aside from the economic and technical sustainability requirements, intensified participation by the civil society and the alignment of political forces to compromise on solutions to problems in the achievement of universal coverage seem necessary to ensure the sustainability of a social health insurance plan (Borgonovi and Compagni 2013, S36–7). Using the metaphor of the five control knobs (Roberts et al. 2004, 26–8), DJSN is expected to help the president in synchronizing: (1) the financing of health care; (2) payment to health care providers; (3) organizational aspects of health care provision; (4) regulation of BPJS, health care providers, beneficiaries, and employers; and (5) behaviors of individual patients and providers. Because the president may authorize ministers to deal with these tasks, DJSN may face ambiguity of its roles if there is not enough power and technical capability bestowed to the council.

Membership and Premium Fee

Members of BPJS in 2014 are mostly poor households fully subsidized by the government (98,900,000 people out of an overall BPJS coverage of 124,338,408 people). It is estimated that coverage of JAMKESDA (local social health insurance), medical insurance by companies, and private health insurance, will include a total of 50,074,461 people. Overall, 174,412,869 people (71.18 percent of the Indonesian population) will be covered by some kind of health insurance in 2014.

DJSN is supposed to suggest a premium fee for poor households fully subsidized by the government. A recent dispute between the Ministry of Finance, which committed to only U.S. $1.35 premium per person per month, and the Ministry of Health, which demanded U.S. $1.97 premium per person per month of government subsidy to poor households, suggested that DJSN did not have enough authority nor technical support to resolve important issues in the implementation of social health insurance as stipulated by the SJSN Law. The Minister of Finance argued that the government had paid only U.S. $0.42 for JAMKESMAS since 2008, so a threefold increase of the previous premium fee would be more than enough. The Minister of Health contended that with the low premium level suggesting limited revenues of BPJS, it would be hard to expect a reasonable case-based reimbursement system. Eventually it was decided that the subsidy for poor people for premium payment would be U.S. $1.67. Financial constraints experienced by public hospitals and community health centers will be overcome using the government budget. Meanwhile, the premium rate for Jakarta Health Card, subsidized by the Jakarta provincial government, is already U.S. $1.96.

Presidential Regulation No. 111 of 2013 instructed that workers employed by the government, such as civil servants, police officers, and military members, would pay 2 percent of their salaries, while a premium amounting to another 3 percent of their salaries would be covered by the government. Premium payments for workers other than those employed by the government is only 0.5 percent of their salaries, and the other 4.5 percent is paid by the employers until July 1, 2015. After that date, the premium rate for these workers (not employed by government) is 1 percent of their salaries.

Benefits Package

The basic benefits package offered by BPJS consists of outpatient care and inpatient care only at third-class wards for those fully subsidized by the government. Civil servants and military or police officers (middle and higher ranks) are entitled to better amenities at second- or first-class wards. The medical component of the benefits package will be the same for all beneficiaries of BPJS. Utilization review and verification of DRG (known as INA-CBG, described below) billing will be analyzed by BPJS to evaluate whether the hospital care adequately addressed the need of patients without providing unnecessary care.

Many beneficiaries of ASKES have expressed concern that access to higher medical technologies, including medicine for cardiovascular diseases and cancers, will be limited due to the case-based reimbursement system fully implemented in 2014. ASKES has developed and continuously updates its drug lists containing generic and branded pharmaceuticals; some are quite expensive proprietary medicines. In the era of BPJS, the use of generic medicines will be predominant as a part of the cost-containment strategy.

A Chronic Disease Management Program, better known as PROLA-NIS, was started in 2010 by ASKES as a proactive approach in secondary and tertiary prevention of disabling chronic diseases. The program is designed to improve quality of life and empower beneficiaries to manage their own chronic health problems, especially those related to diabetes mellitus, high blood pressure, cardiovascular diseases, and chronic renal diseases. ASKES supports its participants with prescribed medicine for one month (including branded anti-hypertensive and insulin), laboratory tests, health education, and community self-help through associations or clubs. This program is spearheaded by primary care doctors or family physicians.

Although a chronic disease management program may not reduce health care expenditure (de Bruin et al. 2011, 119), members of PRO-LANIS admitted that the program could potentially improve their lifestyles and medication compliance, and many members of ASKES worried that the program will be terminated when BPJS is implemented in 2014. In fact, medication for patients in the PROLANIS program initially was prescribed only for one week; due to many complaints, it now is prescribed for one month, as was the case under ASKES. Beneficiaries of ASKES and JAMSOSTEK have now begun to think of buying coin-surance, as they worry that the benefits package will be downgraded as the social health insurance is implemented. There is pressure on the government to allow members of ASKES and JAMSOSTEK to retain the same benefits they are receiving now when the new BPJS is in place.

Payment to Health Care Providers

A capitation fee will be paid to primary care providers, comprising community health centers, private clinics, and practicing family doctors. The capitation fee is 8,000 rupiah (U.S. $0.70) per member per month. Primary care needs considerable investment, and may provide better value for money compared with its alternatives (WHO 2008, xvii). The capitation fee offered by BPJS is too small for private primary care providers, who may also dispense medicines, so they might possibly treat only emergency visits and more frequently admit patients to secondary care facilities to avoid financial loss. Public community health centers are supported by government budgets, so that promotive, preventive, and curative activities could be carried out in a larger number of patients, including those not yet covered by any health insurance plan.

Payment to outpatient and inpatient services in hospitals will be made based on a case-based reimbursement or case-mix system formerly known as INA-DRG. The system was implemented for JAMKES-MAS in 2006 using diagnosis grouping software purchased from 3M. Nearly 1,350 public and private hospitals offered outpatient and inpatient services paid under the case-mix system. In 2010, INA-DRG was replaced by INA-CBG, an open-source software developed by the United Nations University International Institute of Global Health and was used as the grouper for a modified case-mix system, taking into account subacute and chronic diseases, special drugs, special investigative procedures, prostheses, and ambulatory care packages. INA-CBG was designed to be more flexible and acceptable to health care providers.

There are 798 inpatient and 288 outpatient diagnosis groups directly associated with INA-CBG tariffs, adjusted for eleven hospital types and classes and four regions in Indonesia—(1) Sumatera, (2) Java and Bali, (3) Borneo-West Nusa Tenggara-Celebes, and (4) Molucca-Papua-East Nusa Tenggara. By design, fees for medical doctors have not been specified in the case-mix system, and it is left to the health care providers to decide the remuneration rate of the doctors, who are used to the fee-for-service system.

Payment to health care providers based on diagnosis-related group in low- and middle-income countries needs adjustment of the imported system to the local context (Mathauer and Withenbecher 2013, 7). BPJS should be prepared to handle unwanted incentives for increased hospital admission and readmission, up-coding of cases to gain higher remuneration, underprovision of necessary care, and rejection of more costly cases (Langenbrunner et al. 2009, 195–6).

THE HEALTH CARE QUALITY SYSTEM IN SOCIAL HEALTH INSURANCE

Evidence concerning the impact of health insurance on health care quality is limited (Spaan et al. 2012, 688). There are legal regulatory frameworks to endorse quality of health care. The Ministry of Health plays the dominant role for continuously improving the quality of health care through standard setting, continuous education, health technology assessment, infrastructure development, and monitoring/evaluation. Quality of care is "the degree to which health services for individuals and populations increase the likelihood of desired health outcomes and are consistent with current professional knowledge" (Institute of Medicine 1990, 21). There are two main components of quality of care: (1) the technical aspect (based on current medical knowledge) and (2) the interpersonal aspect as perceived by patients (Donabedian 1979, 277). The governance of quality of care includes setting standards for health care (such as adequacy of resources) and attributes of services as perceived by patients, such as responsiveness, courtesy, and capacity to fix health problems (Agency for Healthcare Research and Quality 2005, 1).

Regulations for Health Care Quality

Public health regulations have been considered an essential public health function, one of the knobs of the health system intended to improve performance (Roberts et al. 2004, 248) and strengthen health system capacity (Mills et al. 2006, 91). Law Number 44 of 2009, Article 36, indicates that good governance of hospital services should include transparency, accountability, independence, responsibility, equity, and appropriateness. The Ministry of Health Regulation Number 755 of 2011 mandates that every hospital establish a medical committee to assure quality of clinical care and patient safety. The promotion of patient safety in a hospital is regulated through Ministry of Health Regulation Number 1691 of 2011. A team that consists of hospital administrators, doctors, and nurses should be responsible for monitoring, evaluating, and improving patient safety initiatives in the hospital.

Ministry of Health Regulation Number 411 of 2010 indicates that clinical laboratories are obliged to carry out internal quality control and be accredited every five years by an accrediting committee in order to uphold safety and security in the workplace and to assure compliance with the requirements for personnel, facilities, and clinical procedures.

The supply and availability of drugs and vaccines are regulated through Ministry of Health Regulation Number 830 of 2009. Guidelines for selecting and prescribing the most appropriate antibiotics with strict indication, narrow spectrum, adequate dose, safety, and cost-effectiveness are provided through Ministry of Health Regulation Number 2406 of 2011. The diagnosis and treatment of malaria are endorsed in the Ministry of Health Regulation Number 05 of 2013. Detection and case management of MDR TB is suggested in Ministry of Health Regulation Number 13 of 2013.

Many other regulations are also meant to improve quality of care, such as hemodialysis in hospital (Ministry of Health Regulation Number 812 of 2010), anesthesiology and intensive care in hospital (Ministry of Health Regulation Number 519 of 2011), referral system for individual patient (Ministry of Health Regulation Number 01 of 2012), hospital-based health promotion (Ministry of Health Regulation Number 04 of 2012), and a hospital accreditation system (Ministry of Health Regulation Number 12 of 2012). Comprehensive guidelines on the prevention and control of cardiovascular diseases were issued as Ministry of Health Regulation Number 854 of 2009. Local health offices and health care organizations are mandated to enforce these regulations.

With the implementation of social health insurance under BPJS more regulations will be promulgated by the Minister of Health to enhance quality of care and patient safety. Compliance with these regulations will become the basis of contractual agreements between BPJS and health care providers (DJSN 2012, 95). A cautionary note addressed by Aspinall (2014, 1) suggests that "oligarchic power relations and the corruption they spawn still undermine health care quality, despite expansion of coverage."

Contributions of Professional Associations in Quality of Care Assurance

Professional associations (of doctors, nurses, pharmacists, and others) should play significant roles in education and human resource development, endorsement of best practices, and development of practice guidelines flexible enough to accommodate the socioeconomically and culturally diverse Indonesian population. Ministry of Health

Regulation Number 1438 of 2010 mandates that national clinical care guidelines should be developed by professional associations and signed by the health minister. Hospital administrators are responsible for developing standard operational procedures, including clinical pathways and clinical protocols or algorithms, which are coordinated by the medical committee and revised every two years. Clinical pathways, considered key elements in assuring quality of care through evidence-based practices, are potentially also a tool for cost containment through prevention of unnecessary care. Standardized clinical pathways should become the consensus among doctors and nurses, at least for those working in the same hospital or locality.

Health care professionals have participated individually and in committees contributing to regulatory frameworks to promote quality of care. The role of professional associations is mainly to protect the interests of the members and to sponsor accredited continuing education symposia, seminars, and online education programs. The Indonesian Medical Association discussed with the parliament specifically how health workers should be compensated for their services under the BPJS plan (Aritonang 2012).

Professional associations, especially the Indonesian Medical Association, are often criticized for not doing enough to protect the public from medical malpractice and negligence, which could be the consequences of the worst quality problems. Medical malpractice is often considered a criminal matter rather than a civil matter, as the Indonesian Penal Code (article 359) may classify medical negligence causing bodily injuries as an offense. The help of the Indonesian Medical Association has often been called for when a member is subject to a lawsuit. A separate Indonesian Medical Disciplinary Council was formed to uphold the standards of medical practice and levy disciplinary sanctions on doctors proven to be guilty of malpractice. The Indonesian Medical Association and the Indonesian Medical Disciplinary Council did very little to prevent malpractice (Faizal 2011). The health care professional associations could be more proactive, for example, in developing quality-of-care assessment tools and health care quality improvement strategies, and in providing opportunities for continuous learning by all health care personnel.

Quality of Care Perspectives Among Beneficiaries

Quality of care is also measured as satisfaction of beneficiaries. The quality of medical care defined by Steffen is the "capacity of elements of that care to achieve legitimate medical and nonmedical goals, set by the patients in consultation with the physician" (1988, 56). The BPJS Law set a target of 85 percent of beneficiaries reporting satisfaction with health services by 2019. Repeated surveys of the satisfaction of beneficiaries will be conducted by BPJS every six months. Benefits and services to beneficiaries will be evaluated annually.

According to Presidential Act Number 12 of 2013, Article 45, beneficiaries of social health insurance who are not satisfied with benefits or services may file a complaint with the respective health facility or with BPJS Health. If the response to the complaint is still unsatisfactory, the beneficiaries of BPJS may submit the complaint to the Minister of Health.

DISCUSSION

A social health insurance system is not entirely new in Indonesia. However, universal coverage is a challenging goal that is being pursued by the government of Indonesia in a short period of time (only five years, from 2014 to 2019). Countries like Austria, Germany, Costa Rica, Israel, Japan, and the Republic of Korea needed many decades to accomplish the transition from partial to universal health coverage (Carrin and James 2005, 47).

Universal health coverage movements in Indonesia have been fueled by political interests at the central and local (provincial and district) government levels, and are associated with the increasing demand for social welfare in general as stipulated by the Constitution and SJSN Law. Economic resources, existing institutions, and societal division (including geographic distribution of resources) play significant roles (McKee et al. 2013, S41) in achieving universal health coverage. The social insurance administrator and health professional associations demanded that the Indonesian government should spend at least 50 percent more than currently agreed by the Ministry of Finance to cover premium fees for the poor and indigent. Eventually, U.S. $1.67 was the agreed amount, which still fell short of what was demanded. Total health expenditure in Indonesia was 2.6 percent of its GDP in 2010, the third smallest in Asia after Myanmar and Pakistan (OECD/WHO 2012, 71). Unequal distribution of resources across areas in Indonesia, which encompasses more than 17,000 islands, such as misdistribution of specialists, who favor big cities in Java and Bali (Meliala et al. 2013, 32), necessitates specific policies to address better resource allocation to remote areas, including efforts to encourage the private sector to develop more health care facilities in these areas.

ASKES, a major state-owned social health insurance company, is being transformed to a single payer trust fund known as BPJS Health, beginning in 2014. The social health insurance will expand its membership from 17 million members to more than 124 million members in 2014. With an extensive network of branch offices in all districts, used to serve public employees and military/police personnel, BPJS Health will be capable of managing the single-payer system, as long as it is equipped with the resources needed to serve a more than sevenfold increase in its membership. Advantages of a single-payer system include possible financing of promotive and preventive services with benefits (such as lower morbidity) in the long run, development of a unified computerized database, assessment of quality of care through medical record analyses without breaching the privacy of doctor-patient relationships, cost saving, and better resource allocation to improve public health (Schiff et al. 1994, 5–7; Hsiao 2011, 1188).

Under the SJSN Law, DJSN is mandated to help the president ensure that health care provision will be more cost effective and accessible without sacrificing the quality of care. The BPJS Law underscores the role of DJSN as a monitoring and research agency with no decision-making authority regarding important policy issues on social health insurance and universal coverage. DJSN is also mandated to become an external supervisor of BPJS, together with the State Financial Audit Board and Financial Services Authority, without functions clearly specified for each of the three organizations. Internal supervisors of BPJS will consist of a board of commissioners (comprising government representatives, employees' representatives, employers' representatives, and public figures) and an internal audit department. The board of directors, consisting of five qualified professionals, will manage BPJS Health.

Health professional associations mainly see their role as protecting the interests of their members. They should be involved in the assessment of technical efficacy and the quality of health care provision, based on summaries of health care outcomes recorded in the databases maintained by BPJS Health. Currently, health professional associations are participating in the development of the national clinical guidelines stipulated by Ministry of Health Regulation Number 1438 of 2010.

Beneficiaries of ASKES and JAMSOSTEK who are satisfied with their current benefits package demand that BPJS will provide at least the same benefits that they have received so far, since they pay a higher premium rate (2 percent of their salaries or wages) compared with the premium contribution paid by the government for poor households. The beneficiaries of ASKES and JAMSOSTEK may be entitled to better amenities according to their premium level, but are entitled to the same basic medical care provided equally to all members of BPJS. Presidential Regulation Number 12 of 2013 allows coinsurance and co-payment for benefits uncovered by BPJS Health, such as orthodontics treatment, complementary and experimental medicine, and treatment for infertility. The two-tier system under BPJS Health as a single payer may incur additional burdens of administrative costs for the coordination with private health insurance and co-payment for services not covered by the BPJS plan.

The social health insurance plan mandated by SJSN Law and BPJS Law may not successfully lead to universal coverage in five years' time. The provision of universal coverage emerges from negotiation rather than design, and always takes time (Savedoff et al. 2012, 926). At its best, the insurance plan will significantly expand social protection to the poor and indigent. Important governance issues include the prevention of leakage to the nonpoor and adverse selection of those not eligible for a subsidized premium but in need of costly treatment and health care procedures. Increased government spending to boost the total amount of pooled resources for health care would not improve population health, if the targeting of funds is not in accordance with the needs of the population (Moreno-Serro and Smith 2012, 918). A robust information system for insurance membership and health care utilization needs to be implemented at the earliest point possible, before BPJS Health starts.

According to Presidential Regulation Number 12 of 2013, the central, provincial, and district governments are responsible for providing adequate health care facilities through public resources or in collaboration with private health care centers and hospitals. Primary care facilities need strengthening, for example, through the improvement of laboratory services as mandated by Ministry of Health Regulation Number 37 of 2012. Improved quality of care will lead people to trust primary care services as functional and effective health-service providers, and to not see them only as gatekeepers for referral to secondary health care. As shown by the example of Thailand, universal health coverage can be achieved through a pro-poor subsidy and strengthening the primary health care network at the district level so that it effectively serves the rural poor (Limwattananon et al. 2012, 10). Public health activities, such as school health promotion, sanitation and environmental health inspection, and outbreak investigation, could be integrated with the primary care services. In conclusion, Indonesia needs to learn from the experiences of other countries to strengthen the capacity of its primary care facilities so that they can effectively deliver good-quality services to people who live on the periphery, thereby moving the nation toward universal health coverage.

REFERENCES

Agency for Healthcare Research and Quality. 2005. *Guide to Health Care Quality: How to Know It When You See It.* Washington, D.C.: U.S. Department of Health and Human Services.

Ananta, A. 2012. "Sustainable and Just Social Protection in Southeast Asia." *ASEAN Economic Bulletin* 29 (3): 171–83.

Arifianto, A. 2006. "The New Indonesian Social Security Law: A Blessing or Curse for Indonesia?" *ASEAN Economic Bulletin* 23 (1): 57–74.

Aritonang, M. S. 2012. "Doctors Want Higher Pay Under Social Security Providers (BPJS) Scheme." *Jakarta Post,* June 20.

Aspinall, E. 2014. "Health Care and Democratization in Indonesia." *Democratization* dx.doi.org/10.1080/13510347.2013.87379.

Borgonovi, E., and A. Compagni. 2013. "Sustaining Universal Coverage: The Interaction of Social, Political, and Economic Sustainability." *Value in Health* 16: S34–S38.

Carrin, G., and C. James. 2005. "Social Health Insurance: Key Factors Affecting the Transition Towards Universal Coverage." *International Social Security Review* 58 (1): 45–64.

de Bruin, S. R., R. Heijnk, L. C. Lemmens, J. N. Struijs, and C. A. Baan. 2011. "Impact of Disease Management Programs on Health Care Expenditures for Patients with Diabetes, Depression, Heart Failure or Chronic Obstructive Pulmonary Disease: A Systematic Review of the Literature." *Health Policy* 101 (2): 105–21.

Dewi, S. W. 2013. "Jakarta Mulls Topping up Health Care Premium." *Jakarta Post,* May 22.

DJSN. 2012. *Peta Jalan Menuju Jaminan Kesehatan Nasional 2012 – 2019.* Jakarta: DJSN.

Donabedian, A. 1979. "The Quality of Medical Care: A Concept in Search of a Definition." *Journal of Family Practice* 9 (2): 277–84.

Fauzi, E. B. 2011. " 'Conspiracy of Silence' in Malpractice Cases." *Jakarta Post,* April 28.

Harimurti, P., E. Pambudi, A. Pigazzini, A. Tandon. 2013. *The Nuts and Bolts of Jamkesmas: Indonesia's Government-Financed Health Coverage Program,* UNICO Studies Series 8. Washington D.C.: World Bank.

Hsiao, W. C. 2011. "State-Based Single-Payer Health Care—A Solution for the United States?" *New England Journal of Medicine* 364: 1188–90.

Institute of Medicine. 1990. *Medicare: A Strategy for Quality Assurance, Vol. 1.* Washington D.C.: National Academy Press.

Kondo, A., and H. Shegeoka. 2013. "Effects of Universal Health Insurance on Health Care Utilization, and Supply-Side Responses: Evidence from Japan." *Journal of Public Economics* 99 (1): 1–23.

Lagomarsino, G., A. Garabrant, A. Adyas, R. Muga, and N. Otoo. 2012. "Moving Towards Universal Health Coverage: Health Insurance Reforms in Nine Developing Countries in Africa and Asia. *Lancet 380* (September 8): 933–43.

Langenbrunner, J. C., C. Cashin, and S. O'Dougherty. 2009. *Designing and Implementing Health Care Provider Payment Systems, How-To Manuals.* Washington D.C.: The World Bank.

Limwattananon, S., V. Tangcharoensathien, K. Tisayaticom, T. Boonyapaisarncharoen, and P. Prakongsai. 2012. "Why Has the Universal Coverage Scheme in Thailand Achieved a Pro-Poor Public Subsidy for Health Care?" *BMC Public Health* 12 (suppl): 56.

Mathauer, I., and F. Wittenbecher. 2013. "Hospital Payment Systems Based on Diagnosis-Related Groups: Experiences in Low- and Middle-Income Countries." *Bulletin of the World Health Organization*, article ID: 91:746–56.

McKee, M., D. Balabanova, S. Basu, W. Ricciardi, and D. Stuckler. 2013. "Universal Health Coverage: A Quest for All Countries but Under Threat in Some." *Value in Health* 16: S39–S45.

Meliala, A., K. Hort, L. Trisnantoro. 2013. Addressing the Unequal Geographic Distribution of Specialist Doctors in Indonesia: The Role of the Private Sector and Effectiveness of Current Regulations." *Social Science & Medicine* 82: 30–34.

Mills, A., F. Rasheed, and S. Tollman. *2006. Strengthening Health System, in Disease Control Priorities in Developing Countries, 2nd edition,* edited by D. T. Jamison, J. G. Breman, A. R. Measham, G. Alleyne, M. Claeson, and D. B. Evans. New York: Oxford University Press.

Moreno-Serro, R., and P. C. Smith. 2012. "Does Progress Towards Universal Health Coverage Improve Population Health?" *Lancet* 380: 917–23.

OECD/WHO. 2012. *Health Expenditure in Relation to GDP in Health at a Glance: Asia/Pacific 2012*. Paris: OECD.

Roberts, M. J., W. C. Hsiao, P. Berman, and M. R. Reich. 2004. *Getting Health Reform Right. A Guide to Improving Performance and Equity*. New York: Oxford University Press.

Savedoff, W. D., D. de Ferranti, A. I. Smith, V. Fan. 2012. "Political and Economic Aspects of the Transition to Universal Health Coverage." *Lancet* 380: 924–32.

Schiff, G. D., A. B. Bindman, T. A. Brennan. 1994. "A Better Quality Alternative: Single-Payer Health System Reform." *Journal of the American Medical Association* 272: 803–08.

Spaan, E., J. Mathijssen, N. Tromp, F. McBain, A. ten Have, and R. Baltussen. 2012. "The Impact of Health Insurance in Africa and Asia: A Systematic Review." *Bulletin of World Health Organization* 90 (9): 685–92.

Sparrow, R., A. Suryahadi, and W. Widyanti. 2013. "Social Health Insurance for the Poor: Targeting and Impact of Indonesia's ASK-ESKIN Program." *Social Science & Medicine* 96: 264–71.

Widjaja, M. 2012. "Indonesia: In Search of a Placement-Support Social Protection." *ASEAN Economic Bulletin* 29 (3): 184–96.

World Health Organization. 2008. *Primary Health Care (Now More Than Ever)*. Geneva: WHO.

CHAPTER 8

Governance and Health System Performance: National and Municipal Challenges to the Brazilian Family Health Strategy

Luiz A. Facchini, Elaine Thumé, Bruno P. Nunes, Suele M. Silva, Anaclaudia G. Fassa, Leila P. Garcia, and Elaine Tomasi

INTRODUCTION

The Brazilian Unified Health System, or SUS, was created in 1988, following the enactment of a new Constitution, which was approved as a framework for the democratic regime in Brazil after twenty-one years of military dictatorship. The Brazilian 1988 Constitution recognizes health as a civil right and a state duty (Elias and Cohn 2003; Brazil 2010). SUS was implemented to guarantee the constitutional mandate of a public health care system, aimed at achieving universal coverage, equity, uniformity, and equivalency of benefits to both urban and rural populations (Giovanella et al. 2008; Fleury et al. 2010; Noronha et al. 2010; Thumé et al. 2010; Paim et al. 2011). Dating back to 1975, SUS inception and design has its roots in the Brazilian health reform and the political movement for democracy involving stakeholders ranging from intellectuals and health services researchers to workers' organizations and political parties (Elias and Cohn 2003).

Since 1988, laws, ordinances, agreements, and pacts have been strengthening SUS organization based on equality in the division of expenditures; diversification in revenue sources to finance health services; and democracy and participatory health system governance with the inclusion of workers, employers, retirees, and government agencies. The rules of SUS governance and institutional development emphasize a strategic vision in policy planning and assessment, highlighting the usefulness of epidemiology to determine priorities, resource allocation, and programmatic guidance (Brazil 2010; Noronha et al. 2010; Brazil 2011; Brazil 2012).

SUS is a decentralized public health system, coordinated by the federal government but managed at three levels through a continuous interaction of municipal, state, and federal authorities as well as stakeholders participating in commissions and councils where decisions are made by consensus (not by vote). Triple governance is a constitutional rule and is implemented through intergovernmental negotiation for the development of public health policies, resource allocation, and priority setting oriented by consensus and accountability. The national goal is to invest in a strong primary health care system with organized access to its secondary and tertiary levels (Brazil 2010; Brazil 2012). Decentralization has made the municipalities responsible for developing governance capacity to competently organize, direct, and deliver health system resources, assess performance, and promote stakeholder participation at the local level. Municipal government also organizes health service physical structure, equipment, and professional teams. State and federal governments must provide financial and technical support to the municipalities, particularly smaller and poorer ones.

In 1994, the Ministry of Health launched the Family Health Program (now called Family Health Strategy, or FHS) as the federal strategy to improve primary health care (PHC) delivery and SUS performance regarding universal and comprehensive care. FHS was inspired by the Community Health Workers Program and the Family Doctors Program, started in Brazil in the beginning of the 1990s as a local initiative, mainly in small towns in the country's inner Northeast region. Since then, Family Health has become the priority strategy to scale up PHC, delivering health actions addressing health promotion, preventive exams, and health care to poorer and vulnerable population groups. Currently, FHS has 33,998 family health care teams assigned to specific geographic areas and defined populations as the first point of contact for health issues (1,000 families or 4,500 persons per team). From the smaller to the bigger cities throughout the country, the teams provide integrated care and outreach into patients' homes and the community. FHS has become the structural basis for a decentralized approach to municipal SUS management, reaching 5,298 (95 percent) municipalities and 107,517,065 people (56 percent of the Brazilian population).

Like all SUS initiatives, FHS is triple governed. At the federal level, the Ministry of Health, the Council of State Health Secretaries, and the Council of Municipal Health Secretaries are the leading authorities, alongside the National Health Council. A similar arrangement is found at state and municipal levels of governance (Facchini et al. 2006; Giovanella et al. 2008; Paim et al. 2011; Brazil 2012).

Health status and health services indicators have improved in the last twenty years in Brazil, as have the SUS health care network and FHS coverage. The infant mortality rate fell by 75 percent between 1990 and 2012—the 2012 rate reached 12.9 per 1,000 live births. In the same period, the under-five mortality rate declined from 62 to 14 per 1,000, corresponding to a 77 percent reduction (UNICEF 2013). In the last five years alone, hospital admissions due to diabetes or stroke have decreased by 25 percent, the proportion of children under 5 years old who are underweight has fallen by 67 percent, over 95 percent of women receive prenatal care, and diphtheria, tetanus, and pertussis (DTP) vaccine coverage in children less than one year old is greater than 95 percent in most municipalities (Facchini et al. 2008; Harris and Haines 2010; Paim et al. 2011). Evidence shows a consistent association between FHS coverage growth and decrease in child mortality and hospitalization for PHC sensitive conditions, especially in relation to the most vulnerable groups (Macinko et al. 2007; Nedel et al. 2008; Aquino et al. 2009; Guanais and Macinko 2009; Mendonça 2009). Furthermore, FHS has also been developed to increase SUS performance, and there are analyses that it promotes better PHC delivery, facilitating the access of most vulnerable people to better quality health care (Facchini et al. 2006; Facchini et al. 2008).

Public health care is provided through SUS either by public or outsourced private services. Complementary to the SUS, there is the private sector, dominated largely by private insurance companies. They mainly provide specialized care, reaching 47,900,000 people, corresponding to coverage of approximately 25 percent (ANS 2013), ranging from around 40 percent in the bigger and richer cities of the Southeast region to less than 20 percent in smaller and inner cities in the North and Northeast regions (Giovanella et al. 2008; Brazil 2010; Paim et al. 2011). The public and private components of the system are distinct but interconnected, and people can use services delivered by different providers, depending on their access or paying capability (Paim et al. 2011). It is important to note that the private sector is supported by the public sector in various ways. One is through duplicate coverage, in which individuals contributing to private insurance plans use public services, mainly for higher complexity and more expensive procedures, as well as for PHC activities such as immunization and health surveillance. Another way is through tax remission for service providers considered to be "philanthropic services" as well as for individuals paying for private services and contributing to private insurance plans.

However, in Brazil, as in most countries, a context of financing constraints and demands for accountability from citizens and social organizations is increasing interest in understanding governance contributions to health system performance (Mikkelsen-Lopez et al. 2011). These financing constraints are aggravated by public resources being assigned to private health services and insurance companies. There are several governance initiatives and efforts at the federal and municipal levels of SUS, but they are relatively new and scarcely assessed.

As a contribution, this chapter examines FHS governance at national and municipal levels and its relationship with SUS performance in different municipal contexts. A theoretical framework was designed to search for patterns and trends in health system performance related to different levels of FHS coverage, selected as a proxy of governance dimensions. The chapter also discusses governance challenges to be addressed at federal and municipal levels in order to improve SUS performance.

Health System Governance

The World Health Organization (WHO) has broadly defined health systems as including "all organizations, institutions and resources that are devoted to producing health actions" (WHO 2000, xi). In a step to increase analytical clarity, WHO has further advanced the notion that health systems can be disaggregated into six major subsystems or building blocks: (1) governance, (2) financing, (3) human resources, (4) information, (5) medicines and technologies, and (6) service delivery (WHO 2007). These categories, while helpful in identifying and tracing key functions that any health system should be able to perform, nevertheless do not represent mutually exclusive boundaries. Furthermore, it is not clear how the different building blocks relate to one another and what actions should be taken with them to improve performance. It is not clear what kind of health system could be built with the building blocks, nor is the hierarchy regarding them apparent.

Governance has been defined as the initiatives and means adopted by a society to promote collective action and deliver collective solutions to reach common goals (Dodgson et al. 2002). Governance is also recognized as the exercise of political, economic, and administrative authority in the management of a country's affairs at all levels (UNDP 1997). This broad concept encompasses the many ways in which individuals and groups organize themselves to achieve approved goals. It comprises complex mechanisms, processes, and institutions through which citizens and groups articulate their interests, mediate their differences, and exercise their legal rights and obligations. Such organization requires agreement on a range of matters including membership within the cooperative relationships, obligations and responsibilities of members, the making of decisions, means of communication, resource mobilization and distribution, dispute settlement, and formal or informal rules and procedures concerning all of these (UNDP 1997; Dodgson et al. 2002).

Health governance is identified as a function of the health system, encompassing principles regarding strategic vision, policy formulation and planning, social participation and consensus orientation, rule of law, transparency, responsiveness, equity and inclusiveness, effectiveness and efficiency, accountability, regulation, information, assessment capacity, and intelligence as well as ethics (Islam 2007; Roberts et al. 2004; Mikkelsen-Lopez et al. 2011).

In a context of resource constraints in many countries, attention has been focused on the leading role of governance in health system performance and health care delivery (Roberts et al. 2004; Baez-Camargo and

Jacobs 2011; Mikkelsen-Lopez et al. 2011). A major concern relates to the relevance of contextual characteristics determining the differences in governance issues, as well as in health system performance, between and within countries, regions, and municipalities (Murray and Frenk 2000; Roberts et al. 2004; Mikkelsen-Lopez et al. 2011).

In the last decade there has been relevant improvement in the theoretical and methodological means to evaluate governance shortcomings and support adequate interventions. Successful health care delivery requires effective institutions, and management has led government officials, academic and funding actors to emphasize governance as a key element for strengthening health system performance (Dodgson et al. 2002; Siddiqi et al. 2006; Baez-Camargo and Jacobs 2011; Mikkelsen-Lopez et al. 2011).

Theoretical Framework

Health-sector frameworks proposed to assess governance are increasingly available. All of them offer insights into the way governance may affect health outcomes and suggest which elements associated with governance are important to be considered (Brinkerhoff 2008; Roberts et al. 2004; Lewis and Pettersson 2009; Siddiqi et al. 2009; Vian et al. 2010; Baez-Camargo and Jacobs 2011; Mikkelsen-Lopez et al. 2011).

The frameworks are useful for addressing governance, despite the differences in their dimensions and indicators (Mikkelsen-Lopez et al. 2011). Nevertheless, there is a consensus that governance is about the rules that distribute the roles and responsibilities among social actors, shaping the interactions among them (Brinkerhoff 2008). As applied to health systems, the rules are formal and informal means and initiatives that provide incentives and constraints for certain types of behavior for relevant actors and stakeholders regarding health system goals. From this point of view, governance refers to the institutions that define and regulate the processes through which health systems manage human resources, acquire and distribute medicines and technologies, generate and disseminate information, and provide means to finance the provision of health services to the population (Baez-Camargo and Jacobs 2011).

Our framework (Figure 8.1) analyzes FHS governance as a particular issue of the health system (Baez-Camargo and Jacobs 2011). FHS is examined as a governance initiative and population coverage is a proxy for governance accountability/ethical commitment/social responsibility, strategic vision, consensus orientation, and policy design (WHO 2007; Mikkelsen-Lopez et al. 2011) to deliver primary health care in municipalities with different population sizes, this being a contextual synthesis of wealth and infrastructure (Brazil 2012).

Financing, health workforce, information, medicines, and technology to deliver PHC to the population are health system inputs or essential means to determine SUS performance at the municipal level (Viana et al. 2006; WHO 2007; Mikkelsen-Lopez et al. 2011). Health system inputs are determined by governance options and decision making,

FIGURE 8.1 Framework to Approach FHS Governance and Health System Performance

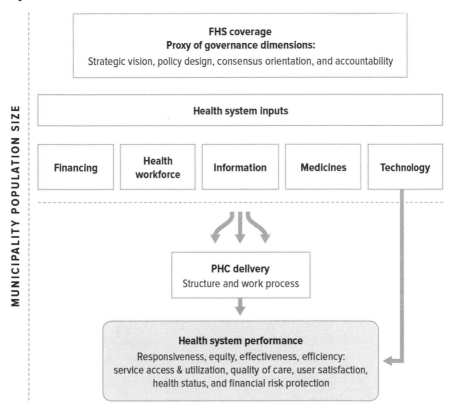

shaping the structure and the work process at PHC centers (Donabedian 1988), as well as connecting governance initiatives to daily care. The framework acknowledges the interconnectedness of actors and functions in health systems across different levels of analysis. No one dimension, category, indicator, or issue is absolutely independent and autonomous. The framework assesses governance at the municipal and the national policy levels. Health system performance is assessed through service access and utilization, quality of care, user satisfaction, health status, and financial risk protection (Donabedian 1988; Roberts et al. 2004). It expresses governance outcomes, such as responsiveness, equity, effectiveness, and efficiency (Siddiqi et al. 2009; Mikkelsen-Lopez et al. 2011).

The model addresses formal governance while recognizing the relevance of informal institutions and stakeholder networks as significant phenomena affecting public governance processes (Viana et al. 2006; WHO 2007; Mikkelsen-Lopez et al. 2011). However, it is useful to explore governance initiatives and means and their connections with PHC delivery and health system performance in Brazil. The framework maps the relevant categories and indicators on health system inputs, PHC delivery, and health system performance, allowing the examination of patterns and trends according to FHS coverage, this being a proxy of governance.

METHODOLOGY

This chapter examines whether governance decision making at federal and municipal levels to scale up FHS coverage as a priority is improving PHC delivery and health system performance in different contexts. Better SUS performance could be a form of feedback on governance decision making at the national and municipal levels regarding FHS financing and resource allocation. Data from several sources were used to show a complex panel of patterns and trends related to the categories and indicators proposed in the theoretical framework (Table 8.1).

In order to analyze trends in FHS indicators, coverage was classified as low (less than 30 percent), intermediate (30 percent to 64.9 percent), and high (65 percent and over). Only 11 percent of municipalities presented low population coverage, 17 percent had intermediate coverage, and 73 percent had high coverage. FHS covered 100 percent of the population in 2,455 municipalities (44 percent of the total) (Brazil 2012a).

Municipality population size was characterized in terms of four groups: up to 30,000 inhabitants; 30,001 to 100,000; 100,001 to 500,000; and more than 500,000 (Table 8.1). Brazil comprises 5,565 municipalities, one federal district and twenty-six states divided into five regions: North (8 percent of the total population), Northeast (28 percent), South (15 percent), Southeast (42 percent), and Central-Western (7 percent). According to the 2010 Census, the Brazilian population amounts to 190,732,694 persons (IBGE 2013). Of the total number of municipalities, 23 percent had up to 5,000 inhabitants (n=1,298) and the vast majority of municipalities had up to 30,000 inhabitants (81 percent). Only thirty-eight municipalities had more than 500,000 inhabitants.

FHS coverage stratified by municipality population size was used as a proxy for governance. Context was approached through three indicators regarding the socioeconomic characteristics of the municipalities. Furthermore, we have selected forty-eight indicators to approach the different categories presented in the theoretical framework. The health system inputs were assessed through four financing indicators, three health workforce indicators, three information indicators, two medicines indicators, and four technology indicators. To assess PHC delivery we selected five structure indicators and seven work process indicators, with emphasis both on general issues relating to the services and also their adequacy regarding health care. Finally, health system performance was examined through twenty indicators, including nine health service access and utilization indicators, six health care quality indicators, one patient satisfaction indicator, one financial risk protection indicator, and two health-status indicators (Table 8.1).

Total prevalence of the selected indicators was used to highlight the level of implementation of priority health actions, classified as universal and fully implemented (over 75 percent), highlighted in medium gray; partly implemented (50 percent to 75 percent), highlighted in light gray and scarcely implemented (up to 50 percent), highlighted in dark gray. The analytical approach looks for trends and patterns in the indicators regarding FHS coverage and municipality size.

To analyze the difference among all the indicators of health system inputs, PHC delivery and health system performance regarding FHS coverage and municipality size, we looked for the linear trend in indicator prevalence using the chi-square test. Trends shown in medium gray had a significantly positive trend; those shown in light gray had no significant trend; those with dark gray had a significantly negative trend. Tables 8.2 and 8.3 summarize the patterns and trends regarding increasing FHS coverage according to each municipal population size.

Data were obtained from several sources. Data from the Brazilian Institute of Geography and Statistics (IBGE 2010) were used to stratify the municipalities by population size (IBGE 2013).

The United Nations Development Program (UNDP) Human Development Index (HDI) was used to describe the country's socioeconomic characteristics. HDI is composed of data on life expectancy at birth, education, and gross domestic product per capita. The index ranges from 0 (no human development) to 1 (total human development). Low municipal HDI is between 0 and 0.499, middle HDI is between 0.500 and 0.799, and high HDI between 0.800 and 1 (UNDP 2010).

The project entitled Health Service Access and Quality (AQUARES) (Siqueira et al. 2011; Piccini et al. 2012) was used to determine part of the socioeconomic context by classifying the population according to years of schooling and economic class. The economic classification identifies people as belonging to classes A (richest) to E (poorest), taking into account the ownership of goods and the level of education of the head of household (www.abep.org).

In order to explore some characteristics of the financing, health workforce, information, technology, medicines, structure, and work process of PHC services and health service performance, data were used from the Program for Improving Primary Care Access and Quality (PMAQ), launched in 2011 by the Brazilian Ministry of Health (Brazil 2011a). The program aims to induce the establishment of processes to enhance the capacity of federal, state, and local administrations as well as that of the primary health care teams to deliver services ensuring greater access and quality, according to the population's needs. It has been organized into four phases that complement and form a continuous cycle of improving access and quality (Adherence and Contract, Development, External

TABLE 8.1 Categories, Indicators, and Sources of Information to Examine Family Health Strategy Governance in the Brazilian Unified Health System

CATEGORY	INDICATORS	SOURCES/YEAR/TYPE/SAMPLE
Governance	FHS coverage	Primary Health Care Department—Ministry of Health (2012)
Municipality Population Size	Municipality population size	IBGE (2010)
Socioeconomic Context	HDI	UNDP (2010)
	Economic class	AQUARES (2009)
	Years of schooling	AQUARES (2009)
Financing	Ministry of Health financial resources allocated to PHC (%)	Primary Health Care Department - Ministry of Health (2012)
	Ministry of Health financial resources allocated to PMAQ (US$ dollars)	Secondary 5,565 municipalities
	Municipal budget spending on health (%)	Public Health Budgets Information System—SIOPS (2012)
	Municipal adherence to round one and two of PMAQ	Primary Health Care Department - Ministry of Health (2012) Secondary 5,565 municipalities
Health Workforce	Teams with physician, nurse, nursing technician or auxiliary and community health agent (%)	Program for Improving Primary Care Access and Quality—PMAQ-AB (2012) Primary
	Full team with university education (physician, nurse, dentist) (%)	33,149 Primary Health Care Services
	Teams with physician and nurse (%)	
Information	Existence of ombudsman (%)	Program for Improving Primary Care Access and Quality—PMAQ-AB (2012)
	Professionals' working hours (%)	
	Information about services publicized to patients (%)	Primary 33,149 Primary Health Care Services
Medicines	Medicines to treat hypertension (%)	Program for Improving Primary Care Access and Quality—PMAQ-AB (2012)
	Medicines to treat diabetes (%)	Primary 33,149 Primary Health Care Services

CATEGORY	INDICATORS	SOURCES/YEAR/TYPE/SAMPLE
Technology	Computer availability (%)	Program for Improving Primary Care Access and Quality—PMAQ-AB (2012)
	Internet access (%)	
	Access to telehealth (%)	Primary
	Electronic medical records (%)	33,149 Primary Health Care Services
Structure of PHC Services	Exclusive bathroom for employees (%)	Program for Improving Primary Care Access and Quality—PMAQ-AB (2012)
	Bathroom adapted for disabled persons (%)	Primary
	Appropriate structure for conducting Pap test[1] (%)	33,149 Primary Health Care Services
	Appropriate care structure for people with hypertension[2] (%)	
	PHC center structure being improved—building works (%)	
Work Process of PHC Services	Appropriate work process for performing Pap test [3] (%)	Program for Improving Primary Care Access and Quality—PMAQ-AB (2012)
	Appropriate work process for caring for people with hypertension (%)	Primary
	Municipal management support to FHS teams[4] (%)	16,820 health teams
	Local management of FHS[5] (%)	
	Health center opening hours meet patients' needs (%)	
	Patients report the physician's presence at the health center or in neighborhood activities during all hours of operation (%)	
	Patients know the physician's name (%)	

CATEGORY	INDICATORS	SOURCES/YEAR/TYPE/SAMPLE
Health System Performance	Women with postpartum care (%)	SUS Development Index – IDSUS (2011)
		Secondary
	Patients having medical consultation for hypertension at the health center (%)	5,565 Municipalities
	Hypertensive patients having electrocardiograms (%)	
	Patients having medical consultation for diabetes at the health center (%)	
	Diabetic patients having foot examination (%)	
	Women with 7 or more prenatal appointments kept (%)	
	Pap test ratio for every 100 women aged between 25 to 59	SUS Development Index—IDSUS3 (2011)
	Hospitalization for ambulatory care-sensitive conditions (%)	Secondary
		5,565 municipalities
	Proportion of cure of pulmonary tuberculosis > 85%	
	Coverage of anti-polio vaccination	
	Infant mortality rate	
	Use of medical consultation in the last 3 months (%)	Public Health Action Organizational Contract—COAP (2012)
	Use of hospitalization in the last year (%)	Health Service System Access and Quality Project—AQUARES (2009)
	Use of emergency room in the last year (%)	Primary
		12,402 adults
	Use of home health care in the last 3 months (%)	
	Advice on health promotion	
	Patient satisfaction (%)	
	Advice on the use of condoms in all sexual relations	
	Advice to quit smoking	
	Counseling on physical activity	

Note:
[1] Availability in PHC of at least six of the following items: spotlight, gynecological table, disposable speculum, endocervical brush, Ayre's spatula, slide fastener, glass slide, and specific form to request exam.
[2] Availability of at least eight of the following items: tape measure, specific register form, adult weighing scales, adult sphygmomanometer and stethoscope, atenolol, captopril, losartan, calcium channel blocker, and diuretics.
[3] Presence of all the following items: Pap Test performance, the existence of smear collection records, exam result, and follow-up with women after treatment.
[4] Investigated through the following questions: "Is there a continuous education program involving FHS teams in the municipality?"; "Does the team receive support for work process planning and organization?"; "Does management staff provide basic health care information to assist in analyzing the health situation?"; "Does the team receive support from municipal governance to discuss the FHS information monitoring system?"; "Does municipal governance support the FHS team self-assessment process?"; "Does management support/has it supported the organization of the work process to implement or qualify standards of health care access and quality?"; "Does your FHS team receive permanent institutional support from staff or from an individual?"; "Does the primary care team receive support from other professionals to aid or assist in the resolution of clinical cases considered complex?"; and "Did the municipal governance consider risk and vulnerability criteria when defining the number of people under the responsibility of the FHS team?"
[5] Investigated through the following items: health action planning, problem identification, priority casting, implementation activities, results and targets monitoring and analysis, map of the area/territory, reducing access barriers, multiprofessional shared agenda, schedule for priority groups, and recording of referrals.

Evaluation, and New Agreement). This chapter has used the Ministry of Health database and the External Evaluation carried out from June to August 2012, when 33,149 PHC services were visited and 61,233 patients were interviewed. (Brazil 2012b) (Table 8.1).

Data from the Public Health Budgets Information System (SIOPS) were used to estimate municipal spending on health in 2012. This system was institutionalized in 2000 by the Ministry of Health and contains financial information generated and maintained by states and municipalities regarding revenues and expenditures (Brazil 2011).

The SUS Performance Index (IDSUS) was used to analyze the performance of the Unified Health System with regard to the effectiveness of primary health care services, including prenatal care, Pap test, hospitalization for ambulatory care-sensitive conditions, and anti-polio vaccination, as well as the proportion of cure of pulmonary tuberculosis (Brazil 2011b).

The Health Service Access and Quality project (AQUARES) (Siqueira et al. 2011; Piccini et al. 2012) was also used to evaluate health care service utilization, performance, and quality. The project used a cross-sectional design and was carried out in 2008–2009, including a sample of children aged under five years, adults aged twenty to fifty-nine, and elderly citizens aged sixty and older in one hundred municipalities from all five of the country's regions.

The Public Health Action Organizational Contract (COAP) is a cooperative agreement signed between federal, state, and municipal governments aimed at the organization and integration of activities and services within health regions in order to ensure universal and comprehensive care. It has been used to assess the infant mortality rate (Brazil 2011c).

RESULTS

Country Context

The average Human Development Index (HDI) was 0.70 in Brazil in 2010, increasing linearly with municipality population size. In municipalities with fewer than 30,000 inhabitants, average HDI was 0.69, increasing to 0.71 in municipalities with 30,001 to 100,000 inhabitants and 0.78 in cities with between 100,001 and 500,000 inhabitants, reaching 0.81 among the largest cities (Table 8.2). When divided into quartiles it was observed that municipalities with lower HDI scores ranged from 0.47 to 0.63, while in the top quartile municipalities ranged between 0.77 and 0.94.

As shown in Table 8.2, using economic classes from the AQUARES project (Siqueira et al. 2011; Piccini et al. 2012), 28.3 percent of adults

TABLE 8.2 Characteristics of Brazilian Municipalities

	Municipality Population Size (Inhabitants)				
	Up to 30,000	30,001 to 100,000	100,001 to 500,000	More than 500,000	Total
Municipalities (n)	4,487	790	250	38	5,565
FHS coverage (%)					
Low	7.4	18.0	39.2	44.7	10.6
Middle	11.1	37.2	46.0	44.7	16.6
High	81.4	44.8	14.8	10.5	72.8
HDI (mean)	0.69	0.71	0.78	0.81	0.70
Economic class (ABEP)					
A/B	17.3	26.8	28.1	37.0	28.3
C	48.5	47.9	54.9	51.9	51.5
D/E	34.3	25.2	17.0	11.1	20.2
Schooling (years of study)					
None	12.1	8.1	4.2	3.3	6.3
1 to 4	21.4	18.8	15.8	10.3	15.7
5 to 11	56.4	59.7	66.2	66.4	63.1
12 or more	10.1	13.4	13.8	20.0	14.9

Note: HDI = Human Development Index

belong to classes A and B, 51.5 percent to class C, and 20.2 percent to D and E. It was also found that 6.3 percent of adults had not completed one year of school, 15.7 percent had between one and four years of schooling, and 14.9 percent had completed twelve or more years. The proportions of adults in classes A and B, as well as those with a higher level of education, increase with the size of the municipality. However, in municipalities with up to 500,000 inhabitants, FHS coverage is increasing in areas where the proportion of adults without schooling is growing and where the proportion of people classified in classes D and E is higher.

FHS Governance

FHS is present in 95 percent of the Brazilian municipalities. In 1998, FHS was present in 1,134 municipalities (20 percent), with 3,062 teams covering a population of 10,459,259 inhabitants. At the end of 2008 it was present in 5,235 municipalities (94 percent), with 29,300 teams covering a population of 93,178,011 inhabitants. Currently (July 2013), the Family Health Strategy operates in 5,309 municipalities (95 percent), with 34,185 teams reaching 108,096,363 inhabitants (Brazil 2013).

FHS coverage increases in smaller municipalities and in poorer areas all over the country, although particularly in the Northeast region. As a result, the difficulties in achieving better performance in municipalities with higher FHS coverage are likely to be greater.

Health System Inputs

Financing

Federal spending on PHC reached U.S. $6.35 billion in 2011 following a significant increase over the last ten years, coinciding with FHS coverage extension in larger municipalities (over 100,000 inhabitants). In 2002, only 12.0 percent of Ministry of Health spending on health care was allocated to PHC, increasing to 14.3 percent in 2007, and reaching almost 19 percent in 2012. The percentage of federal spending on hospital inpatient and outpatient care remained stable over the years at around 50 percent. However, prophylactic, diagnostic, and therapeutic tests and supplies increased more than six times over the period, from 1.6 percent in 2002 to 10.1 percent in 2012.

Municipal spending on health has increased significantly over the last ten years, coinciding with FHS coverage extension and the increasing number of specialized services delivered by SUS (Brazil 2011). It accounted for 13.4 percent of total municipal budgets in 2000, reaching 20.3 percent in 2010, without significant difference in municipality population size. It also decreased in a small proportion in relation to increased FHS coverage. FHS therefore appears to be an efficient option for municipal spending on health, particularly if it promotes better health system performance.

PMAQ is a federal governance initiative to encourage policy design at the municipal level, increasing financial resources associated with better FHS access and quality. From 2010 to 2013, federal primary health care financing increased by U.S. $1.57 billion, and 48.2 percent of this amount was transferred to the municipalities via PMAQ. The remaining amount was distributed to expanding teams (around 7 percent), increasing salaries (26 percent), and supporting new programs (19 percent) such as the School Health Program, Home Health Care, and Telehealth (Brazil 2012a).

Municipality adherence to rounds one and two of PMAQ were 71 percent and 89 percent, respectively. This can be considered to be a well-implemented governance strategy because of the increased proportion of financial incentives received by municipalities as a result of improving service access and quality. These percentages improved as FHS coverage increased (Table 8.3).

Health Workforce

Covering about 56 percent of the Brazilian population, FHS provides over 34,000 physicians, 34,000 nurses, and 21,000 dentists to deliver PHC in more than 95 percent of the country's municipalities (Brazil 2013).

The PMAQ external evaluation studied a selected sample of 16,820 FHS teams participating in the financial incentive assessment. Of all primary health care services in Brazil, 77 percent had a complete team (doctor + nurse + nursing technician/auxiliary + community health worker). Regardless of municipality size, the rates of full primary health care teams increased with FHS coverage. Furthermore, 64 percent of PHC services

TABLE 8.3 Patterns and Trends of the Indicators of FHS Governance, Health System Inputs, and PHC Delivery as FHS Coverage Increased in Municipalities with Different Population Sizes

Indicators	Total Prevalence	Municipality Population Size (inhabitants)			
		Up to 30,000	30,001 to 100,000	10,001 to 500,000	More than 500,000
GOVERNANCE					
FHS coverage	56%	–	–	–	–
FINANCING					
Adherence to PMAQ round one	71%	↑	↑	*	*
Adherence to PMAQ round two	89%	↑	↑	*	*
HEALTH WORKFORCE					
Full team (physician, nurse, nursing technician or auxiliary and community health agent)	77%	↑	↑	↑	↑
Full Team with university education (physician, nurse, and dentist)	64%	↑	↑	↑	↑
Full team with university education (physician and nurse)	86%	↑	↑	↑	↑
INFORMATION					
Existence of ombudsman	34%	↑	↑	↑	*
Professionals' working hours	37%	↑	↑	↑	*
Patients informed about services	48%	↑	↑	↑	*
MEDICINES					*
To treat hypertension	90%	*	*	*	*
To treat diabetes	94%	↓	*	*	*
TECHNOLOGY					*
Availability of computer	53%	↓	↓	↓	*
Internet access	37%	↓	↓	↓	*
Access to telehealth	14%	↑	↑	*	↑
Existence of electronic medical records	14%	↓	*	↑	↑

Indicators	Total Prevalence	Municipality population size (inhabitants)			
		Up to 30,000	30,001 to 100,000	100,001 to 500,000	More than 500,000
PHC DELIVERY					
Structure of Health Facilities					
Exclusive bathroom for employees	85%	*	↓	↓	↑
Bathroom adapted for disabled persons	16%	↓	↓	↓	↑
Appropriate structure for conducting Pap test	34%	↑	↑	↑	↑
Appropriate structure for caring for people with hypertension	28%	↑	↑	↑	↑
PHC centers improving structure —building works (%)	41%	↑	↑	↑	↑

Note:

Total prevalence = shows the patterns of twenty-seven different indicators, expressing the degree of health system issue implementation or population coverage regarding health system performance. An overall rate of up to 50 percent was classified as scarcely implemented and highlighted in dark gray; a rate of 50 percent to 75 percent was classified as partly implemented and highlighted in light gray; and a rate of over 75 percent was classified as fully implemented and highlighted in black.

Trend regarding the implemented action or health system performance indicators, controlled by the municipality population size (linear trend assessed through chi-square test)

↑ significantly positive trend   * non-significant trend   ↓ significantly negative trend

had at least one physician, one nurse, and one dentist available, and 85.8 percent had a doctor and nurse on their permanent staff (Table 8.3). This proportion also increased according to population size, from 84 percent in municipalities of up to 30,000 inhabitants to 90 percent in cities with more than 500,000 inhabitants. Even in a selected sample, there is less availability of physicians and nurses in the smaller cities.

Information

We analyzed the proportion of information provided to users of the Ministry of Health Ombudsman telephone service (34 percent), professionals' working hours at the PHC service (37 percent), and services offered by the teams (48 percent). These three indicators were all poorly implemented (<50 percent) regardless of municipality size, although these proportions improved as FHS coverage increased (Table 8.3).

Medicines

Essential drugs for hypertension and diabetes have been fully implemented in SUS since 2011 and are supported by the Popular Pharmacy Program. Ninety percent of medicines to treat hypertension were obtained from the SUS, and 65 percent of these in SUS primary health care services. Similarly, 94 percent of drugs to treat diabetes were obtained via SUS. In the case of drugs to treat hypertension and diabetes, these proportions did not show significant differences as FHS coverage increased (Table 8.3).

Technology

Computers were available at 53 percent of FHS services, but only 37 percent had access to the Internet and only 14 percent used electronic medical records and telehealth. Computers and Internet access were less available as FHS coverage increased. In the bigger municipalities, around 80 percent of FHS teams had access to computers and 64 percent had access to the Internet. Access to telehealth increased as FHS coverage grew. Electronic medical records decreased as FHS coverage increased in municipalities with fewer than 30,000 inhabitants. In the bigger municipalities, the presence of electronic medical records grew as FHS coverage increased (Table 8.3).

PHC Services Delivery

Structure of Health Facilities

Generally, the structure of PHC services in Brazil is problematic. As a marker of structural conditions, an exclusive bathroom for employees and a bathroom adapted for disabled persons were available in 85 percent and 16 percent of the PHC centers, respectively. These structural characteristics tended to become worse as FHS coverage increased, although in the bigger municipalities they grew as FHS coverage increased (Table 8.3).

An appropriate health facility structure for performing Pap smears was found in 34 percent of services. In all sizes of municipalities, this indicator was better where FHS coverage was higher (Table 8.3).

An appropriate health facility structure for providing care to people with hypertension was observed in 28 percent of cases. This indicator improved when FHS coverage was higher, regardless of municipality size (Table 8.3).

Incentives related to building new FHS centers and to renovating and expanding current services have been implemented since 2011 as a federal response to the structural problems of FHS services. Currently, 41 percent of municipalities have at least one FHS center being built, 33 percent have one or more being renovated, and 42 percent have one or more being expanded. In the bigger municipalities the proportions increased as FHS coverage grew (Table 8.3).

Work Process

The appropriate work process for performing Pap tests was assessed using the following items: Pap test performance, the existence of smear collection records, records of altered examinations, and follow-up with women after treatment. Only 37 percent of health professionals reported all items characterizing the proper work process. It was not possible to demonstrate any pattern of variability in this indicator by FHS coverage among different population sizes (Table 8.3).

Only 27 percent of PHC services had the appropriate work process for caring for people with hypertension, which includes the following items: record/register of hypertensive patients, register of high-risk hypertensive patients, scheduled consultation through risk stratification, and regular monitoring of patients with hypertension. For all population sizes, appropriate work processes increased as FHS coverage became greater (Table 8.3).

Some 30 percent of teams responded affirmatively to all nine questions about municipal management support to FHS teams. In municipalities with up to 500,000 inhabitants support has grown as FHS coverage has increased (Table 8.3).

Proper health management in the health centers was 14 percent. No patterns were observed considering the different municipality population sizes and FHS coverage (Table 8.3).

The main determinant of the population's access to PHC services is the hours they are open to the public. It is essential that health centers are open at times when people need them. Service users were asked if health center opening hours meet their needs, and 86 percent responded affirmatively. In general, FHS coverage improves this indicator (Table 8.3).

Other indicators of access and continuity of care are the recognition that the doctor is linked to the particular community and the patient knows his or her name. These indicators can be considered to be a guideline of the FHS strategy. Throughout Brazil, 67 percent reported that the physician is present at the health center or in neighborhood activities during all hours of operation and 70 percent of patients knew the physician's name. These proportions decrease with FHS coverage for all municipality population sizes, except municipalities with 500,000 or more inhabitants (Table 8.3).

Health System Performance

Health Services Access and Utilization

The prevalence of seven or more prenatal care appointments kept was 60 percent, showing a decreasing trend as FHS coverage becomes greater. Postpartum care was received by 60 percent of women who had children in the past two years. This indicator decreased as FHS coverage rose in all municipality sizes. The Pap test ratio per one hundred women between twenty-five and fifty-nine years of age was seventy-one, increasing as FHS coverage becomes greater (Table 8.4).

Access to medical consultation for hypertension and diabetes has reached a high degree of implementation. At least 85 percent of patients with hypertension and 89 percent with diabetes consulted a physician in the six months prior to the interview. In all population sizes, higher proportions of these indicators were observed with the increase of FHS coverage (Table 8.4).

Among adults, medical consultation increased significantly with FHS population coverage in municipalities with between 30,000 and 100,000 inhabitants as well as in those with over 500,000 inhabitants. In municipalities with between 100,000 and 500,000 inhabitants, medical consultation decreased as FHS coverage grew. There were no differences in municipalities with up to 30,000 inhabitants (Table 8.4).

Adult utilization of emergency rooms decreased linearly as FHS coverage grew in almost all municipality sizes. Home health care of adults increased significantly with FHS coverage in all municipality sizes (Table 8.4).

Polio vaccine coverage greater than or equal to 90 percent was observed in 58 percent of municipalities. In general, the rate increased where FHS had high coverage (Table 8.4).

Health Services Quality

Fewer than half of patients with hypertension had undergone an electrocardiogram in the last six months (46 percent). Increased FHS coverage improved this percentage, except in municipalities with between 100,001 and 500,000 inhabitants. However, only 30 percent of patients with diabetes had had their feet examined in the last six months, showing an increasing trend as FHS coverage becomes greater (Table 8.4).

Counseling on the promotion of a healthy life is an essential part of FHS activities. Advice on the use of condoms in all sexual relations increased due to the increase in FHS coverage, with a significant increase in municipalities having up to 500,000 inhabitants. Advice on quitting smoking increased due to the growth in FHS coverage in all municipality sizes. Counseling on physical activity increased due to the increase in FHS coverage in municipalities with between 30,000 and 100,000 inhabitants and in those with more than 500,000 inhabitants. There was significant reduction in municipalities with between 100,000 and 500,000 inhabitants (Table 8.4).

The prevalence of hospitalization for ambulatory care-sensitive conditions was 36 percent in relation to the country's total hospital admissions. This decreased as FHS coverage rose in all municipality sizes (Table 8.4).

Patient Satisfaction

In the AQUARES evaluation study, opinion as to medical consultations being good and excellent was high among all municipality sizes and FHS

TABLE 8.4 Patterns and Trends of the Indicators of Health System Performance per Increased FHS Coverage in Municipalities with Different Population Sizes

Indicators	Total Prevalence	Municipality population size (inhabitants)			
		Up to 30,000	30,001 to 100,000	10,001 to 500,000	More than 500,000
HEALTH SYSTEM PERFORMANCE					
Health Services Access and Utilization					
Women with 7 or more pre-natal care appointments kept (%)	60%	↓	↓	↓	↓
Women with postpartum care	60%	↓	↓	↓	↓
Pap test ration per 100 women aged between 25 to 59	71%	↑	↑	↑	↑
Patients with medical consultation for hypertension at the health center	85%	↑	↑	↑	↑
Medical consultation for diabetes at the health center	89%	*	*	*	*
Medical consultation	34%	*	↑	↓	↑
Emergency room utilization	18%	↓	↓	↓	↓
Home health care	5%	↑	↑	↑	↑
Coverage of polio vaccination (greater than or equal to 90%)	58%	*	↑	↑	↑
Health Services Quality					
Hypertensive patients having electrocardiograms	46%	↑	*	↓	*
Diabetic patients having foot examination	30%	*	*	*	↑
Counseling for patients to use condoms in all sexual relations	40%	↑	↑	↑	↑
Advice to quit smoking	51%	↑	↑	↑	↑
Counseling on physical activity	30%	*	↑	*	↑
Hospitalization for ambulatory care-sensitive condition (%)#	36%	↓	↓	↓	↓

Indicators	Total Prevalence	Municipality population size (inhabitants)			
		Up to 30,000	30,001 to 100,000	10,001 to 500,000	More than 500,000
HEALTH SYSTEM PERFORMANCE					
Patient Satisfaction					
Good and excellent opinion on the medical consultation	88%	↓	↓	↓	↓
Financial Risk Protection					
Free medical consultation provided by SUS	54%	↑	↑	↑	↑
Health Status					
Proportion of cured pulmonary tuberculosis (> 85%)	43%	*	↑	*	*
Infant mortality (<15/1000 live births)	48%	↓	↓	↓	↓

Note:

Total prevalence = shows the patterns of nineteen different indicators, expressing the degree of health system issue implementation or population coverage regarding health system performance. An overall rate of up to 50 percent was classified as scarcely implemented and highlighted in black; a rate of 50 percent to 75 percent was classified as partly implemented and highlighted in light gray; and a rate of over 75 percent was classified as fully implemented and highlighted in gray.

Trend regarding the implemented action or health system performance indicators, controlled by the municipality population size (linear trend assessed through chi-square test)

= without defined cutoff

↑ significantly positive trend   * non-significant trend   ↓ significantly negative trend

coverage patterns. However, a significant decreasing trend was found throughout the entire country as FHS coverage increased (Table 8.4).

Financial Risk Protection

Among adults, free medical consultation provided by SUS showed a linear increase with FHS population coverage in the entire country. The increase was statistically significant in smaller municipalities with up to 500,000 inhabitants. In municipalities with over 500,000 inhabitants the difference was not significant, but the trend was the same (Table 8.4). Therefore, higher FHS coverage was effective in promoting financial risk protection.

Health Status

Eighty-five percent was considered to be an acceptable proportion of cured pulmonary tuberculosis cases. This proportion occurred in 43 percent of Brazilian municipalities. In municipalities with between 30,001 and 100,000 inhabitants the indicator improved with FHS coverage. In other municipality sizes, best performance occurs at coverage extremes (Table 8.4).

An infant mortality rate below 15/1000 live births was considered to be acceptable. This rate was recorded in 48 percent of municipalities. The indicator improved as municipality size increased, but worsened as FHS coverage increased (Table 8.4). This trend is well justified considering that municipalities with higher FHS coverage are poorer than those with lower coverage.

DISCUSSION

The results show coherence with the hypothesis under assessment. There was a significant trend of health system performance improving as FHS coverage became greater, with some contextual effect modifications. These findings reinforce the relevance of FHS as an accountable and effective strategy to promote equity, despite all the problems regarding structure and work process within the PHC centers.

FHS coverage association with health system performance frequently showed different patterns depending on the context, according to the municipality population size. In small municipalities SUS performance generally increased with FHS coverage extension. In middle-sized municipalities the patterns were sometimes the opposite, with SUS performance declining as FHS coverage increased, while in the biggest municipalities the positive association was present once more.

The trends were well pronounced in small towns, but in the largest cities they were also identified in relation to several issues under assessment. Considering that municipalities with higher FHS coverage are poorer (as shown by HDI, economic class, and education) and smaller, the findings also express equity and inclusiveness. High FHS coverage seems to promote an effect across the whole system whereby performance, even if it is not better, is no worse when compared to municipalities with lower FHS coverage. Furthermore, the proportion of municipalities' own budget invested in health does not increase with increased FHS coverage, showing this to be an efficient and effective governance decision-making strategy.

Moreover, results have also highlighted some fully implemented health actions with universal coverage, such as care for people with hypertension and diabetes and access to medicines to treat these conditions. However, other health actions are strongly neglected, such as postpartum care, reaching only 60 percent of mothers, even considering that it is included in a traditional health action, like prenatal care. Moreover, there are quality-related problems regarding universal health actions, such as examining the feet of people with diabetes or electrocardiograms for people with hypertension. In general, even the poorly implemented health actions were similar or even better as FHS coverage increased. However, 40 percent of the mothers have no gynecological postpartum care whatsoever, worsening as FHS coverage increased. This is an overlooked issue in SUS and in PHC in Brazil. Solving it is relatively easy, as about 95 percent of all pregnant women and newborn babies are monitored by FHS team prenatal care and baby health care programs. Having women attending PHC centers after child delivery is crucial to improving maternal and baby health and identifying problems regarding breastfeeding, hemorrhages, infections, and mental health, particularly depression.

The worst performance indicators on implementation identified missing health actions in daily care that could be solved immediately if all PHC and FHS teams included them as compulsory actions at each programmed contact with the registered population. Protocols and guidelines are increasingly available and should be promoted and easily accessed by health care management and staff.

This chapter emphasizes FHS governance at national and municipal levels and its relationship with SUS performance in a broad perspective, this being a relatively scarce approach in the Brazilian health system. The chapter used up-to-date information (2009–2012) from several sources to show a complex panel of patterns and trends related to the categories and indicators, many of them relating to all 5,565 Brazilian municipalities. Furthermore, the stratified analysis by municipality size was appropriate for improving the assessment of the effect of different levels of FHS coverage on health system performance.

On the other hand, a potential weakness of the study relates to the variability of data sources, particularly the secondary data, which may differ according to municipality size and country region. Despite that, there is an increasing effort to standardize data collection, mainly in the national surveys, like the PMAQ, that are providing complete and comprehensive information regarding PHC delivery and SUS performance.

In conclusion, the findings show that FHS is having a remarkable systemic effect on SUS, reducing emergency room and hospital use and promoting home health care. The greater FHS coverage, the better health system performance. This applies to almost all municipality sizes, particularly the smaller and the biggest ones (metropolitan areas). The findings are even more relevant regarding equity, if we consider that municipalities with highest FHS coverage are poorer and smaller, generally in the country's inner and remote areas. In light of these findings, in order to achieve the challenging status of care coordination leadership, FHS should be universalized as quickly as possible as the main gateway to SUS.

Despite reaching almost 110 million people, FHS covers only 56 percent of the Brazilian population. Considering its effectiveness, responsiveness, equity, and efficiency, it is sound to suppose that its universal coverage represents accountable and ethical decision making, reinforcing the strategic vision of FHS governance. Federal governance is required to recruit some thirty thousand physicians, nurses, and dentists in order to achieve universal coverage. To achieve this gradually, at least fifteen thousand would need to be recruited to achieve 75 percent coverage initially.

There are increasing expectations by the population and policy makers in municipalities regarding some MoH initiatives, such as the More Doctors Program. This program integrates a national effort to improve PHC delivery and SUS performance in remote and suburban areas, mainly through three-year fellowships to Brazilian and foreign physicians, in addition to investments in infrastructure. The initiative is helping municipalities, not only regarding the health workforce recruiting process but also with regard to its potential to improve FHS coverage in forthcoming years.

REFERENCES

Aquino, R., N. F. de Oliveira, and M. Barreto. 2009. "Impact of the Family Health Program on Infant Mortality in Brazilian Municipalities." *American Journal of Public Health* 99 (1): 87–93.

Baez-Camargo, C., and E. Jacobs. 2011. *A Framework to Assess Governance of Health Systems in Low Income Countries.* Working paper No 11. Basel Institute on Governance.

Brazil. 2010. Constitution of the Federative Republic of Brazil: constitutional text of October 5, 1988, with the alterations introduced by Constitutional amendments no. 1/1992 through 64/2010 and by Revision Constitutional Amendments no. 1/1994 through 6/1994. Brasília: Chamber of Deputies, Documentation and information Center, 3rd ed.: 435.

Brazil. 2011. Estimates of the Impact of Constitutional Linkage of Health Resources: Constitutional Amendment. n° 29/2000. Brasília: Ministry of Health.

Brazil. 2011a. *IDSUS—Index Performance Unified Health System.* Brasília: Ministry of Health.

Brazil. 2011b. Portaria n° 1.654, from 19 June of 2011. Brasília: Ministry of Health. http://bvsms.saude.gov.br/bvs/saudelegis/gm/2011/prt1654_19_07_2011.html.

Brazil. 2011c. Presidential Decree No. 7508, Chapter V, Section II, of the Public Health Action Organisational Contract (COAP). Brasília.

Brazil. 2012. Ministry of Health web page. http://portalsaude.saude.gov.br.

Brazil. 2012a. *National Policy of Primary Health Care.* Brasília: Ministry of Health, Primary Health Care Department.

Brazil. 2012b. *National Programme for Improving Access and Quality of Primary Care (PMAQ): Instructional Manual.* Brasília: Ministry of Health, Primary Health Care Department.

Brazil. 2013. *Coverage Evolution of Family Health Strategy.* Brasília: Ministry of Health, Primary Health Care Department. http://dab.saude.gov.br/historico_cobertura_sf.php, accessed August 8, 2013.

Brinkerhoff, D. W., and T. Bossert. 2008. *Health Governance: Concepts, Experience, and Programming Options. U.S. Agency for International Development.* Health Systems 20/20, policy brief.

Dodgson, R., K. Lee, and N. Drager. 2002. *Global Health Governance: A Conceptual Review.* Centre on Global Change & Health, London School of Hygiene & Tropical Medicine and Department of Health & Development ,World Health Organization.

Donabedian, A. 1988. "The Quality of Care: How Can It Be Assessed?" *JAMA* 260 (12): 1743–48.

Elias, P. E. M., and A. Cohn. 2003. "Health Reform in Brazil: Lessons to Consider." *American Journal of Public Health* 93 (1): 44–48.

Facchini, L. A., R. X. Piccini, E. Tomasi, E. Thumé, D. S. Silveira, F. V. Siqueira, and M. A. Rodrigues. 2006. "Performance of the PSF in the Brazilian South and Northeast: Institutional and Epidemiological Assessment of Primary Health Care." *Ciência & Saúde Coletiva* 11(3): 669–81.

Facchini, L. A., R. X. Piccini, E. Tomasi, E. Thumé, V. A. Teixeira, D. S. Silveira, M. F. S. Maia, F. V. Siqueira, M. A. Rodrigues, V. V. Paniz, and A. Osório. 2008. "Evaluation of the Effectiveness of Primary Health Care in South and Northeast Brazil: Methodological Contributions." *Cadernos de Saúde Pública* 24 (suppl. 1): s159–s172.

Fleury, S., A. L. M. Ouverney, T. S. Kronemberger, and F. B. Zani. 2010. "Local Governance in the Decentralized Health Care System in Brazil." *Revista Panamericana de Salud Pública* 28: 446–55.

Giovanella, L., S. Escorel, L. V. C. Lobato, J. C. Noronha, and A. I. Carvalho. 2008. *Policies and Health System in Brazil.* Rio de Janeiro: Fiocruz.

Guanais, F., and J. Macinko. 2009. "Primary Care and Avoidable Hospitalizations: Evidence from Brazil." *Journal of Ambulatory Care Management* 32 (2): 115–22.

Harris, M., and A. Haines. 2010. "Brazil's Family Health Programme." *BMJ* 341.

IBGE. 2013. *Atlas of Census 2010.* Rio de Janeiro: Ministry of Planning, Budget and Management/Brazilian Institute of Geography and Statistics: 160.

Islam, M. 2007. *Health Systems Assessment Approach: A How-To Manual.* Submitted to the U.S. Agency for International Development in collaboration with Health Systems 20/20, Partners for Health Reformplus, Quality Assurance Project, and Rational Pharmaceutical Management Plus. Arlington, VA: Management Sciences for Health.

Lewis, M., and G. Pettersson. 2009. *Governance in Health Care Delivery: Raising Performance.* October 1. World Bank Policy Research Working Paper No. 5074.

Macinko, J., F. Marinho de Souza Mde, F. C. Guanais, and C. C. da Silva Simoes. 2007. "Going to Scale with Community-Based Primary Care: An Analysis of the Family Health Program and Infant Mortality in Brazil, 1999–2004." *Social Science & Medicine* 65 (10): 2070–80.

Mendonça, C. 2009. *Use of Hospitalizations for Ambulatory Care Sensitive Conditions for the Assessment of Family Health Strategy in Belo Horizonte/ MG.* Porto Alegre: Universidade Federal do Rio Grande do Sul.

Mikkelsen-Lopez, I., K. Wyss, and D. de Savigny, D. 2011. "An Approach to Addressing Governance from a Health System Framework Perspective." *BMC International Health and Human Rights* 11 (1): 13.

Ministry of Health. 2013. *Caderno de Informação da Saúde Suplementar – Beneficiários, Operadoras e Planos.* Rio de Janeiro: Agencia Nacional de Saúde Suplementar.

Murray, C. J. L., and J. Frenk. 2000. "A Framework for Assessing the Performance of Health Systems." *Bulletin of the World Health Organization* 78: 717–31.

Nedel, F. B., L. A. Facchini, M. Martín-Mateo, L. A. S. Vieira, and E. Thumé. 2008. "Family Health Program and Ambulatory Care-Sensitive Conditions in Southern Brazil." *Revista de Saúde Pública* 42 (6): 1041–52.

Noronha, J. C., I. S. Santos, and T. R. Pereira. 2010. *Relations Between the Unified Health System and Health Insurance: Problems and Alternatives for the Future of the Universal System.* Gestão Pública e Relação Público Privado na Saúde. 154. N. R. d. Santos and P. D. d. C. Amarante. Rio de Janiero: CEBES.

Paim, J., C. Travassos, C. Almeida, L. Bahia, and J. Macinko, J. 2011. "The Brazilian Health System: History, Advances, and Challenges." *Lancet* 377 (9779): 1778–97.

Piccini, R. X., L. A. Facchini, E. Tomasi, F. V. Siqueira, D. S. Silveira, E. Thumé, S. M. Silva, and A. S. Dilelio. 2012. "Promotion, Prevention and Arterial Hypertension Care in Brazil." *Revista de Saúde Pública* 46 (3): 543–50.

PNUD. 2010. *Values e Human Development 2010.* Brasília: United Nations Development Programme.

Roberts, M. J., W. Hsiao, P. Berman, and M. R. Reich. 2004. *Getting Health Reform Right: A Guide to Improving Performance and Equity.* New York: Oxford University Press.

Savedoff, W. D. 2011. *Governance in the Health Sector: A Strategy for Measuring Determinants and Performance.* Washington, D.C.: World Bank.

Siddiqi, S., T. I. Masud, S. Nishtar, and B. Sabri. 2006. *Framework for Assessing Health Governance in Developing Countries: Gateway to Good Governance.* Cairo: Eastern Mediterranean Regional Office, World Health Organization.

Siddiqi, S., T. I. Masud, S. Nishtar, D. H. Peters, B. Sabri, K. M. Bile, and M. A. Jamaet al. 2009. "Framework for Assessing Governance of the Health System in Developing Countries: Gateway to Good Governance." *Health Policy* 90 (1): 13–25.

Siqueira, F. V., L. A. Facchini, D. S. Silveira, R. X. Piccini, E. Tomasi, E. Thumé, S. M. Silva, and A. Dilélio. 2011. "Prevalence of Falls in Elderly in Brazil: A Countrywide Analysis." *Cadernos de Saúde Pública* 27 (9): 1819–26.

Thumé, E., L. A. Facchini, E. Tomasi, and L. A. S. Vieira. 2010. "Home Health Care for the Elderly: Associated Factors and Characteristics of Access and Health Care." *Revista de Saúde Pública* 44 (6): 1102–11.

UNDP. 1997. *Governance for Sustainable Human Development: A UNDP Policy Document.* New York: United Nations Development Programme.

UNICEF. 2013. *Levels and Trends in Child Mortality: Report 2013.* New York: United Nations Children's Fund.

Vian, T., W. D. Savedoff, and H. Mathisen. 2010. *Anticorruption in the Health Sector: Strategies for Transparency and Accountability.* Boston: Kumarian Press.

Viana, A. L. d. Á., J. S. Y. Rocha, P. E. Elias, N. Ibañez, and M. H. D. Novaes,. 2006. "Models of Primary Health Care in Large Cities in the State of São Paulo: Effectiveness, Efficaciousness Sustainability and Governableness." *Ciência & Saúde Coletiva* 11: 577–606.

WHO. 2000. *The World Health Report 2000: Health Systems: Improving Performance.* Geneva: World Health Organization.

WHO. 2007. *Everybody Business: Strengthening Health Systems to Improve Health Outcomes: WHO's Framework for Action.* Geneva: World Health Organization.

CHAPTER 9

Challenges in Reforming the Health System to Prevent Maternal Deaths in Low-Income Countries: A Case Study of Nigeria

Friday Okonofua

INTRODUCTION: THE HISTORICAL CONTEXT

Nigeria was first identified as a country with one of the highest rates of maternal mortality in the world in the mid-1980s. The groundbreaking paper by Kelsey Harrison (1985) that reported the determinants of maternal deaths among nearly 23,000 deliveries in northern Nigeria was what the world needed in order to understand the enormity of the problem in low-income countries. The paper described the association between social inequity, economic deprivations, and illiteracy and the high rate of maternal mortality in the region, and highlighted the importance of focusing on broad-based development and governance issues in efforts to prevent maternal mortality. The worldwide dissemination of the paper's results was followed by the convening of the International Conference on Safe Motherhood in Nairobi, Kenya (Cohen 1987). The conference galvanized global commitment to reduce maternal mortality by half by 2000. The increased recognition of the influence of socioeconomic determinants, cultural experiences, and the low status of women led to a paradigm shift from the hitherto narrow focus on family planning as the main weapon to fight overpopulation to a more broad-based agenda focusing on human development and the empowerment of women.

Two major international conferences then followed—the International

Conference on Population and Development (UNFPA 1994) and the Fourth World Conference on Women (UN Women 1995)—that centered on the need to address the broader issues that lead to poor outcomes for women's reproductive health. Both conferences emphasized the need to address the social, economic, and cultural determinants of reproductive health, with particular attention paid to rights, gender equity, and the advancement of socioeconomic justice. As policy makers from both developed and developing countries attended the conferences, the outcomes paved the way for governments to understand the multidimensional nature of the issue and to hopefully develop policies and programs to address them in the years ahead.

Unfortunately, by 2000 it was evident that, contrary to expectations, maternal mortality in Nigeria had increased rather than declined (Wall 1998). This was due in part to insufficient efforts paid to addressing the multiple governance, health systems, and cultural factors that led to persisting malfunctioning of the health system. The military interregnum during the period from 1985 to 1999, characterized by a lack of democratic governance, effectively ensured that none of the recommendations from the global conferences could be implemented in Nigeria. The attendant abuse of human rights and the muzzling of alternative voices weakened all institutions of governance and led to a systematic deterioration of all human living indicators in the country.

It was therefore not surprising that by the end of 1999, Nigeria was reported to account for 10 percent of global estimates of maternal deaths and up to 40 percent of maternal morbidity due to obstetric fistulae (AbouZahr and Wardlaw 2000). Although the country signed the Millennium Declaration (2000), which included a pledge by nations to reduce maternal mortality by 75 percent by 2015, its weak health care system posed a major barrier to the achievement of this goal. In 2000, the World Health Organization summary index of performance of health systems (WHO 2000) ranked Nigeria 187th out of 191 surveyed countries. The WHO assessment found the Nigerian health system to have major problems in the level and distribution of health as well as other indicators of health system performance (WHO 2000, 154). The reemergence of democratic governance in 1999 provided an opportunity to address these problems and to prioritize health as an essential item in the country's developmental agenda.

However, the new government did not begin to prioritize maternal health until the tail end of its first term, 1999–2003. Professor Eyitayo Lambo was appointed the new Minister of Health in 2003. As a health systems expert, he understood the connection between health systems effectiveness and the improvement of health indicators. He was therefore able to identify health systems reform as the new strategic direction for the Federal Ministry of Health for improving the governance of the health system and reducing maternal mortality. Consequently, over the following years, the Ministry, in collaboration with local and international partners, developed a strategic framework and implemented various policies and programs for strengthening the country's health care system. The period also witnessed increased political commitment to addressing maternal health at the highest level of governance (Shiffman and Okonofua 2007).

Partly due to improved health system governance, the country witnessed a decline in maternal mortality by 41 percent between 1990 and 2010 (Hogan et al. 2010). However, the progress made was still less than the proportionate decline needed to achieve the MDG 5. Nigeria is still counted as one of six developing countries that account for 50 percent of global maternal deaths, with the country's burden of maternal death rising to 14 percent of global estimates (Lozano et al. 2011). This chapter describes the processes, methods, and strategies that the country adopted during the first eight years of its new democratic experience (1999 to 2007) to strengthen the governance of its health system and to reduce its high rate of maternal mortality. It provides some explanation for the successes and achievements made, identifies several challenges that remain to be overcome, and makes recommendations on ways to reorganize the health system to reduce the high rate of maternal mortality in the country.

DATA SOURCES

Data were obtained from various policy documents generated by the Federal Ministry of Health of Nigeria during the period 1999 to 2007, when it focused on improving the governance of its health care system (Lambo 2005). We also reviewed various published and unpublished data sources and articles from different parts of the country that documented the performance of the health system and maternal health indicators before and after the period. The Women's Health and Action Research Center (WHARC, www.wharc-online.org), a nongovernmental organization founded in 1993, took specific steps to document the processes both in its annual reports and publications as well as through its flagship international journal, the *African Journal of Reproductive Health* (AJRH, www.ajrh.info). We drew heavily from data accumulated in WHARC's archives to support the information and data presented in this report.

The Nigerian presidency organized two health retreats in 1999 and 2006 as part of its efforts to build political understanding of Nigeria's health system and to proffer appropriate solutions. As a key participant in these workshops, the author of this chapter used the results and recommendations of these meetings, as well as the reports of the presidential adviser on health and the special presidential adviser on MDGs, in analyzing maternal health activities in Nigeria and their effects.

We also reviewed the reports and data from various agencies of government specifically established to improve Nigeria's health system over the past fifteen years. These include the National Agency for Food and Drug Administration (NAFDAC), the Nigerian Health Insurance Scheme (NHIS), the National Primary Health Care Development Agency (NPHCDA), the National Agency for the Control of HIV/ AIDS (NACA), and the Office of Senior Special Adviser to the President on the MDGs (OSSAP-MDGs). Finally, our data sources also include results of several demographic and health surveys (National Population Commission 1992, 1999, 2000, 2004, 2009) that were conducted during the ten-year period, as well as our own understanding of political and social events in the country.

GENERATING POLITICAL COMMITMENT FOR MATERNAL HEALTH IN THE POST-DEMOCRACY ERA

After decades of neglect, a policy window opened for the promotion of maternal health in 1999 at the advent of Nigeria's second attempt at democratic governance, giving hope for future maternal mortality reduction. Raising the profile of a social justice issue such as maternal mortality reduction that affects mainly poor and marginalized citizens can be a difficult undertaking in developing countries. The fact that such countries often grapple with the allocation of limited resources in the face of competing demands means that strategic political calculations have to be made to bring such issues to the attention of policy makers. The relevant question therefore is how maternal mortality reduction came to feature as an important priority item in the national development agenda of Nigeria during the period 1999 to 2007. This can be attributed to three strategic developments, opportunities, and milestones that occurred during the period. The first was the declaration of the Millennium Development Goals (MDGs) by world leaders, which took place within the first year of the new democratic experience. The attendant publicity and release of several international data that suggested that Nigeria was doing poorly in maternal health as compared to the rest of the world steered the top leadership of the new administration to find solutions to the problem.

Second, as President Obasanjo had a background in social justice activism, having been on the board of the Ford Foundation, he was openly sympathetic to issues related to poverty, social marginalization, and socioeconomic injustice. Therefore, in his early speeches as president (Obasanjo 1999) he spoke passionately about the need to end pervading social injustice, economic opportunism, and widespread impunity, and to level the social playing field for all citizens. He also promised to get citizens involved in decision making, especially on issues that affect their daily living. It was therefore not surprising that one of the first steps the president took was to invite citizens and stakeholders to identify priority areas for reform and to make specific recommendations on ways to achieve change in relevant sectors. Tagged *Saturday Forum with Mr. President*, one such retreat, held in July 1999, two months after the administration came into office, focused on the needs of the health system. As a participant in that retreat, the author witnessed the frankness and openness of the discussions and the patriotic fervor with which the president moderated the meeting. The meeting was essentially conducted in a learning mode, which enabled the president to better understand the challenges facing the health system.

The third event that stimulated political consciousness for maternal health was a United Nations MDG Progress Report presented to heads of government at a meeting in New York in 2006. The report showed that

Nigeria was doing poorly in human development and health indicators compared with other developing nations. The country was pinpointed as having the second-highest absolute numbers of maternal and under-five deaths, and, with very low immunization rates, was one of a few countries still harboring the wild polio virus. Life expectancy in the country had also declined to one of the lowest rates in the world. With this information, the president convened a second health retreat in August 2006 with the theme, "Achieving Accelerated Increase in Life Expectancy in Nigeria: The Way Forward" (FMOH 2006). The retreat identified the high rate of maternal and child mortality as the major reason for the declining life expectancy in the country (Okonofua 2006). It identified three priority areas for immediate intervention to reverse the trend. These include the provision of a health safety net to offer women and children access to evidence-based care, the introduction of a midwifery program to improve the staffing of primary health centers (PHCs) throughout the country, and increased funding of maternal and child health care.

STRENGTHENING THE NATIONAL HEALTH SYSTEM AND IMPROVING HEALTH GOVERNANCE: 1999–2007

Some of the specific activities undertaken to strengthen the country's health system between 1999 and 2007 included: (1) declaration of a health reform agenda, (2) enunciation of new health policies, (3) increased health funding, (4) the establishment of the National Health Insurance Scheme (NHIS), (5) specific programming in maternal health, (6) improved human resources for health and infrastructural development, (7) the improvement and consolidation of the country's drug regulatory and enforcement agency, and (8) the establishment of a national HIV/AIDS control agency.

Health Reform Agenda

Health system reform was an important component of the efforts to improve health governance and reduce maternal mortality during the second half of the administration. The Health System Reform Program (HSRP) (Lambo 2005) was designed in 2003 as part of the National

Economic Empowerment and Development Strategy (NPC 2001), with a goal to prioritize health for the accelerated achievement of the MDGs, especially with respect to reduction in infant, neonatal, and maternal mortality rates. The objective of the HSRP was to correct all the factors that led to the poor performance of the Nigerian health system in previous years, propelling it to greater cost effectiveness and efficiency.

The health system reform agenda was developed through a participatory process that involved various stakeholders, including policy makers at national and subnational levels, development partners, and program implementers from across the country. The seven strategic objectives of the HRSP were to: (1) improve the performance of the stewardship role of the government, (2) strengthen the health system and improve its management, (3) improve the availability of health resources and their management, (4) improve the physical and financial access to evidence-based health services, (5) reduce the burden of disease attributable to priority health problems, (6) promote effective public–private partnerships in health, and (7) increase consumers' awareness of their health rights and obligations.

During the period from 2004 to 2007, substantial progress was made in implementing different components of the health system reform agenda. The national health policy was updated, and a national strategic plan for health system reform was approved by the Federal Executive Council. As shown in Table 9.1, several policy documents to guide the implementation of programs and actions in health care were also developed. By mid-2007, eighteen ancillary policies, eight medium-term strategic plans, and four guidelines for implementing the reform agenda were either completed or were at various stages of completion.

The plans and activities of the HSRP have been subjected to various reviews. Despite the good intentions of the reform framework, the actual implementation of the policies and programs contained in the strategy have remained a major challenge.

Emergence of New Health Policies

The period of military rule (1985–1999) that preceded the enactment of the new democracy era in Nigeria was characterized by poor health policy formulation, inadequate legislation on matters relating to health, and

TABLE 9.1 National Policies and Programs Developed as a Consequence of the Health Reform Agenda, 2004–2007

1.	National Health Policy
2.	Health Promotion
3.	Infant and Young Child Feeding
4.	Comprehensive Child Survival and Development
5.	Health Care Financing
6.	Human Resources for Health
7.	Noncommunicable Diseases
8.	Public-Private Partnerships
9.	Integrated Disease Surveillance and Response
10.	Traditional Medicine Practices
11.	National Health Equipment
12.	National Health Management Information System
13.	National Antimalaria Treatment
14.	National Blood Transfusion Services
15.	Integrated Maternal, Newborn, and Child Health Strategy (IMNCH)

the lack of a strategic plan of action for promoting various components of health. As part of the new democratic experience, the two houses of the National Assembly enunciated various health laws and revised old ones during the period. Table 9.2 presents the current health laws and legislative acts in Nigeria, which indicate that a substantial number were formulated after 1999 (FGN 2004; FMOH 2001, 2002, 2005, 2007).

The policies ranged from those that make indirect contributions to health, such as the National Economic Empowerment Development Strategy (NEEDS), to those that promote best practices in health and those that deal directly with the control of specific diseases such as HIV/AIDS. The most noteworthy of these policies with direct implications for maternal mortality prevention were: the national reproductive health policy, the health system reform policy, strategic plan for the accelerated attainment of the MDGs, the revised national health policy, and blueprints for the revitalization of primary health care and the national health insurance scheme. The regime also developed strategic plans for priority health problems such as the Roll Back Malaria policy, which have direct implications for preventing maternal deaths.

TABLE 9.2 A List of Current Policies and Legislative Acts on Health in Nigeria

1998	National Policy on Population for Development, Unity, Progress, and Self-Reliance
1999	National Economic Empowerment Development Strategy (NEEDS)
2001	National Reproductive Health Policy
2002	National Reproductive Health Strategic Framework
2002	National Guidelines for Women's Health
2003	Health Sector Reform Policy
2003	National Strategic Plan for Reproductive Health Commodity Procurement
2004	Strategic Plan for Accelerating the Attainment of the Millennium Development Goals
2004	Recommendations on Repositioning the Federal Ministry of Health
2004	Revised National Health Policy
2004	Blueprint for Revitalization of Primary Health Care in Nigeria
2005	Blueprint for Accelerating the Implementation of the National Health Insurance Scheme
2007	National Health Act (approved in 2009)

Progress in Health Financing

A review of Nigeria's major economic indicators and health expenditure profiles between 1999 and 2013 shows that the country witnessed steady economic growth over the past years from a low of GDP growth rate of 0.69 percent in 1999 to a high of 8.6 percent in 2010. Between 2009 and the first quarter of 2013, Nigeria had one of the fastest-growing economies in the world, largely due to increased international pricing of petroleum, the country's main income earner. However, a major problem has been the lopsidedness in the country's expenditure profile, whereby a large proportion of its budget is devoted to recurrent expenditure. More than 70 percent of the country's annual budget is now dedicated to personnel and overhead costs, from a low of 53.2 percent in 1999. This is in large part due to a three-tier form of government made up of national, state, and local government levels, and to a bloated government labor force.

Despite the booming economy, it is worrisome that Nigeria still spends less than U.S. $63 per capita on health. When compared to the United States, which spends up to U.S. $8,608 per capita on health, the extent of continued underfunding on health in the country becomes evident. The political commitment announced by the government to address maternal health during the period did not appear to have influenced this indicator, as the per capita expenditure rose briefly, from U.S. $44.40 in 2004 to U.S. $79.30 in 2008, only to fall to its currently low figures. To this day, Nigeria's per capita expenditure on health remains one of the lowest in the world.

In 2001, African heads of government agreed at a conference in Abuja (the Abuja Declaration) to allocate 15 percent of their government funding for health in their various countries. Nigeria has yet to meet this target. Its total health funding as a percentage of government expenditure was highest in 2003, when it allocated 7.55 percent, just about halfway to meeting the Abuja target. This indicator fell to 5.5 percent in 2010, its lowest level in a decade.

A major achievement of President Obasanjo's administration was the reduction in the nation's debt burden. Since the 1980s, the country had been indebted to international creditors to the tune of U.S. $35 billion, for which the sum of U.S. $2 billion was spent each year for debt servicing. The debt burden limited the ability of the government to meet the health and social needs of its citizens. In 2005, the Paris Club of creditors agreed to cancel U.S. $18 billion of the country's total indebtedness. The government then directed that the accrued gains (called Debt Relief Gains, DRG) should be used to finance pro-poor programs and the achievement of the Millennium Development Goals in the country. The health system was a beneficiary of this relief. The savings amounted to N100 billion (U.S. $757 million) annually, from which the sums of N21.3 billion and N15 billion were allocated to improve the health system in 2006 and 2007, respectively, while HIV/AIDS control received the sum of N1 billion. During this period, health ranked second to education in allocations made to various sectors from the DRG. However, this only slightly increased the per capita expenditure on health after 2005, while a further slide has appeared since 2009.

The first National Health Accounts was published by Soyibo et al. in 2006. The results showed that household expenditure is the major source of health financing in Nigeria, providing up to 65.9 percent of the total health care costs. By contrast, the federal government provides 12.4 percent; states, 7.4 percent; local government councils, 6.4 percent;

and firms, 6.1 percent; while development partners contribute 1.8 percent to health care financing. Private health expenditure as a percentage of GDP was 5.58 percent in 2002, but declined to 3.71 percent in 2009, which amounts to more than half of the total GDP health expenditure. The data also show that out-of-pocket expenditure as a percentage of private health expenditure remains high, reaching a staggering 95.34 percent in 2010. Thus, high household expenditure on health remains a major challenge in Nigeria, and is a persisting contributor to the high burden of disease in the country. By contrast, external contributions to health care (from donor and related sources) amounted to a paltry 5.07 percent in 2010, representing a nearly 3 percent decline between 2003 and 2010.

Within this context of overall inadequate funding for health, it is to be noted that maternal health received less funding during the period, despite the increased rate of policy developments aimed at addressing the problem. Indeed, the underfunding of maternal health has remained a major subject of discourse in the past decade. In 2007, the government attempted to address this by drafting a national health bill, aimed at ensuring that up to 2 percent of the nation's GDP is set aside for the implementation of primary health care, a major component of maternal health care. The bill was approved by the National Assembly in May 2011, but since it was not signed into law by President Goodluck Jonathan at the stipulated time, it now lacks legislative validity. Despite the pledge by the government to increase funding for maternal health as part of its implementation of the Subsidy Re-Investment Empowerment Program (Nigerian Presidency 2013) for promoting a social safety net for citizens when the government partially removed the subsidy from petroleum products in January 2012, very little evidence of its high-impact value has been seen.

The National Health Insurance Scheme

The National Health Insurance Scheme (NHIS) was established by Military Decree No. 35 of 1999 to reduce the burden of health financing on households and individuals. However, it was not until 2005, during the second half of the new administration, that the plan was finally launched. The scheme is now fully operational, with more than two million registered participants in 2008. By mid-2012, only 3 percent of the population (five million individuals) had been covered (Dutta and Hongoro 2013), indicating a slow pace of progress in scaling up the insurance plan.

An additional limitation of the NHIS is the fact that it does not cover unemployed persons, especially those in rural areas, who tend to have a higher burden of disease and less access to health services. In a country where up to 70 percent of the population lives on less than one dollar a day, this must be one major deterrent to accessing evidence-based care. It was for this reason that the government evolved the Community-Based Health Insurance (CBHI) scheme, to be administered mainly in rural and urban-poor areas. However, even this scheme has yet to take off as a result of resistance to government-led contributory mechanisms.

To engender private contributions to health financing, the administration launched a national policy on public–private partnerships for health (FMOH 2005a). The policy was an offshoot of the health system reform agenda, and was designed to promote collaboration between public and private sectors in providing affordable and sustainable health services. However, there is no concrete evidence to show that the policy has had significant effects in increasing private-sector investments and contribution to health promotion in the country.

Public-Sector Programming in Maternal Health

Alarmed by the daunting statistics on maternal and child health and buoyed by patriotic instincts, President Olusegun Obasanjo decided to personally take steps to reverse the trend. His first decision was to appoint a senior special adviser on the Millennium Development Goals (OSSAP-MDGs), with a specific mandate to prioritize the achievement of the health-related MDGs. However, the concurrent legislative nature of health governance in the country posed a major challenge. While the federal government is in charge of policy development and the management of tertiary care institutions, the states and local government councils manage the health system in their areas of jurisdiction. By this arrangement, the federal government has no direct influence in matters relating to health in the states and local government councils, and yet these subnational levels of government need to function more effectively if positive changes are to be achieved in maternal health. Indeed, it was widely recognized that the deteriorating maternal indicators in the country were largely attributable to the poor performance of states and local government councils in implementing their specific mandates in health.

In order to address this problem, the president appointed an honorary presidential adviser on health in 2006, with the responsibility of mobilizing political commitment at subnational levels of government for implementing appropriate policies and programs for promoting maternal health. Thus, beginning in 2006, the office of the presidential adviser (SPA) worked with the OSSAP-MDGs, the Federal Ministry of Health (FMOH), the National Primary Health Care Development Agency (NPHCDA), and state governments to implement maternal health projects at both the national and subnational levels. Some of the activities implemented included the following:

• The implementation of a policy on free maternal health services at all levels of the health care system to promote increased utilization of evidence-based maternity care by women. This was based on evidence suggesting that only 30 percent of Nigerian pregnant women are assisted at delivery by skilled birth attendants, mainly due to women's lack of economic resources (Okonofua 2006; Okonofua 2007a). By 2010, as many as eighteen of the thirty-six Nigerian states provided free maternal health services (Okonofua and Lambo 2011). President Obasanjo also directed that free medical services should be offered to pregnant women attending federal health institutions across the country.

• The creation of a Midwifery Services Scheme (MSS), whereby retired and recently qualified midwives would serve in rural primary health centers for at least one year on a rotating basis. This was to address the lack of midwives in rural health centers, where a majority of rural deliveries take place. This policy is currently being implemented by the NPHCDA, with recent evidence indicating that more than 26,000 midwives have been recruited, retrained, and are providing services in rural communities across the country. Under this program, 815 health facilities (652 PHCs and 163 general hospitals) have been engaged, with funding coming mainly from the federal government (NPHCDA 2012).

• The country's Integrated Maternal, Newborn, and Child Health (IMNCH) Strategy document was launched in 2007 to strengthen the implementation of integrated maternal and child health services in the country. The program was designed to deliver a package of comprehensive and evidence-based interventions to mothers and children from the time of conception through pregnancy, delivery, and the newborn period, through infancy, and continuing until the child was five years of age. The strategy identified a number of interventions for reducing maternal and child mortality. However, despite its compelling nature, the program has not advanced sufficiently due to inadequate plans made for its implementation (Okonofua 2013). Aside from inadequate financial allocations made for its implementation, there has been complete failure to integrate the processes and methods of its implementation into the health care system. For it to be operational, health workers need to be retrained or oriented to its use, while protocols, procedure manuals, and algorithms are still not in place to support its implementation.

Human Resource and Infrastructural Development

One factor responsible for poor access to maternal health care in Nigeria is the inadequate number of health personnel in the country. Only about 33 percent of pregnant woman are assisted at delivery by skilled birth attendants (doctors and midwives), with less than 10 percent delivered by doctors (Okonofua 2006). With such low skilled birth attendance rates, it would be difficult to dramatically reduce rates of maternal mortality. The challenge has always been in producing an adequate number of health professionals and motivating and retaining them to work in different locations in the country. The 1999–2007 period witnessed a rapid growth in the number of doctors in Nigeria, from a total of 14,754 in 1989 to 52,408 doctors in 2007. The number of nurses, midwives, pharmacists, and other health workers also doubled during the period. The number of obstetricians and gynecologists increased from 250 to more than 1000, while the number of specialist doctors in disciplines such as pediatrics, internal medicine, surgery, community medicine, pathology, and radiology also increased significantly. This was due to increased funding that enabled academic and health institutions to provide undergraduate and postgraduate medical education within the country, rather than candidates going abroad for training, with the likelihood that they would not return.

Despite the growth in health personnel, the period also witnessed an increase in out-migration of health workers. Data from the U.K. National Health Service showed that the number of Nigerian nurses registering to work in the United Kingdom increased from 180 in 1998–1999 to more than 500 in 2003–2004. Similar trends were recorded for emigration of various health professionals to other developed economies around the world.

A further development was the unequal distribution of health workers in various locations across the country, whereby many health professionals either work in exclusive urban communities to the neglect of rural areas or work in lucrative private facilities rather than in public hospitals devoted to the treatment of the poor. Out-migration and the poor distribution of health professionals was a major subject of discourse as part of efforts to improve the health systems. Debate focused on the nature, causes, and consequences of the problem, and on how the situation might be changed to ensure the provision of high-quality maternal health care in the country. The most immediate corrective measure employed by the government was to increase the salaries and emoluments of health workers. However, this did little to address the problem, as the salaries offered were still not competitive with those in the international market.

Another problem was that younger professionals sought to migrate to well-equipped hospitals abroad with modern diagnostic and curative facilities in order to gain additional skills and experience. To address this demand, the government refurbished facilities and infrastructure in all sixteen federal tertiary hospitals in the country through a contract made with VAMED, a German engineering firm. Unfortunately, there was little provision for additional training of personnel to use these facilities, which tended to reduce the quality of service delivery that was obtained from this initiative.

Intensified Drug Regulatory Policy

One major area where the new democratic administration made considerable impact in health promotion was the control of counterfeit and adulterated drugs. For years, Nigeria had the highest rate of adulterated drugs in West Africa. The National Agency for Food and Drug Administration and Control (NAFDAC) was established by Decree No. 15 of 1993 (Federal Ministry of Health 1993). However, prior to 1999, the agency made limited progress in reducing the prevalence of fake and adulterated drugs in the country due to its weak administrative structure. At the time, high rates of adulterated antimalarial and antibacterial drugs contributed to the high burden of maternal ill health in the country.

President Obasanjo appointed Professor Dora Akunyili, a fearless university pharmacy professor, as the director of NAFDAC in April 2001. Following this appointment, NAFDAC intensified its efforts and had significant success in reducing the number of counterfeit, substandard, and illegal drugs in the country. During the period, NAFDAC regulatory activities included the control of counterfeit drugs, the prosecution of persons found contravening the nation's drug laws, and public enlightenment campaigns, with statistics showing increased effectiveness of the agency. In the five years preceding 1999, only 2,539 products were registered by NAFDAC, whereas between 1999 and 2003, 10,584 products were registered, a nearly fourfold increase. NAFDAC also destroyed more than 115 substandard and counterfeit products worth over U.S. $150 million during this period (NAFDAC 2009), with as many as fifty people convicted.

Due to the increased effectiveness of NAFDAC, the level of counterfeit drugs in circulation dropped from an average of 41 percent in 2001 to 16.7 percent in 2006, while the proportion of NAFDAC unregistered drugs in the country declined from 68 percent in 2001 to 19 percent in 2006. Although substantive data are unavailable, this development led to improved control of diseases such as malaria that help account for maternal mortality in the country. The success of NAFDAC in controlling illegal drugs was widely acknowledged by national and international agencies (Roberts and Reich 2011), and was one of the most visible efforts made to transform Nigeria's health system during the period.

The Control of HIV/AIDS

HIV/AIDS control was a major beneficiary of the health reform agenda of Nigeria's democracy period. At the time the new administration came into office in 1999, the national HIV seroprevalence rate had increased to 5.4 percent (see Figure 9.1), with the government having no definite plan for controlling the disease. There was also widespread ignorance (at both the individual and policy levels) about the disease and its true impact. Indeed, in 1998, only the sum of U.S. $2,000 was allocated for HIV/AIDS control, but even this amount was not released.

At the first Presidential Health Retreat held in July 1999, the neglected state of HIV control was presented to President Obasanjo, who immediately offered to lead the fight against the disease. Presidential support led to the development of the expanded HIV/AIDS national multi-sectoral response and the establishment of the Presidential Council on AIDS (PCA) in 2000. The committee (and now the agency) developed several policies, including the National HIV/AIDS Policy, the HIV/ AIDS Emergency Action Plan, and the National Strategic Framework, as well as several guidelines and protocols to fast-track control of the disease (NACA 2004, 2005, 2009).

Since its founding, NACA has received substantial funding from several sources for the control of HIV/AIDS. Apart from increased federal budgetary allocations, HIV/AIDS also benefitted from the DRG made available after the Paris Club cancelled the country's debt in 2005. The country also received HIV assistance funding from the World Bank, President's Emergency Plan for AIDS Relief (PEPFAR), the Global Fund, and several international development organizations. Furthermore, political commitment to tackle the disease reached a new tempo in 2002, when the government provided its own funds to get ten thousand adults and five thousand children on free antiretroviral treatment within one year. More funds were provided through a presidential order in 2005 to place 250,000 (out of the then-estimated 500,000) HIV-positive adults and children in treatment.

Despite increased funding and programmatic activities, decline in HIV/AIDS prevalence has failed to progress at the same rate. Data from NACA (see Figure 9.1) showed that HIV prevalence increased to 5.8 percent in 2001, but declined to 4.4 percent in 2005. Further increase to 4.6 percent occurred in 2008, with a decline to 4.1 percent in 2010. Current estimates indicate a slight drop to a prevalence rate of 4.0 percent in 2013, confirming the slow pace of progress. With an estimated 3.4 million persons living with HIV/AIDS, Nigeria is currently rated as the country with the second-highest burden of the epidemic in the world.

The contribution of HIV/AIDS to maternal health also worsened during the period. HIV/AIDS is now the leading cause of maternal mortality in major hospitals in the country (Aisien et al. 2010). Recent reports from NACA (2013) also show that of the estimated six million annual pregnancies in Nigeria, about 230,000 women are HIV positive.

FIGURE 9.1 National HIV Prevalence Trend, 1991-2013

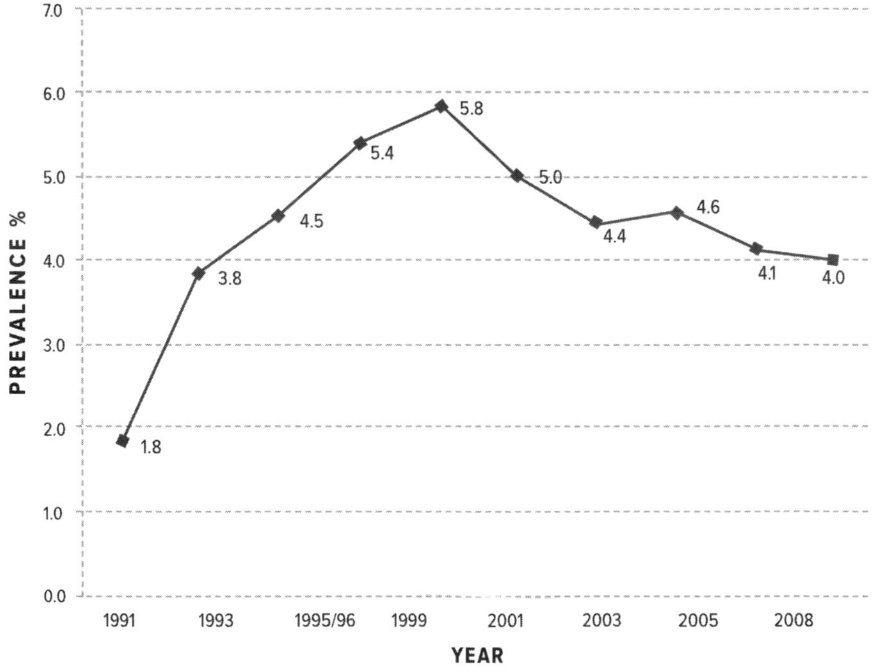

Source: National AIDS Control Agency, Abuja, 2013.

With only 18 percent of women receiving prophylaxis against mother-to-child transmission of HIV, up to sixty thousand HIV-positive babies are born each year. Although an 8 percent drop in HIV among Nigerian children from birth to age fourteen occurred between 2009 and 2012, with about ten thousand fewer children and women acquiring HIV during the period, the country is still counted as having the slowest decline in HIV transmission in children and women of reproductive age. The report also showed that only one in ten HIV-infected children receives lifesaving antiretroviral treatment. Thus, Nigeria currently has one of the highest burdens of pediatric HIV/AIDS, with little progress in the prevention of mother-to-child transmission of the virus.

PROGRESS IN MATERNAL HEALTH INDICATORS

As a result of increased political commitment, the prevention of maternal mortality was the second most mentioned health intervention by government officials during the period between 2004 and 2007. President Obasanjo, for example, personally led the campaign and made several speeches to key public- and private-sector stakeholders on the need to realistically tackle the high rate of maternal mortality in the country. Several state governors and legislators also did the same, especially those seeking reelection to public offices. Indeed, maternal mortality became a buzzword in the country's political lexicon, with the media being very active in the ensuing discussions and debate. However, only a few subnational-level governments backed this up with specific strategic programming on maternal health. Although as many as eighteen state governments declared policies on the implementation of free maternal health (Okonofua and Lambo 2011), the lack of substantial allocation of funding reduced the program's impact. Indeed, Chama commented on the implementation of the free maternal health program in Borno State, in northeastern Nigeria, as follows:

> The program is characterized by severe shortages in resources needed to promote maternal health.... Although an amount was budgeted for the program in 2009, the program had died by the beginning of that year. It appears the program is only a political gimmick aimed at aligning with the current wave of

declaration for free maternal health by state governments across the country. There does not appear to be any sincerity on the part of government to execute the program with purposefulness and tenacity. (2010, 51)

However, a notable exception was Ondo State Government, under Governor Mimiko (a medical doctor), which launched the Abiye maternal health program in 2010 (Mimiko 2010). Under Abiye, intense public health education was provided to women and community gatekeepers on the need for evidence-based maternity care; free maternity services were provided in all public health facilities in the state; health rangers were trained and assigned to specifically monitor twenty-five pregnant women per health ranger throughout pregnancy and delivery; toll-free mobile phones were provided for pregnant women to contact their health rangers when pregnancy complications occurred; and ambulances were provided to rapidly transport pregnant women to health facilities when they experienced complications. The state also built two mother and child hospitals in two major cities at which all pregnant women experiencing pregnancy complications were offered high-quality routine and emergency-referral obstetric care.

Within the first year of its implementation, the program treated 31,000 pregnant women, with 1,224 women delivered by caesarean section, with no recorded cases of maternal death. A more than 200 percent increase in attendance in prenatal clinics and a nearly 250 percent increase in deliveries were recorded in public maternity hospitals during the first twelve months of the implementation of the program, with a corresponding decline in the proportion of women using faith-based clinics and traditional birth attendants (Ondo News 2013).

With the slow pace of implementation of maternal health programs in other states, it was not surprising that the rate of improvement in maternal health indicators has not been encouraging. Although maternal mortality declined to 630 per 100,000 women in 2013, the fact that intermediary indicators (contraceptive prevalence rate, percent of women attending to prenatal care, and proportion of home birth) did not change substantially during the period implies that the fall in maternal mortality may not be sustained. By contrast, there was some improvement in child health indicators as epitomized by the nearly 30 percent decline in infant mortality between 2003 and 2013, and the decline in the under-five mortality rate from 201 per 1,000 live births in 2003 to 143 in 2013. Similarly, the proportion of children aged twelve to twenty-three years who are fully immunized increased to 71 percent in 2013, which may have accounted for the decline in infant and under-five mortality rates experienced during the period 2003–2013.

DISCUSSION AND RECOMMENDATIONS

The objective of this chapter is to describe how political commitment was mobilized in an attempt to reduce the high rate of maternal mortality in Nigeria, and to identify the lessons learned in the process. Although several international development partners and local nongovernmental organizations implemented various activities for preventing maternal mortality in the country in previous years, the lack of government ownership of such programs tended to reduce their sustainable long-term impact. Efforts to engage governments to prioritize the reduction of maternal mortality between 1990 and 1999 were unsuccessful due to the military dictatorship that ran the country during the period. The advent of democratic administration in 1999 provided a window of opportunity, which was utilized very extensively by both local and international partners working on the issue.

Several lessons were learned in the process. The first lesson is that an issue such as maternal mortality that has multifactorial components will require political mobilization at the highest level of governance for any effective traction to be achieved. President Obasanjo, as coordinator of the executive arm of government, needed to be the principal focus of the advocacy activities.

Second, we learned that the best way to begin the advocacy process is to build the awareness and understanding of the president about the issue, without necessarily assuming that he had prior knowledge of the determinants of the problem. This we did with the new president, under the platform provided by the *Saturday Forum with Mr. President*. Additionally, there is a tendency for change advocates to use an adversarial approach in an attempt to gain priority political attention for an issue, believing that government officials know the problem already and that they are merely failing to act. The results of this intervention indicate that this is not always the case, and that considerable time and patience need to be devoted to building policy makers' understanding of the problem. As an example, Dr. Mimiko was able to develop the highly successful Abiye maternal health program in Ondo State because of his prior knowledge of the issue, being a medical doctor himself.

The third lesson we gained from this effort was the need to offer simple and layered solutions to the problem rather than those based on a multicomplex analysis and interpretation of the problem. Policy makers have little time for high-level academic pontification of the solutions to a problem. By contrast, government officials, especially those in developing countries, would be more likely to act if simple and inexpensive solutions are provided in such a way that they can address them in a back-to-back manner, rather than being required to provide omnibus solution to a problem that has taken time to accumulate. The need to rank solutions in order to gain government's attention to the problem is therefore an important and critical strategy.

However, the program faced several challenges. Despite gaining high-level political commitment for maternal mortality prevention, the approach did not result in substantial deployment of resources to address the problem, nor was there a sustainable decline in rates of maternal mortality. Although new policies that addressed maternal health were developed, very few of these policies were actually implemented. Budgetary allocations for health were also marginal, with very little devoted to addressing maternal health.

A major question, therefore, is: What was responsible for this disconnect between the high-level political commitment and the actual implementation of policies and programs in maternal health? Our first explanation for this was the failure to infuse the bureaucratic system with the same zeal and passion shown by the president for reform in the health sector. Indeed, a major lesson we learned is that political commitment at the highest level of government should be followed up with second-layer advocacy and capacity-building activities for program implementers (e.g., program directors at the Ministry of Health) to ensure that they are able and willing to carry out the program activities. This is the only way to improve the quality of health systems governance necessary to reduce the burden of ill health in countries with manifestly low capacity to deliver health interventions.

A second problem was that many of the presidential ideas and thoughts about health were not completely integrated into the political discourse at the time. Health, being a multidimensional issue, has its own political calculations, which needed to be considered in efforts to attract attention to the sector. In a country like Nigeria, where the limited resources are often competed for by several sectors, the allocation of resources to a sector has its own political considerations. Although the president demonstrated a decisive will to address health issues, the failure to include health in his broad-based political strategy meant that his vision for health was not carried through following his exit in 2007. This oversight became glaring when the president who succeeded him failed to include health in his seven-point strategic agenda, despite the fact that the two administrations were products of the same political party.

According to Kaufman and Nelson (2004) and Roberts et al. (2004), the policy reform cycle can be better contemplated under four working cycles: (1) the initial placement in the policy agenda (agenda setting), (2) technical design of the reform process, (3) legislative consideration and passage of the reform bill, and (4) implementation of the adopted policy (implementation). While our efforts succeeded in placing the maternal mortality issue in the policy agenda, we failed to complete the entire policy reform cycle. In particular, our failure to include legislation as part of the reform diminished the sustainability and large-scale impact of the program. Also Fox and Reich (2013) identify four variables that are critical for achieving successful reform. These include institutions, ideas, interests, and ideology. Therefore, I believe that this initiative was also imperiled by the lack of effort to infuse relevant institutions and stakeholders with the ideas and ideology needed to consolidate the reform process. Going forward, these variables need to be taken into account in efforts to deepen political commitment for institutionalizing best practices for preventing maternal mortality in the country.

A third problem was the inadequate understanding of the connection between poor health outcomes and the national economy. Although the nation's economy improved considerably in the second half of the administration, there was no concomitant improvement in the nation's health indicators. This was in part due to a skewed distribution of the nation's wealth, as a considerable proportion of the population remained poor despite the improving economy. Although the administration attempted to relieve the health burden of the poor by allocating much of the debt relief gains to pro-poor policies, there was little evidence that such allocations actually benefitted the poor. Despite the improved economy, living conditions in the country did not improve due to the effects of pervasive poverty, illiteracy, and deteriorating infrastructure. Access to environmental sanitation, clean water, a healthy environment, good nutrition, transportation, and a ready source of energy remained inadequate, which considerably reduced the opportunity to create good health in the country. As part of a composite demonstration of political commitment, efforts should be devoted to rectify these intermediating determinants of maternal health.

CONCLUSIONS

We conclude this analysis by positing that political commitment is necessary to strengthen health systems and promote maternal health in democratizing low-income economies with high rates of maternal mortality. Achieving political commitment will be relevant for gaining community ownership of programs designed to address maternal health, leading to greater effectiveness and sustainability of such programs. It will also ensure the deployment of substantial state resources for addressing maternal health and for promoting accountability and transparency in the use of available resources. A stepwise approach based on building political actors' knowledge and understanding of the problem, identifying simple and cost-effective solutions to the problem, demonstrating the benefits that can accrue to political actors by addressing the problem, and entrenching the reform in the legislative process are some ways to advance social change for the issue.

However, political commitment alone is not sufficient. Sustainable progress can only be made if attention is paid to building policy entrepreneurs able to infiltrate the political system with ideas for reforming the health system to prevent maternal deaths. Maternal health experts also need to improve their expertise to constantly engage policy makers in creating the necessary changes. Furthermore, maternal health would have to be developed as part of a comprehensive agenda for achieving broader developmental goals. Strategic efforts, when devoted to addressing broader issues such as the promotion of basic education, empowering women, reducing the rate of poverty, and countering harmful cultural beliefs and practices, will contribute to accelerated declines in rates of maternal mortality in Nigeria and other low-income countries.

REFERENCES

AbouZahr, C., and T. Wardlaw. 2000. *Maternal Mortality in 2000: Estimates Developed by WHO, UNICEF and UNFPA.* Geneva: Family and Community Health Department, WHO. www.wqlibdoc.who.int/hq/2000/a81531.pdf/.

Aisien O. A., J. T. Akuse, L. O. Omo-Aghoja, S. Bergstrom, and F. E. Okonofua. 2010. "Maternal Mortality and Emergency Obstetrics Care in Benin City, South-South Nigeria." *Journal of Clinical Medicine Research* 2 (4): 55–60.

Chama, O. C. 2010. "An Assessment of Policies and Programs for Reducing Maternal Mortality in Borno State, Nigeria." *African Journal of Reproductive Health* 14 (3): 63–72.

Cohen, S. A. 1987. "The Safe Motherhood Conference, Special Report." *International Family Planning Perspectives* 13 (2): 68–70.

Dutta, A., and C. Hongoro. 2013. *Scaling up National Health Insurance Scheme in Nigeria: Learning from Case Studies of India, Colombia and Thailand.* Washington D.C.: Futures Group.

Federal Government of Nigeria. 1998. National Health Insurance Scheme Decree No. 35, May 10, 1999. Laws of the Federation of Nigeria.

Federal Government of Nigeria. 2004. *National Policy on Population for Sustainable Development.* Abuja, Nigeria: Federal Government of Nigeria.

Federal Ministry of Health. 1993. National Agency for Food and Drug Administration and Control (NAFDAC) Decree No. 15. Abuja, Nigeria: Federal Ministry of Health.

Federal Ministry of Health. 2001. *National Reproductive Health Policy and Strategy.* Abuja, Nigeria: Federal Ministry of Health.

Federal Ministry of Health. 2001a. *National Reproductive Health Policy and Strategy to Achieve Quality Reproductive and Sexual Health for All Nigerians.* Abuja, Nigeria: Federal Ministry of Health.

Federal Ministry of Health. 2002. *Nigeria National Reproductive Health Strategic Framework and Plan, 2002–2006.* Abuja, Nigeria: Federal Ministry of Health.

Federal Republic of Nigeria. 2005. *A Blueprint for Revitalizing Primary Health Care in Nigeria.* Abuja, Nigeria: Federal Ministry of Health.

Federal Ministry of Health. 2005a. *National Policy on Public-Private Part-nerships for Health in Nigeria.* Abuja, Nigeria: Federal Ministry of Health.

Federal Ministry of Health, 2006. *Presidential Retreat on Accelerated Reduc-tion of Maternal Mortality in Nigeria.* Abuja, Nigeria: Federal Ministry of Health.

Federal Ministry of Health. 2007. *The National Policy on the Health and Development of Adolescent and Other Young People in Nigeria.* Abuja, Nigeria: Federal Ministry of Health.

Federal Ministry of Health. 2007a. National Integrated *Maternal, New-born, Child Health Strate*gy, Government of Nigeria. Abuja, Nigeria: Federal Ministry of Health.

Fox, A. M., and M. R. Reich. 2013. "Political Economy of Reform." In *Scaling Up Affordable Health Insurance: Staying the Course*, edited by Alexander S. Preker, Marianne E. Lindner Dov Chernichovsky, and Onno P. Schellekens. Washington, D.C.: World Bank.

Harrison, K. 1985. "Childbearing, Health and Social Priorities: A Sur-vey of 22,774 Consecutive Hospital Births in Zaria, Northern Nige-ria." *BJOG: An International Journal of Obstetrics and Gynaecology 1985* 92, Supplement 5: 1–119.

Hogan, M. C., K. J. Foreman, K. J. Foreman, M. Naghavi, S. Y. Ahn, M. Wang, S. M. Makela, A. D. Lopez, R. Lozano, C. J. L. Murray. 2010. "Maternal Mortality for 181 countries, 1980–2008: A System-atic Analysis of Progress Made Towards Millennium Development Goal 5." *Lancet* 375 (9726): 1609–23.

Kaufman, R., and J. Nelson. 2004. "Conclusions: The Political Dynam-ics of Reform." In *Crucial Needs, Weak Incentives*, edited by R. Kaufman and J. Nelson, 473–519. Washington, D.C.: Woodrow Wilson Center Press.

Lambo E. 2005. *Breaking the Cycle of Poverty, Ill-Health and Underdevelop-ment in Nigeria.* Paper presented at a Guest Lecture of the College of Medical Sciences, University of Benin, Benin City, Nigeria.

Lozano R., H. Wang, K. J. Foreman, J. K. Rajaratnam, M. Naghavi, J. R. Marcus, L. Dwyer-Lindgren, K. T. Lofgren, D. Phillips, C. Atkinson, A. D. Lopez, C. J. L. Murray. 2011. "Progress Towards MDG 4 and 5 on Maternal and Child Mortality: An Updated Anal-ysis." *Lancet* 378 (9797): 1139–65.

Mimiko O. 2010. *Mobilising Resources for Achieving MDG-5: The Ondo State Example.* Paper presented at the 2nd Annual Safe Motherhood Lecture, organised by the Women's Health and Action Research Centre (WHARC). Abuja, Nigeria.

National Action Committee on AIDS. 2004. *Guidelines for Prevention of Mother to Child Transmission of HIV/AIDS in Nigeria.* Abuja, Nigeria: NACA.

National Action Committee on AIDS. 2005. *Nigerian National Response Information Management System (NNRIMS).* Abuja, Nigeria: NACA.

National Action Committee on AIDS. 2009. *National HIV Trend 1991– 2008.* Abuja, Nigeria: NACA.

National Action Committee on AIDS. 2013. *National HIV Trend 1991– 2008.* Abuja, Nigeria: NACA.

National Planning Commission (NPC). 2001. *National Economic Empowerment and Development Strategy.* Abuja, Nigeria: Federal Ministry of Planning.

National Population Commission [Nigeria]. 1992. *Nigeria Demographic and Health Survey 1990.* Calverton, Maryland: National Population Commission and ORC/Macro.

National Population Commission [Nigeria]. 2000. *Nigeria Demographic and Health Survey 1999.* Calverton, Maryland: National Population Commission and ORC/Macro.

National Population Commission [Nigeria]. 2004. *Nigeria Demographic and Health Survey 2003.* Abuja, Nigeria: National Population Commission, Federal Republic of Nigeria, and MEASURE DHS+ ORC Macro.

National Population Commission [Nigeria]. 2009. *Nigeria Demographic and Health Survey 2008.* Abuja, Nigeria: National Population Commission, Federal Republic of Nigeria, and MEASURE DHS+ ORC Macro.

National Primary Health Care Development Agency. 2012. *MSS—Midwives Service Scheme.* Abuja, Nigeria: National Primary Care Development Agency.

Obasanjo, O. O. 1999. *The New Dawn.* President Obasanjo's inaugural address to the nation, Abuja, Nigeria. www.dawodu.com/obas1 .htm.

Okonofua, F. E. 2006. *Report of a Survey of Policies of State Governments on Costing of Health Services, with Special Reference to Maternal and Child*

Health. Report presented to the presidency. Abuja, Nigeria: Federal Ministry of Health.

Okonofua, F. E. 2006a. *Maternal Health.* Brief for Nigeria Health Review (NHR 2006). Abuja, Nigeria: Health Reform Foundation of Nigeria (HERFON).

Okonofua, F. E. 2007. *Increasing Life Expectancy Through Improved Maternal and Child Health Programming in Nigeria.* Paper presented at the breakfast meeting with President Chief Olusegun Obasanjo GCFR at Aso Rock Villa, Abuja, Nigeria, organized by the Nigerian Development Forum.

Okonofua, F. E. 2007a. *Report on a Survey of Policies Of State Governments on Costing of Health Services, with Special Reference to Maternal and Child Health.* Report presented to the presidency. Abuja, Nigeria: Federal Ministry of Health.

Okonofua, F. E. 2013. "The Health Sector." *In Olusegun Obasanjo—The Presidential Legacy 1999–2007*, edited by O. O. Akinkugbe, A. Joda, O. Ibidapo-Obe, F. E. Okonofua, and T. Idowu, 218–257. Ibadan, Nigeria: Book Craft.

Okonofua, F. E. 2013a. "Integrated Maternal, New-Born and Child Health (IMNCH) Strategy: How Has It Advanced in Africa?" *African Journal of Reproductive Health* 17 (1): 9–14.

Okonofua, F. E., and E. Lambo. 2011. "Advocacy for Free Maternal and Child Health Care in Nigeria—Results and Outcomes." *Journal of Health Policy* 99: 131–38.

Ondo News. 2013. "Ondo Abiye: USA Conference Gets Success Report." *Ondo News,* January 16. www.ondonews.com/tag/abiye.

Roberts, M. J., W. C. Hsiao, P. Berman, and M. R. Reich. 2004. *Getting Health Reform Right: A Guide to Improving Performance and Equity.* New York: Oxford University Press.

Roberts, M. J., and M. R. Reich. 2011. "Counterfeit Medicines in Nigeria." In *Pharmaceutical Reform: A Guide to Improving Performance and Equity.* Washington D.C.: World Bank. http://documents.world bank.org/curated/en/2011/01/15156075.reform-guide-improving-performanve-equity.

Shiffman, J., and F. E. Okonofua. 2007. "The State of Political Priority for Safe Motherhood in Nigeria." *British Journal of Obstetrics and Gynecology* 114: 127–33.

Soyibo A., O. Odumosu, F. Ladejobi, A. Lawanson, B. Oladejo, S. Alay-ande. 2005. *National Health Accounts of Nigeria, 1998–2002.* Report submitted to the World Health Organization. Ibadan, Nigeria: University of Ibadan.

United Nations Millennium Declaration. 2000. 8th Plenary Meeting, No 55/2 (A/55/L.2). Geneva: United Nations.

UN Women. 1995. Fourth World Conference on Women, Platform for Action. www.un.org/womenwatch/daw/beijing/.

UNFPA. 1994. *ICPD Program of Action.* www.unfpa.org/public/global/publications/pid/1973.

Wall, L. L. 1998. "Dead Mothers and Injured Wives: The Social Context of Maternal Morbidity and Mortality Among Hausa of Northern Nigeria." *Studies in Family Planning* 29 (4): 341–59.

World Health Organization. 2000. *World Health Report 2000—Health Systems: Improving Performance.* Geneva: World Health Organization.

CHAPTER 10

Governing the Reform of the United Nations Health Systems for Palestine Refugees: Moving Mountains

Akihiro Seita

INTRODUCTION

Governing national health reform is always complex. Available resources are relatively, if not absolutely, limited, and the social and political environment does not always support change. Health sector reform is a "profoundly political process" according to Roberts et al. (2004, 61), thus it requires both technical and political feasibility analysis. The United Nations (UN) Relief and Works Agency for Palestine Refugees in the Near East (UNRWA) has been engaged in the reform of its health delivery system for the last two years, and we continue to assess its progress. UNRWA manages the largest health delivery system of all UN agencies, serving around five million Palestine refugees at present. UNRWA's health system is in the unique position of operating in multiple states while being managed not by the governments of those states, but by the UN. Additionally, because the situation of the Palestine refugees is heavily influenced by conflicting political forces in the region, the health system will likely persist for many years to come, and will need to adapt to the evolving environment.

Note: The data in this chapter are current as of July 2013 when it was written.

This chapter analyzes the reform process of UNRWA's quasi-governmental health system, highlighting the lessons we learned for the effective governing of health reform. Because this is the first major reform of UNRWA's health system, the chapter will answer questions regarding the motivations for reform, implementation of the family health team model, and how UNRWA is monitoring its progress.

BACKGROUND

UNRWA was established in 1949 following the 1948 Arab–Israel conflict, and became operational in 1950 to provide relief, human development, and protection services to Palestine refugees. Sixty-three years later, the agency continues to provide education, health, relief, and social services to more than five million registered Palestine refugees in five fields of operation: Gaza, West Bank, Lebanon, Syria, and Jordan. UNRWA has its headquarters (HQ) in Amman, Jordan, and in Gaza, which coordinate the activities of the five field offices (FO). The annual operating budget of UNRWA is around U.S. $550 million, which is provided exclusively by donor contributions. Eighteen percent of the operating budget is allocated to operating health services in the five fields.

UNRWA started the agency-wide reform process, called organizational development (OD), in 2006 to strengthen organizational capacity within all programs (health, education, relief, and social services) to serve Palestine refugees more efficiently and effectively. The OD reform process focused on four levels of change as determined by higher management within UNRWA: program management, human resource (HR) management, organizational process and systems, and leadership and management (UNRWA 2009, 51). One significant change during OD was the decentralization and empowerment of field offices in their operations. For example, HQ originally controlled the budget and HR management of all field office programs, however, as a result of the OD, both responsibilities were devolved to the field office level.

UNRWA health systems have three tiers: headquarters, which handle policy and strategy development, field health departments, which are primarily concerned with operational management, and health centers, which provide service delivery. UNRWA follows both United Nations and host country regulations. UNRWA provides primary health care at 139 health centers with three thousand staff, five hundred of whom are doctors. Health centers provide three main services: maternal and child health care (MCH) (including immunizations), noncommunicable disease (NCD) care and management, and general outpatient services. Aside from one in the West Bank, UNRWA does not run its own hospitals; UNRWA contracts with local hospitals in order to provide subsidized secondary or tertiary care. Financing of UNRWA's health services, around U.S. $100 million a year from donor contributions, is usually allocated as follows: 60 percent for staff salary, 20 percent for hospital payment, 15 percent for medicines and supplies, and 5 percent for other needs. All services at health centers, including medicines and laboratory tests, are provided free of charge. Cost of hospital care is shared with refugees. In principle, UNRWA has fee-for-service contracts with hospitals, and covers 70 percent of such payment with certain ceilings: the rest is borne by patients. This plan varies among the five fields based on the local situations.

UNRWA has contributed to sizable health gains for Palestine refugees. The infant mortality rate, for example, declined from 160 per 1,000 live births in the 1950s to less than 25 in the 2000s. Communicable diseases are largely under control, thanks to high vaccination coverage and the early detection and control of outbreaks using a health center–based epidemiological surveillance system. There were no reported cases of poliomyelitis, tetanus, diphtheria, pertussis, measles, or rubella among the refugee population in 2011; additionally, a declining incidence of typhoid and tuberculosis has been reported recently (UNRWA 2013, 36).

However, the context in which UNRWA operates is rapidly changing. Demographic transition within the Palestine population has resulted in a 3 percent growth rate and an increasing NCD burden. The dynamic political and social environment—influenced by the stagnant Arab–Israeli peace process, the current Syrian crisis, and other regional events related to the Arab Spring—also heavily influences the refugee population and UNRWA's ability to provide services. Additionally, the global financial crisis continues to seriously affect UNRWA operations, as it has led to financial constraints in host government health services, increased hospital prices, and reduced donor support.

These contextual changes motivated the reform process for UNRWA's health services in 2010. There is an increasing need to focus on the prevention of the behaviors and lifestyles that lead to an increased risk of NCDs, rather than on simply treating the disease once it has presented. Improvement of efficiency within UNRWA's health services is needed, as it will relieve the pressure experienced by higher costs, especially to treat NCDs, and dwindling funds. In addition, UNRWA recognized the benefit to a primary care model in that the "family doctor" allows families to build a relationship with their doctors over the long term. The hope is that continuous visits with the same doctor over the life course will improve overall family health, eliminating the need for cost-intensive treatments later in life. E-health and the appointment system also serve to reduce wait times and improve overall efficiency, creating a smoother client flow and reducing the amount of paperwork for the staff.

HEALTH REFORM STRATEGY DEVELOPMENT

The education program, the largest program of UNRWA, started its reform process in 2010; UNRWA envisaged health reform as the second phase. We at the health department of UNRWA began exploring health reform strategy in January 2011 as part of the OD, which was three months after the author joined UNRWA. The OD indicated that health reform should make health services more efficient and effective, particularly in response to the changing context in which UNRWA operates (UNRWA 2013, 16). We eventually adopted the family health team (FHT) model as the core health reform strategy by mid-2011, after six months of preparations, including extensive discussions, stakeholder analysis, and consultations. What follows is a summary of the steps taken to initiate and advance the reform.

Political Analysis (Stakeholder Analysis)

We began the initial discussions on UNRWA health reform with a full understanding that it is not only a technical but also—probably more importantly—a political process. At first, there was visible skepticism, if not resistance, to health reform among UNRWA health staff at all levels. While OD had brought important changes to UNRWA operations, health services at the delivery level had largely remained the same, and in some cases, declined, due to financial difficulties. A reform was thus perceived as reduction of services, and not improvement. In an effort to mitigate this kind of thinking, we conducted a stakeholder analysis and consultations from the very beginning of the process.

We began the political analysis by considering the main players and stakeholders in the reform process. In UNRWA's operations, there are four key stakeholders: Palestine refugees (beneficiaries), UNRWA staff (thirty thousand in total, with three thousand in health, and almost exclusively Palestine refugees), host governments, and donors. Their power, positions, and perceptions on reform are complex. They are, in principle, supportive of the improvement of UNRWA services. However, going about health reform the wrong way could easily change that support to opposition. Refugees, already dissatisfied with the reduction of services available due to financial constraints, were skeptical about reform, concerned that it signaled an even greater reduction of services. UNRWA staff were also skeptical of health reform, as they shared many of the concerns of the refugee population (the majority being refugees themselves). Seeing the dissatisfaction of both patients and staff, host governments shared concerns that health reform might do more harm than good. Donors, for their part, were concerned that UNRWA had not yet made decisive reform, in spite of the fact that the environment and needs of the population served had changed drastically.

After the political analysis, we decided on two key strategies. The first was to put the refugees at the center of the reform. The argument was that if the refugees were happy, the staff would, in turn, be happy. A happy staff and client base would, in turn, satisfy the concerns of host countries. Seeing the improvements among staff and client satisfaction, coupled with a supportive and satisfied host country might, in turn, compel donors to provide additional support. Our goal was primarily to facilitate the stakeholders' buy-in and equally, if not more importantly, avoid strong opposition.

The other strategy was to identify strong agents of change—within UNRWA's context, these are the heads of UNRWA health services, or chief of field health program (CFHP), in the five fields. They themselves are members of the refugee population, and have a strong influence on the staff in their fields. They are also well respected by and have good communication with refugees. Above all, they were to be the implementers of the reform once it started. This was particularly important within the context of OD, where field offices have largely autonomous operations.

Identification of the Problems in Palestine Refugee Health and Health Services of UNRWA

We then conducted an analysis on the problems that UNRWA health services were facing with both the data we had and the previous reviews on UNRWA health services (UNRWA 2013, 16). We strongly engaged UNRWA staff, particularly CFHP, in the situation analysis.

Among the refugee population, the demographic transition is under-way, which means that populations are living longer; aging populations have changing health care needs. Additionally, the epidemiological transition among refugees has already taken place; the main causes of mortality and morbidity for the population are no longer communicable diseases. The data clearly confirmed that the health priority for the refugee population is now noncommunicable diseases such as diabetes mellitus, hypertension, and cancer. NCDs account for 70 to 80 percent of the causes of morbidity and mortality among the refugees. In fact, the number of diabetes and hypertension patients cared for at UNRWA health centers has been continuously increasing by 3 to 5 percent per year; there were more than 210,000 NCD patients being cared for in 2012 (UNRWA 2013, 33).

However, UNRWA health services had not been responding to these changing needs; it was continuing to provide the same health services it had provided for decades. The services had been rather disease- or condition-specific and fragmented within the health center: MCH, NCD (diabetes and hypertension), and general walk-in clinic. Additionally, the health centers were overwhelmed with patients; the average daily medical consultations per doctor has long been around one hundred, too high to provide quality services in both principle and practice. UNRWA has had appointment systems in place for years, and also started e-health (electronic medical records) in several centers beginning in 2009: however, they have yet to show impact on the overall workload of doctors, though improvements were noted in the MCH clinics.

Initial Discussions on Health Reform and the Family Health Team Model

Based on the above analysis, we started initial discussions on health reform within and outside of UNRWA. The key question we sought to answer was, "What is the best way to address NCDs at our health centers?" This became the question we focused on because, as stated above, as a result of the demographic and epidemiological transitions, NCDs have become the core health problem for Palestine refugees; health centers continue to be the most important institutions in UNRWA health services. We raised this question to the CFHP, as they were among the key persons in health reform.

During the discussions, the idea of adopting family medicine, particularly in the form of a family health team (FHT) emerged as a response to our key question: "What is the best way to address NCDs at our health centers?" FHT is practiced in Ontario, Canada, where a FHT provides primary health care through a team of family doctors, nurses, and other health care providers. Each team is set up based on local health and community needs, and focuses on chronic disease management, disease prevention, and health promotion (Rosser et al. 2011, 165). FHT has also been introduced in Brazil, where it was expanded rapidly and produced a significant impact on infant mortality reduction and improved access to treatment and prevention for NCDs (Macinko and Guanais 2006; see also chapter 8 in this book). Adopting FHT in UNRWA health centers was strongly supported within the organization, as it is a progressive primary health care model, it addresses the burden of NCDs on the refugee populations, and it emphasizes the importance of families, a key cultural value for Palestine refugees.

In order to ensure we kept our key stakeholder, namely the refugees, in mind during the reform, we envisioned "Fatima," a fictional refugee woman and her family. We illustrated how Fatima and her family would benefit from the improvement of services before (Figure 10.1) and after (Figure 10.2) the introduction of FHT at health centers. We translated FHT into Arabic carefully as "فريق صحة العائلة". This is a literal translation (from right to left "team" "health" and "family"). "Family" is a very important notion in the Palestine refugee society, as is "health," and thus the translated phrase has very positive connotations within the

FIGURE 10.1 Pre-Reform: Fatima, Mohamed, and Their Children at the Health Center

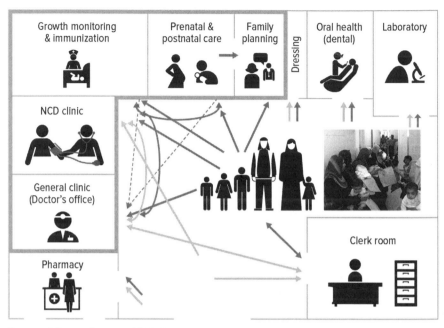

Photograph Source: Courtesy of UNRWA

FIGURE 10.2 Post Reform: Fatima, Mohamed and Their Children at the Health Center

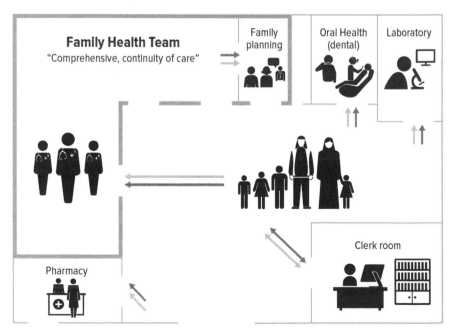

Note. Most icons in Figures 10.1 and 10.2 courtesy of TheNounProject.com.

Palestine culture. In March 2011, we organized a retreat with CFHP and adopted FHT as the reform strategy. We defined FHT as a family- and person-centered approach designed to provide holistic primary care at UNRWA health centers. Families are registered with and assigned to a provider team, or FHT, which consists of a doctor(s), nurse(s), and midwife(s). The provider team is responsible for all health care needs of the family registered over the life cycle.

Development of the Initial Log Frame (Results Chain) of Reform

After the initial agreement, we developed the first reform strategy document in July 2011 (UNRWA 2011). The target of the reform was to implement FHT in all 139 health centers by 2015. Provisional key outputs were: the reduction of doctors' workload, utilization of the appointment system as demand control, and improvement in the rational use of antibiotics. E-health was also an important support element. Copayment or prepayment of services at health centers was not an option, as it would have been politically impossible to implement under the environment at the time of reform. Improvement of NCD care was an important goal, but this could not happen without first reducing the workload per doctor. This led us to select the average daily medical consultations per doctor as one key quality improvement indicator, in conjunction with five others, discussed below in more detail.

As the FHT was a new venture within UNRWA, we first started with a pilot group of health centers, which allowed us to work out any unforeseen issues and build a logistical framework, or "log frame" (also known as "results chain"), which frames the FHT approach and supports its implementation at other health centers. This log frame would contain inputs necessary for implementing the FHT, as well as the process components, outputs (service improvement), outcomes (health status improved), and overall desired impact of the FHT. The goal was to develop a log frame that contained all the indicators necessary to determine the efficiency and effectiveness of the new model.

Financing Health Reform

Throughout the process outlined above, we engaged potential donors, including the governments of Austria, Japan, Luxembourg, and the United States. We dialogued with key donors to understand their perceptions of UNRWA and its health services, as well as their views of the FHT model. In discussions with donors, it was mentioned that this was the easiest idea to sell. The United States demonstrated their strong interest in supporting FHT and e-health by providing additional funds of approximately U.S. $400,000 to start the FHT pilot in 2011. The United States has continued to support the FHT and e-health expansion, with a total of U.S. $1.2 million to date. While not directly designated for FHT expansion, funds from other donors were often earmarked for the Health Department within the general fund, which covers all operational expenses for UNRWA.

HEALTH REFORM STRATEGY IMPLEMENTATION

Piloting of the Family Health Team

In October 2011, we started the FHT pilot in two health centers, one each in Gaza and Lebanon. Both centers were chosen because they met three selection criteria we set: they both had the presence of competent heads of the centers (senior medical officer, or SMO), both had strong support from the community, and both were close to their respective field office, allowing for proper supervision. CFHP took the lead in preparing for and conducting the pilot.

In Gaza, Beit-Hanoun health center was selected. It is located in a semi-urban area, serving approximately forty-five thousand registered refugees. The SMO spent two months preparing to implement FHT by first engaging health center staff and community representatives. Once he successfully gained buy-in from the staff, he created three FHTs in the center, each composed of two doctors, two nurses, and one midwife. He then divided the refugee population geographically into three groups, assigning each to a team. This process took a total of two weeks.

In the next six weeks, he focused on three main tasks. First, health center staff, particularly the doctors and nurses, had to be retrained. Under the old health model, caregivers specialized by experience in either MCH, NCD, or general health services. Under the new FHT model, they would have to be able to provide all three services to all patients if needed. Training was conducted via rotations, giving staff exposure to each specialty. The second task was to renovate and reorganize the health center so that each team was located together. Throughout this process, the SMO and health center staff continued the third task, dialogue with the community, by visiting community centers, schools, and other important institutions. Similar preparations took place at Rashidieh health center in Lebanon.

The pilot started in October 2011 in both centers, and the results of the pilots were encouraging. Patients showed very high overall rates of satisfaction. One patient in Lebanon said, "This new system is excellent. The time that nurses and doctors devote to me and my family is much more than before" (UNRWA and Columbia University 2012). Doctors also showed a good response to the new model (Figure 10.3).

FIGURE 10.3 Patients and Staff (Doctor) Satisfaction with FHT Pilot

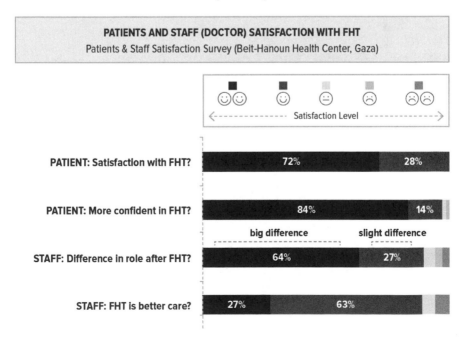

The number of average daily medical consultations showed a significant decrease in the health center in Lebanon: from around eighty consultations per day per doctor, to around fifty. Gaza showed a mild decrease from around one hundred to ninety consultations per day, per doctor, however there was a fairer distribution of workload among doctors in the health center. In the past, doctors at the walk-in/general services clinic had the bulk of the patient load, often as many as 120 patients a day, while MCH doctors had a much lower number of patients, often fewer than fifty patients a day. After FHT implementation, all doctors in the center had around ninety patients a day (because each team covers one-third of the population served). It became apparent that this equal distribution of the workload was one of the main reasons that doctors supported the FHT transition.

Innovations taken by the health center staff, particularly in collaboration with the community, were inspiring. The community played a large role in contributing to the preparation of FHT; for example, they collaborated with one another to decorate the walls of the health center with various health messages. This innovation also inspired some friendly competition between the three health teams in the health center in Gaza, who decorated the walls of their offices according to their team's logo and colors.

Expansion of the Family Health Team

Encouraged by the initial results from the pilot, we expanded the FHT model to other health centers in a staggered manner from early 2012. West Bank started its first FHT in January 2012, followed by Jordan in March 2012. Each field expanded the FHT model gradually but steadily, and by the end of the first quarter of 2013, a total of forty-one health centers had introduced the FHT model. The two-month preparation for implementing the FHT model that took place in both pilot health centers has been standardized to "Ten Steps to Start FHT" (Figure 10.4).

Due to the ongoing conflict in Syria, introduction of the FHT model has been suspended at those health centers. Consequently, all data below exclude Syria.

Responses from both communities and health center staff have been

FIGURE 10.4 Ten Steps to Start FHT

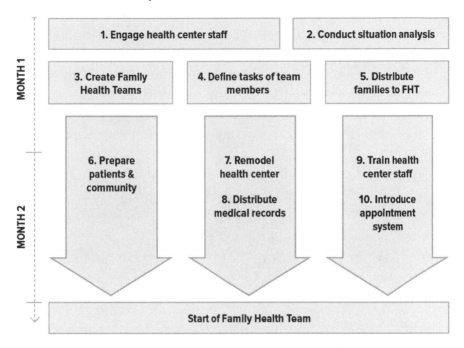

NOTE: The 10 steps are linked. Timing and sequencing of the steps may vary according to the local situations and needs.

largely positive. We have observed improvements similar to those in the pilot health centers in terms of number of daily medical consultations, and in other quality improvement indicators, discussed in more depth below. E-health was also expanded in many of these centers. As of the end of the first quarter of 2013, twenty-one of the forty-one health centers with FHT also have e-health—fifty-one health centers, total, have e-health.

In July 2012, the UNRWA health department, in partnership with the Mailman School of Public Health at Columbia University (New York, United States), conducted a joint assessment of the FHT implementation in three health centers, one in Jordan, one in Lebanon, and one in West Bank (UNRWA and Columbia University 2012). These centers were selected because they were among the first to implement FHT, and would likely have more measurable results. This assessment aimed to generate evidence on the impact of the FHT model by monitoring:

average daily medical consultations per doctor, patient wait time, duration of consultation, and rational use of medicines.

The assessment concluded that, as a result of FHT, patients were able to get information about their different health needs from one provider rather than seeing multiple specialists, thus decreasing repeat visits. FHT led to a decline in the number of daily consultations for doctors in all sites assessed. In Lebanon, the number of consultations per doctor, per day decreased from 123 to 83 as a direct result of FHT implementation (Figure 10.5).

Patient waiting time also decreased significantly (Figure 10.6). In Aqbat Jaber health center (West Bank), waiting time decreased from twenty-four minutes to six minutes per patient, on average. However, the contact time between doctor and patient did not notably increase, except at the center in Lebanon. The assessment indicated that the improvement in Lebanon was likely because its health center has the most functional appointment system with e-health, while others did

FIGURE 10.5 Average Daily Consultations per Doctor, Rashidieh (Lebanon) and Aqbat Jaber (West Bank)

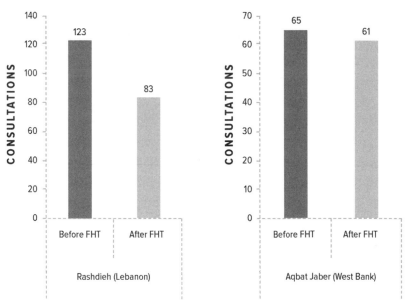

Source: UNRWA–Columbia University (USA) collaboration

FIGURE 10.6 Average Waiting and Consultation Time, Rashidieh (Lebanon) and Aqbat Jaber (West Bank)

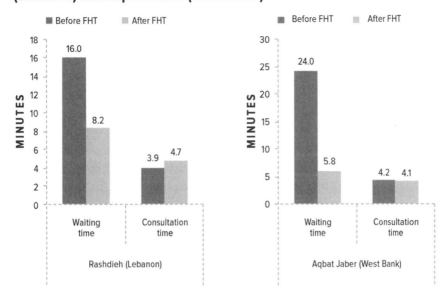

Source: UNRWA Columbia University (USA) collaboration

not. The lack of increase in patient/doctor interaction time remains a major concern, and is designated for further analysis and action.

DEVELOPMENT OF INNOVATIVE COHORT MONITORING SYSTEM FOR DIABETES AND HYPERTENSION

In the meantime, to help us improve the care of NCDs, we developed a new monitoring system for diabetes and hypertension care by adopting the quarterly cohort analysis methods of tuberculosis care and by using the e-health system (Khader et al. 2012, 1165). UNRWA has long provided care for diabetes and hypertension, as treatment of these NCDs is more manageable at the primary care level, and does not require extensive surgeries or specialists. The cohort analysis was initiated to answer "two deceptively simple questions: How many patients have been diagnosed and what happened to them?" Such simple questions were generally neither asked nor answered in the care of diabetes and hypertension. The methodology and results were published in *Tropical Medicine and International Health* in September 2012 (Khader et al. 2012). UNRWA's ability to successfully adopt the cohort analysis methods of tuberculosis care received a positive response from the global public health community in the *Lancet* (Mullins 2012), in an editorial in *Tropical Medicine and International Health* (Maher 2012), and the *International Journal of Tuberculosis and Lung Disease* (Seita and Harries 2012).

Finalization of the Health Reform Log Frame (Results Chain)

With the results obtained, we expanded and finalized the health reform log frame document in early 2013, including efficiency analysis of the reform using input and output indicators. The Department

FIGURE 10.7 FHT Log Frame and Results Chain

economy

Costs	Inputs	Process	Outputs	Outcome	Impact
$x	• Staff	• FHT	• Consultations	• NCD: control, prevalence; complications; premature deaths averted	• Long, healthy life expectancy
$x	• Medicines	• e-Health	• Rational prescribing		
$x	• Hospital services	• Renovation	• Lab diagnoses • Hospital treatment		
$x	• Other direct inputs	• General • NCD services	• NCD Rx compliance • NCD exams		
$x	• Indirect inputs	• MCH services	• FP commodities • Prenatal care • EPI vaccination • Essential medicines	• MMR • IMR • Contraceptive prevalence rate • EPI disease prevalence	

efficiency

effectiveness

for International Development (DFID) of the United Kingdom has supported this exercise by providing a health economist. The log frame/ results chain, shown in Figure 10.7, beginning with costs, inputs, process, outputs, and outcome, will help us illustrate UNRWA's desired impact. The key concepts used were economy (converting costs into inputs), efficiency (converting inputs to outputs), and effectiveness (converting inputs into outcomes and eventually impact). The logic behind the log frame is that, with proper implementation of FHT and e-health, quality of care will improve because the FHT will provide better consultations, will lead doctors to make more rational prescriptions, will help patients avoid unnecessary hospitalizations, and will improve NCD care compliance (outputs). This will, in turn, result in better control of NCDs and other conditions as outcomes, which will ultimately lead to the desired impact of a long and healthy life expectancy.

Six lead indicators were selected to gauge progress in the implementation of health reform through assessing input economy, output efficiency, and outcome effectiveness (Table 10.1). These six main indicators were selected by analyzing the specific ways in which we hoped FHT would improve efficiency in the health centers; they will be measured on an annual basis.

TABLE 10.1 Lead Indicators

	ISSUE	INDICATOR	WHY?
A1	Input economy	Total cost/capita	Overview of inputs per head (and main components)
A2	Output efficiency	Consultations/doctor/day	Doctor productivity; quality; also relevant for referrals/prescriptions
A3	Output efficiency	PHC cost/consultation-minute	Cost-efficiency of main output; "minute" rather than consultation for quality
A4	Output efficiency	Hospital referrals/capita	Fast-growing cost component, suspected unnecessary element; FHT approach should produce lower level
A5	Output efficiency	Prescriptions/capita	Suspected unnecessary element; FHT approach should produce lower level
A6	Outcome effectiveness	NCD patients controlled/NCD patients diagnosed	Major current/future disease area; suspected lack of quality/effectiveness; outcomes driver

Moreover, an additional fifteen indicators of secondary importance were selected for monitoring the reform progress in even more detail (Table 10.2).

The log frame report (UNRWA 2013, 7) concluded that the initial modeling suggested that "UNRWA's health services reform, based on family health team systems, aims to build on past achievements and has several elements that can clearly be justified on efficiency and

TABLE 10.2 Secondary Indicators

	ISSUE	INDICATOR	WHY?
B1	Input economy	Salary cost/doctor	Proxy for all salaries, largest single cost driver
B2	Input economy	Unit cost/15 tracer medicines	Proxy for all medicines, significant cost driver
B3	Input economy	Doctors/served population	Allocative efficiency
B4	Output efficiency	Cost/consultation	Supplementary to cost/consultation-minute
B5	Output efficiency	Wait time/consultation	Quality aspect for patients
B6	Output efficiency	Duration/consultation	Relevant for quality (doctor and patient), referrals and prescriptions
B7	Output efficiency	Consultations/capita	Behavioral cost driver; suspected variance between demographic groups
B8	Output efficiency	Cost/hospital case	Significant driver of hospital cost; itself negotiation-driven
B9	Output efficiency	Antibiotic + analgesics/all prescriptions	Significant driver of medicines cost; suspected unnecessary utilization
B10	Output efficiency	NCD patients compliant/all NCD diagnoses	Driver of NCD outcomes
B11	Outcome effectiveness	Served population/registered population	Utilization measure; patient satisfaction
B12	Outcome effectiveness	Maternal mortality rate	Ensure past outcome gains maintained
B13	Outcome effectiveness	Infant mortality rate	Ensure past outcome gains maintained
B14	Outcome effectiveness	Contraceptive prevalence rate	Long-term cost driver (and other gains)
B15	Outcome effectiveness	NCD late complications/NCD diagnoses	Major current/future disease area; indication of treatment quality

effectiveness grounds" (UNRWA 2013, 99). The log frame and the report helped us to document the sustainability and efficiency of the FHT reform. Our initial budget projections indicated that the expansion of FHT and e-health would require an initial investment of U.S. $7.5 million through 2015, with an additional U.S. $500,000 per year to maintain FHT and e-health after 2015 (UNRWA 2012). Donors' concerns are often that an improved quality of care will mean more expensive care. However, from the start, our focus has been on creating more efficient care, not more expensive care.

DISCUSSION, CONCLUSIONS, AND WAY FORWARD ON HEALTH REFORM

We at UNRWA have managed to reform the largest health system within the UN (quasi-governmental health system) quickly and effectively. Introduction and rollout of the reform was fast, efficient, and results-oriented. Over the course of two years, we were able to formulate the strategy for reform, acquire the buy-in of key stakeholders (six months), pilot the FHT in two sites (six months), and ultimately implement the FHT model in thirty-five health centers throughout UNRWA's service areas, excluding Syria (one year). As described above, joint assessments with partners and feedback from staff and clients confirmed that the desired results were achieved and underlined the potential efficiency, effectiveness, and sustainability of the reform.

The presence of a number of factors facilitated such impressive results. From the start, we conducted a clear political analysis on UNRWA's work environment, challenges, and strengths, which included a thorough understanding of the various stakeholders, their positions, and how they work and interact. Our stakeholders are in a unique position, as they are both client and staff. It was clear from the start that they needed to be the focus of this reform; we had to focus on making the client happy. Fatima and her family emerged as a way for UNRWA to keep the refugee at the center of the reform while also accounting for the shift in health needs among our target population, namely to the care and control of NCDs. The FHT model was the clear solution for Fatima and her family, and their various health needs.

We moved to pilot quickly, once the initial log frame of FHT was formulated. Our reasons for this were to try to find the modalities of the FHT implementation and, perhaps more importantly, to begin producing positive results in order to generate momentum within UNRWA. As a direct result of the CFHP's leadership and innovations by the health center staff, we managed to successfully implement FHT in the four fields where UNRWA is currently operating at full capacity. The presence of e-health in nineteen of thirty-five health centers implementing FHT was very helpful, as it helps facilitate the work of staff and conveys a sense of efficiency and convenience to patients. Additionally, we were well equipped to respond quickly to requests from donors for efficiency and effectiveness analysis.

Perhaps one of the best consequences of this reform was that it highlighted the capabilities and strengths within the UNRWA health system. UNRWA has provided uninterrupted health services to Palestine refugees for sixty-three years. Throughout that time, our services have expanded as the needs of the population have changed, and shortages of medicine are rare. Our staff are present and committed to their work, as almost all of them are Palestine refugees themselves. For these reasons, the successful, rapid expansion of FHT was possible, when it might not have been feasible in other settings around the world. UNRWA's success in implementing the FHT model relatively seamlessly in such a short time has also revealed its potential to serve as a model for future health reform worldwide.

There are, of course, a number of significant challenges facing UNRWA's health reform. The overall political context within the five fields in which the agency operates is extremely complex, unpredictable, and at times unstable. The current crisis in Syria is a prime example of the volatile nature of our work. A June 16, 2013, Syria crisis situation update from UNRWA stated that at least 235,000 of more than 500,000 Palestine refugees living within Syria have been displaced within the country since the conflict began in early 2011 (UNRWA 2013). In a UN news report from June 17, 2013, UNRWA Commissioner-General Filippo Grandi stated that "seven out of twelve of the agency's camps [within Syria] are now virtually inaccessible...killings, kidnappings, poverty, destruction, and fear have become part of daily life" (UN News Centre 2013). UNRWA estimates that 62,000 Palestine refugees from Syria had fled to Lebanon, while more than 7,500 had crossed into neighboring Jordan (UNRWA 2013). The stalemate in the peace process in the occupied Palestinian territory has also negatively affected both the health of refugees and UNRWA's ability to operate at full capacity in those regions. A report by the World Health Organization (2012) stated that the fundamental rights of Palestinians to access health care is often unprotected; "delays and denials of access violate patients' right to access and may lead to a deterioration of their health status" (2012, 6).

The global financial crisis has put more stress on UNRWA's exclusively donor-funded operation; financial deficits are anticipated at the beginning of every fiscal year. At the same time, the refugee population increases 3 to 5 percent every year, and the cost of operations likewise has continuously increased. This stretches the already tight UNRWA operating budget further. For example, UNRWA's health expenditure per refugee was U.S. $31.70 in 2011, which is quite low in this level of economy, even though we do not manage hospitals (WHO 2001).

In addition to the financial challenges facing UNRWA, we also face a barrier regarding the capacity of our staff. The majority of doctors at UNRWA are ordinary practitioners who are not trained family doctors, nor are they trained specialists. The insufficient capacity of our medical staff may potentially limit the doctors' ability to respond to patient needs under the FHT model.

Such challenges and our responses can be summarized by referring to the five control knobs for health reform, introduced by Roberts et al. (2004, 9)." ... [c]ontrol knobs describe discrete areas of health system structure and function that matter significantly for health system performance and are subject to change as a part of health reform." In this case, the five knobs of health reform are: financing, payment, organization, regulations, and behavior.

Financing refers to "the mechanisms by which money is mobilized to fund health-sector activities" (Roberts et al. 2004, 153). In UNRWA's case, 100 percent of funds are donor financed. We do not charge a tax or take insurance, and no fee for service is taken from the patients at any of our 139 health centers. In the event that a patient is admitted to the hospital, UNRWA shares the cost of the hospitalization with the patient. Any change to these policies could be devastating for health reform, as they are incredibly politically sensitive issues for both refugees and host governments. Rather than making changes to these policies at this stage, we will continue to deliver results to donors in an efficient and effective manner, displaying the sustainability inherent in this model. Additionally, we will continue to work through the FHT to strengthen our collaboration and trust with the communities and host governments in which we work. It is possible that in time we can explore additional funding mechanisms acceptable to all stakeholders.

Payment refers to "alternative mechanisms for distributing...funds" (Roberts et al. 2004, 212). UNRWA provides a standardized salary to its staff, which varies among fields, due to the host country's salary scale. Respective field offices control staff salaries, procurement of goods, and operational costs for institutions like health centers. This means that individual health centers do not have control over their budget. While not an issue to date, this could prove problematic if in the future senior medical officers have no incentive to produce results beyond baseline expectations. We are in the process of reforming the role of the health center in the UNRWA structure, which will hopefully give the SMO the authority to manage the health center and funds independently; we plan to expand the system once we have stabilized it. Additionally, we plan to bring in technical advisers who can help us reform our current system of hospital payments, an exercise started at one health center in the West Bank in February 2013. Currently, UNRWA covers 70 to 90 percent of the cost of patient hospitalizations. A goal of the FHT model is to reduce the number of unnecessary hospital admissions, which will hopefully reduce this out-of-pocket cost to UNRWA.

Organization refers "both to the overall structure of the health care system and to the individual institutions that provide health care services" (Roberts et al. 2004, 212). Thus far, UNRWA has only focused on the improvement of health centers through implementation of FHT, however this new model may necessitate a change at the field office and HQ level as well. Technical officers who specialize in NCDs and MCH at the health center, field office, and HQ level may no longer be essential to the daily functions of a health center operating under the FHT model. These personnel changes will need to be discussed at a later date.

Regulation refers to "the use of the coercive power of the state to change the behavior of individuals and organizations in the health care sector" (Roberts et al. 2004, 247). UNRWA follows the regulations of the United Nations in principle, and also, as appropriate and needed, follows their host country's regulations. So far, this has not impacted the health reform and FHT expansion.

Behavior refers to the "methods for changing individual behavior through population based interventions...[specifically,] how the behavior control knob [can] be used to improve health system performance and promote public health goals" (Roberts et al. 2004, 281). This is an area in which UNRWA has yet to make significant strides. As the above assessment confirms, FHT has been very successful at reducing patient waiting time, yet face time with the doctor has not increased as expected. There are several issues affecting this lack of behavior change. First, UNRWA has no continuous professional development (CPD) system of its own. Instead, staff are forced to rely on the CPDs of host countries, which are often inconsistent. Additionally, UNRWA doctors are trained as ordinary practitioners, not family doctors. Academically, family medicine is a four-year postgraduate specialty in the Middle East, something UNRWA does not have the capacity to provide. We could bring our doctors up to professional standards by providing one-year, on-the-job training in family health for at least five hundred UNRWA doctors initially, followed by training for support staff. However, a standard template for this training is not available, and tailored courses are quite expensive: it could cost approximately U.S. $10,000 per doctor. Despite these challenges, we recognize the need for such training, and will continue to work with partners to come to a suitable solution.

Governing health reform is a domain of political and social science. Technical correctness has no meaning unless it becomes politically correct, or at the very least *not incorrect*. UNRWA operates in one of the most politicized parts of the world, yet we have managed to deliver results by carefully creating an agenda that does not invite opposition and that is supported and promoted by key stakeholders and interested parties. Despite our impressive progress during the initial FHT reform, UNRWA continues to face steep obstacles in a climate of reduced donor

funding and changing demographics of our target population; additionally, each of the five control knobs for health reform poses its own challenges. Nevertheless, the enthusiasm and dedication with which our staff
operates on a daily basis is profoundly encouraging. It is this motivation
and drive that gives UNRWA the confidence to continue to improve
our services through health reform in order to better serve the five million Palestine refugees in our network.

REFERENCES

Hsaio, W. H. 2003. *What Is a Health System? Why Should We Care?* Cambridge, MA: Harvard School of Public Health.

Khader, A., L. Faraiallah, Y. Shahin, M. Hababeh, I. Abu-Zayed, S. Kochi, A. D. Harries, R. Zachariah, A. Kapur, W. Venter, and A. Seita. 2012. "Cohort Monitoring of Persons with Hypertension: An Illustrated Example from a Primary Healthcare Clinic for Palestine Refugees in Jordan." *Tropical Medicine and International Health* 17 (9): 1163–70.

Macinko, J., and F. C. Guanais. 2006. "Evaluation of the Impact of the Family Health Program on Infant Mortality in Brazil, 1990–2002." *Journal of Epidemiology and Community Health* 60 (1): 13–19.

Maher, D. 2012. "The Power of Health Information—The Use of Cohort Monitoring in Managing Patients with Chronic Noncommunicable Diseases." *Tropical Medicine and International Health* 17 (12): 1567–68.

Mullins, J. 2012. Cohort Reporting Improves Hypertension Care for Refugees. *Lancet* 380 (9841): 552.

Roberts, M. J., W. Hsiao, P. Berman, and M. R. Reich. 2004. *Getting Health Reform Right: A Guide to Improving Performance and Equity.* New York: Oxford University Press.

Rosser, W. W., J. M. Colwill, J. Kasperski, and L. Wilson. 2011. "Progress of Ontario's Family Health Team Model: A Patient-Centered Medical Home." *Annals of Family Medicine* 9: 165–71.

Seita, A., and A. D. Harries. 2012. "All We Need to Know in Public Health We Can Learn from Tuberculosis Care: Lessons for Non-Communicable Disease." *International Journal of Tuberculosis and Lung Disease* 17 (4): 429–30.

United Nations News Centre. 2013. "Palestinian Refugee Camps in Syria Now 'Theatres of War'—UN Agency Chief." United Nations News Centre, June 17. Retrieved June 27, 2013, http://www.un.org/apps/news/story.asp?NewsID=45198#.Ucv0-6JHJOg.

UNRWA and Columbia University, Mailman School of Public Health. 2012. *Update on Health Reform.* Amman, Jordon: UNRWA.

UNRWA and DFID. 2013. *Health and Education Efficiency in UNRWA.* Amman, Jordan: UNRWA.

UNRWA Health Department. 2011. *Modern and Efficient UNRWA Health Services: Family Health Team Approach.* Amman, Jordan: UNRWA.

UNRWA Health Department. 2013. *Annual Report 2012.* Amman, Jordan: UNRWA. http://www.unrwa.org/userfiles/2013052094159.pdf.

UNRWA. 2009. *UNRWA Medium-Term Strategy: 2010–2015.* Amman, Jordan: UNRWA. http://www.unrwa.org/userfiles/201003317746.pdf.

UNRWA. 2012. *Implementing the Family Health Team Approach in UNRWA Clinics: Case Study Reports from Lebanon, West Bank, and Jordan.* Amman, Jordan: UNRWA.

UNRWA. 2013. "Syria Crisis Situation Update: Issue 51." June 16. Amman, Jordan: UNRWA. Retrieved June 27, 2013. http://www.unrwa.org/etemplate.php?id=1789.

World Health Organization (WHO). 2001. *Macroeconomics and Health: Investing in Health for Economic Development.* Geneva: WHO.

World Health Organization (WHO). 2012. *Right to Health: Barriers to Health Access in the Occupied Palestinian Territory, 2011 and 2012.* Geneva: WHO.

CHAPTER 11

The Challenges of Governing the Korean National Health Insurance System and Its Implications: Financial Sustainability and Accountability

Hacheong Yeon

INTRODUCTION

No one questions that Korea's national health insurance performance has been truly phenomenal by the standard of time taken to achieve universal health insurance. The planning, adoption, and implementation of Korea's various health policy measures within a short period have been so impressive that many analysts have attempted to identify the secrets of Korea's success: whether government officials were wise and did the right things or whether Korea just got lucky. The strengths of Korea's health insurance system have been acknowledged in international evaluations. A recently conducted international comparison of national health systems by Conn Hamilton (2006, 26) ranked Korea's health system as fifth out of twenty-four major OECD countries. Korea's National Health Insurance Corporation has shared its knowledge and information on Korea's experiences through an international training program for the last five years. (In 2013, the agency changed its name to the National Health Insurance Service; this chapter uses the name NHIC throughout to refer to the organization.) In this program, 235 representatives from ninety-five developing countries were introduced to the Korean health insurance system; from 2005 to 2009, 498 guests from fifty-four countries also visited the NHIC to learn about the system (NHIC 2011).

Despite Korea's recognized achievements in developing its health insurance system, the process was not straightforward, involving significant trial and error before it developed into a system with universal eligibility. Furthermore, the national health insurance system (NHIS) still has many problems that require further improvement and financial reform.

This chapter explores lessons learned in the development of Korea's NHIS, while looking at current challenges of financial sustainability and accountability. The study begins with an examination of the existing socioeconomic factors in Korea leading to the adoption of NHIS and the process of implementing national health insurance. To this end, the chapter briefly examines the key characteristics of NHIS implementation. Next, the chapter reviews the current policy reforms related to administrative governance and operations. We then analyze the achievements and challenges of financial sustainability and governance of the NHIS today. The chapter concludes with the implications of financial sustainability and accountability and proposes a series of policy recommendations. By analyzing the lessons learned in developing Korea's NHIS, this study hopes to assist other developing countries in introducing and implementing their own national health insurance systems.

MAJOR MOTIVATIONS OF ADOPTION AND CHARACTERISTICS OF THE NHIS

Important elements in the early planning and adoption of Korea's NHIS were establishing medical institutions and building a collaborative system with medical service providers, strengthening political will and government financial support, and promoting public support for the new system. This section focuses on these three topics while examining the major socioeconomic factors that motivated Korea to introduce NHIS.

The Decision-Making Process for the Adoption of the NHIS

A major factor behind Korea's development of the NHIS was the country's economic development (shown in Figure 11.1). The first three

FIGURE 11.1 Transformation of the Korean Economy and NHIS

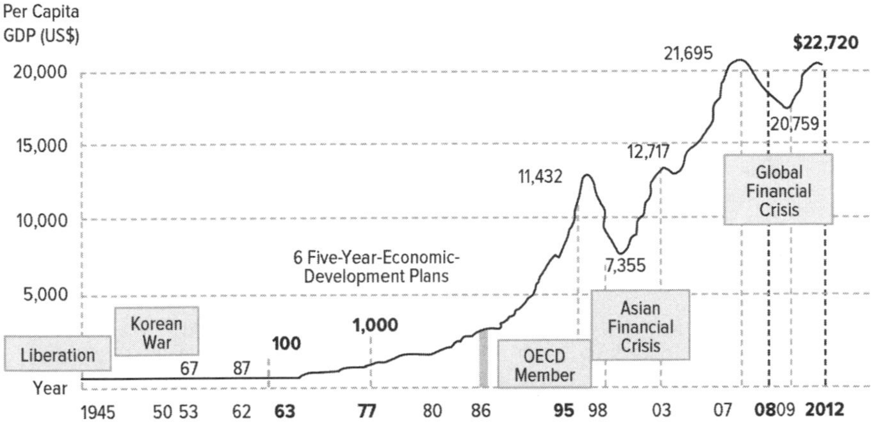

Note: Compulsory NHIS introduced in 1977; universal eligibility achieved in 1989.

Five-Year Economic Development Plans (1962–76) achieved their objectives and raised per capita income, providing the material foundation that enabled an accelerated adoption of four major social insurance institutions, one of which was health insurance. The government was aware that low-income groups confronted huge socioeconomic burdens in their access to medical care and sought to respond to these demands by setting the health sector as a national priority. In other words, successful economic development and the political decisions made by government leaders enabled the institutional foundation for the adoption of compulsory health insurance in Korea. Korea's social health insurance system thus originated from efforts to address the problems confronted by the relatively impoverished classes overshadowed in the trajectory of growth.

To implement compulsory health insurance, which began on July 1, 1977, the government needed to establish the relevant infrastructure and institutions. The most urgent priority was to develop medical facilities that could provide adequate medical services all over the nation. At the time, more than 80 percent of medical institutions were located in large cities. The government sought to address this imbalance by supporting the building of private hospitals and expanding the availability of medical equipment in rural regions and near industrial complexes with inadequate medical services while also modernizing the medical equipment in national and public hospitals. This approach was adopted as formal policy in a resolution passed at the Economic Ministerial Council in March 1978 to establish and invest in hospitals in industrial complexes and underserved rural areas, and also in a resolution at the Economic Ministerial Council passed in December 1980 to implement investment and a loan plan to support private hospital facilities. As part of this plan, from 1978 to 1992, Korea acquired loans from Japan's Overseas Economic Cooperation Fund (OECF), Germany's Kreditanstalt für Wiederaufbau (KFW), and the International Bank for Reconstruction and Development (IBRD) to provide financial support to a total of 239 institutions, including 168 private hospitals (Ministry of Health and Welfare 2006).

In the 1970s, the government decided to organize a study tour of Japan to learn about its health insurance system and governance methods. A special research team on Japanese medical insurance was organized jointly between the Korean Medical Association (KMA), the Korean Hospital Association (KHA), and the Ministry of Health and Welfare (MOHW). They made several visits to Japan culminating in a special report, *The Medical Insurance Fees and the Insurance System in Japan*, on December 16, 1976. This report had a significant influence on the legislation for health insurance fee payments and on the structure and operations of the NHIS in Korea, especially the use of a modified version of Japan's point system for setting reimbursement fees. The KMA and KHA, in collaboration with the MOHW, determined that payment should be charged by a fee-for-service (FFS) method while maintaining Korea's customary level of fees. This was probably the only plausible way to introduce a health insurance system without a large break from the customary fee system. As requested by the KMA and KHA, the FFS system was adopted for determining fees to pay for medical services in the new insurance system.

To secure and build a collaborative system with medical institutions, the MOHW and the Health Insurance Council collaborated with key representatives of the medical services sector (KMA and KHA) to request that each medical institution participate in an official contract for providing treatment. By late December 1977, the government had secured an average of fifty designated medical institutions for each health insurance cooperative, thus launching a system that provided policyholders with increased access to medical services.

To ensure public adoption of insurance, the government and the health insurance cooperative association launched promotional campaigns. In the early years of health insurance, eligibility was given to employment-based policyholders at workplaces with five hundred or more employees based on strict criteria, which allowed the system to operate without any great conflicts and precluded the need for strong promotional campaigns from the government. However, the introduction of health insurance for self-employed people in rural communities required citizens to understand the unique features of social insurance, and public promotion was a very important task to emphasize that the new insurance program was a governmental program and not from a private company or a local project. The promotional campaign intensified from July 1987 to the end of that year. During this period, new regional medical insurance cooperatives were established and public officials, school personnel, and industrial complexes were incorporated as members, and the national medical insurance system became unified.

In short, the factors that led to the emergence of Korea's universal NHIS in 1988–1989 were the historical outcomes of: (1) strong political decisions and financial support from the national government, (2) legislation in the form of the Medical Insurance Act (1963), (3) the implementation of seventeen demonstration pilot projects for both the employed and self-employed during 1965–76, (4) efforts in policy research, including a study tour abroad and plans to prepare the institutional foundation of national health insurance, (5) the establishment of medical insurance cooperatives and implementation of employment-based health insurance at workplaces with five hundred or more members, (6) the active participation of the KMA, KHA, and civil society, and (7) active promotional initiatives and efforts directed toward citizens (1987–88). All of these factors contributed to the achievement of national health insurance, which Korea accomplished in 1989.

MAJOR CHARACTERISTICS OF NHIS

Korea's national health insurance system had four major characteristics at the time of its introduction.

First, risk pooling through the compulsory entry of all citizens: The purpose of this measure was to pool risks, by responding to social risks collectively and by avoiding adverse selection such as cherry-picking or poaching of enrollees, which pushes health insurance costs up. This was a lesson learned from several demonstration projects, which motivated Korea to disperse the risk, which is regarded as the joint responsibility of the entire society as a whole, through compulsory insurance for all citizens.

Second, scaled insurance premium based on financial ability and provision of identical benefits: The NHIS took into consideration the financial ability of each individual when securing its funding through insurance premiums by scaling the amount of insurance premiums assessed and collected based on income. But it then provided the same benefits to members regardless of the individual contribution. These rules, along with the compulsory participation of all citizens, have allowed the health insurance system of Korea to strengthen health solidarity while effectively redistributing income from high-income groups to low-income groups. When the health insurance premium charges are compared to the benefit costs, the effect of income redistribution on different income classes (as indicated by insurance premium tiers) can be clearly observed (NHIC 2011, 2–11).

Third, governmental financial support: Initially, the employment-based health insurance plan was designed to evenly split the insurance premium charges between the employer and the policyholder, enabling the system to operate without support from the government. However, when health insurance was introduced for the rural self-employed in 1988 and for urban self-employed in 1989, these policyholders raised concerns about the 50 percent support for insurance premiums received by the employment-based policyholders. Moreover, the difficulties in assessing the incomes of self-employed policyholders and in collecting premiums through a withholding system placed a burden of excessive insurance premiums on the self-employed in lower income groups. In response to these inequities, political parties and the government engaged in negotiations about subsidizing the costs of some insurance benefits, and insurance management and operations, using funds from the government budget. The insurance system underwent a process of operating with a partial dependence on financial support from the government. The financing system thus became a hybrid model, which is not financed either completely by taxes (Nordic model) or by social insurance premiums (German model) (Bonoli 1997, 351–72).

Fourth, debate over the single insurer: A major reform to the NHI system occurred in 2003, when the numerous cooperative-based groups that provided governance for Korea's NHIS became financially and administratively unified under a single insurer represented by the NHIC. This structural reform of the system in 2003 constitutes one of Korea's most important health reforms (along with the reform that separated dispensing from the prescribing of medication and gave doctors and pharmacists separate roles in the health system).

The debate over the single insurer for the NHIS in Korea was heavily influenced by the prevailing ideas about health policy—ideas that had been floating around and bumping into one another after democratization began in the country (during the 1980s). Also, as Fox and Reich (2013) explain, ideology affects partisan competition and political bargaining strategies. Ideologically driven partisan competition in Korea affected this debate over a single insurer. In general, parties on the left of the ideological spectrum supported more redistributive proposals, including financing through general tax revenue and publicly delivered health services. Parties on the right preferred the status quo or more regressive forms of financing, with private-sector involvement and limited government participation.

The debates in Korea on the policy decisions to unify the health insurance cooperatives took place over two decades (1980–2003), involving complex entanglements of various social forces with interests at stake. In particular, the opposition political party (liberal) used the NHIS reform to galvanize public support by making it an election platform in the late 1990s, promising a sweeping approach that would replace the unpopular multiple insurance cooperative systems with an integrated single-insurer system. The electoral victory of the liberal party in 1997 provided the political basis for this major reform.

The process of integrating the management, operations, and finances of Korea's insurance systems began on October 1, 1998, with the creation of a National Health Insurance Management Corporation that targeted 227 regional medical insurance cooperatives, including public officials and private school personnel (Table 11.1). However, this integration occurred only at the administrative level; the finances remained separated, so that the public and school health insurance and the self-employed health insurance operated from two different funds. Then,

TABLE 11.1 The Road to Single Insurer of the NHIS

Category		Prior to Oct. 1, 1998	After Oct. 1, 1998	After July 1, 2000	After July 1, 2003
Management Integration	Self-employed cooperative	227	National Medical Insurance Management Corporation (1 unit)	National Health Insurance Corporation (1 unit)	
	Public and school corporation	1			
	Employment-based cooperative	142	142		
Financial Integration	Self-employed cooperative	227	1	1	Health insurance finances (1)
	Public and school	1	1	1	
	Employment-based	142	142		

Source: National Health Insurance Corporation, 2012.

on July 1, 2000, a second national integration took place, which combined the National Medical Insurance Management Corporation with 142 employment-based medical insurance cooperatives, to establish the single insurer represented by the NHIC, thereby accomplishing the complete unification of management and operations. At the same time, some degree of financial integration was also achieved. The funds for the public and school medical insurance and the employment-based health insurance (EHI) were integrated into a single fund; the regional health insurance remained separate financially. Then, in July 2003, the regional-based health insurance (RHI) and the EHI merged their finances, finally completing the integration and consolidation of the NHIS (Table 11.2).

It is worth noting, however, that even after Korea launched a health insurance system completely integrating both administrative and financial operations, the criteria for assessing insurance premiums were not integrated and remained as a binary structure. This organizational separation has caused persistent problems of inequity between EHI policyholders and RHI policyholders regarding insurance premiums, a point we return to below.

TABLE 11.2 The Major Characteristics of the NHIS (2012)

Types	Universal Social Insurance System – A Single Insurer
Population coverage	Whole population except the poor ('medicaid'); two types of coverage ('accounts') a. Employees: ordinary employees, civil servants, private school teachers, and military personnel dependents b. Residents: self-employed, temporary or daily workers, farmers, etc.
Financing	Contributions plus government subsidy a. Employees: 5.64% (total): 2.82% employee, 2.82% employer, and government subsidy b. Residents: contributions depending on taxable income, property, sex, age, and household size, plus government subsidy * Sources of government subsidy consist of general tax revenue and surcharge on tobacco
Benefits	Benefit package is uniform • Statutory benefits: (mainly in-kind) medical examination, drugs, surgery, nursing, ambulance, and check-ups. Duration: unlimited • Patients co-payment: 20% of hospitalization fees, and certain rates of co-payment of outpatient fees (30% clinic and pharmacy, 40% hospital, 50% general hospital)
Reimbursement	• Fee-for-service based on RBRVS (Resource-Based Relative Value Scale) scheme; fees are negotiated in a committee participating consumers, providers, and government • Additional fee allowed (15% clinic, 25% hospital, 30% tertiary hospital) and special consultation fees for specialists at hospitals • DRG based fees are applied in 7 types of DRG (Compulsory from July 2012)
Organization	Ministry of Health and Welfare Affairs: Supervision and policy decision NHIC (National Health Insurance Corporation): eligibility of policyholders, collection of premium and reimbursement HIRA (Health Insurance Review Agency): examine claims and review

Governance and Administrative Accountability

Figure 11.2 shows the governance structure of Korea's NHIS, outlining the relationships among the main parties according to their key accountabilities. The MOHW is the main governmental agency responsible for supervising NHIS policies and directing operations. The Ministry organizes and operates the Health Insurance Policy Deliberation Committee (HIPDC), which decides on key issues, including the criteria for treatment costs covered by insurance, the assessment of treatment costs, the level of insurance premiums for policyholders, and final decisions on

FIGURE 11.2 Governance Accountability of the NHIS

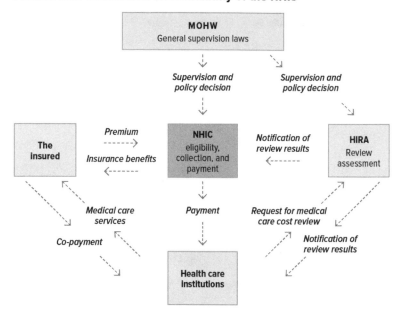

health insurance fees. The HIPDC is composed of twenty-five members, with the vice-minister of the MOHW serving as the committee chair and the other members constituted by eight representatives of policyholders, eight representatives of providers, and eight representatives of the public interest.

The NHIC is the single insurer (and payer) for the NHIS, and is the public agent of operation and management. The NHIC manages the eligibility of policyholders and dependents, assesses and collects insurance premiums, reimburses and handles post-management of insurance benefits fees, offers health promotion and prevention programs, pursues educational training and promotional efforts on health insurance, conducts research, and pursues international collaboration. The NHIC also provides oversight and regulation against fraud and abuse, which includes: (1) individual guidance for potential inappropriate charges and practices, (2) disciplinary actions by cancelling contracts (de facto expulsion from medical practice), and (3) criminal prosecution of severe fraud cases. Their work on benefits includes negotiations with pharmaceutical companies on drug prices, reimbursement of insurance benefit fees, and the conclusion of contracts determining the price per relative value unit (the conversion factor used for reimbursement points). In addition, the

NHIC is responsible for operating and managing the Finance Operation Committee, which decides on financial issues relating to contracts on covered treatment costs, changes in the insurance premium rate, the adjustment of the insurance premium, and review and resolution of insurance premium deficits, among other things.

Another major entity is the Health Insurance Review and Assessment Service (HIRA), which is independent from the NHIC. Almost all medical and pharmacy claims are submitted electronically, which is an effective means of lowering the administrative costs of claims review. Korea has already achieved nearly 100 percent computerization of the claims review process; the use of computerized claims will, it is hoped, provide an effective tool for cost containment.

The claims review and reimbursement functions in the Korean NHIS are separate (unlike in Japan). Treatment institutions submit claims for reimbursement to the HIRA for services, the HIRA reviews the claims and reports its findings to the NHIC, which reviews the findings and adjusts the reimbursement before paying the treatment institution. Claims review in Japan does not evaluate the quality of care; however, the Korean HIRA is legally authorized to assess the quality of care of providers. HIRA reviews the claims for treatment costs covered by insurance, evaluates the suitability of treatments, and confirms the eligibility for treatment coverage. HIRA also determines the resource-based relative value scale (RBRVS), the amount of reimbursements for treatment costs and pharmaceutical costs, and the ceiling on treatment material costs. HIRA is also responsible for operating and managing the Specialized Evaluation Committee on New Medical Technologies that determines the range of benefits for new medical technologies.

EVALUATION OF THE ACHIEVEMENTS AND FINANCIAL SUSTAINABILITY

From 1988, in the wake of democratization, Korea's NHIS has continuously expanded the population covered and range of benefits. Under the previous authoritarian regimes, health insurance was gradually expanded in a piecemeal fashion, which primarily benefited economically vital coalitions and sectors. After democratization began in 1988, increased political competition resulted in a more dramatic expansion of benefits. Specifically, the political party in power used universal coverage as a strategy to gain popular support. While Korea's health insurance is regarded as having successfully achieved its original objectives of "diffusing and reducing the burden of medical fees by means of medical insurance" (as stipulated in 1977 in the early period of its establishment), in reality the NHIS has fallen short of these goals. This section evaluates the achievements and financial sustainability of Korea's NHIS.

Evaluation of Achievements

Expansion of Population Eligibility

Universal population coverage in Korea was achieved by moving health insurance membership from voluntary to compulsory, with the establishment of NHI in 1977, and by moving from insurance linked to formal employment to insurance that included the self-employed. Compared to other countries, Korea attained nationwide health security in the fastest time. Germany took 127 years to achieve nationwide medical insurance, Austria took seventy-nine years, and Japan took thirty-six years (1927–61). Meanwhile, Korea took only twenty-six years from the time of adoption of the Medical Insurance Act in 1963, and just twelve years from the time of the institution of employment-based health insurance in 1977 to achieving universal coverage in 1989.

Table 11.3 shows how population eligibility (the ratio of the insured to total population) changed from 1977 to 2012. In 1977, there were 3.2 million eligible people, constituting only 8.8 percent of the total population; thereafter, the eligible population continually increased, rising to 24.2 percent in 1980 and then to 98.2 percent in 2012. In 2011, Korea's insured population was composed of the following groups: employees (54.8 percent), civil servants and private school teachers (9.2 percent), self-employed (32.7 percent), and Medicaid recipients (3.3 percent).

In addition, there was an increase in the number of foreigners in Korea and Korean citizens residing abroad eligible for national health insurance. As of late 2010, the total number of foreigners and citizens residing abroad who held health insurance policies totaled 481,088, consisting of 456,932 foreigners and 24,156 citizens residing abroad. Since 2001, when health insurance eligibility was extended to these groups, the number of people covered in these groups has increased nearly sevenfold.

TABLE 11.3 Health Insurance Eligible Population

Category		1977	1980	1985	1990	2000	2006	2008	2009	2011
Total Population		36,412	38,124	40,806	42,869	47,008	48,297	48,597	48,760	50,757
Health Insurance	Total (eligibility rate)	3,200 8.8%	9,226 24.2%	17,995 44.1%	40,180 93.7%	45,896 97.6%	47,410 98.2%	48,160 99.1%	48,614 99.7%	49,127 96.8%
	Employment-based	3,140	5,381	12,215	16,155	17,578	23,724	25,774	26,761	28,426
	Private schools	–	3,780	4,210	4,603	4,826	4,721	4,642	4,651	4,632
	Regional	60	65	1,570	19,422	23,492	18,965	17,743	17,201	16,068

Note: Medicaid enrollees are excluded in this table.
Source: National Health Insurance Corporation, Homepage of NHIC, 2012.
Unit: 1,000 persons

Expansion of the Range of Insurance Benefits

Improvement has also been achieved in the coverage of health insurance benefits, which has steadily expanded to include high-cost, severe illnesses. Benefits were also extended to previously uncovered services such as examinations performed with high-cost equipment using advanced technology (CT in 1996, MRI in 2005). Financial support has also been provided (through reduced co-payments or lower ceiling on total co-payments) for individuals with high-cost, severe illnesses or rare or incurable diseases, and socially vulnerable groups such as people with low incomes, elderly citizens, children, disabled persons, and pregnant women.

In addition, Korea has gradually expanded the time period of coverage each year for expenses that could be charged to the insurer. In 1989, when the nationwide health insurance system was first launched, the period of benefits coverage was limited to 180 days per year, but Korea began to incrementally extend the annual time limit on treatment covered by insurance beginning in 1994. (The 180 days limit for coverage included the number of treatment days for inpatient and outpatient services as well as the number of prescription days per medicine; coverage thus included, for example, daily hypertension medication for six months and then the patient needed to pay out of pocket.) From July

1994, the time limit was extended to 210 days for elderly citizens aged sixty-five or over, and from 1996, the time limit on benefits was eliminated for the elderly aged sixty-five or over, citizens with registered disabilities, designated persons of national merit with injuries, and patients receiving treatment for tuberculosis.

The number of days for benefits coverage also increased for ordinary policyholders, expanding by increments of thirty days to 210 days in 1995, 240 days in 1996, 270 days in 1997, 300 days in 1998, and 330 days in 1999, finally reaching 365 days in 2000. The limit on the number of benefit coverage days was eliminated entirely beginning in 2001. However, after the implementation of the policy separating the dispensing of medicines and medical services, Korea's national health insurance suffered deteriorating financial conditions and the government reinstated a limit to the number of days of benefit coverage per year. This system to limit coverage to a certain number of days was completely eliminated beginning in 2006 (Won 2008, 286).

Another important reform was the introduction of a "co-payment ceiling system" in 2004, which allowed for refunds on request of co-payments that exceeded the ceiling (or cap). The co-payment rate for ordinary patients (without special vulnerabilities) is 20 percent of the treatment fee for inpatients, and for outpatients the rate is 30 percent at clinics, 40 percent at hospitals, 50 percent at tertiary care hospitals, and 30 percent for pharmaceutical expenses. In addition, in cases where the co-payment for insurance benefits exceeds 1.2 million won spent within thirty days, a co-payment compensation system can return 50 percent of the amount exceeding the cap post facto. However, the deadline to apply for this system was short and there was no upper limit to the 50 percent rule, hence the coverage for patients with high-cost, severe diseases was poor.

This system was later replaced with a supplemented co-payment ceiling system, which provides for differential limits on the maximum amount of out-of-pocket payments that can be charged based on income level. In other words, policyholders in the lower 50 percent tier for insurance premiums are annually waived 2 million won or more on co-payments, policyholders in the 30–50 percent tier for insurance premiums are waived 3 million won or more on co-payments, and policyholders in the upper 20 percent tier of insurance premiums are waived 4 million won or more on co-payments. Thus, health insurance policyholders with relatively lower income levels are provided with a greater degree of medical security. But still, medical services are not as accessible as they could be for low-income classes and socially marginalized groups. Consequently, Korea should conduct evaluations of this co-payment ceiling system policy and gradually expand its scope, while further strengthening measures to support vulnerable social groups that may currently be marginalized from the benefits of health insurance.

In the inpatient sector, while the nominal rate of coverage has remained around 80 percent since 1995, the effective rate of coverage only reached around 65 percent in the early 2000s, and thereafter fell to around 55 percent. From 1995 to the early half of the 2000s, the gap between the nominal coverage rate and the actual effective coverage rate tended to decrease, but then the gap widened again. In the case of outpatient treatment, both the nominal coverage rate and the actual effective coverage rate are improving, and the discrepancy between the two is also diminishing (Kim 2011, 87).*

At the same time, the rate of individual co-payment has decreased, which alleviated some of the financial burden of medical care on the household budget. According to OECD Health Data, the percentage of total medical expenditures charged as co-payments to policyholders in Korea decreased from 56.5 percent in 1985 to 36.9 percent in 2004. During the same period, the percentage of individual co-payments in OECD countries slightly increased from 16.3 percent to 19.8 percent. Although Korea's co-payment percentage remains high when compared to the OECD average, remarkable progress has been made in narrowing the gap between Korea and OECD countries, from 40.2 percent in 1985 to 17.1 percent in 2004 (NHIC 2007, 15).

Access to medical services has also improved from 1977 to 2010. Coverage for the inpatient sector exhibited a slight increase, while coverage for the outpatient sector improved by a relatively large margin. (Detailed information is available from the author.) Compared with

---

* *Nominal coverage rate (Coverage rate for areas included in health insurance benefits) = Statutory co-payment/(Payment by the insurer + Statutory co-payment)*

Actual effective coverage = (Statutory co-payment + Out-of-pocket payment for uninsured benefits)/ (Payment by the insurer + Statutory co-payment + Out-of-pocket payment for uninsured benefits)

outpatient visits in 1977, when health insurance was first introduced, the number of outpatient visits per person has risen from 0.65 days to 16.4 days in 2010, and this is more than double the average number of 7.3 days in OECD countries. If we compare country averages for outpatient treatment days per individual, we see that for Korea the average was 11.8 days, for Sweden it was 2.8 days, for the United States 3.8 days, for France 6.6 days, and for Germany 7.0 days, while the OECD average was 6.8 days in 2010 (NHIC 2011). Moreover, the number of days for inpatient hospitalization per person has also increased from 0.11 days to 2.12 days, which is above the OECD average of 1.2 days (OECD Health Data 2012).

Evaluation of Financial Sustainability

Health insurance is financed primarily through monthly insurance premiums contributed by policyholders and to a lesser degree through government subsidies from general tax revenue and a surcharge on tobacco. Meanwhile, financial expenditures consist of the insurance benefits costs charged by the medical providers as compensation for the patients' usage of medical services and the administrative expenses to maintain the insurance system.

Table 11.4 shows that the NHIS financial environment is questionable now. Recently, expenditures have increased much faster than the revenues as the benefits covered have expanded and the population ages. The substantial increase in benefit expenditures and premium levels can be explained partly by the increase in medical service fees and increasing patient visits, but also partly by the rapid increase in medical service spending for the elderly population. It is projected that Korea will be an aged population society by 2018 and that medical service costs for the elderly population may account for more than 40 percent of the total by then. If the low fertility trend (the total fertility rate for Korea was 1.23 in 2010 and 1.30 in 2012) continues, there are grave concerns about the sustainability of the NHIS through revenues from insurance premiums as the growing elderly population must be supported by comparatively fewer members of the system and society (Sah 2010, 4).

TABLE 11.4 Financial Status of the NHIS

		Annual Growth Rate	2002	2003	2004	2005	2006	2007	2008	2009	2010	2011
Revenue	Total	12.55	138,903	168,231	185,722	203,325	223,876	252,697	289,079	311,817	335,265	379,744
	Contributions	13.85	108,764	133,993	150,892	166,377	185,514	215,979	248,300	263,717	281,489	323,955
	Government subsidies	7.01	25,747	27,792	28,567	27,695	28,698	27,042	30,540	37,838	39,123	51,697
	Surcharge on tobacco	9.43	4,392	6,446	6,263	9,253	9,664	9,676	10,239	10,262	10,630	4,082
Expenditure	Total	10.28	146,510	157,437	170,043	191,537	224,623	255,544	275,412	311,849	348,599	373,766
	Benefits	10.57	138,993	149,522	161,311	182,622	213,893	245,614	264,948	301,461	336,835	361,890
	Administrative cost	5.28	7,517	7,915	8,732	8,915	9,730	9,930	10,464	10,388	11,764	11,976
Balance			Δ7,607	10,794	15,679	11,788	Δ747	Δ2,847	13,667	Δ32	Δ12,994	6,008
Cumulative Balance			Δ25,716	Δ14,922	757	12,545	11,798	8,951	22,586	22,586	9,592	15,600

Unit: 100 million won

Source: National Health Insurance Corporation. Annual Statistics of NHI, 2012.

Financial Revenues of the NHI

The assessment and collection of insurance premiums in Korea is shown in Table 11.5. As of 2010, 83.9 percent of the total funding for health insurance came from insurance premiums, 11.6 percent from government support, 3.2 percent from the tobacco levy, and 1.3 percent from other sources. Since health insurance is primarily funded through premiums, the task of accurately and equitably assessing the premium level for each policyholder and collecting the premium through a reasonable method is very important for the governance (maintenance and operation) of the system. Here, we will examine the procedures and conditions for the assessment and collection of insurance premiums.

Premium–imposing system: Korea has a number of problems related to premiums arising from the "one insurer–two imposing systems," meaning one system for self-employed and another for formal workers. Those problems include inequities between the two systems, differences between imposing components of the two systems, differences between qualifying conditions for beneficiaries, differences between criteria to

TABLE 11.5 Sources of the NHI Fund (2012)

	EMPLOYEE INSURED (EHI)	SELF-EMPLOYED (RHI)
Contribution Rate (%)	5.64%	Certain amount by grade (100 grades with ceiling)
Base for Imposing Contribution	Taxable Income	Taxable Income, property, automobile, sex, age, household size
Share of Contribution	Employer and employee each 50% (30% by school and 20% by government for private school teachers)	
Government Subsidy (including surcharge on tobacco)	20% of total premium revenue	

Source: National Health Insurance Corporation, 2012.

assess income, regressive premiums for the self-employed, complexity of the systems, and income sources not applicable to impose contributions of more than 40 percent of total income sources (NHIC 2011).

Method of determining the insurance premium for EHI policyholders: The assessment system for the employment-based health insurance (EHI) was basically an earnings-related method, where the income was multiplied by a certain value to calculate the insurance premium. The actual income was converted to a standardized income through an income standardization method, so that the standardized monthly wage amount was multiplied by the insurance premium rate, and the employer and the employee each contributed 50 percent of this amount. As noted above, the current insurance premium rate is set at a single rate after the integration of all health insurance cooperatives into a single organization (NHIC) in 2000. The single insurance premium rate after integration has been continuously increasing, rising from 3.63 percent in 2002, and reaching 5.64 percent in 2012—although this is still much lower than the premium rates in Japan, which vary from 8 percent to 9.5 percent depending on the plan (Okamoto 2011, 3).

Method of assessing the insurance premium for self-employed policyholders: While the EHI applied a unified system scaled by income level for determining the premium level, the self-employed regional-based insurance (RHI) calculated the premium based on income plus a combination of other items. This approach was adopted due to inadequate information and the absence of accurate data on income for self-employed policyholders. The RHI method of assessing insurance premiums uses "insurance premium assessment score points," which reflect the policyholder's income, assets (including leases and monthly rentals and cars), and rate of participation in economic activities, and the score points are then multiplied by an amount charged per point. Next, deduction rates are applied to calculate the final insurance premium for the household unit. In other words, all members of the household to which the policyholder belongs have the joint responsibility to pay the premium. However, underage people (defined according to the criteria stipulated in the Presidential Decree) are exempt from the obligation to pay.

Government subsidy: At the time the RHI system was designed, the government's plan was to provide support not only for the management and operation costs but also for part of the expenses for insurance benefits coverage costs. Accordingly, the government promised national subsidies for 50 percent of the self-employed insurance financing.

In 2000, when the financial situation of the NHIS deteriorated, there was a need for increased governmental financial support. In 2002, the Special Act on Sound Finance of National Health Insurance was passed. From then on, government funding for health insurance expanded to include not only support from the general budget but also support through the national health promotion fund created by a surcharge on tobacco. Also, the size of the government funding was clearly stipulated. The size was fixed at 50 percent of the funding for self-employed RHI, within which 35 percent was allocated to general accounts (as of 2005–2006, but then decreased to 40 percent for 2002–2004), and 15 percent support through the health promotion fund (as of 2005–2006, which then decreased to 10 percent for 2002–2004). Finally, 20 percent of the total contribution of the NHIS (both EHI and self-employed RHI) was legislated as the amount of the government subsidy (including health promotion fund). But the actual amount is less than 20 percent, as the level of subsidy is decided before the next year's contribution amount (estimated) is set.

The contributions of policyholders thus accounted for 83.3 percent in 2011, based on their income (wage income, financial income, income from rent, transfer income, etc.), properties, cars, and demographics (sex, age). The total government subsidy including the health promotion fund (surcharge on tobacco) was 16.6 percent of total revenue in 2011. This level compares favorably with other countries, since the share of government subsidy (NHI + Medical Aid) is 23.29 percent in Korea, which is less than Taiwan (25.5 percent of total revenue), France (47 percent of total revenue), and Japan (35.3 percent) (MOHW 2012; OECD Health Data 2012).

Expenditures of the NHI

Korea is now faced with serious challenges due to the increasing share of total national health expenditure (THE) to GDP, the increasing NHI treatment expenditure, and increasing benefit coverage costs of NHIS, while the growth rate of THE is higher than that of GDP. In relation to these trends, one of the key policy issues now is how Korea can build up proper cost containment measures when faced with a crocodile's mouth pattern between increasing income and skyrocketing health care costs. As shown in Table 11.6, between 2005 and 2010, the annual growth rate of the GDP was 6.28 percent, while the NHI benefit expenditure's annual growth rate was substantially higher at more than 14.3 percent for the same time period. Table 11.6 also shows that the percentage average annual growth rate of THE per GDP (D/A) was 4.64 percent, which was higher than the OECD average of 2.0 percent (Shin 2011, 2).

TABLE 11.6 Health Care Expenditure and GDP

	2005	2006	2007	2008	2009	2010	Annual Growth
GDP (A)	865,240	908,743	975,013	1,023,937	1,063,059	1,173,275	6.28
THE (D)	49,227	54,783	61,888	66,700	-	82,927	11.22
Treatment (B)	20,742	22,506	24,862	28,410	32,389	34,869	11.07
B/A	2.87	3.13	3.32	3.41	3.70	3.72	4.53
Benefit (C)	18,262	21,489	24,561	26,499	30,146	33,570	14.36
D/A	5.69	6.03	6.35	6.51	6.92	7.10	4.64

Unit: billion won, %

Note: Annual growth rate (2001–2010). OECD average for D/A was 9.5% in 2010.

Sources: BOK, National Income, 2012. Yearbook of statistics, each year, NHIC 2001-2011. Health Insurance Review & Assessment Service, Homepage of the Health Insurance Review & Assessment Service, 2011. OECD Health Data, 2012.

THE=Total Health Expenditure.

Analysis of Treatment Expenditure (2001–2010)

An analysis of treatment expenditures between 2001 and 2010 can help identify the contribution of different factors to rising costs. The annual number of beneficiaries increased by 0.59 percent during this time period, annual visit days per capita increased by about 3.86 percent per year, and annual treatment cost per visit day increased by 6.48 percent per year from 2001 to 2010. Therefore, Table 11.7 shows that total annual growth rate of treatment expenditure increased by 10.94 percent per year. Table 11.7 also indicates relative roles of different factors to increasing expenditures from 2001 to 2010: the contribution by number of beneficiaries is 5.38 percent, visit days per capita is 35.32 percent, and treatment cost per visit day is 59.3 percent.

This analysis shows that, since the implementation of medical insurance in 1977, the usage of medical services by citizens has surged explosively and has now reached a point where the use of medical services has become a serious concern.

Now let's consider how patients use different medical services and the expenditure implications. Table 11.8 shows that there is a strong concentration of outpatients in secondary and tertiary hospitals. This pattern reflects the absence of any regulations on service choice, which may cause unnecessary use of medical resources and a rise in health care

TABLE 11.7 Levels of Contribution by Factors Increasing Expenditures (2001–2010)

	Total		Inpatient		Outpatient		Pharmaceutical	
	Growth rate	Contribution rate	Growth rate	Contribution rate	Growth rate	Contribution rate	Growth rate	Contribution rate
Number of beneficiaries	0.59	5.38	0.59	3.93	0.59	6.96	0.59	5.18
Visit days per capita	3.86	35.32	10.50	69.95	3.25	38.33	1.94	17.05
Treatment amount per capita	6.48	59.30	3.92	26.12	4.64	54.72	8.85	77.77
Treatment amount	10.94	100	15.01	100	8.48	100	11.38	100

Unit: %

Note: Growth rate is annual, and contribution rate represents levels of contribution.

TABLE 11.8 Expenditure for Outpatients, by Type of Health Care Institute

	2006	2007	2008	2009	2010	Annual Growth Rate
Tertiary hospital	1,201,625 (10.80)	1,436,858 (11.60)	1,684,175 (12.48)	1,844,169 (12.91)	2,288,408 (14.22)	17.47 (7.12)
General hospital	1,271,584 (11.43)	1,480,410 (11.95)	1,666,329 (12.35)	1,882,323 (13.17)	2,075,072 (12.89)	13.02 (3.06)
Hospital	648,771 (5.83)	737,947 (5.96)	878,326 (6.51)	929,578 (6.51)	1,122,216 (6.97)	14.68 (4.58)
Clinic	5,919,406 (53.20)	6,486,972 (52.36)	6,894,908 (51.09)	7,137,975 (49.95)	7,790,382 (48.41)	7.11 (-2.33)
Total	11,126,704 (100.00)	12,389,783 (100.00)	13,496,086 (100.00)	14,288,951 (100.00)	16,092,582 (100.00)	9.66

Unit: million won, (%)

Note: Except pharmacies and oriental health clinics (hospital).

Source: National Health Insurance Corporation, Major Statistics on Health Insurance, 2011.

costs. Without an effective mechanism and regulations for patient referral, there exists an incentive for overconsumption (shopping around for medical services) for policyholders. However, benefits for them may be far less than the costs because of the time and discomfort cost to spending time in the hospital or going to the doctor. In other words, Korea's NHIS creates moral hazard for policyholders and in addition there exists "considerable discretion (choice)" in treatment for service providers. Also, the reimbursement system for providers favors general or tertiary hospitals, which also contributes to rising costs.

Other Related Policy Issues: Payment System

Korea's fee-for-service system (using Resource-Based Relative Value Scale) has served as the main method of payment for treatment costs in the NHIS. The system sets relative value units for each specifically categorized medical service, and these units are then multiplied by the conversion factor (value unit per fee unit). These two elements determine the fee paid by the NHIS for each medical service. Currently, the conversion factor is determined by agreements concluded between the NHIC and each specific type of medical institution. Each year representatives of seven provider organizations (such as clinics, hospitals, dentists, traditional herbal medicine institutions, pharmacies, and mid-wifery clinics) conclude contracts through negotiations with the NHIC. In cases where an agreement cannot be reached, the HIPDC deliber-ates and reaches a decision that is then publicized by the minister of the MOHW.

Despite having several advantages, the FFS system also poses vari-ous problems. Among these problems, the greatest issue is that the FFS system fails to control treatment costs, due to: (1) providers' behavior to maximize their revenue and (2) information asymmetry. Under FFS, providers tend to increase the quantity of medical services to maximize their revenue, as the price (medical fee) is fixed (providers' revenue = fee for service x quantity). In addition, because of information asym-metry, providers have the power to decide medical service quantity (ser-vice frequency and intensity). Table 11.9 shows the implications for this argument.

To address the problems arising from the FFS system, beginning in 2002 Korea introduced the case payment system based on diagnosis-related groups (DRGs) for seven types of illnesses. Initially in Korea, the case payment system was not applied compulsorily but through voluntary adoption by the medical institutions, and as of August 2010, 2,321 institu-tions (69.4 percent of the applicable institutions) were voluntarily partici-pating in this system. The system has been applied compulsorily since July 2012.

TABLE 11.9 Decomposing Growth in Health Care Expenditure

Source	Growth Rate	Decomposing Growth (%)			
		Total	Age Effect	Income Effect	Residual Effect
OECD (2006): Base on public health expenditure	OECD average, 1981-2002	3.6	0.3	2.3	1.0
	OECD average, 1970-2002	4.3	0.4	2.5	1.5
	Korea, 1982-2002	10.1	1.4	6.1	2.4
NHI benefit	Korea, 2000-2009	12.65	1.83	5.83	4.99

Source: OECD (2006), Projecting OECD Health and Long-term Care expenditures and NHIC, Korean NHI yearbook of statistics from each year.

NEWLY EMERGING POLICY ISSUES AND CHALLENGES AHEAD

Financial Projection

When NHIS was introduced in Korea, it was initiated with three characteristics: low premiums, low range of benefits coverage, and low medical costs. Korea then built a universal health insurance system within a remarkably short time. Today, in spite of these achievements, Korea's NHIS is confronting many challenges, such as strengthening the range of benefits coverage, improving the system's accountability and governance, and achieving financial sustainability.

There have been various financial projections about the future of Korea's NHIS, showing quite different results depending on the researchers. One study projected that the proportion of national health expenditure to GDP could reach 13 percent as of 2050, and concluded that the proportion of the NHI budget to GDP should be controlled below 5 percent for sustainable national financing (Kim and Kim 2007, abstract). Shin (2012) also estimated the required premium contribution rate is 8.21 percent to 9.73 percent, based on his different scenarios for the year 2020 (Shin 2011, 22).

Table 11.10 shows that the proportion of benefits coverage cost of NHI to GDP from 2010 to 2020 is projected to increase by 2.87 percent to 4.94 percent. Even under assumptions that the percentage share of government subsidy (including the surcharge on tobacco) in total NHI revenue is kept at 20 percent, the required contribution rate in 2020 is accordingly estimated as higher than 9.7 percent. That is 1.82 times the contribution amount in 2010. However, currently, 8 percent is legislated as the premium ceiling. These results suggest that the financial sustainability of Korea's NHIS is questionable under the current governance and finance system, and the government needs to increase its financial resources.

Policy Recommendations for Financial Sustainability

We recommend that Korea consider six policy recommendations to improve the financial sustainability of the NHIS for the future.

TABLE 11.10 Financial Projection of NHI Expenditure

Year	THE (1)	THE/GDP (2)	Benefits Coverage NHI (3), (3)/GDP	Gov. Subsidies	Total Premium	Premium Rate (%)
2010	83	7.10	33.57 (2.87%)	4.98	29.70	5.33
2013	96	7.91	44.31 (3.65%)	7.63	38.14	6.60
2014	103	8.07	48.85 (3.82%)	8.41	42.05	7.07
2015	110	8.30	51.76 (3.90%)	8.91	44.56	7.27
2016	118	8.49	57.35 (4.12%)	9.87	49.37	7.82
2017	127	8.84	62.37 (4.34%)	10.73	53.69	8.26
2018	136	9.11	68.00 (4.55%)	11.70	58.54	8.74
2019	146	9.38	74.78 (4.80%)	12.87	64.38	9.33
2020	156	9.60	80.40 (4.94%)	13.84	69.22	9.74

Unit: trillion won, %

Note: Based on the following assumptions that (1) annual increasing rate of income applicable to impose contribution is 3%, (2) share of population 65+ is 15%, (3) benefits coverage rate of 2010 at 65% is maintained, and (4) annual government subsidy (16.6%) is maintained (including health promotion fund; surcharge on tobacco).

THE = Total Health Expenditure

1. Reform the health care delivery system: In principle, to enhance the macro-level efficiency in the utilization of resources, Korea needs to establish a policy for the management of medical resources at the governmental level that will encourage or mandate a balanced distribution of high-quality medical resources by type and by region. Korea needs to develop and institute a referral system befitting the country's circumstances to perform a gatekeeping function, so that citizens will be provided with lifetime health management services centered on primary care. At the same time, Korea needs to provide incentives to reduce reliance on clinic-level hospital beds and outpatient treatment at general and tertiary hospitals, and establish obligatory provisions regarding patient referral and patient transference among medical institutions.

For this purpose, as short-term strategies, the following measures are recommended: first, for policyholders, Korea needs to differentiate the co-payment rate of outpatients more strongly by types of institutes: increase co-payment of outpatient services in general and tertiary hospitals to control outpatients' use of these facilities and to motivate primary care utilization. Second, for providers, Korea should abolish fees for selective medical treatments for outpatient services, and control the number of outpatients in tertiary hospitals. As long-term strategies, first an emphasis on primary care is needed. A designated doctor system (especially for patients with frequent service use) is recommended to guarantee primary care as a gatekeeper to manage chronic diseases. Second, specialized and/or base hospitals are recommended. Competitive hospitals are to be disease-specific specialized hospitals, competitive regional hospitals to be regional base hospitals, and in the long-term, induce a first and third delivery system without the second level. Third, specialized facilities for intensive care are also recommended. Large general hospitals should be reorganized into specialized hospitals for intensive care.

2. Expand resources available for NHI finance: It is well known that Korea's percentage of public funding remains at a low level compared with those of advanced countries. As of 2008, the percentage of public funding for national medical expenditure was 55.3 percent, which was very low compared to the OECD average of 71.7 percent (Kim 2011a, 99). First, increasing the government subsidy for the NHIS benefits coverage expenditure of older beneficiaries ("old–old," referring to those eighty years of age or older) is recommended. By 2020, Korea is expected to become an "aging society" (one where the percentage of those aged sixty-five or older is 14 percent or higher), with the elderly population reaching the level of 15.6 percent and the financial sustainability of the NHIS aggravated by rapid aging of the population. To address the dual problems of low fertility and aging population in Korea, it is necessary to strengthen and prepare national policies for the aging population, and also build a system to provide high-quality services to senior citizens in urgent need of such care by accelerating the consolidation of the long-term care insurance system for the elderly and institutionally supplementing and improving this system, which seeks to transition the burden of care from the family to the society as a whole.

Korea now has to engage in a serious debate on what the new financing system should be to provide health care for the elderly. Currently, the debate appears to be going nowhere, and the future of the current health care system for the old is quite uncertain. We should start a debate over whether long-term care for elderly should be financed from tax (Nordic model) or by social insurance (German model). Meanwhile, for this purpose within the NHIS, Korea must improve the system for classifying the category of long-term care and diversify the benefits coverage support for senior citizen treatment expenses, such as subsidizing 50 percent of benefit expenditure through co-payment of health insurance for the elderly of sixty-five years and over. According to Shin's estimation, if implemented, the amount of government subsidy in 2020 is estimated at 19,080 billion won (21.83 percent of total) as the benefit amount of older beneficiaries (over sixty-five years) is estimated at 38,160 billion won (43.66 percent of total) (Shin 2011, 34). Second, it is recommended that Korea expand the premium system and levy insurance premiums on earnings omitted from a contribution-based system (thereby including pension income, capital gain financial income, rent income, and transfer income).

3. Improve the premium-imposing system: Korea also faces the challenge of improving its system for charging insurance premiums. Discrepancies in insurance premium charges for formal sector EHI and self-employed RHI insurance policies have given rise to problems of fairness in premium contributions, including problems related to free-riding coverage for the dependents of employment-based policyholders. To solve these problems, first, as a short-term improvement, Korea needs to simplify the complex contribution-imposing system, especially for the self-employed, and reduce the "regressiveness" of the contribution system for the self-employed. As a long-term improvement measure, Korea needs to first introduce an income-based unified form of contribution-imposing system. Second, the dependent status approval standards should be improved. Excluding siblings from the category of dependents is recommended, in accordance with the National Basic Livelihood Security Act. Siblings who are excluded should be transferred to self-employment insurance, and those who are eligible for Medical Aid should be transferred to Medical Aid. Excluded dependents with considerable property should be seen as having some economic ability, and they should pay an insurance premium based on the principles of social insurance.

Korea also needs to incrementally increase the current level of insurance premiums to strengthen the range of benefits coverage. The rate of insurance premiums in Korea is relatively low compared with rates found in major countries that implement a health insurance system. As of 2008, the premiums were 14.0 percent in Germany, 13.8 percent in

France, and 9.5 percent in Japan (plus an additional 1.5 percent for Long-Term Care Insurance for those forty years and over in 2011), whereas the rate in Korea remained at 5.64 percent in 2011 (NHIC, internal materials, 2012; Okamoto 2011, 3).

However, it will be almost impossible for Korea to maintain a stable fiscal balance by relying *only* on revenues from insurance premiums in the future. Therefore, Korea must identify sources of revenue in addition to the insurance premiums. In order to expand the benefits coverage of health insurance in the future to the level of advanced countries as mentioned above, Korea must secure structurally stable sources of financial revenue. In addition, adverse factors that directly harm health, such as alcohol and smoking, and fossil fuels that cause atmospheric pollution leading indirectly to health risks result in socioeconomic costs. There are currently discussions regarding the possibility of measures to reduce these social costs by assigning the economic opportunity costs and by instituting or expanding the implementation of health taxes on socioeconomic activities that create negative health externalities.

4. Improve the reimbursement system: In addition to demand-side factors that are driving increases in treatment expenses, Korea is also confronting supply-side factors, such as the cost-inducing payment system based on fee for service. Consequently, Korea needs to design efforts to rationally reform the payment system for treatment costs to resolve these problems.

It is recommended that Korea place more responsibility on providers through the payment system (such as DRGs and global budgets) to help contain costs. In the long term, a prepayment system (e.g., global budgeting, capitation, or DRGs) should be used rather than a post-payment system (e.g., FFS), to induce providers to reduce unnecessary use of expensive medical equipment and services. First, for outpatients, there is a need to decide the amount of the total budget through capitation and a family or individual doctor system, and for inpatients, there is a need to introduce a new mechanism (one that decides the medical fee in accordance with the number of cases) in addition to the introduction of a DRG system. Second, Korea needs to differentiate medical fees between acute care and chronic disease care; in addition, it must increase the budget according to GDP growth, aging, benefits coverage extension, the Consumer Price Index, and input from the association of providers since they have knowledge and clinical experiences that allow them to make specific budget distribution plans (including the review and assessment of benefit expenditures).

5. Strengthen primary care and health promotion: In Korea, primary care is placed in a structure of wastefulness due to excessive competition and an excessive input of resources, with services often limited to the treatment of illnesses. A major policy issue is the absence of preventive and promotional programs. Korea's national health insurance system has devoted a very small proportion of its expenses to prevention and health promotion programs, and aside from health screening exams, there are no separate programs targeted to improve health.

Care to prevent the occurrence of illnesses in advance can be more effective than ex post facto treatments, and it is also the most cost-effective method for reducing medical expenses on a national scale. It is therefore necessary for Korea to adopt a new method for managing illnesses, namely the method of advanced prevention that allows early detection of illnesses and health-promoting approaches to improve the health-related behaviors of individuals. To develop a lifelong health-screening program for all age groups, it will be necessary to further systematize the contents and the processes of the screenings and bolster their value so as to improve the efficiency of the screening system's management and operation.

6. Rationalize management of insured pharmaceutical costs: Finally, Korea needs to address policy issues related to the lagging efficiency of pharmaceutical expenditures. The share of pharmaceutical expenditures to THE were 24.3 percent in 2001 and 21.6 percent in 2010, reflecting a decrease of 2.73 percent. However, according to OECD Health Data (2012), Korea expends much more on pharmaceuticals than other major countries—compared to the OECD average percentage of pharmaceutical expenses to THE (OECD average 16.6 percent), Japan at 20.8 percent, and the United States at 11.9 percent in 2010. Also, the price of generic medicines in Korea (68 percent of original drug) is higher than in other countries. To compare, the price of generic drugs is 50 percent of that of the original drug in France, 52 percent in Austria, 55 percent in Italy, 60 percent in the Netherlands, and 70 percent in Japan (Shin 2011, 14). The major causes for the high percentage dominated by pharmaceutical expenses and the rate of increase are that medical institutions lack the incentive to purchase low-priced pharmaceuticals, the system for identifying accurate data on actual transactions is inadequate, and the pharmaceutical price discounting system is insufficient (Kim 2011, 100).

To rationally manage the costs of insured pharmaceuticals, Korea needs to transition from the previous micro-level method of managing drug prices for individual items to a macro-level method of managing pharmaceutical expenses by setting a total target value. Meanwhile, Korea also needs to bring greater transparency to the distribution structure for pharmaceutical products and track actual transactions to rationalize the criteria for determining pharmaceutical prices. We must strengthen the drug utilization review to establish mechanisms that will enable appropriate use of pharmaceuticals, and these efforts must be accompanied by measures to expand bioequivalence tests and to prepare an institutional foundation providing incentives to medical institutions, thereby encouraging the use of affordable and high-quality generic pharmaceuticals.

CONCLUSION: SOME LESSONS AND IMPLICATIONS

In this section, we examine the lessons and implications of the development process of Korea's NHIS for other countries as they seek to implement their own national health insurance system.

Looking back on early stages of health insurance in Korea, we can identify two elements that made it possible for all citizens to have health insurance within such a short period and for the system to achieve such notable success. First is the government's strong leadership and commitment (political will) in undertaking a series of social reform measures to respond to the citizens' demands regarding economic and social developments. Second is the successful economic development in Korea. These were the key factors that propelled the development of Korea's four major social insurance systems, including the NHIS.

Korea adopted an incremental approach to expanding health insurance eligibility and strengthening benefits to prevent potential complaints from health care providers and policyholders. From the beginning, there were three key characteristics of the NHIS: low premiums, limited range of benefits covered, and low medical costs. These conditions allowed Korea to build the groundwork for a soft landing and also avoided any initial large government burdens in financing and managing the NHIS. This method was administratively convenient for the system's governance (management and operations) and also made it possible to create a framework for consolidating the insurance system without incurring excessive strain in terms of financing or the management of expenditures.

To secure funding, Korea initially charged employers contributions for employment-based policyholders in the early stages of implementing health insurance. It was only later, in the process of expanding eligibility to self-employed residents in rural and urban communities, that the government provided financial support. Such financial support ensured that in the early stages of health insurance implementation, the policyholders were offered low premium rates (a low-burden approach) as an incentive to increase participation in the insurance plan, which allowed Korea to consolidate the basis for stably expanding the health insurance to a national scale.

Despite these positive decisions, however, there were also aspects in which greater deliberation in the early stages of the system's introduction could have improved the system's performance. Here we consider the current policy issues (problems) of the NHIS and how they might have been avoided if certain issues were deliberated better in the process of implementation.

First was the decision to adopt a FFS payment system. This decision was made without in-depth discussion of systems used in other countries, aside from Japan. This has resulted in many challenges that impede efficiency in financial management. It is clear from Korea's experience that a broader discussion is needed of the various systems available for handling fee payments, especially in the early stages of implementing a health insurance system. For example, Taiwan offers an excellent example of this kind of deliberation of different payment methods and its decision to move its current payment system through a stage-by-stage transition into a global budget payment system (Yang 2011, 9–10).

Second are the methods for setting insurance premiums. The criteria for assessing insurance premiums was not integrated, and remained in a binary structure that caused problems of inequity between EHI policyholders and RHI policyholders. The complexity of this method of charging insurance premiums and the discrepancy in the amount of insurance premiums that arise when employment-based policyholders change to a self-employed insurance policy or vice versa have increased complaints from citizens. This might have been avoided if the assessment system had been unified in the initial stages of instituting health insurance and if the criteria for premium charges had been simplified.

Third is the way health insurance is managed and operated by the NHIC, while Medicaid benefits for low-income people are handled by the government. This approach has been criticized for its shortcomings in operational efficiency. Also, in the early period following the introduction of health insurance, the group eligible for Medicaid benefits comprised 10 percent of the total national population, but under conditions in which the beneficiaries of these medical services receive support for the insurance premium from the government nearly without responsibilities for co-payment, there may arise the problem of moral hazards leading to increases in expenditures. For these reasons, it is impossible to increase the number of people eligible for such support, and the percentage of the population receiving this support has declined to around 3 percent. Governments that are introducing health insurance should establish long-term plans for how far to extend the number of Medicaid beneficiaries, and should consider the risk of moral hazard due to the very low level of insurance premiums compared with those of ordinary health insurance policyholders. For this reason, there must be mechanisms for efficiently managing the eligibility for Medicaid benefits and controlling the potential for rising expenditures for these benefits.

Fourth is the management and utilization of databases. Korea's health insurance was first implemented at the unit of cooperatives and was gradually expanded to include all citizens in the NHIS, and initially there was little effort to create a database of information. Moreover, although information in the early period of Korea's NHI was collected into a database, this resource was not analyzed and used for policy decisions. Therefore, another lesson for countries that are introducing national health insurance is to organize pertinent information into a database from the early stages of implementation and to seek ways to utilize the data to inform policy.

Fifth, while Korea aimed to incrementally expand both the scope of eligibility and the range of benefits for health insurance, the NHIS did not succeed in expanding benefits to the degree anticipated, although eligibility did expand to all citizens within twelve years after introduction. Governments must deliberate whether to concentrate on expanding eligibility among the population or to focus on expanding the range of benefits in tandem with the expansion of eligibility. This decision deserves serious consideration, because the issue is closely linked to insurance premium revenues. In light of Korea's experiences, it appears best to begin with low insurance premiums in the early years of instituting health insurance to secure the participation of policyholders, and some governmental support in certain areas seems necessary. However, once the health insurance system has stabilized to a certain degree, then efforts must be made to actively persuade policyholders of the justification for raising the insurance premium to a more reasonable level and to ensure that the insurance premium provides sufficient financing for the system so as to minimize governmental support. In addition, clear provisions must be made to regulate the purposes for which government subsidy funding is used.

Lastly, financing care of the elderly has been the Achilles heel of Korea's fragmented health insurance system (up to 2000), because the rates of enrollment among the elderly vary considerably from insurer to insurer. The EHI cooperative has the lowest enrollment of the elderly, while the self-employed-based RHI cooperative has the highest. How to balance this inequality of elderly enrollment to sustain the NHIS has always been at the center of health policy debates. A complete unification of all insurers is an obvious and ultimate solution for the Korean NHIS. We should note that Korea began operating its health insurance through a cooperative method in the early years, and later, following the integration of multiple fragmented cooperatives, the government's role grew.

In operating a national health insurance system, there are both advantages and drawbacks depending on the agents of the operation. We can consider the example of Taiwan, where the government exercises complete authority in the operation of health insurance, or the case of Germany, where the National Health Insurance Corporation is given the responsibilities of an insurer along with autonomy in governing benefits and financial decisions. If we opt for the method of operation based on cooperatives, where the autonomy of each cooperative is respected as much as possible, there will need to be methods for pursuing efficiency in management while minimizing inequities that arise among the cooperatives in terms of revenues and expenditures. On the other hand, systems operated by a single, integrated insurer demand mechanisms to ensure internal competition in management and operations.

In conclusion, the international community has positively valued Korea's NHIS as one of the most efficient systems in the world that provides universal health security for all of the country's citizens at a low cost. This study has examined the development of the health insurance system in Korea and the implications of Korea's experiences for developing countries. Although Korea has created an outstanding institution worthy of the admiration of other countries, it is also true that Korea still faces many challenges ahead. Korea's past decisions to implement various policies in accordance with the country's socioeconomic conditions illustrate that each country must consider certain issues in the process of introducing health insurance and that those decisions must fit local circumstances. This chapter suggests that there is no such thing as the "best health care reform" or the best national health insurance system in the world—and also that the health care and health insurance systems of one country cannot be directly transplanted into another country. These national systems evolve over time, along with people's choices and with national policies, through a process of trial and error and successes and failures.

REFERENCES

Bonoli, G. 1997. "Classifying Welfare States: A Two-Dimension Approach." *Journal of Social Policy* 26 (3): 351–72.

Commission for the Advancement of Health Security, National Health Insurance Corporation. 2010. *Report on the Activities of the Commission for the Advancement of Health Security.* Seoul: Commission for the Advancement of Health Security, National Health Insurance Corporation.

Fox, Ashley M., and Michael R. Reich. 2013. "Political Economy of Reform." In *Scaling Up Affordable Health Insurance: Staying the Course,* edited by A. S. Preker, M. E. Lindner, D. Chernichovsky, and O. P. Schellekens. Washington, D.C.: World Bank, 395–434.

Hamilton, Conn. 2006. *Healthy Provinces, Healthy Canada: A Provincial Benchmarking Report.* Ottawa, Canada: The Conference Board of Canada.

Homepage of the National Health Insurance Corporation. Accessed: July 2012. http:// www.nhic.or.kr.

Homepage of the Health Insurance Review & Assessment Service. Accessed: July 2012. http:// www.hira.or.kr.

Jo, Won-Tak. 1999. *The Project to Implement Integrated Medical Insurance: With a Focus on the Context Behind the Deferment of the Legislation on Medical Insurance Integration, Social Welfare Policy Volume 9.* Seoul: Korea Academy of Social Welfare Policy.

Jung, Hyung-Sun. 2012. *Korean National Health Accounts and Total Health Expenditure in 2010.* Seoul: Ministry of Health and Welfare and Yonsei Institute of Health and Welfare.

Kim, John M., and Kim Woocheol. 2007. *A Model of Long-term Health-care Costs,* abstract, 2. Seoul: Korea Institute of Public Finance.

Kim, Seon-Hee. 2009. "A Morphogenetic Approach to Policy Changes: With a Focus on Medical Insurance Fee Policies." *Korea Public Administration Journal* 43 (2): 227–56.

Kim, Jin-Su. 2011. *The Operation of National Health Insurance and Its Implications.* Seoul: Korea Development Institute.

Kim, Jin-Su. 2011a. *Mid and Long Term Financial Projections of Health Insurance System (2009-2030).* Seoul: Korea Institute for Health and Social Affairs. WP 2011.

Kim, Jin-Su, Su-Ra Seo, In-Deok Choe, and Jae-Sin Kim. 2009. *Comparative Research on Income Identification Systems Used in Korea and Abroad for the Purpose of Stabilizing the Finances of the Health Security System*. Seoul: National Health Insurance Corporation.

Korean Statistical Information Service. www.Kosis.kr.

Ministry of Health and Welfare. 2006. Ministry of Health and Welfare Press Release Data, 7.10, Seoul: Ministry of Health and Welfare.

Ministry of Health and Welfare. 2010. *2009 White Paper on Health and Welfare*. Seoul: Ministry of Health and Welfare.

Ministry of Health and Welfare. 2010. *Statistical Yearbook on Health and Welfare*. Seoul: Ministry of Health and Welfare.

Ministry of Health and Welfare and Korea Institute for Health and Social Welfare Affairs. 2010. *The Future Strategies for Health and Welfare*. Seoul: Ministry of Health and Welfare and Korea Institute for Health and Social Welfare Affairs.

Ministry of Health and Welfare and Korea Institute for Health and Social Affairs. 2012. OECD Health Data. Seoul: Ministry of Health and Welfare and Korea Institute for Health and Social Welfare Affairs.

National Health Insurance Corporation. 2007. *Health Insurance Review & Assessment Service: A Statistical Review of the Past 30 Years of Health Insurance*. Seoul: National Health Insurance Corporation.

National Health Insurance Corporation. 2008. *Financial Projection*. Seoul: National Health Insurance Corporation.

National Health Insurance Corporation. 2011. *Major Statistics on Health Insurance for 2010*. Seoul: National Health Insurance Corporation.

National Health Insurance Corporation. 2011. *Analysis of the Current Data on Benefit Costs Compared to Insurance Premium Charges in 2010*. Seoul: National Health Insurance Corporation. National Health Insurance Corporation. 2011. *Major Statistics on Health Insurance for the 1ˢᵗ Quarter of 2011*. Seoul: National Health Insurance Corporation.

National Health Insurance Corporation. 2011. *Internal Data of the Cross-Country Comparison; Annual Statistics on the Number of Days for Outpatient Treatment Per Individual*. Seoul: National Health Insurance Corporation.

Okamoto, Etsuji. 2011. *Japan's Health Care Financing and Cost-Containment*. Tokyo: National Institute of Public Health.

OECD. 2006. *Projecting OECD Health and Long-Term Care Expenditures.* Paris: OECD.

OECD. 2010. *Health at a Glance 2009: Key Findings for Korea.* Paris: OECD.

OECD. 2012. *OECD Health Data 2012.* Paris: OECD.

Park, Il-Su, and Dong-Heon Lee. 2010. *Research on the Mid-term and Long-term Prospects for the Health Insurance System.* Seoul: National Health Insurance Corporation.

Reich, M. R. 2002. "The Politics of Reforming Health Policies." *Promotion and Education* 9 (4): 138–42.

Reich, Michael R., Keizo Takemi, Marc J. Roberts, and William C. Hsiao. 2008. "Global Action on Health Systems: A Proposal for the Toyako G8 Summit." *Lancet* 371: 865–69.

Roberts, M. J., W. Hsiao, P. Berman, and M. R. Reich. 2004. *Getting Health Reform Right: A Guide to Improving Performance and Equity.* New York: Oxford University Press.

Sah, Gong-Jin. 2011. *Blue Print and Road Map for Modernizing Korea's Sustainable Health Insurance System*, working paper, 2011–13. Seoul: Korea Institute for Health and Social Affairs.

Shin, Young Seok. 2011. *Financial Projection of National Health Insurance (NHI) in Korea and Policy Measures for Sustainable NHI.* Seoul: Korea Institute for Health and Social Affairs.

Sin, Hyeon-Woon. 2003. *Methods for Reforming the Health Insurance Management System and Reestablishing the Role of the Insurer, Health and Welfare Forum.* Issue No. 82. Seoul: Korea Institute for Health and Social Affairs.

Tsutsui, Takako. 2011. *Perspective on Long-term Care Insurance for an Aged Society in Japan.* Tokyo: National Institute of Public Health.

Won, Seok-Joo. 2008. *Theory of Social Welfare Policy.* Seoul: Yangseowon.

Wong, Joseph. 2004. *Healthy Democracies: Welfare Politics in Taiwan and South Korea.* Ithaca, NY: Cornell University Press.

Yang, Ming-Chin. 2011. *Health Care Financing and Cost-Containment in Taiwan.* Institute of Health Policy and Management, National Taiwan University.

Yang, Myeong-Saen. 1999. "History of Changes in the Governmental Regulation of Medical Fees." *Journal of the Korea Hospital Association* 262: 95–103.

Yeon, Hacheong. 1985. *Who Gains and Who Loses: An Overview of Equity and Efficiency in Korea's Health Insurance System.* Takemi Program in International Health discussion paper. Boston: Harvard School of Public Health.

Yeon, Hacheong. 1986. "Social Welfare Policies in Korea." *International Social Security Review* 2 (86).

Yeon, Hacheong. 1989. "An Approach to Developing Primary Health Care in Korea." In *International Cooperation for Health: Problems, Prospects, and Priorities,* edited by M. R. Reich and E. Marui. Dover, Massachusetts: Auburn House Publishing Company.

Yeon, Hacheong. 1996. "A New Vision of National Welfare toward the 21st Century: Harmonizing Global Trends and Traditional Values in Korea." *Korea Institute for Health and Social Affairs, Research Monograph:* 96–09.

Yeon, Hacheong. 1997. "Future Reform Strategies of the Health Insurance Program in Korea." Future Prospect of Health Insurance Program in Developing and Developed Countries, Tokai University, WHO Regional Office for the Western Pacific, Japan.

Yeon, Hacheong. 2012. *Divided Korea: Social Security and Welfare Issues for Reunification.* Paper presented at U.S.–Korea Institute-Johns Hopkins University 1st SAIS-KDI Forum on Development and Transition Economies, September 6, 2012, Johns Hopkins working paper—forthcoming.

Yeon, Hacheong. 2013. *Lessons from Korea's Experience V: Social Security & Welfare Policy.* Seoul: KDI School of Public Policy and Management.

Yeon, Hacheong, and Chong Kee Park. 1981. "Recent Development in the Health Care of Korea." *International Social Security Review* 2 (82).

Yoo, Seung-Heum, ed. 2008. *60 Years of Health and Medicine in the 60 Year History of the Republic of Korea: The Direction for the Future Development of Health and Medicine.* Seoul: Ministry of Health, Welfare and Family Affairs, National Academy of Medicine of Korea.

CHAPTER 12

Participation of the Lay Public in Decision Making for Benefits Coverage of National Health Insurance in South Korea

Juhwan Oh, Young Ko, and Soonman Kwon

INTRODUCTION

Although South Korea successfully established national health insurance (NHI) in 1977, and has maintained universal coverage since 1989, it has long been criticized for insufficient benefits coverage (Cho 1989; Kwon 2009). For example, computed tomography (CT) was not covered until 1995; medications for chronic conditions (such as diabetes mellitus) were only covered for six months per year per patient until 1994 and were not fully covered until the year 2000. Magnetic resonance imaging (MRI) to diagnose cancer and establish preoperative cancer stage was not covered until 2005, and ultrasonography is still not covered.

Korean society thus decided on a trade-off between universal population coverage and the coverage extent of medically necessary benefit packages in the early phase of NHI, based on a perception that both were not affordable at the same time. This insufficiency affected not only benefits coverage for the subscriber but also reimbursement to providers. The insufficient nature seemed not to be a major issue for subscribers in the early phase of NHI, as it still helped lessen people's burden at the point of medical services utilization, but the insufficient nature of reimbursement did create dissatisfaction among providers at the time. Benefits coverage unfortunately had no chance to incrementally improve its insufficiency over time since the establishment of national health insurance in Korea. Korean policy does not allow providers to practice balance billing (where providers could bill patients for the difference between their charges for insured services provided and a lower amount reimbursed under the NHI plan); but it does allow extra billing (where the provider gives an uninsured service, at the same time as the insured services, and patients pay an additional amount out of pocket). This extra billing functions as a kind of compensation tool to improve the income of providers.

In 2010, out-of-pocket payments accounted for 32 percent of total health expenditure in Korea (OECD 2012). NHI does not adequately protect citizens from a financial crisis caused by severe illness (Park et al. 2006; Kwon 2009). Various public requests to expand benefits coverage have been made since the early 1980s. In 2005, the government expanded benefits coverage by lowering co-payment rates in selected "severe" illnesses. These "severe illnesses" included cancer, some cases of stroke, and cardiovascular diseases. The above policy for targeting a few severe illnesses triggered debates with regard to: (1) the appropriateness of the operational definition of "severity," considering potentially equally severe diseases such as liver diseases, and (2) the priority of clinical severity over the severity of financial risk caused by less critical disease.

This dispute about coverage is not limited to Korea but is a common problem of priority setting throughout the world (Daniels 1993). A social consensus on distributive principles (which benefits should be covered) for health policy making is difficult to achieve for both the expansion and reduction of benefits coverage. A crucial component of health care governance relates to who makes decisions and what criteria and process they use.

Framework for Priority Setting

Accountability for reasonableness (A4R) has been proposed as a guiding framework for priority setting with limited resources (Daniels 2000; Daniels and Sabin 2008; Maluka et al. 2010; Stafinski et al. 2011). A4R defines practical conditions for reasonableness when a society needs to make decisions in a limited-resource setting. A4R consists of four components, according to Daniels and Sabin (2008). The first condition for reasonableness is *relevance*: decisions need to have fair reasons expressed by fair-minded people. The second condition is *publicity*: relevant content related to the decision should be open to the public at all times. The third condition is *revisability*: the ability to make revisions based on condition changes or important information that was omitted during the initial decision making. The fourth condition is *enforcement*: the aforementioned conditions should be enforced by laws or institutional structure.

Social Value Judgments by Lay Public Participation

According to Rawlins and Culyer (2004), social value judgments are decisions based on what is good for society and are crucial to determining whether resources are distributed fairly (Rawlins and Culyer 2004). Participation of the lay public in the policy-making process ensures that the social value judgments regarding health care represent the opinions of "average" citizens (Rawlins 2004; Contandriopoulos 2004). Participation of the lay public also promotes transparency in the decision-making process and can address concerns among individuals who have grown distrustful of decisions made solely by government officials (Daniels 2000). This lay public participation framework has not traditionally been accepted in Asian societies like Korea because the Confucius-based culture has prioritized expert-driven decision making. Support for public input, however, has recently gained growing acceptance due to Korea's difficulty in achieving efficient and equitable benefits coverage for health insurance.

Deliberative Theory

Deliberation enables participants to share perspectives and build consensus. The process is common throughout the world in legal systems where citizens' juries deliberate over a verdict based on testimony provided during a trial. The goal of deliberation in policy formation is to obtain more informed and robust feedback than what is available through basic data-collection mechanisms like surveys. A controlled investigation conducted by Abelson et al. (2003) found that deliberation produces a dose-effect-like response; in that study, the views of participants were more amenable to change as increased amounts of deliberation were introduced. The authors noted that this outcome illustrates that deliberation leads to consensus building and information exchange. The authors also noted that dominant views are less likely to change through deliberation and may actually become more entrenched. An important aspect of the deliberative process is that all individuals are provided information on the topic before the deliberation. This ensures that the discussion can be informed by evidence (Abelson 2003).

PREVIOUS EXAMPLES OF PUBLIC PARTICIPATION IN HEALTH POLICY FORMATION

Several Western countries have institutionalized lay public participation in health policy formation to improve social consensus. The state of Oregon in the United States made the first attempt to explicitly establish a boundary of resource utilization, in 1989 (Golenski and Thompson 1991). During the first prioritization attempt, the Health Services Commission of Oregon used a cost/utility formula that ultimately produced a prioritization list that was inconsistent with the commissioners' perceived importance (i.e., the commissioners' value judgment). After confronting unsuccessful results through this cost-utility formula approach, the commission decided to stress public value judgment in the first step and cost-effectiveness accounting in the next step. A priority list was finalized in 1991 based on public hearings, questionnaire-based interviews, and focus-group interviews (Kitzhaber 1993). The Oregon case was the first instance of public engagement in the prioritization of benefits coverage in the world; however, only four of the eleven commissioners were actually members of the lay public. The other commissioners were experts, such as physicians, nurses, and social workers.

The United Kingdom (UK) adopted a citizen council in the mid-1990s based on the experience of using citizens' juries in the court system (Lenaghan et al. 1996). The UK was the first in the history of health policy formation to establish a commission comprised entirely of members of the lay public (Lenaghan et al. 1996). The commission, called the citizens' jury, which later became the citizen council, consists of thirty members of the lay public who reside in various places within the UK. Following selection, the council members listen to testimony from experts of their choosing and are provided sufficient time to discuss and cross-check the witnesses' opinions. During the final phase, the commission is responsible for publishing a social value judgment. Two-and-half days are given to the council to deliberate each requested agenda item, and each year one-third of the council members are moved off the committee (after a three-year term).

Lay public participation in health policy formation has since diffused to several countries with some diversity in the form of institution (Bruni et al. 2008; Street et al. 2014). However, there is no example of laypeople's participation in Asian countries except for the involvement of civic groups (Deng and Wu 2010). Like the rest of Asia, the Republic of Korea does not have a formal method for lay public involvement in health policy decisions. The Korean health policy debate has occurred exclusively within expert societies, including experts in civic groups, because of the lack of institutions for lay public participation.

In addition, to our knowledge, there have been few instances to date of lay public participation in national-level governance of health systems in developing countries (Maluka et al. 2010).

Aim

South Korea has been under public pressure to increase its benefits coverage for NHI, while also facing controversies over the appropriateness of items that were newly added to the benefits package. A4R could be a useful framework for decision making within the Korean health insurance system. Based on the A4R conceptual framework, the Korean government decided to establish a citizen's council to help incorporate social value judgments in health-coverage priority setting. The council uses clear procedures, which are based on the scientific literature in the field. For example, care was taken to allow sufficient time for deliberation, a process that has proved beneficial in councils in other countries (Abelson 2003). The procedures for the council were tested and refined through an experimental council held several months in advance of the real council.

This chapter reviews the achivments and remaining challenges following the implementation of this approach to deliberative democracy in South Korea.

EXPERIMENTS OF LAY PUBLIC PARTICIPATION IN DECISION MAKING FOR HEALTH INSURANCE BENEFITS IN 2008, 2010, AND 2012

In Korea, two authors of this chapter (J.O. and S.K., both former Takemi Fellows) have been involved in the efforts to improve health insurance governance by implementing public participation interventions based on the A4R framework. Professor Norman Daniels of the Harvard School of Public Health supported this initiative because of his expertise in this field. Three experiments were conducted to determine feasible policy options for decision making regarding benefits coverage and willingness to pay for increased insurance contribution. The experiments were conducted in 2008, 2010, and 2012. The experiments consisted of two components: information provision and sufficient deliberation. During the intervention, participants were first provided full and updated information by a team of experts (information provision component); participants then discussed the issues with one another for a moderate amount of time (deliberation component).

First Experiment

In 2008, the first experiment dealt with willingness to pay and preferences among various expansion options of benefits coverage, such as targeting patients with severe diseases, targeting vulnerable populations (e.g., elderly), bringing individual uninsured service items into the benefits package, introducing cash benefits options, and decreasing the ceiling on cumulative out-of-pocket (OOP) payments (Kwon et al. 2012a). In the survey before participation, 46 percent of the participants were willing to increase their premiums to expand benefits coverage. After participation in the deliberation, 63 percent of the participants were willing to pay increased contributions. Preferences for different approaches to expand benefits coverage were measured by the proportion of participants who were willing to pay increased contributions to expand the benefits based on the specified approach. Targeting vulnerable populations and targeting patients with severe diseases were the most preferred options (88 percent of participants and 86 percent, respectively, were willing to pay an increased premium for these options); targeting individual uninsured service items was the next preferred option (67 percent); decreasing the ceiling on OOP payments and introducing cash benefits approaches were the next preferred options (58.3 percent and 54.2 percent, respectively). With regard to targeting vulnerable populations, the elderly were the most preferred group and the disabled were the least preferred, when compared with children or the poor.

Second Experiment

The second experiment was conducted in 2010. The experimental lay citizen committee members, who were selected via a stratified random sampling method using age, gender, and residential area, were asked to decide whether to newly cover certain uninsured services. There were two sets of questions. The first questions were applied for twelve disease group categories, and the second questions were for sixteen specific service items. Participants were fully informed by experts from academia and had a sufficient length of time to discuss the issue within two separate small groups based on gender (Kwon et al. 2012b).

For the first questions, the most supported disease group category, after information and deliberation, was *chronic, severe disease requiring continuous treatment*, and the supporting level increased after information and deliberation compared with the level of support before provision of those two elements (from 93 percent to 96 percent). The least preferred category was *prevalent but not severe disease*, and the supporting level decreased after the meeting (from 46 percent to 25 percent).

For the second questions, willingness to cover currently uninsured service items generally decreased after information and deliberation, compared with initial intention to newly cover, before information and deliberation opportunities were provided (e.g., from 96 percent to 59 percent for vaccinations, which were already provided free of charge in public health centers), except for some items such as extra charges for specialist services (from 46 percent to 71 percent).

Third Experiment

The third experiment, conducted in March 2012, dealt with maternal health service coverage options. The policy questions were two: first, whether people prefer continuing a cash benefits policy for pregnant women with increased amounts of cash for covering more uninsured services or substituting the cash benefit policy with an in-kind benefits coverage policy. The other question was whether people intended to expand in-kind benefits to newly cover certain uninsured services, such as amniocentesis, nonstress fetal monitoring test, iron medicine for anemia prevention, folic acid for neural-tube-defect prevention, gestational diabetes mellitus screening, and prenatal ultrasonography.

For the first policy question, lay people preferred in-kind benefits coverage to cash benefits, to reduce potential consumer moral hazards. For the second question, support to cover screening tests for gestational diabetes mellitus was increased after information and deliberation compared with initial intention (from 55 percent before the meeting to 83 percent after information and deliberation) based on participants' improved understanding of interventions to prevent disease progression. Most citizens did not support covering amniocentesis for confirming fetal Down syndrome and other chromosomal anomalies (from 52 percent to 13 percent), considering that no treatment options exist following prenatal diagnosis.

MOVING FROM THE EXPERIMENT TOWARD AN OFFICIAL COMMITTEE

The three experiments showed people's willingness to *increase* their financial contribution to NHI to achieve better coverage. At the same time, they were willing to *reduce* support of expanding service coverage for some cases after full information was provided and they had sufficient deliberation and discussion. During the experimental committees, participants replaced their original wishes (more benefits than currently offered and as-low-as-possible contribution) with revised wishes (more benefits than currently offered, however, *fewer* benefits compared with their initial wishes, and greater willingness to contribute).

While these three experimental decisions showed consistent results, in the real policy arena there were repeated challenges with respect to acceptable ways of reaching reasonableness while benefits coverage decisions were going on every year. Coverage decisions each year did not satisfy laypeople and academia sufficiently, and diverse criticism about new decisions was pervasive, regardless of the newly covered services to be offered. Following the consistent and fruitful results of the three experiments, in September 2012, the Korea NHI Service eventually established the Citizen Committee for Participation, with the hope that this new committee would provide a better benefits coverage decision-making mechanism, with appropriate levels of reasonableness, considering the dissatisfaction and criticism that had arisen in previous years.

During the experimental period, two conditions of A4R (the *relevance* condition and the *revisability* condition) were adapted to implement lay public participation in Korea. The other two conditions (the *enforcement* condition and the *publicity* condition) have not yet been applied because the NHI Service was not confident that it could implement them as an institutional activity with regular intervals at the time they decided to implement the lay public committee.

Experience of the First Citizen Committee for Participation in South Korea in September 2012

The first Citizen Committee for Participation was held in September 2012 and included thirty people who were randomly selected out of a group of 2,650 applicants. Before random selection was conducted, people who did not meet the definition of "lay public" were excluded. The lay public was defined as those with neither expertise nor strong financial interest in the policy decision. For example, the criteria excluded people with a family member working for either private health insurance companies or the public health insurance authority. The purpose of the committee was to make recommendations on forty-five medical service items for potential benefits expansion. Professional associations related to the service items provided the most updated knowledge and information to the committee members on September 22, 2012. The members had deliberative discussions the next day. "Disease severity" and "financial burden on patients with the related condition" were the values that the members thought were most important during the deliberative conference.

The Citizen Committee for Participation expressed its willingness to *increase* their financial contribution to NHI. They also *decreased* their demand to cover some service items in the benefits package after the conference compared to their initial demand. This pattern is consistent with the outcomes of the previous three experiments. Almost 80 percent of the committee members supported increasing the premium for better benefits coverage at the end of the conference, in comparison with the 72 percent who supported increasing the premium before the conference. Of the forty-five medical service items under discussion, twenty-three service items were agreed to be covered by more than 50 percent of the members at the end of the meeting, compared with twenty-six items that were supported for coverage in the pre-survey (before both information and deliberation were provided).

The official policy-making body for coverage decisions (Health Insurance Policy Committee or HIPC) ultimately accepted nine service items that were at the top of the priority list of the twenty-three items supported by the lay public committee for coverage expansion in 2013. By accepting the recommendations of the Citizen Committee, the Health Insurance Policy Committee delisted an item (a medication indicated for osteoarthritis) that was planned to be covered in 2013. It means that the *revisability* condition of A4R worked out in the coverage decision. The official body (HIPC) selected a total of thirteen items for coverage expansion. Of these thirteen items, nine items (69 percent) were recommendations of the Citizen Committee for Participation, while two items (15 percent) had been predetermined through a previous decision process before the Citizen Committee was implemented. The remaining two items (15 percent) selected by the official body were not on the top priority list of the Citizen Committee. One of the items (for a surgical treatment) was, in fact, disapproved by 55 percent of the members because it could be eventually defined as a cosmetic surgery; the other (a cancer drug) was also disapproved by 52 percent of the members because it had minimal benefit compared to its cost. However, these two items were chosen for coverage by the official decision body despite the reasoning of the Citizen Committee for Participation.

Considering that 69 percent of the newly covered items were chosen through the Citizen Committee for Participation, lay public participation had an important role in benefits coverage decisions even in the first year of its operation. Making decisions on benefits coverage is a key component of governing a health system, especially a national health insurance system. More than 1 trillion Korean won (equivalent to U.S.

$1 billion) were allocated to cover the new items in the year 2013, with no political criticism or policy debate, partly because they were supported by the lay public participation body in the year 2012.

All four conditions of A4R were eventually applied in the implementation of the Citizen Committee for Participation, in various degrees. The *enforcement* condition was partially met, as the Citizen Committee was institutionalized as an annual conference by the health insurance agency NHIS; during the experimental phases this condition was not met at all. The *relevance* and *revisability* conditions also worked quite well, as they did in the experimental phase. However, improvements are still needed for the *publicity* condition, because the results of the Citizen Committee for Participation were not accessible by the public. This absence of the *publicity* condition commitment was partly rooted in the lack of active political groups to encourage this commitment; in addition, NHIS confronted no active criticism with respect to its lack of commitment, except for a few scholars, including the authors (S.K .and J.O.). Increased commitment on the *publicity* condition could help strengthen the newly institutionalized committee as it would provide greater opportunity for sharing policy intention and process with subscribers.

MAKING THE CITIZEN COMMITTEE FOR PARTICIPATION WORK MORE EFFECTIVELY

There is still some room to improve the new policy of participatory decision making and deliberative democracy through the Citizen Committee for Participation with respect to benefits coverage decisions in Korea. The following section examines these issues.

Sufficiency of Time

The authors worried that two days would not be sufficient time for the committee participants to become fully informed about and deliberate over the forty-five items proposed for benefits coverage. A three-day meeting was not approved due to timeline constraints. Because of this, efforts were made to arrange the most suitable experts with sufficient knowledge, effective communication skills, and neutral attitude, to inform the Citizen Committee for Participation while transferring the official opinion of the professional associations with regard to each uncovered service item (forty-five items). For the Citizen Council of the UK (the first established lay citizen-based committee), the lay public chooses the experts who will provide information about the topics. However, in the Korean case there was not sufficient time, so the preparation task force selected the experts. This strategy saved time and resulted in the committee members receiving sufficient information and time for deliberation, as confirmed in the post-committee survey. About 66 percent of participants felt that the time span was appropriate for discussion, while 24 percent felt it was too long and 10 percent thought it was too short, according to post-conference survey. The deliberation time was one full day, and the discussion duration for each agenda item was assigned by the participants themselves; duration was flexible, based on participants' needs, and the discussion was moderated by one of the lay participants, who was elected as the moderator of the day by the participants. Discussion was limited to participants, without influence from those beyond the committee membership.

Based on different levels of complexity and varying amounts of information provided by the experts, agenda items required different lengths of time in order for people to develop adequate understanding (Table 12.1). One item—coverage for second (additional) cosmetic facial surgery for patients who had already received covered cosmetic surgery after curative surgery for cleft lip and/or palate—required less than three minutes for participants to gain an understanding of the procedure; however, this item required quite a long time for deliberation, about thirty minutes, before members had fully weighed the variety of considerations and logic among the participants. A dental treatment option (utilization of photosynthetic material for dental caries treatment), however, required a long period of explanation before it was understood, but needed a relatively short time for deliberation after participants' understanding was complete. Another item (subcutaneous intravenous route for anticancer drug delivery) required a short time for participants to understand the information given and to deliberate: less than three minutes for both. Additionally, members were given the option to state that they were unable to make a decision. Most of the items were answered by the participants, though one of the items was not answered (deferred) regarding whether "to cover or not." In this sense, two consecutive days for forty-five items was not too short a time for the participants.

Ease of understanding for items seemed to be related to both the sufficiency of knowledge and the communication skill of the expert, whereas ease of deciding depended more on the issue's own characteristics, which could not be changed and rather legitimates the call for people's value judgment. In other words, the ease of understanding could be increased through better preparation by the experts, whereas the ease of deciding reflected the challenges of assessing a treatment's worth and judging its social value. The time for understanding could be reduced by better preparation (by the expert); the time for deciding, however, sometimes required providing sufficient time for full deliberation of complex value judgments in the committee meeting.

The Second Citizen Committee for Participation was held on May 25 and 26, 2013, for benefits coverage decisions that would be effective beginning in the year 2014. However, the post-committee survey following the Second Citizen Committee meeting of 2013 showed that the amount of time provided was "short" (41 percent), which is higher

TABLE 12.1 Level of Ease for Benefits Coverage Decisions in the Citizen Committee for Participation

	HARD TO UNDERSTAND	EASY TO UNDERSTAND
Hard to decide	• A herbal medicine • A lung cancer test	• Second cosmetic surgery for cleft lip and palate • Dental implant • MRI for hand injury • Ultrasonography • Language treatment for development retardation
Easy to decide	• Use of photosynthetic material for dental caries treatment • Sex hormone assay • Sleep disturbance test	• Subcutaneous intravenous route for anticancer drug delivery • Self-catheterization for spina bifida • Self-test for blood sugar level in type 2 diabetes mellitus • Consumables for burn treatment • Scaling of teeth • An anticancer drug for breast cancer

than that in the first committee in 2012 (10 percent). In the 2013 meeting, 52 percent of the participants perceived that it was adequate and 3 percent viewed it as long, probably because twelve additional items were inserted at the last minute at the request of Ministry of Health and Welfare. An appropriate number of items should be assigned to the committee based on the available time, so as not to rush the members' decision process.

Dominant Social Values of Lay Public Participants

With respect to social values to be considered in the benefits decisions, the participants considered *financial risk protection* and *disease severity* as the top two priority values. The next social values were *health outcome*, followed by *size of unmet need* and, lastly, *cost-effectiveness* and *scientific evidence of effectiveness*. This order of preferred value was created by participants after discussing the preferences, considering the value of each one, redefining each concept, and then naming their own value with these exemplified key word concepts. The key words were given with a predetermined form of naming. Members could only choose among the given six concepts, which were listed by the preparation group. Giving participants an opportunity to understand what they value while they are considering new benefits coverage for the next year would help people deliberate with one another while respecting others' values, which may differ from their own. Keeping this time slot during the committee meeting would help manage the time for deliberative decision.

Acceptance by the Rest of the Lay Public

If the lay public in the Citizen Committee for Participation endorses an additional item for NHI coverage and agrees to pay a higher contribution, does that mean the general public would also accept such an endorsement? The authors thought the deliberative informed decision process would not be enough if the report was not publicly available, given two aspects. One aspect is the *publicity* condition of A4R. The other is that the United Kingdom already allows people who are not participants of the Citizen Council of NICE (National Institute for Health and Clinical Excellence) to easily access and read the report of the council via web posting; this policy may serve the currently stable health policy of the UK in several ways. The publicly available report helps people comprehensively think the issues through by presenting good information and diverse values. The rest of the public may thus feel their concerns were well covered in the Citizen Committee for Participation by reading about the decision-making processes of the committee's members. To achieve support from the general public, the members of the Citizen Committee for Participation need to cover as many potential arguments and counterarguments as possible. In this way, the committee could be viewed as a functionally accumulative sample of prospective opinion of the public when the whole citizenry is sufficiently informed and deliberate.

The *publicity* condition, one of the four requirements of A4R, should be emphasized to improve the lay public participation process in Korea. If the public feels that the committee's deliberations were thoughtful enough, new policy decisions such as increasing the amount of premium contribution may be successfully implemented and accepted by the rest of the public.

Expected Social Benefit Through Lay Public Committee

The authors hope this new policy initiative to implement A4R in making decisions about benefits will be effective in achieving value for money (out of a constrained budget) and attaining social consensus on a willingness to pay higher contributions. Officials will hopefully be on the same page with the authors in this respect. The approach of the Citizen Committee for Participation (an informed, deliberative procedure) would benefit the people more in terms of macro-efficiency, compared with the previous decision process, which did not allow a sufficient amount of time to consider the appropriateness of benefits coverage. This was the basis of controversy and criticism regarding the previous decisions on benefits coverage expansion before the year 2012. More in-depth evaluations after several rounds of benefits coverage changes via this newly established committee would be worthwhile to disclose the effectiveness of this approach of citizen participation. This may include satisfaction score follow-up surveys with respect to benefits coverage extent for every year.

POLICY IMPLICATIONS

The recent experience in South Korea with the Citizen Committee for Participation has important implications for NHI coverage decisions in many countries where public participation remains a pending health policy issue. Korea's experiences are especially important considering the past experience in Oregon, where an attempt to list the benefits package through a formula confronted obstacles from the public; the objections arose chiefly due to a discrepancy between the lay public's value perceptions and the priority list, which was generated mainly by cost-effectiveness. Korea's approach provides a feasible example of implementing A4R in institutional governance under limited resources. People's values may vary at different times and circumstances, which may make it difficult to implement a formula-based decision process (as in Oregon).

The experience of the Citizen Committee for Participation in Korea shows that people may be willing to increase their premium contributions to expand benefits if a deliberative democratic decision-making process exists. The general public does not necessarily demand ever-increasing benefits, but can decide to keep benefits at a reasonable level once they understand the nature of public funding, financial sustainability, and cost-effectiveness. If these results are the product of common human values and experiences—and not from the unique context of Korea—then this approach to deliberative democracy may help reduce policy failure in other cultural settings as well. The mid-term and long-term effectiveness of this effort to implement deliberative democracy still needs to be evaluated, but it deserves broad recognition around the world for its innovative approach to making difficult social decisions.

REFERENCES

Abelson, J., P. G. Forest, et al. (2003). "Deliberations About Deliberative Methods: Issues in the Design and Evaluation of Public Participation Processes." *Social Science & Medicine* 57 (2): 239–51.

Bruni, R. A., A. Laupacis, W. Levinson, and D. K. Martin. 2008. "Public Engagement in Setting Priorities in Health Care." *Canadian Medical Association Journal* 179 (1): 15–18.

Cho, S. 1989. "The Emergence of a Health Insurance System in a Developing Country: The Case of South Korea." *Journal of Health & Social Behavior* 30 (4): 467–71.

Contandriopoulos D. 2004. "A Sociological Perspective on Public Participation in Health Care." *Social Science & Medicine* 58: 321–30.

Daniels, N.. 1988. *Am I My Parents' Keeper? An Essay on Justice between the Young and the Old*. New York, Oxford Univerisity Press.

Daniels, N. 1993. "Rationing Fairly: Programmatic Considerations." *Bioethics* 7 (2–3): 224–33.

Daniels, N. 2000. "Accountability for Reasonableness." *BMJ* 321 (7272): 1300–01.

Daniels, N., and J. E. Sabin. 2008. "Accountability for Reasonableness: An Update." *BMJ* 337: a1850.

Daniels, N. 2011. "Legitimacy and Fairness in Priority Setting in Tanzania." *Global Health Action* 4.

Deng, C. Y., and C. L. Wu. 2010. "An Innovative Participatory Method for Newly Democratic Societies: The 'Civic Groups Forum' on National Health Insurance Reform in Taiwan." *Social Science & Medicine* 70 (6): 896–903.

Florig, H. K. 2006. "An Analysis of Public-Interest Group Positions on Radiation Protection." *Health Physics* 91 (5): 508–13.

Golenski, J. D., and S. M. Thompson. 1991. "A History of Oregon's Basic Health Services Act: An Insider's Account." *Quality Review Bulletin* 17(5): 144–49.

Kitzhaber, J. A. 1993. "Prioritising Health Services in an Era of Limits: The Oregon Experience." *BMJ* 307 (6900): 373–377.

Kwon, S. 2009. "Thirty Years of National Health Insurance in South Korea: Lessons for Achieving Universal Health Care Coverage." *Health Policy and Planning* 24 (1): 63–71.

Kwon, S., J. Oh, Y. Jung, and J. Heo. 2012. "Citizen Council for Health Insurance Policy-Making." *Korean Journal of Health Economics and Policy* 18 (3): 103–119 (in Korean).

Kwon, S., M. You, J. Oh, S. Kim, and B. Jeon. 2012. "Public Participation in Healthcare Decision Making: Experience of Citizen Council for Health Insurance," *Korean Journal of Health Policy and Administration.* 22 (4): 467–496 (in Korean).

Lenaghan, J., B. New, and E. Mitchell. 1996. "Setting Priorities: Is There a Role for Citizens' Juries?" *BMJ* 312 (7046): 1591–93.

Maluka, S., P. Kamuzora, M. S. Sebastiån, J. Byskov, Ø. E. Olsen, E. Shayo, B. Ndawi, and A.-K. Hurtig. 2010. "Decentralized Health Care Priority-Setting in Tanzania: Evaluating Against the Accountability for Reasonableness Framework." *Social Science & Medicine* 71 (4): 751–59.

OECD. 2012. *OECD Health Data 2012—Frequently Requested Data.* Paris: OECD.

Park, C. S., H. Y. Kang, I. Kwon, D. R. Kang, and H. Y. Jung. 2006. "Cost-of-Illness Study of Asthma in Korea: Estimated from the Korea National Health Insurance Claims Database." *Journal of Preventive Medicine and Public Health* 39 (5): 397–403.

Rawlins, M. D. 2004. "NICE and the Public Health." *British Journal of Clinical Pharmacology* 58: 575–80.

Rawlins, M. D., and A. J. Culyer. 2004. "National Institute for Clinical Excellence and Its Value Judgments." *BMJ* 329 (7459): 224–7.

Rawls, J. 1971. *A Theory of Justice.* Cambridge, MA: Harvard University Press.

Stafinski, T., D. Menon, C. J. McCabe, and D. Philippon. 2011. "To Fund or Not to Fund: Development of a Decision-Making Framework for the Coverage of New Health Technologies." *Pharmacoeconomics* 29 (9): 771–80.

Street, J., K. Duszynski, S. Krawczyk, and A. Braunack-Mayer. 2014. "The Use of Citizens' Juries in Health Policy Decision-making: A Systematic Review." *Social Science & Medicine* 109: 1–9.

Yang, B. M. 1996. "The Role of Health Insurance in the Growth of the Private Health Sector in Korea." *International Journal of Health Planning and Management* 11 (3): 231–52.

PART III

Concluding Remarks

Reflections (i)

Richard Horton

I am not a Takemi Fellow and I am not on the Harvard faculty. So I did wonder why I had been invited to this remarkable celebration—until the magic word "publication" was mentioned. There is no free lunch— or anniversary symposium—for a medical editor. In truth, of course, I have been a privileged spectator here, and I have learned a great deal about your work and the tremendous achievements of this program. I am also here (and I hope this is true) because of two friends—Keizo Takemi and Michael Reich. Their leadership of the Takemi Program, and indeed their leadership in the scholarly discipline of public health and in politics as an expression of a public commitment to public health, is exceptional. I am honored to be able to stand shoulder to shoulder with both men, and I pay tribute to their leadership.

You can learn a great deal about a country from its proverbs, and Japan has a rich source of proverbs and sayings. Here is one (and you will be glad to know that I am not going to attempt to recite it in Japanese). The English translation is this: "A frog in a well knows nothing of the great ocean." Now this is a very significant proverb in Japan. The meaning of it, if one thinks about it for a second, is quite clear. A frog in a well knows nothing of the great ocean, which means that people are satisfied to make judgments about the world based upon their own narrow experience and without taking any account of the world beyond the narrow setting of their own lives.

During the past two days, this meeting has been all about the world outside. It has been about broadening our experiences and it has been about saying that we are not satisfied to judge without a full appreciation of the experiences that we share, one with another. So my first conclusion from these two days is that we are not frogs in a well—and I trust that is surely welcome knowledge.

I want to say a word about Japan as well. It is no accident that Japan has led, with thirty years of support for the Takemi Program and, most recently, with the stunning commitment of Prime Minister Shinzo Abe to universal health coverage. This year a great discovery was made and reported in the pages of *Nature*. The discovery concerned the earliest use of pottery in any human society, fifteen thousand years ago. Where was this earliest use of pottery? It was in Japan, of course. Why is it important to talk about pottery from Japan fifteen thousand years ago at a meeting here in the Harvard School of Public Health? There is a reason, and a very good reason at that. Fifteen thousand years ago, human beings were hunter-gatherers. We roamed wildly across the lands of the Earth until a few groups of people (whom we now call Japanese) stopped and started making pottery. That moment marked the end of humans as hunter-gatherers. Pottery making was the beginning of human civilization. It was the beginning of human settlement. It was the beginning of building communities. As far as we know today, that moment began in Asia. It signifies a commitment over fifteen thousand years, not just the past thirty, to innovation, to technology, to human development, to sustaining human development. And those are the same values, fifteen thousand years later as we sit here today, that inform the Takemi Program, to which I offer my admiration and congratulations.

This meeting has been a revelation to me. We have had authentic reportage from the front lines of global health—work that, in truth, we rarely hear about. In Geneva and in Seattle, the two great capitals of global health today, you do not often hear about this kind of work. That, I think, has been a tremendous success of the Takemi Program, to draw these experiences and this evidence out and present it in the way we have heard.

The theme of this meeting has been *governance,* and I want to make five brief observations about what we have heard. Let me begin first with a word that has been mentioned repeatedly. That word is *community.* I want to step back a moment from the word community, because the point at which you analyze any problem is very important. I can describe Boston according to the unit of the brick. Boston is built of bricks, and I could describe Boston in terms of the bricks that make up the city. It would be perfectly accurate to do so. But this would not be, I think we can agree, a very helpful way to describe the city of Boston. We need a larger unit of analysis to understand what Boston is as a city. The community is a very important unit of analysis for this. But there is another unit of analysis that, in global health, we almost never talk about—and yet seems to me to be absolutely crucial. Communities are the building blocks of *civilizations.*

I want to reflect for a moment on the notion of the civilization, because the science of human civilizations has largely been marginal to our discussions in global health, and that may be a mistake. We must change the nature of our conversation in global health to put civilizations as collections of communities much more at the center of our concerns.

Why should we pay more attention to the notion of civilizations? Because the science of civilizations tells us something important about our sustainability as a species. Oftentimes, we talk about grave threats, whether they be epidemics, war, or climate change. And we think of these external threats as dangers we somehow have to defeat. But when you look at the science of civilizations, that point of view might be mistaken. What this science seems to tell us is that, far more important than these external threats, it is the quality of the social and political institutions we create, together with the way in which we make decisions within those institutions and within our society.

The great challenge, therefore, is not the threats outside of us. The challenge is within us. It lies in this room; it lies in the structures and institutions we create as human beings. The threats to our civilizations, whether they be corruption, incompetence, economic crisis, social division, urban decline, or state fragmentation, are our responsibility as problems to solve. If our unit of analysis was the sustainability and future of our civilizations, we might make governance a much more important political priority than it is today.

The second issue is *accountability.* It was said yesterday that accountability is the key to governance, but then we had a semantic debate about the meaning of accountability. We created a false dichotomy between outcomes and process. Accountability is about both. An example: there is a tentative experiment taking place in global health today that was initiated by Ban Ki-moon's program "Every Woman, Every Child." This

program is the UN secretary-general's signature initiative to accelerate progress on Millennium Development Goals 4 and 5. And to cut a
slightly long story short, two years ago a small group was given a very
long and unattractive name: an independent Expert Review Group
(iERG) on Information and Accountability for Women's and Children's
Health. The task of the iERG, on which I serve with my colleague Joy
Phumaphi (who is currently also executive secretary of the African
Leaders Malaria Alliance) and others, is to define "accountability."

So what does it mean? The definition we take comes from the human
rights community and is divided into three distinct activities. First, *monitoring*. Monitoring means having a health information system. We do
not talk much about the importance of a high-quality health information system to monitor the progress and performance of the health sector. We should. We should be concerned about monitoring indicators of
health performance with a particular focus on equity—disaggregating
data as much as we can, whether it be across income quintiles, sex, rural
or urban residence, or level of education.

Often when we think about accountability, we stop at monitoring.
We want to get data from whatever source we can, and then say that we
have delivered accountability. That would be a mistake. The next step in
accountability is what we have been doing here: *review*. In other words,
a democratic, participatory, and transparent process wherein different
groups in society—governments, civil society, private sector, professionals—come together to discuss and debate the meaning of the data and
information acquired through monitoring. That mechanism can take
place in many different ways in countries. It could be a National AIDS
Commission or a health sector review, or there could be an ombudsman
or a parliament, or there might be a human rights institution. There is
no prescribed way of achieving a successful review. Each country ought
to proceed in its own way. But even monitoring and review are not
enough. The third part of accountability is *action* or *remedy*. There needs
to be an effector arm, a mechanism by which monitoring and review are
turned into some kind of response.

In the work we at the iERG have done in women's and children's
health, we have concluded in our two published reports that there is a
huge accountability gap globally and in countries. Indeed, we believe
that one of the biggest obstacles to making progress in health is the

weakness of accountability mechanisms in countries and globally. So the message I take from our discussion at this meeting is that we have to find a better way to get the theory and practice of accountability more aligned.

It was also said yesterday that accountability ultimately comes back to people. So that's my third observation: *people.* We have heard it again and again—almost every presentation has been about the vulnerability of people to political, economic, social, and even environmental shocks. And therefore the need for protection is a huge motivating force as we think about the agenda for health post-2015, in a new era of sustainability. But let's be careful in our excitement to rush toward sustainable development goals. It is an exciting moment, a new big idea, to be sure. It is about the environment and climate change.

Please be careful, though, because poverty has not gone away. Poverty remains with us. Why is poverty still important? Because poverty has a critically damaging effect on governance, although maybe not in the way you have imagined. What has emerged from one international collaboration, part of which is based here in the Department of Economics at Harvard, is this: being poor matters because it impedes our intellectual function. It impedes our cognitive capacity; it stops us from thinking; it stops us from thinking in a smart way. Being poor reduces our cognitive performance. Being poor, the fact of poverty, consumes our mental resources, leaving us with less capacity to dedicate ourselves to other concerns in our society.

This effect is not only through the stress of being poor. There is something about being poor itself that consumes our mind and stops us from being able to do other things. Poverty is a tax on our intellectual capacity, and the erosion of that cognitive capacity is also an erosion of our ability to govern effectively. Defeating poverty, even in an era of sustainable development, is an absolutely essential prerequisite for better governance.

Why is a tax on our intellectual capacity for governance important? The answer lies partly in the fourth word that has been used frequently in the past two days—*knowledge.* If the Takemi Fellowships are about anything, they are about producing reliable knowledge. But reliable knowledge does not come out of thin air. Reliable knowledge depends upon institutions of knowledge production, including, most importantly, our universities. Strengthening higher education and our research institutions has been massively neglected in development policy, at a great cost to our opportunities to make progress in health. Investment, or rather the lack of investment, in higher education and research has been a neglected dimension of governance.

My untested hypothesis is that the quality of governance very much depends upon the quality of higher education institutions, universities, and research institutes in a particular setting. I can point to country examples to attempt to prove my hypothesis. I can point to Mexico, for example, and especially the role of Mexico's National Institute of Public Health. I can point to Turkey—and the former Minister of Health of Turkey is sitting in this room now. A crucial success factor for Turkey in its quest to achieve universal health coverage was the demand for reliable information, which required strong institutions of higher education research and data production. Japan's success in achieving universal health coverage in 1961, and its responses to ongoing challenges and its successes in developing domestic and international health policies, depend upon the strength of its higher education and research institutes. One can point to many examples where national transformations in health have depended upon key investments in national institutions for data gathering, research, and knowledge for policy. We need to take our universities much more seriously for governance, accountability, and for global progress in health.

So what has all this knowledge actually taught us? This question brings me to my fifth and final observation. We are living at a time of diverse *global risks*. We have heard many of them discussed these past two days—regional and global financial crises, the effects and the aftereffects of war, social division, nuclear disaster, AIDS, aging, maternal and child ill health, how one provides care to refugee populations. These risks are not mutually exclusive. They are highly interconnected. One risk will affect another. A small change to one risk can lead to a large change to another risk. And what this network of risks tells us today is that we live in a highly unstable world. We must accept highly unstable national and global systems, which are defined by the characteristics of their risks.

One of our greatest challenges today is to understand the risk culture we are living in. Central to that challenge is, of course, governance. How do we manage these risks?

I think there are at least two ideas that are relevant to our thinking about how to manage global risks from the perspective of governance. The first, and this statement is perhaps a little frightening, is that there is no simple solution. The best we can hope for is to be knowledgeable about the risks around us, to have what one might call "risk competence"—to be able to analyze risks, and to think about scenarios and opportunities for resilience in adapting to the risks we face. The second idea is that we have to devise mechanisms to promote cooperation and collaboration between countries and between peoples. Networks of risk demand networks of risk-competent actors.

If anything typifies the ethos of the Takemi Fellowships it is the creation of this community of individuals who work—across nations, across peoples, across cultures—to understand the risks we face as a species. The clarion call that came yesterday, to intensify the Takemi network, is right not only for the Takemi Fellowship but also for the broader challenges we confront in the world today.

Let me conclude with one further Japanese proverb: "An apprentice near a temple will recite the scriptures untaught." In other words, it is the environment that makes us who we are. It is the unique environment that you as Takemi Fellows have created that has helped to shape and influence the characters of more than two hundred fellows—a truly remarkable achievement. It's an achievement I salute.

Reflections (ii)

Masami Ishii

I am very pleased that the symposium in October 2013 commemorating the thirtieth anniversary of the Takemi Program was a great success. The same year (2013) was also a milestone for the Harvard School of Public Health: the school's one hundredth anniversary. The Takemi Symposium thus was positioned as part of a series of celebratory events.

I am sure that the Takemi Fellows who gathered in Boston from around the world greatly appreciated their discussions with Professor Michael Reich and other Harvard community members. This event was more than a chance to discuss key issues about governing health systems and catch up with old friends; it was also an invaluable opportunity to take a new step toward the Takemi Program's thirty-first year and its future in global health.

On behalf of the Japan Medical Association, I would like to sincerely recognize the tremendous efforts of everyone at Harvard University and around the world who has worked to support this program for so many years, especially Professor Michael Reich. I am also happy to affirm today that the Takemi Fellows are continuing to work hard in their research and policy efforts, challenging difficult health issues in countries across the globe. The papers presented at the symposium, and collected in this book, provide evidence of their impressive contributions to research and policy that improves health systems performance.

Thirty years is a long time, but I believe that this is just the starting point for the Takemi Program as it moves forward to future activities. I hope that all Takemi Fellows will continue to support the program and its further contribution to global health.

The Japan Medical Association (JMA) has supported this program for many years, especially since 1994, when it began to select and provide scholarships to send two Japanese Takemi Fellows to take part in the program each year. I have been in a position at the JMA supporting this program for eight years now. During this time I have done my best to assure stable and continuous support for the Takemi Program, from the JMA and from other groups in Japan.

In light of the program's accomplishments, I am especially honored to be named an Honorary Takemi Fellow; the award was conferred on me at the Takemi Symposium, in recognition of the dedicated efforts of the Japan Medical Association, led by President Yoshitake Yokokura, and my contributions to those efforts, and as a symbol of Harvard University's appreciation for the JMA's support over many years.

I close my remarks with the Japanese saying, "Endurance makes you stronger." The Takemi Program has shown it can endure, and the examples in this book more than demonstrate the fellows' strength. We look forward to a long and successful future for the continued activities of the Takemi Program at Harvard University, and of the Takemi Fellows doing good work in the world.

Reflections (iii)

Lincoln Chen

I was there at the beginning. Well, almost! I became the Taro Takemi Professor of International Health in January 1987, joining the vision launched by Dr. Taro Takemi and Dean Howard Hiatt, and I held that position for the next ten years. I was recruited to the HSPH faculty by Dean Harvey Fineberg, and I benefitted enormously from the mentoring of David Bell, the first director of the Takemi Program, and someone we remember with respect and affection. On my arrival at HSPH, I assumed the role of program director, but Bell and I soon agreed on appointing Michael Reich into this position, a wise decision.

I never met the legendary Taro Takemi, but I traveled to Japan early on and worked with Dr. Takemi's colleagues at the Institute of Seizon and Life Sciences in Tokyo. I tried to understand: What is "seizon"? Eventually, I concluded that "seizon," a distinctively Japanese concept, is a sort of sociobiology of human beings that goes beyond simply the biology of life. From those trips, as well, I remember the warmth of the Takemi family—Mrs. Takemi and her children, including Keizo Takemi, his two sisters, his brother, and their families. Over the ensuing decades, my friendship and collaboration with Keizo grew, in Japan, throughout Asia, and also at Harvard on numerous occasions, as he became a major policy figure in global public health.

HARVARD AS A CROSSROADS

The Takemi Program became the bedrock for our HSPH "grand strategy" in international health, which Dean Fineberg and I developed and called the "crossroads" strategy. This strategy did not posit Harvard as the ultimate repository of knowledge. Rather, we explicitly recognized the rich diversity of knowledge around the world; Harvard would both learn and contribute by operating as a hub for knowledge sharing, exchanging, and creativity.

The Takemi Program played a central role in this strategy, seeking to attract the best and brightest to the Harvard crossroads. The program also enabled Harvard to move from "international" to "global" health. Now global health is a crowded, popular, and competitive field. But when I arrived at HSPH in 1987, the school's Office of International Health faced high student demand but weak funding, few faculty, and low academic status. Steve Joseph and Joe Wray had already departed, leaving only Richard Cash. The Takemi Program enabled us to move from international to global health, since the program did not divide the world into "North versus South" or "East versus West." Global flows of all kinds were accelerating—1980 witnessed the fall of the Bamboo Curtain, and 1990 witnessed the fall of the Iron Curtain. Similarly, Takemi Fellows came from both poorer and richer countries, were global in intellectual scope, and explicitly recognized global health interdependence. Over time, Takemi Fellows have had major impacts around the world. One of the geniuses of Harvard is leadership development. The strategy seems to be to do no harm, but attract the best and brightest and, after they succeed, claim credit for their good works!

Our growing group at HSPH crafted many crossroad initiatives with our partners. The Commission on Health Research for Development, which released its report at a Nobel Symposium in 1990, was chaired by John Evans and included such luminaries as V. Ramalingaswami of India and Adetokunbo Lucas of Nigeria, both of whom would eventually join the school. We invited Saburo Okita, the former foreign minister of Japan and a renowned development economist, to join the commission, and he agreed, through the intermediation of Keizo Takemi. A Takemi Fellow, Eiji Marui, was assigned to assist Okita to keep track of the commission's details.

The Health Transitions Program similarly brought together important leaders in global public health at Harvard, including Jack and Pat Caldwell from Australia and Julio Frenk from Mexico, along with Harvard faculty members Arthur Kleinman and Amartya Sen. We worked with Dean Jamison and Larry Summers (then chief economist at the World Bank) on the landmark *1993 World Development Report* on health and development. At the same time, research fellow Chris Murray produced the first estimates of the global burden of disease for 1990. David Hunter led the AIDS and Reproductive Health Network, consisting of a half dozen partners, just before Jonathan Mann came to Harvard to lead the School's AIDS work following his departure from WHO. Peter Berman directed the Data for Decision-Making Project supported by USAID. Perhaps Harvard's major contribution to health policy has been the Flagship Program in Health Reform for the World Bank, led by Professors Bill Hsiao and Marc Roberts along with the Takemi Program's longtime director, Michael Reich.

The Takemi Program was so successful that we also copied it for the MacArthur and Bell leadership fellows programs based at the Harvard Center for Population and Development in Cambridge.

OUTREACH THROUGH JAPAN'S LEADERSHIP

In addition to the Takemi Fellows, the Takemi Program has also had important outreach through Japan. I would like to note three initiatives in particular, related to the Takemi Program, that have had major impacts in the world through the activities of Keizo Takemi. When Keizo Takemi was based at Tokai University in the mid-1990s, he initiated a series of workshops that led to the concept of "human security." Emma Rothschild and I joined these workshops, which seeded the UN Commission on Human Security cochaired by Sadako Ogata and Amartya Sen; their important report was released in 2003.

A few years later, Keizo played a major role in setting the global health agenda through the 2008 G8 meeting held in Japan. He chaired an unusual Japanese interministerial and public-private sector committee that focused on the challenges of advancing "health systems strengthening" around the world. Their report shaped the Japanese government's proposal on global health that was ultimately adopted by the G8.

More recently, Keizo led the research team that produced the *Lancet* Japan series, a comprehensive report on Japan's fifty years of universal health coverage. This 2011 publication was strongly supported by *Lancet* editor Richard Horton, and was no doubt helped by Takemi Fellows. Keizo has continued on as a major global health policy maker, for example, working with Prime Minister Abe on the 2013 UN General Assembly on universal health coverage.

LOOKING TO THE FUTURE

We live in a changing global health world, with the onset of the "triple tsunami" of aging, noncommunicable diseases, and growing disability. At the same time, the public is more engaged in health, and global health has become a major stream of work in international diplomacy.

The Takemi "brand" is undoubtedly the famous Takemi Fellows Program, which is now recognized around the world. And the way the fellowship program evolves in the future will depend on its leadership. The current leaders will be a hard act to follow. Michael Reich, a pioneer in health policy analysis, has been a dedicated mentor and teacher to the Takemi Fellows—always generous with his time, and academically demanding and rigorous. Also, underappreciated are his constant efforts (working with Japanese partners) to ensure the program's survival; it takes much perseverance to keep a high-quality program alive for three decades.

His collaboration with Keizo Takemi has been a key source of the program's continuity and success. Keizo Takemi, a policy maker and politician, has served as Japan's deputy foreign affairs minister, deputy health minister, and global health leader. Keizo pursues his social passions through policy and politics. In his work on human security, he has highlighted the importance of human security among people in local communities, especially among the poorest. In his work on health systems, he has stressed the insufficiency of disease control alone and argued for a broader view of strengthening the entire health system. He has been a passionate champion of health equity and universal health coverage around the world.

Part of the Takemi Program's commitment to global health is using public health as an instrument for peace. This commitment connects directly to Taro Takemi's tradition and legacy. Once, at an international meeting, Keizo introduced himself as a Takemi; when it was my turn, I reported that I had been a Takemi Professor. Another participant observed that "you are stepbrothers."

In this regard, we are all part of the extended Takemi family, connected biologically, professionally, and socially. This network, of family and fellows who carry the Takemi name, shares the Takemi ethos: health with security, peace with justice, and social solidarity. That fusion, that "seizon," ultimately is both the power and future of the Takemi dream.

APPENDIX

Short History of the Takemi Program in International Health and List of Takemi Fellows, 1984–2013

SHORT HISTORY OF THE TAKEMI PROGRAM IN INTERNATIONAL HEALTH

Founding

The Takemi Program in International Health emerged from the shared interests of Dr. Taro Takemi in Japan and Dr. Howard Hiatt in the United States. Each had long been concerned about the problems of promoting health and preventing disease, both in industrialized nations confronted by rising health costs and in developing countries burdened by persistent poverty.

FIGURE A.I Professor Bell, Dean Hiatt, and Dr. Takemi in Tokyo, December 1981.

Dr. Takemi, as president of the Japan Medical Association, emphasized the need to bring together experts from medicine, public health, economics, law, politics, and other fields to find effective and equitable solutions to the development and distribution of health care resources. Dr. Hiatt, as dean of the Harvard School of Public Health, similarly stressed the development of interdisciplinary approaches to the study of health problems and health policy.

In 1981, Dr. Takemi invited Dean Hiatt to Tokyo to address a meeting of the World Medical Association on the development and allocation of medical care resources. Out of their discussions grew the idea of the Takemi Program in International Health at Harvard. To move the ideas forward, Dean Hiatt included Professor David Bell, who was chair of the Department of Population Sciences.

Dr. Takemi and Dean Hiatt agreed that the program would concentrate on the problems of *mobilizing, allocating, and managing scarce resources to improve health*, and of *designing effective strategies for disease control and prevention and health promotion, with a focus on the world's poorer countries*. Each year the program would bring together at Harvard a small group of Takemi Fellows from around the world, with an emphasis on participants from developing countries.

Leadership

The program started in July 1983 with funds donated by two private companies in Japan, and was named after Dr. Taro Takemi. The funds provided for an endowed chair named after Taro Takemi, and for start-up funds for the Takemi Program. Professor Bell served as acting director of the program, and Dr. Michael Reich was hired as the program's assistant director, to organize the program and make it run. In 1986, Dr. Lincoln Chen was hired as the first Taro Takemi Professor of International Health at Harvard. In 1988, Dr. Reich became director of the program—a position he continues to hold—and in 1997 he became Taro Takemi Professor of International Health Policy.

FIGURE A.2 The first group of Takemi Fellows (left to right): Lukas Hendrata (Indonesia), Hacheong Yeon (South Korea), Prakash Gupta (India), Hong-chang Yuan (China), and Keiji Tanaka (Japan)

Takemi Fellows in International Health

The first group of Takemi Fellows, pictured at the right, arrived in late summer 1984 to begin their research fellowship year at HSPH. Their research topics remain relevant even today: effective family planning and community participation in Indonesia; economic analysis of Korea's health system; controlling the health consequences of nonsmoking tobacco use in India; strategies for schistosomiasis control in China; and how the fee schedule works for paying physicians in Japan.

Between its founding and 2013, the Takemi Program at Harvard welcomed 241 Takemi Fellows from fifty-one countries around the world (the complete list is provided in Table A.1 below). Their subsequent accomplishments are impressive. Many Takemi Fellows have achieved leadership positions in their own countries, and have pushed the frontiers of knowledge and action. These leaders include: the minister of health of Indonesia; the commissioner of the State Food and Drug Administration in China; the secretary of Health and Family Welfare in India; deans, department chairs, and professors in many universities; and the founders of innovative nongovernmental organizations and private companies related to health. Takemi Fellows have come together from time to time over the years in multiday international symposia (listed on page 378) dedicated to reflecting and pushing the global public health policy forward. Each has resulted in a publication similar to this current book. The 30th Anniversary Symposium took place in October 2013.

Supporters

Many organizations have contributed to sustaining the activities of the Takemi Program at Harvard over the past thirty years. The longstanding partnership with the Japan Medical Association continues to provide a solid foundation for the program. A generous annual donation from the Japan Pharmaceutical Manufacturers Association has contributed most of the program's annual operating expenses for many years. Since 2000, most Takemi Fellows have raised their own fellowship funds in order to participate in the program, from many different sources. In the previous decade, the Carnegie Corporation of New York and the Merck Company Foundation made generous grants to the program that provided financial support to individual Takemi Fellows from low- and middle-income countries. These contributions are greatly appreciated.

Other fellows have received financial support from their universities, governments, or other foundations, or have self-financed.

The Program Model

Over the past three decades, the Takemi Program at Harvard has evolved into a unique example of U.S.-Japan private cooperation to advance global health goals and the health policies and conditions of developing countries.

The weekly Takemi Seminar is the primary teaching activity of the fellowship program. It examines the question of how to set priorities under conditions of limited resources and evolving technology. Fellows explore such techniques as quantitative, institutional, bioethical, and social analyses. Seminar materials stress comparative case studies in international health, with problems drawn from both developed and developing countries. Seminars are led by faculty members from the School of Public Health and other Harvard faculties, and by outside specialists.

In addition to the core seminar, fellows participate in courses, seminars, and other activities relevant to their interests at the School of Public Health, throughout Harvard University, and at other universities in the Boston area. These provide opportunities to strengthen fellows' knowledge of economics, epidemiology, policy formulation, political analysis, organizational behavior, or evaluation with an emphasis on the application of quantitative analytic methods. The activities also provide fellows with the opportunity to interact extensively with students, faculty, and other professionals, which in some cases has led to funded collaborative research projects.

The Takemi Program is nondegree oriented, as degree course requirements would substantially reduce the time for research and writing. Fellows may also be invited to join in the teaching of global health courses at the School of Public Health, and in this and other ways will have opportunities to interact with students at the school. Takemi Fellowships generally have a duration of ten months. However, this may be adjusted in special cases. Upon completion of the program, Takemi Fellows receive a certificate.

TABLE A.1 Takemi Fellows in International Health, 1984–2013

COUNTRY	NAME	YEARS
AZERBAIJAN	BAGIROV, Rasul	2002–2003
BELGIUM	DE NEVE, Jan-Walter*	2012–2013
BRAZIL	BERTOLDI, Andréa	2005–2006
	CARRET, Maria Laura	2005–2006
	CESAR, Juraci A.*	1997–98, 1998–99
	DE BARCELLOS, Ana Paula	2012–2013
	FACCHINI, Luiz Augusto*	1996–97
	FASSA, Anaclaudia*	1998–99
	FILHO, Jose Rodrigues	1991–92
	FIORI, Nadia Spada*	2013–2014
	IUNES, Roberto Fontes	1995–96
	POSSAS, Cristina de A.*	1991–92
	SASSI, Raul Mendoza*	2000–01; March–Aug 2012
	THUME, Elaine*	Jan 2009–Feb 2010
BURKINA FASO	BAYA, Banza	2002–2003
CAMEROON	NTANGSI, Joseph	1997–98
CANADA	BHATTACHARYYA, Onil	2006–2007
	KENDALL, Tamil*	2013–2014
CHINA	CAI, Jin–wen	1988–89
	CORNELY, Zhuo Zhang	2012–2013
	DENG, Ming	1992–93
	HAO, Chun*	2013–2014
	JIA, Zhongwei*	2012–2013
	LI, Yanping	2008–2009, 2009–2010
	LIN, Hui-qing	1994–95
	LUO, Juhua	2000–01
	MA, Jingdong	2009–2010
	MAO, Zhenzhong	1999–2000
	RAO, Keqin	1996–97
	SUN, Xiaoming	2007–2008
	WANG, Hong*	1994–95
	WANG, Zeng–sui	1986–87
	WU, Jing*	2007–2008, 2008–2009
	XU, Xiping	1988–89
	XUE, Qinxiang*	2006–2007

*indicates attendance at the 30th Anniversary Symposium

COUNTRY	NAME	YEARS
CHINA	YIN, Li	2002–2003
	YUAN, Hong-chang	1984–85
COLOMBIA	ALZATE, Alberto S.	1987–88
	URIBE-MOSQUERA, Tomas	1985–86
	VILLANUEVA, Alvaro	2003–2004
COTE D'IVOIRE/ CANADA	TANON, Anais	2009–2010
DENMARK	SCHAPIRA, Allan	1987–88
EGYPT	EL-ADAWY, Maha*	1997–98
FRANCE	HUTTIN, Christine*	1994–95
	PERIN, Ines	2000–01
	RAINHORN, Jean-Daniel	1990–91
GERMANY	SUPADY, Alexander	2009–2010
GHANA	AWEDOBA, Albert	1997–98
	COLEMAN, Nii Aylte*	1996–97
HONG KONG	HO, William*	2005–2006
	LEUNG, Gabriel	2004–2005
INDIA	BANATI, Prerna	2010–2011; 2011–2012
	BHAT, Ramesh	1990–91
	BODAVALA, Ranganayakulu*	1999–2000
	D'SOUZA, Marcella	2000–01
	DURVASULA, Ramesh S.	1987–88
	GARG, Charu	1997–98
	GUMBER, Anil	1993–94
	GUPTA, Prakash C.	1984–85
	KARAN, Anup	2006–2007
	MAHAPATRA, Prasanta	1991–92
	MAX, Emmanuel	1987–88
	MISHRA, Udaya*	2003–2004
	MOHANTY, Jatish	1996–97
	MURALEEDHARAN, V.R.	1995–96
	NAIDU, B.M.	2002–2003
	PRAKASAMMA, Mallavarapu*	1992–93
	PRAKASH, Charu	1997–98
	PURUSHOTHAMAN, Mohankumar	1992–93
	RANGANAYAKULU, Bodavala*	1999–2000
	RAO, K. Sujatha*	2001–02

*indicates attendance at the 30th Aniversary Symposium

COUNTRY	NAME	YEARS
INDIA	SELVARAJ, Sakthivel	2006–2007
	SIVALENKA, Srilatha	2001–02
	SRILATHA, Venkatalakshmi	1989–90
	UPLEKAR, Mukund*	1988–89
	VARATHARAJAN, Durairaj	1999–2000
	YESUDIAN, C.A.K.	1990–91
INDONESIA	BIMO, Bim	1991–92
	HENDRATA, Lukas	1984–85
	KUSNANTO, Hari*	2001–02
	MBOI, Nafsiah	1990–91
IRAN	FARVID, Maryam*	2013–2014
	MEHRDAD, Ramin	2008–2009
	RAMEZANI, Fahimeh	2004–2005
ISRAEL	COGGAN, Diane	1997–98
	FACTOR, Roni	2009–2010, 2010–2011
	KITRON, Uriel*	1985–86
	MISHAL, Shaul	1995–96
ITALY	GNESOTTO, Roberto*	1995–96
JAPAN	ADACHI, Motoi	1998–99
	FUJII, Mitsuru	1985–86
	GOTO, Aya*	2012–2013
	HAMAMOTO, Mieko	2008–2009
	HIRAYAMA, Megumi	1995–96
	HORI, Kazuichiro*	2012–2013
	HOSHI, Hokuto*	1996–97
	HOSODA, Miwako	2008–2009, 2009–2010
	HOZUMI, Dairiku	1997–98
	IDE, Hiroo	2007–2008
	IMAMURA, Hidehito*	1999–2000
	ISHIKAWA, Noriko	2003–2004
	JIMBA, Masamine	2001–02
	KANAGAWA, Shyuzo	1995–96
	KIMOTO, Kinuko*	2000–01
	KOBAYASHI, Hajime	2002–2003
	KOBAYASHI, Yasuki	1989–90
	KONDO, Naoki	2006–2007
	MARUI, Eiji*	1986–87

*indicates attendance at the 30th Anniversary Symposium

COUNTRY	NAME	YEARS
JAPAN	MIYOSHI, Chiaki	1994–95
	MOJI, Kazuhiko*	1991–92
	NAGATA, Takashi	2004–2005, 2005–2006
	NAKAMURA, Yasuhide*	1996–97
	NOMURA-BABA, Marika*	2013–2014
	NOTO, Yuji*	1998–99
	NOZAKI, Ikuma	2010–2011
	NUMASAWA, Katsumi	1997–98
	OMAE, Kazuyuki	1987–88
	ONO, Michio	2000–01
	OSAKA, Ken	2001–02
	OSANAI, Yasuyo	2004–2005
	SAKAI, Rie*	2011–2012, 2012–2013
	SAKAMOTO, Naoko	1999–2000
	SAKISAKA, Kayako	2009–2010
	SASAKI, Asami	2008–2009
	SASE, Eriko	2005–2006
	SEITA, Akihiro*	2003–2004
	SHIMIZU, Mayumi	2007–2008
	SHIRAI, Kokoro	2010–2011
	SUGIURA, Yasuo	2005–2006
	TAKAHASHI, Tai	1994–95
	TAKEMI, Keizo*	2007–2008, 2008–2009
	TANAKA, Keiji*	1984–85
	TOMIOKA, Shinichi*	2013–2014
	TOMIZUKA, Taro*	2010–2011
	TSUTANI, Kiichiro	1990–91
	UCHIYAMA, Shusaku	2012–2013
	UEHARA, Naruo	1988–89
	YAGYU, Fumihiro	2006–2007
	YAMAMOTO, Taro*	2002–2003
	YODA, Takeshi*	2009–2010
	YOSHIDA, Tohru	1992–93
KENYA	MAKUMI, Margaret	2003–2004
	WAMAI, Richard*	2006–2007, 2007–2008
KYRGYZSTAN	BIIBUSUNOVA, Damira	2003–2004
MALAWI	MTIMUNI, Beatrice	1990–91

*indicates attendance at the 30th Anniversary Symposium

COUNTRY	NAME	YEARS
MALAYSIA	KHOR, Geok Lin*	1988–89
MEXICO	AVILA-FIGUEROA, R. Carlos	1995–96
	GONZALEZ, Luz Maria	2012–2013
MOROCCO	MEKKI-BERRADA, Abdelwahed	2000–01, 2001–02
NICARAGUA	VELAZQUEZ, Aurora	1989–90
NIGERIA	ADEDIMEJI, Adebola	2004–2005
	ALUBO, Ogoh	1999–2000
	AMAZIGO, Uche*	1991–92
	DARE, Lola	1999–2000
	LAWOYIN, Taiwo	1999–2000
	NWAKOBY, Boniface	1989–90
	NWAORGU, Obioma*	1994–95
	OBIKEZE, Daniel	1992–93
	ODIMEGWU, Clifford	2001–02, 2002–03
	OGBUOKIRI, Justina	1994–95
	OKAFOR, Chinyelu R.	1988–89
	OKEIBUNOR, Joseph*	2010–2011
	OKONOFUA, Friday*	1991–92
	ONOKERHORAYE, Andrew	1998–99
	ONWUDIEGWU, Uchenna*	1993–94
	OZUMBA, Benjamin*	1995–96
	WALKER, Mary	2002–2003
PAKISTAN	KHAN, Amanullah	1995–96
	QURESHI, Asma Fozia	1987–88
PHILIPPINES	DANGUILAN, Marilen*	1998–99
	ORBETA, Aniceto	1996–97, 1997–98
	SOLON, Jose Orville	1988–89
POLAND	NABIALCZYK-CHALUPOWSKI, Malgorzata*	1993–94, 1995–96
RUSSIA	VARAVIKOVA, Elena	1995–96
S. KOREA	JOH, Hee-Kyung	2010–2011; 2011–2012
	JU, Yeong-Su	2005–2006
	KIM, Chang-yup	2004–2005
	KIM, Jin Hyun	1996–97
	KIM, Minah Kang*	Feb 2010–March 2012
	KIM, Sujin*	2013–2014
	KIM, Yoon	Feb 2011–March 2012

*indicates attendance at the 30th Anniversary Symposium

COUNTRY	NAME	YEARS
S. KOREA	KWON, Soonman	2001–02
	LEE, Tae-Jin*	2006–2007
	OH, Juhwan*	2008–2009, 2009–2010
	PARK, Sang Min	2007–2008
	SHIN, Young-jeon	2002–2003, 2003–2004
	SONG, Young Joo*	2008–2009
	YANG, Bong-min*	1989–90, 1995–96, 2006–07, 2007–08
	YEON, Hacheong	1984–85
SIERRA LEONE	GIBRIL, Akim	1996–97
SOUTH AFRICA	HERMANUS, Mavis	1998–99
	HOFFMAN, Margaret	1993–94
	LEBESE, Lebogang F.	1995–96
	LONDON, Leslie*	2001–02
	MYERS, Jonathan E.	1987–88
	PICK, William	1990–91, 1996–97
	PRICE, Max*	1994–95
SRI LANKA	ABEYKOON, Palitha	1989–90
	DE SILVA, Weraduwage Indralal	1996–97, 1997–98
	MENDIS, John Bertrand*	1991–92
	SAMARASINGHE, Sam*	1985–86
SUDAN	EL SAMANI, El Fatih	1985–86
SWITZERLAND	CARRIN, Guy	1985–86
	ZUBER, Patrick	1993–94
TAIWAN	CHAN, Chang-Chuan*	1997–98
	CHANG, Hong-jen	2004–2005
	CHANG, Yao Mao	2006–2007, 2007–2008
	CHEN, Solomon	2011–2012
	KING, Chwan-chuen*	1999–2000
	LAN, Chung-Fu	1986–87
	LU, Jui-Fen Rachel*	2004–2005
TANZANIA	BHACHU, Sem Singh	1989–90
	HAMDANI, Salha	1994–95
	MUHONDWA, Eustace P.Y.	1987–88
	NGUMA, Justin	1991–92
	RUGEMALILA, Joas	1991–92
THAILAND	KUNAVIKTIKUL, Wipada*	2008–2009
	PHONBOON, Kanchanasak	1986–87

*indicates attendance at the 30th Anniversary Symposium

COUNTRY	NAME	YEARS
THAILAND	RATAWIJITRASIN, Sauwakon	1995–96
	SUPAKANKUNTI , Siripen*	1996–97
	VEERAVONGS, Suriya	1993–94
THE GAMBIA	SILLA, Balla Musa	1994–95
THE NETHERLANDS	TOY, Mehlika	2011–2012, 2012–2013
	VAN DEN BORNE, Francine	2002–2003
TURKEY	KAYA, Sidika	1999–2000, 2000–2001
	MOLLAHALILOGLU, Salih*	2007–2008
UGANDA	KONDE-LULE, Joseph*	1990–91
	NANTULYA, Vinand	2000–01
UNITED KINGDOM	CIBULSKIS, Richard*	2000–01
USA	BUMP, Jesse*	2009–2010, 2010–2011
	CAMMETT, Melani	2013–2014
	COLWELL, Stacie	1998–99, 1999–2000
	GOOD, Charles M.	1986–87
	GOROFF, Michael*	2008–2009
	GREEN, Edward	2001–02
	HENNING, Margaret*	2012–2013
	LONG, Kurt	2000–01
	RICHEY, Lisa	1999–2000
	VAVRUS, Frances	1999–2000
VIETNAM	TRAN, Tuan*	1994–95
ZAIRE	RUKARANGIRA, Wa Nkera	1988–89
ZAMBIA	CHITAH, Mukosha Bona	2000–01

*indicates attendance at the 30th Anniversary Symposium

Past Takemi Symposiums in International Health

- **1984: First Symposium:** Health Policy Towards the 21st Century: Health Problems Beyond the National Boundary, Tokyo, Japan, May 19–20, 1984
  - **Publication:** Reich, Michael R., ed., *Health Policy Towards the 21st Century: Health Problems Beyond the National Boundary.* President and Fellows of Harvard College and Institute of Sciences for Human Survival, 1985.

- **1986: Second Symposium:** Health, Nutrition, and Economic Crises: Approaches to Policy in the Third World, Boston, MA, USA, May 20–22, 1986
  - **Publication:** Bell, David E. and Michael R. Reich, eds., *Health, Nutrition, and Economic Crises: Approaches to Policy in the Third World.* Dover, MA: Auburn House Publishing Co., 1988.

- **1988: Third Symposium:** International Cooperation for Health: Problems, Prospects, and Priorities, Tokyo, Japan, July 1–3, 1988
  - **Publication:** Reich, Michael R., and Eiji Marui, eds., *International Cooperation for Health: Problems, Prospects, and Priorities.* Dover, MA: Auburn House Publishing Co., 1989.

- **1990: Fourth Symposium:** *Protecting Workers' Health in the Third World*, Boston, MA, USA, September 29–October 1, 1990
  - **Publication:** Reich, Michael R., and Toshiteru Okubo, eds., *Protecting Workers' Health in the Third World: National and International Strategies.* Westport, CT: Auburn House, 1992.

- **2000: Fifth Symposium:** *Symposium on International Health and Medical Ethics*, Tokyo, Japan, Dec 1–2, 2000
  - **Publication:** Aoki, Kiyoshi, ed., *Ethical Dilemmas in Health and Development.* Tokyo: Japan Scientific Societies Press, 1994.

ACKNOWLEDGMENTS

We wish to express our deep appreciation to the many individuals and organizations who supported the 30th Anniversary Symposium of the Takemi Program in International Health at Harvard University (held in October 2013), and the production of this book, which is based on the papers presented at the Symposium. These supporters are numerous, at Harvard, in the United States, in Japan, and around the world.

The 30th Anniversary Symposium benefited from the Takemi Program's long-standing partnership with the Japan Medical Association. The Symposium and the subsequent production of this book received financial support from the Japan Pharmaceutical Manufacturers Association, the China Medical Board, and the Chiang Mai University Faculty of Nursing, with additional contributions from the Japan-Based Executive Committee of PhRMA, the Japan Medical Devices Manufacturers, and the Japan Federation of Medical Devices Associations. These generous financial contributions made the Symposium and this book possible. We deeply appreciate the support and the opportunities it created.

Many people contributed to the production of this book. We thank each of the authors for their contributions, as well as their willingness to revise their papers and respond to multiple queries in the editing process. We also thank Bibliomotion's publications team, under the leadership of Jill Friedlander. In particular, Jill Shoenhaut guided us and the book through the publication process. Susan Lauzau provided expert copy-editing of the entire volume, helping us smooth the prose from different parts of the world. Carol Maglitta of OneVisualMind created the tables and figures throughout the book, with a magical touch. Erin James helped edit one chapter and transcribe a commentary. Anya Guyer provided extraordinary support throughout the process by helping us edit and format the entire volume, moving the book forward toward completion.

A special note of appreciation is due to Donna DiBartolomeo, who helped organize the Symposium and its papers and assured that all the participants arrived and enjoyed the event, and to Amy Levin, Program Coordinator for the Takemi Program, who organized many aspects of the Symposium in addition to the program's day-to-day administration.

Finally, thanks to all the Takemi Fellows whose dedication to the program over the past thirty years and engagement in the Symposium are the heart of this work.

Michael R. Reich
Keizo Takemi
December 2014

Participants at the 30th Anniversary Takemi Symposium

INDEX